social WELFARE & social development in South Africa

LEILA PATEL

OXFORD
UNIVERSITY PRESS

OXFORD
UNIVERSITY PRESS

Great Clarendon Street, Oxford OX2 6DP

Oxford University Press is a department of the University of Oxford.
It furthers the University's objective of excellence in research, scholarship, and education by publishing worldwide in

Oxford New York

Auckland Cape Town Dar es Salaam Hong Kong Karachi
Kuala Lumpur Madrid Melbourne Mexico City Nairobi
New Delhi Shanghai Taipei Toronto

With offices in
Argentina Austria Brazil Chile Czech Republic France Greece
Guatemala Hungary Italy Japan Poland Portugal Singapore
South Korea Switzerland Thailand Turkey Ukraine Vietnam

Published in South Africa
by Oxford University Press Southern Africa, Cape Town

Social Welfare and Social Development
ISBN 0 19 578433 2 (10 – digit, current)
ISBN 978 0 19 578433 6 (13 – digit, from 2007)

First published 2005

Publishing manager: Marian Griffin
Editor: Lydia Wilson
Design and cover design: Oswald Kurten
Indexer: Ethné Clarke

Published by Oxford University Press Southern Africa
PO Box 12119, N1 City, 7463, Cape Town, South Africa

Set in 8.5 pt Leawood on 12 pt by RHT desktop publishing, Durbanville
Cover reproduction by The Image Bureau
Imagesetting by Castle Graphics
Printed and bound by ABC Press, Cape Town

Contents

Foreword

Although the people of South Africa experienced revolutionary change as the entrenched apartheid system of racial, economic and social oppression disintegrated in the 1990s, South African social workers, social administrators and social policymakers are only too aware of the need to promote policies and programmes that raise living standards, meet basic needs, maximize opportunities, address social problems and create a just society in which the well-being of all is guaranteed. They recognize that political change is only a first step: the challenge now is to press for the formulation, implementation and continued renewal of effective measures that will achieve these goals.

This important book, *Social Welfare and Social Development in South Africa*, shows how much has been achieved, but also how much more needs to be done to translate into reality the hopes and aspirations of millions of South Africans for a better life. Compiled by a group of South Africa's leading social work and social policy scholars, this book offers important insights into social welfare in South Africa, and the policies and programmes that have been adopted in recent years to promote the well-being of the nation's people. The book's authors provide an interesting account of how thoughts on social welfare policy have evolved since the apartheid years. Grounded in historical analysis, the book provides an overview of a wide range of policy measures and services designed to address social needs and enhance social well-being. A number of chapters address specific fields of social work practice and social policy-making, and show how the social services in South Africa are responding to those with special needs. Other chapters are more broadly focused dealing with wider issues of policy and political economy. The book not only meets the needs of South African students, educators, policymakers and others, but will be of interest to an international readership that has long been fascinated with the unique developments that have characterized South Africa's recent transformation.

Of particular interest is the book's synthesis of social work, social welfare and social development. South Africans have been international leaders in promoting a developmental approach to social welfare, and the book's numerous references to this approach show how developmentalist thinking has informed social policy-making and integrated remedial, supportive and change-focused ideals. As the need to renew a commitment to poverty eradication is again being recognized at the global level, the South African experience will not only inform but inspire international thinking. The issues and debates articulated by the contributors to this important book offer helpful insights into the way the social development perspective can be incorporated into social work and social policy around the world.

I am greatly honoured to have been asked to write the foreword to this most readable, thoughtful and important book. I know that social work and social policy colleagues everywhere will join me in congratulating Leila Patel and her colleagues on producing a book that will not only be valued by students and educators, but by those engaged in social work practice, administration and policy-making in both the voluntary and governmental sectors. I know that many readers, like me, will appreciate the book's informative account of social welfare in South Africa, and value the relevance of its insights to social work and social policy in their own countries.

James Midgley
Specht Professor and Dean, School of Social Welfare
University of California, Berkeley

Contributors

Dr Ndangwa Noyoo is Zambian by birth. He is a senior researcher at the Centre for Social Development in Africa, University of Johannesburg. Prior to joining the Centre he lectured at the University of the Witwatersrand School of Social Work and was Principal Researcher at INTERFUND. His academic teaching and research experience is in development studies, monitoring and evaluation, social development, social policy, and social work.

Dr Jean Triegaardt is a senior lecturer at the University of Pretoria in the Department of Social Work and Criminology. She has many years of experience as a lecturer in the field of social security, social welfare policy and social development. She is also a former Director of Social Security in the Department of Welfare, at present known as Department of Social Development.

Theresa Wilson is a consultant to a number of development agencies in the field of HIV/AIDS workplace programmes, home-based care and social development policy and interventions. She is the former Deputy Director of Planning and Parliamentary Service for the Department of Welfare, Pretoria. She has been involved with social development policy and practice issues in both South Africa and Malawi.

Acknowledgements

This book is the culmination of work over almost two decades. Many individuals and organisations contributed their ideas, knowledge and experience which informed the writing of this book. Progressive social service organisations of the 1980s helped shape the idea of development social welfare in South Africa. Many people participated in the development of the White Paper for Social Welfare. Today, many more individuals and organisations continue to work tirelessly under difficult circumstances and with limited resources to realise the vision of a caring, participative, just, people-centred and peaceful society. This book is dedicated to you all.

I am most grateful to Michael Rice, a former Commissioning Editor at Oxford University Press who encouraged me to write this book. A short sabbatical in 2002 at the School of Social Welfare at the University of California, Berkeley provided an opportunity to reflect, conduct research and exchange ideas. Thank you to Jimmy Midgley for facilitating the academic exchange and for his support for the project. I am especially indebted to Derek van der Merwe, the Deputy Vice Chancellor Academic at the University of Johannesburg for his support.

Jean Triegaardt, Ndangwa Noyoo and Theresa Wilson collaborated with me on this project. I am most grateful to you all for your assistance. Jean Triegaardt and Ndangwa Noyoo also co-authored the ancillary material for students. Thank you also to Tanya Santa for assistance with the bibliographies and library searches. Jimmy Midgley, Mel Gray, Antoinette Lombard and Rienie Schenck reviewed the first draft of the book. The manuscript has been enriched by the incisive comments of all the reviewers. Helpful comments were also received from Terry Sacco, Hettie Ellis and Huma Louw on specific chapters. Craig Mackenzie assisted with the editing of the book which was reassuring.

At Oxford University Press, I benefited immensely from the editorial advice and encouragement from Lydia Wilson. Many organisations provided valuable information on projects, photographs and shared documents and reports with the authors for which we are most grateful. Theresa Wilson assisted in gathering the material on the projects and the many examples from practice. Theresa and I have worked together on many research projects over the years and much of this information has found its way into the book. Thank you to my colleagues at the Department of Social Work, University of Johannesburg for creating the space for me to write.

As always, Azhar, you and the girls are my inspiration.

Leila Patel

Introduction

South Africa is one of the few countries that have adopted a developmental approach to social welfare in line with the United Nations World Declaration on Social Development (United Nations 1996). This African experiment with developmental social welfare is an ambitious one given the country's complex social, cultural, economic and political history, which has shaped the character of the social welfare system. This book is about social welfare and social development in South Africa in a changing regional and global world.

The welfare model inherited from colonialism and apartheid was inequitable, discriminatory and relied on inappropriate and unsustainable methods of service delivery. The apartheid welfare system was ineffective in addressing mass poverty, inequality and in meeting the basic needs of the majority of the population. Social policy was modelled on Western European institutional policies for the white minority whilst a residual system of social welfare prevailed for blacks. However, former racially based welfare policies had some positive features such as a delivery infrastructure, the enactment of social legislation, social security benefits and welfare services. A collaborative partnership between government, religious philanthropy, the voluntary and private sector was an important feature of the system.

'The welfare model inherited from colonialism and apartheid was inequitable, discriminatory and relied on inappropriate and unsustainable methods of service delivery.'

Throughout the 1980s, opposition social movements mobilised against a system of institutionalised racial differentiation in social welfare. These social movements advocated a just, equitable and democratic welfare dispensation and experimented with alternative models of social welfare delivery (Patel 1992). A bold new vision for social welfare unfolded which later shaped national social policy in a democratic society.

After the national democratic elections in 1994, the racial, paternalist and residual apartheid welfare system was abolished and a new dynamic approach suited to the demands of the global era was adopted. Inspired by a renewed interest in social development in the literature and the efforts of the United Nations to promote a social development perspective, the South African government adopted its policy – formulated in the *White Paper for Social Welfare* – in 1997 (Department of Welfare 1997). The new policies brought together the positive strands of social welfare theory and practice locally and globally, and these were integrated with country-specific conditions to produce a South African policy that is unique.

The developmental approach to social welfare was intended to modernise the welfare system to be more just, equitable, participatory and appropriate in meeting the needs of all South Africans. Neo-liberal solutions relying on market fundamentalism and minimal government intervention as well as the state-dominant model of the post-war welfare state were rejected as inappropriate in addressing the development needs of the society. The social development perspective attempts to transcend these ideas by harmonising social and economic development goals and investing in human capacities. The developmental approach is a pro-poor strategy promoting participation of the socially excluded in development activities to achieve social and economic justice, a partnership approach to social development, social solidarity and active social citizenship.

The past decade has been marked by momentous social, economic and political change in South Africa. Significant gains have been made in the policy and legislative domain, in the ending of racial discrimination, in access to social benefits and social services and in the creation of an integrated and development-oriented welfare system. Fiscal austerity, accompanied by liberalisation of the economy in order for it to be globally competitive, and the complexity of managing macro-change at all levels of the state and society simultaneously have proved to be immense challenges for all South Africans. Institutional challenges in the administration of social development continue to hamper effective service delivery at a time when the social costs of the transition are growing – as seen in rising unemployment and poverty, the escalation of the HIV/AIDS pandemic and increasing violence and crime. The backlog of services for the poor and the vulnerable as a result of the country's apartheid past, rising popular expectations and advocacy from organised civil society groups to expand social security benefits pose ongoing challenges for policy-makers.

The political and economic transition from apartheid to a non-racial democracy in a more integrated global world has come with increasing social costs. Many of the social problems and social conditions that the South African government, the Southern African Development Community (SADC) and the New Partnership for Africa's Development (NEPAD) are grappling with have national, regional and transnational dimensions. When the *White Paper for Social Welfare* was developed in the mid-1990s, its focus was essentially national. It was designed to overcome the legacy of the country's apartheid past and to promote the reconstruction and development of the society. Today, globalisation is at the centre of economic, political, social and cultural debates. But the implications of globalisation and regionalisation for social welfare and development are not well understood and should be the subject of on-going research – especially in relation to health, education, social welfare services and social security among countries in the Southern African Development Community (SADC).

Since the fall of apartheid, and the ending of South Africa's isolation from the rest of the world, a more cosmopolitan and culturally diverse society has emerged with greater movement between the countries in the African region and beyond. Opportunities exist to exchange ideas and experiences to promote regional and global solidarity, reduce poverty and inequality and achieve human and social development. Whilst globalisation is considered to offer great opportunities for human advancement, grave concerns remain about its threats to human security and the widening disparities between rich and poor within countries and between countries and regions. The marginalisation of Africa from the new global information economy and society has generated new economic, political, health, environmental, social and personal threats to human security. These conditions are considered to emanate from the global diffusion of neo-liberal ideology and the spread of the world capitalist system, which is leading to increased vulnerability of populations. Systems of social provision across the Sub-Saharan African region are under severe pressure to cope with the twin challenges of addressing past disparities and meeting new needs and demands in the present global era. New national and regional solutions that do not take account of the new risks brought about by world-wide and regional economic, political, technological, cultural and social integration will not achieve the desired results.

The social development perspective to social welfare provides the most appropriate and sustainable way to tackle the dual challenge of addressing past disparities and new needs flowing from the risks to human security and development in a global and Southern African regional context. The challenge for the future is to ensure that social and human development goals remain on the African agenda and that policy is implemented incrementally. Experience elsewhere shows that modest but consistent and targeted social investments are more likely to lead to real improvements in the quality of life of the people. Governments have a primary responsibility for ensuring social development as both a means and an end, and a public good. However, the private and voluntary sectors – especially indigenous, informal community-based voluntary organisations – also have a complementary responsibility to meet social goals and promote democracy, proactive citizenship and social solidarity.

There is widespread agreement among South African social work practitioners and educators about the need to reposition the discipline to respond appropriately and effectively to the changing local and global context (Weyers 2002; Lombard 2002; Drower 2002; Noyoo 2001; Gray 1998; McKendrick 1998; Potgieter 1998; Sewpaul 1997). The shift of social welfare towards a development paradigm is based on a constitutional, policy and legislative mandate. The execution of this mandate requires a fundamental transformation of the welfare sector. This has caused considerable tension and uncertainty about the management of change from the old system to the new. This process of change is ongoing and provides the social welfare sector with new opportunities for growth, development and the exploration of new conceptual approaches to social work practice from a development perspective (Louw 2002).

The notion that social work should be concerned with social change, problem-solving in human relations, and empowering and liberating people to enhance social well-being has been reiterated by international education and professional organisations (Hare 2004; International Association of Schools of Social Work 2002; International Federation of Social Workers 2002). These ideas resonate with current South African thinking and have been incorporated into the newly approved standards for social work education. The South African Qualifications Authority (SAQA) has devised standards for qualifications in the Health Sciences and Social Services fields. The SAQA Standards Generating Body for Social Work acknowledges the core purpose and rationale of social work to be in line with international trends and national social development. The SAQA Standards for Social Work are unequivocal about the need for social workers to be equipped with knowledge, skills, values and a critical reflective practice to deal with the consequences of social inequality, poverty and marginalisation (SAQA Standard Generating Body for Social Work 2003).

For the purpose of this book, social work from a social development perspective is the practical and appropriate application of knowledge, skills and values to enhance the well-being of individuals, families, groups, organisations and communities in their social context. It also involves the implementation of research and the development and implementation of social policies that contribute to social justice and human development in a changing national and global context. These are bold new directions for practitioners and the professional educational institutions that are required to bring their academic programmes for undergraduate and postgraduate qualifications in line with the newly adopted standards.

Purpose and scope of the book

The developmental perspective is increasingly being acknowledged as a viable alternative to conventional social welfare policy approaches such as the residual and institutional conceptions of social welfare. Since this is a new and evolving approach, there is considerable scope for its theoretical development and the consideration of its practice and educational implications (Midgley 2001; Midgley & Livermore 1997).

The developmental approach is being implemented in developing contexts and it is here that innovation and good practice lessons can be learnt. There is, however, a paucity of literature on the social development approach to social welfare and social work practice in the African context. A critical success factor in implementing the new approach is quality and appropriately trained social workers and the re-orientation of social service professionals to a social development perspective. The book aims to provide students and practitioners with a sound orientation to the theory and practice of developmental social welfare and social work in South Africa. It will enhance their grasp of the concepts, theories, skills and values of development social welfare and social work and draws on comparative literature and experience locally, regionally and globally. Critical thinking and a reflective approach to practice are emphasised. The content also draws on issues and real-life situations that social workers and social service professionals address all the time at a local level and how these are connected to themes in a changing global context.

The content of the text is in line with the new social development policy adopted by the South Africa government. The book also complies with the purpose of social work education and most of the key outcomes set by the SAQA Standards Generating Body for the Bachelors Degree in Social Work and some outcomes for the Masters Degree in Social Work.

The book is organised into three major parts. Part 1, 'Social welfare and social development in a global and regional context', contains two chapters. Chapter 1 examines the nature and meaning of concepts such as globalisation, social welfare and social development. Different theoretical perspectives that inform social welfare and social development are discussed with reference to their implications for social policy, social development programmes and development practice. Chapter 2 explores the concept of regional integration and its impact on social development in Southern Africa. The region is examined in relation to its historical development, its socio-economic and political context and the human development situation. The implications for regional co-operation, social policy and social development strategies and programmes are also addressed. These two chapters provide an overview of the context and the dual challenges facing South African social development policy-makers and practitioners. On the one hand they are faced with the challenge of addressing the legacy of colonialism and apartheid in the context of regional integration. The challenge on the other hand is to address the implications of globalisation and regionalism for social welfare and development. Students and practitioners are encouraged to examine these challenges and their practice implications.

Part 2, 'Social development in South Africa', contains four chapters. Chapter 3 explains the historical development of social welfare in South Africa including colonialism, apartheid and resistance to apartheid giving rise to the new directions and the transition to a democratic society. Social welfare in a post-apartheid society is discussed in Chapter 4, which focuses on the new context, the South African conception of developmental social welfare and the institutionalisation of the new approach through policy and legislation. The chapter also outlines how the system is structured, organised and resourced. These two chapters provide a context for the next two chapters that focus on the country's two key social development programmes: social security and social welfare services. Chapter 5 focuses on the conceptionalisation of social security, the nature and scope of social security, the policy debates and the developmental approach to social security. Developmental welfare services are discussed in Chapter 6 with reference to the paradigm shift from a social treatment model of welfare service delivery to a developmental approach. Developmental welfare services refer to the delivery of integrated and community-based social services, facilities, social investment programmes and social assistance to promote social justice, build human capabilities and enhance livelihoods and social functioning in order for people to lead productive and fulfilling lives. The chapter provides an overview of the nature and scope of developmental services with reference to children, youth and families, older persons, people with disabilities, HIV/AIDS, crime and violence and substance abuse. The major thrusts of services from a development perspective are also addressed.

Part 3, 'Social development practice', contains 3 chapters. Chapter 7 sets out the two-stage social development practice model that is contextually relevant to meeting needs and addressing social conditions in the South African context. The character and organising themes of social development practice are summarised in stage one of the model and the practice frame of reference is explained in stage two of the model. This chapter also defines the key concepts, purpose, mandate, knowledge, skills and values of developmental social work and social services. Chapter 8 demonstrates the key paradigm shift through documenting and critically reflecting on innovation and good practice lessons based on South African case studies. In Chapter 9, skills to enhance social development practice are examined that are considered critical to practice in the local context: these include micro-development, mezzo and macro skills in initiating and managing organisational change, managing anti-poverty projects and building and sustaining social development partnerships. Mediation, conflict resolution, action research, advocacy and anti-discriminatory practice skills are also addressed. These three chapters build on one another with the aim of enhancing student and practitioner knowledge and skills. The concluding chapter, Chapter 10, considers the future landscape of social development with reference to five themes: social development in a national and global context; regionalism and social development; social policy, institutional issues and social security and welfare services.

Bibliography

DROWER, S.J. (2002). Conceptualizing social work in a changed South Africa. *International Social Work*, 45:1, 7-20.

DEPARTMENT OF WELFARE (1997). *White Paper for Social Welfare*. Government Gazette No 18166 Vol 386.

GRAY, M. (1998). *Developmental Social Work in South Africa*. Cape Town: Phillips Publishers.

HARE, I. (2004). Defining social work for the 21st century. The International

Federation of Social Workers revised definition of social work. *International Social Work*, 47:3, 407-424.

INTERNATIONAL ASSOCIATION OF SCHOOLS OF SOCIAL WORK & INTERNATIONAL FEDERATION OF SOCIAL WORKERS (2002). Discussion Document on Global Qualifying Standards for Social Work Education and Training.

INTERNATIONAL FEDERATION OF SOCIAL WORK (2000). *International Federation of Social Workers' Definition of social work.* Adopted by the IFSW General Meeting 26th July 2000. Montreal, Canada.

LOMBARD, A. (2002). Social work training responding to the challenges of a changing environment. In Weyers, L. (ed.) (2002). *Repositioning Social Work within a Changing Environment. A collection of papers presented at 2002 National Conference of the JUC.* (153-165). Potchefstroom: School for Psychosocial and Behavioural Sciences, University of Potchefstroom.

LOUW, L. (2002). The national developmental paradigm mandates a repositioning of social services practice in South Africa. In Weyers, L. (ed.) (2002). *Repositioning Social Work within a Changing Environment. A collection of papers presented at 2002 National Conference of the JUC.* (3-9). Potchefstroom: School for Psychosocial and Behavioural Sciences, University of Potchefstroom.

MCKENDRICK, B.W. (1998). Social work education and training: from preparing for apartheid society to training for a developing democracy. *Social Work/Maatskaplike Werk*, 34, 99-111.

MIDGLEY, J. (2001). *New Directions in Social Work Practice: Learning from the Developing World.* California: School of Social Work, University of Southern California School of Social Work.

MIDGLEY, J. & LIVERMORE, M. (1997). The Developmental Perspective in Social Work: Educational Implications for a New Century. *Journal of Social Work Education*, 33:3, 573-585.

NEPAD (NEW PARTNERSHIP FOR AFRICA'S DEVELOPMENT) (2001). *New African Initiative.* Pretoria: Government Printers

NOYOO, N. (2001). Social Development in Sub-Saharan Africa: Lessons for social work practice in South Africa. *International Social Work*, 43: 4, 452-465.

PATEL, L. (1992). *Restructuring Social Welfare. Options for South Africa.* Johannesburg: Ravan Press.

POTGIETER, M.C. (1998). *The Social Work Process. Development to Empowerment of People.* South Africa: Prentice Hall Pty Ltd.

SAQA (South African Qualifications Authority) Standards Generating body for Social Work (2003). Bachelor of Social Work NQF Level 7. Government Notice 433 of 2003. Republic of South Africa: South African Qualifications Authority.

SEWPAUL, V. (1997). The RDP: Implications for Social Work Practice and Social Welfare Policy Development in South Africa. *Social Work/Maatskaplike Werk*, 33: 1, 5-18

UNITED NATIONS (1996). *Report of the World Summit for Social Development: Copenhangen,* 6-12 March 1995. New York: United Nations Department of Public Information.

WEYERS, L. (ed.) (2002). *Repositioning Social Work within a Changing Environment. A collection of papers presented at 2002 National Conference of the JUC.* School for Psychosocial and Behavioural Sciences. Potchefstroom: University of Potchefstroom.

PART 1

Social welfare and social development in a global and regional context

CHAPTER
1 Globalisation and social welfare

LEARNING OUTCOMES

After you have read this chapter you should be able to:
- Define the concepts of globalisation and social welfare.
- Describe the nature and meaning of globalisation for social welfare and human security.
- Discuss and compare the philanthropy, neo-liberal, institutional, social justice and social development perspectives on social welfare in terms of various key concepts.
- Give critical comment on what the future of social welfare is likely to be in the global era.

What is globalisation?

The term globalisation is used to refer to fundamental, large-scale, rapid and complex social changes in contemporary societies that have far-reaching consequences for people. Bilton et al. (2002:46) say that globalisation is the 'process whereby political, social, economic and cultural relations increasingly take on a global scale, and which has profound consequences for individuals' local experiences and everyday lives'.

Globalisation is often equated with 'the Great Transformation' (Polanyi 1973) of societies that unfolded during the 19th century global industrialisation process and that gave impetus to the rise of world capitalism. International interdependence can also be traced to the political and economic expansion of imperial powers through colonialism. Unlike globalisation in the industrial and colonial period, globalisation in the late 20th and early 21st centuries is unfolding as the rapid movement of technology, goods, money, people and ideas affecting people all over the world. It has brought into question existing systems of global governance and the role of nation states in determining their own destiny. New markets, technological innovation such as the internet and cellular phones, new actors, networks and new rules and standards are resulting in the growing interdependence of people and societies.

'Globalisation is everywhere and the dynamics of the globalisation process operate at both a local and a global level.'

Globalisation is not an abstract and remote process. The scale, speed and intensity of global connections make its impact immediate. Since it is a multifaceted phenomenon, the meeting of human needs cannot be viewed in isolation from these global changes. Today, the reality of globalisation is widely acknowledged by scholars, commentators and social actors across the globe (Bilton et al. 2002; Castells 2000; Giddens 2000; Friedman 2000; Mishra 1999; Midgley 1997; Rodrik 1997). Globalisation is everywhere and the dynamics of the globalisation process operate at both a local and a global level.

Some of the distinctive features of globalisation, such as the separation of time and space and disappearing borders, link people's lives in a way that has never happened before. Computer networks do not require face-to-face interaction in a particular place, and this leads to invisible social and institutional relations and increasing alienation. These developments have come about as a result of new technology that is considered to be the new engine of development. The era of globalisation is also referred to by some scholars as the information age, the 'network society' or information capitalism (Castells 2000).

Another distinctive feature of globalisation is the way in which industrial production is being globalised through the activities of transnational corporations. As the productive activities of these corporations grow internationally, they tend to be less connected to a place, and national and local community interests come to be of secondary importance. In order to remain globally competitive, their priorities are to curtail production costs, respond to changing market needs and remain innovative through scientific and technological developments. A new international division of labour is occurring (Bilton et al. 2002). One sector is made up of jobs in transnational corporations that require a highly skilled workforce. People occupying such positions are well paid and have secure jobs; they also tend to be male. The other economy consists of low-skilled jobs in the secondary labour market, and these are lower paid, insecure, offer limited opportunities for mobility and tend to be dominated by women, working-class youth, older people, migrant workers and ethnic minorities. In many countries there is now a growing pool of people who are structurally unemployed due to the large-scale restructuring of production processes. The globalisation of production has also been accompanied by the financial volatility of global capital markets, and this has resulted in economic insecurity and economic collapse in some countries.

Economic changes have also been accompanied by significant political and ideological shifts following the end of the Cold War in the late 1980s that led to the collapse of the Soviet Union and Central and Eastern European socialism. The former socialist countries adopted Western liberal-democratic capitalist systems and social welfare arrangements. The end of the Cold War also saw the consolidation of the position of the United States as a world power. The end of the Cold War dominated by two superpowers – the Soviet Union and the United States – did not result in peace and stability in the world. New forms of genocide, ethnic conflict, civil wars and terrorism have escalated, and these are threatening world peace and security and are impacting negatively on human and social development. Bilton et al. (2002) identify two related economic and political processes that are unfolding in the world today. On the one hand, there is a growing economic incorporation of countries into a single world economic system that is unequal and uneven in its development, and that is dominated by the rich and powerful industrial countries. On the other hand, these processes have also been accompanied by the break-up of some countries and regions at the end of the Cold War, and this has led to nationalist struggles and regional political and economic realignments in response to the new global dynamics.

These complex processes are also affecting the power of nationally elected governments, which are accountable to their electorates, to fully control the political, economic and social developments of their societies. Transnational corporations have the freedom to choose to establish manufacturing plants where they can secure cheaper labour. They make their own decisions to invest or to disinvest in particular-countries. Economic and political decisions are also being made in an increasingly regionalist world made up of regional blocs in the Americas, Europe and Asia. Countries outside of the three regional blocs, such as those on the African continent, face the risk of being permanently marginalised from world developments. It is widely believed that globalisation and regionalisation are two complementary processes, although there is considerable debate as to whether regionalism is not simply a response to protect regions from the globalisation process (Lee 2003). National governments are also being constrained in their choices as transnational political authorities and regional formations become more powerful and influential. At the same time there has been a growth of local, regional and global social movements opposing the negative consequences of the globalisation process, and these movements have become especially influential in shaping the global agenda.

The changes that are taking place at a global level are also of a profoundly social and cultural nature. As communication across borders is increasing via the media, through the migration of people and via cultural, intellectual and skills exchanges, more and more people are exposed to new ideas, norms, values, languages and religious beliefs. This awareness of a world greater than one's own has broadened the horizons of many people. It is widely believed that an understanding of cultural difference could lead to a greater appreciation of cultural diversity, tolerance and harmony among the peoples of the world. However, the changes produced by globalisation have also threatened existing cultural identities, and this is manifesting itself in xenophobia, racism, religious fundamentalism, discrimination, oppression, stereotypes and prejudice (Allen & Eade 2000; Borja & Castells 1997).

'The changes that are taking place at a global level are also of a profoundly social and cultural nature.'

Another dimension to the globalisation of culture is the growth of a consumer culture. This consumerism has been accompanied by the diffusion of Western culture, ideas and levels of consumption, and this process is being promoted by the media and the advertising industry to expand markets and the sale of commodities on a worldwide level. The American television series *Days of Our Lives* and *The Bold and the Beautiful*, while entertaining to most South Africans, also disseminate social knowledge and socialise people to the values and norms of a particular society. McDonalds, Levi's, Guess jeans and Nike are some of the international brands that are particularly popular among young people. Brand identification serves to draw them into a global consumer culture that is increasingly perceived to be a monoculture or a form of cultural imperialism (Becker 1987).

The globalisation of culture, regionalism and claims to the right to cultural expression have also given rise to an exponential growth in trade in cultural goods (e.g. books, magazines, multimedia products, software, records, films) and services (e.g. performing arts, cultural information, libraries, museums, documentation centres) (UNESCO 2000). The expansion of international trade in cultural industries has been accompanied by increasing attempts to liberalise trade in cultural goods and services through the World Trade Organisation. As markets are becoming more integrated, consumers are buying goods from many different parts of the world in local shops and supermarkets. Local businesses such as community-based cultural tourism initiatives will also have to compete with foreign goods in their own communities, and this may provide them with new risks and opportunities to increase their export markets. Fundamental to the debate on the commercialisation of culture is the question as to what the relationship between the economic and non-economic value of cultural goods and services is. Can a price tag be assigned to the intangible aspects that culture conveys, such as beauty, heritage, identity, belonging, social cohesion or the meaning of life? Should cultural services such as libraries and museums be considered a public good and be made accessible to all people?

While globalisation has distinctive economic, political and cultural features, the meaning of globalisation at a social level and its implications for social development are not fully understood. Of particular significance is the meaning of globalisation for social care and caring labour (UNDP 1999). The importance of human ties, networks of social relations, trust and the sense of identity and belonging that is engendered from being part of a community or neighbourhood with real-life and face-to-face interactions has been widely acknowledged. Networks of support are considered critical to human development and to the care and support of vulnerable people (Trevillion 1999).

'While globalisation has distinctive economic, political and cultural features, the meaning of globalisation at a social level and its implications for social development are not fully understood. Of particular significance is the meaning of globalisation for social care and caring labour.'

Social care involves the provision of social and emotional support systems and networks in the family and the community and may include the provision of tangible assistance and care for children, the sick, the elderly and people with physical and mental disabilities. Women have traditionally provided social care. As the participation of women in the labour force has increased since the Second World War, it has also changed economic structures and family and household relations with far-reaching implications for the provision of care in the home and the community. Caring labour is generally unpaid work provided by men and women for the benefit of their families and communities. As pressure has mounted on the time of both men and women in the changing world of work, there has been a shift to social care being provided as a public service. There is a growing private market in care services that is dominated largely by women – who are over-represented in caring professions and tend to be lowly paid. The social dynamics of globalisation have contributed to increased pressure on family and community systems of support and this has resulted in the expansion of the private provision of care services. This changing situation presents great challenges for policy-makers. As regards the provision of social support and social care, what should the relations between the family, community, market and the state be? A further problem is promoting gender equality and a more equitable distribution of the costs and burdens of care.

New communications technologies have the potential to strengthen social networks through connecting people from afar and improving social service delivery systems. However, social scientists have argued that as market and human relations become more impersonal and remote, people become disconnected or disengaged from their local communities (UNDP 1999). Much community care has also been provided voluntarily and has been an expression of altruism; such altruism is being undermined by the burgeoning market for private care.

Advocates of civic service, volunteerism and community service are attempting to find new ways of countering these trends through fostering greater civic participation and social citizenship at global, national and local levels. The concept 'civic service' refers broadly to voluntary service and citizen action to promote the public good and extends beyond the family to local communities, national and cross-national arenas (Moore et al. 2003). Civic service is increasingly being recognised as a significant social institution and an emerging social phenomenon in a context of global social, cultural, economic and political change.

These developments have also been accompanied by growing opportunities for civic participation to promote social and democratic development. The 1990s has seen a proliferation of civil society groups, non-governmental organisations, informal institutions, volunteerism and social movements operating outside the state in both the North and the South (UNDP 2002; Fisher 1998; Fowler 1995). The flow of resources through international and transnational NGOs has also increased. Civil society organisations are playing a significant role in providing humanitarian support, advocacy for human development, peace and improved representation of people in democratic institutions (UNDP 2002; Swilling & Russell 2002; Anheier & Salamon 1999; Fisher 1998; Fowler 1995). These trends appear to be emerging due to a decline in traditional forms of civic participation through trade unions and political parties. This decline has also given rise to the search for novel forms of engagement with public issues and for new ways of participation, representation, collective action and self-expression.

Globalisation and human security

The United Nations Development Programme (UNDP) in its *Human Development Report* (1999) argued that globalisation provides new opportunities for addressing poverty, fostering global solidarity, the exchange of ideas, knowledge and a shared commitment to achieve human development. Increased trade and foreign investments in the global era also have the potential to generate economic growth, which is necessary for social development. However, if economic growth does not bring positive social benefits and the enhancement of human well-being and security, then limited social progress would have been achieved.

There are grave fears that these opportunities and benefits will bypass the African continent, effectively pushing poor people, countries and regions to the margins (Castells 2000). Liberalisation and privatisation are shaping access to new markets. Industrial trade rules are feared to be working against the economic interests of poor countries, and have failed to restrain economic protectionism in the developed world. The pressures of global competition could also undermine care and social support systems, and threaten income and job security due to fluctuations in financial markets. Globalisation is widely considered to be a threat to human security in both rich and poor countries (UNDP 1999).

'Globalisation is widely considered to be a threat to human security in both rich and poor countries.'

The risks to human security identified by the UNDP (1999) include economic, political, employment, environmental, physical and social factors. These threats to human security are multidimensional in their impact, and lead to stagnation or reversal of human development indicators in many parts of the world such as sub-Saharan Africa. However, in other parts of the world significant progress has been made and many billions of people have benefited from globalisation (UNDP 2003).

Economic insecurity. Financial volatility in global markets and the economic turmoil and collapse in Mexico, East and South East Asia and Argentina starting in the late 1990s demonstrate the risks to human security that such countries have had to face (Singh 2000). Crises of this nature have become common with the spread of global capitalism with consequences for increasing poverty levels, personal vulnerability and the reversal of gains in human development indicators in those societies. Growing inequality and widening of disparities have been noted between groups within countries and between countries and regions of the world (UNDP 2003).

Global economic integration has also impacted negatively on South Africa's economy. According to Gelb (2005:372), the South African economy like other 'emerging markets' that have embraced greater financial openness in the economy, has not been able 'to avoid the volatility and destabilisation associated with external capital flows'. Since 1996, South Africa has experienced three foreign exchange crises resulting in the reversal of capital flows to the country and exchange rate collapse (Gelb 2005). The rand depreciated by nine and a half percent in 2000 and it has strengthened considerably since then. Currency volatility has been cited as an important reason for creating an unfavourable climate for job creation and economic growth. Substantial economic growth is needed to address the backlog in meeting human needs accumulated through apartheid. Resources have therefore been constrained.

Employment and income insecurity. The economic and corporate restructuring necessary to be globally competitive has resulted in the loss of jobs, incomes, and social protection schemes connected with employment and a weakening of labour standards. Many countries have adopted more flexible labour standards and policies to encourage investment but this has also led to increased vulnerability of workers and households (Mishra 1999; Rodrik 1997).

Employment insecurity also leads to income insecurity and poverty. 'Despite higher living standards that globalisation has delivered in large parts of the world, hundreds of millions of people have experienced economic reversals rather than advances', states the UNDP Report (2003:16).

In the apartheid period, South Africa recorded negative economic growth per capita for close to a decade before the advent of democracy. Since 1994, an average economic growth of 2.8 percent has been recorded, but this has not been accompanied by growth in employment to significantly reduce poverty. The restructuring of the economy and pressures to actively engage with the international economy have resulted in a shift from public services, mining and construction to financial and business service sectors. A dual economy is emerging: one part is made up of skilled workers employed in the financial and business sectors, while the 'second economy' contains unskilled workers in the informal sectors. The benefits of growth are not reaching the 'second economy' and the consequences have been unemployment, lack of skills and marginalisation. This in turn has led to the social exclusion of millions of people who are denied a livelihood. In 2003, approximately 4.2 million (mainly unskilled) people were unemployed (Republic of South Africa 2003). On the other hand, a shortage of skilled workers exists in many sectors. Social exclusion is defined by Castells (2000:71) as a 'process by which individuals and groups are systematically barred from access to positions that would enable them to achieve an autonomous livelihood.'

Health insecurity. Globalisation has given rise to the rapid movement of people across the world through travel and migration, and this has spread diseases such as HIV/AIDS, which has presented a particular challenge to all countries. The disease has quadrupled since the first cases were recorded in the 1980s. Since then, 42 million people globally have been infected with the virus and almost half have died. The UNDP (2003) estimates, moreover, that 13 million children were orphaned in this time. The social and economic impact of HIV/AIDS on individuals, families and communities is enormous: the pandemic constitutes a human tragedy that is immeasurable. Reduced life expectancy, loss of skills, increased poverty, vulnerability and social costs in compromised child development due to loss of parents and caregivers are some of the consequences for human security. Particularly affected by the disease is the world's poorest region, sub-Saharan Africa. The HIV infection rates have increased exponentially in South Africa with grave social and economic consequences which will be discussed in Chapter 6.

'The social and economic impact of HIV/AIDS on individuals, families and communities is enormous: the pandemic constitutes a human tragedy that is immeasurable.'

Environmental degradation and consumer pressures are also leading to the depletion of the earth's natural resources and this is resulting in food and health insecurity – especially in the poorest regions of the world.

Personal and community insecurity. Limited research has been conducted on the impact of globalisation at individual, family and community levels. The supporters of globalisation may argue that social problems and public issues such as crime and violence, child labour, personal vulnerability, poverty and disease are not new and can be traced to the devastating effects of industrialisation in the 18th and 19th centuries. However, Castells (2000) argues that the nature, form and scope of some contemporary social problems are directly related to the social changes brought about by the globalisation of economies and societies. An example of this is transnational crime involving the illicit trade in drugs, women, children and weapons, and the laundering of money. These criminal activities are considered to present some of the greatest threats to personal and community safety and security. Activities of this sort have also threatened the security and economies of nations – especially developing and transitional societies. This is occurring because criminality has been able to flourish in a global environment of deregulated capital markets and has taken advantage of new communications and transportation technologies, especially in drug trafficking and the trade of arms. The internet, for instance, is used for trafficking in women and girls and in the sexual exploitation of children – which is a fundamental violation of human rights. Castells (2000) is of the view that the disintegration of the nuclear family and patriarchy without something else to replace it is one reason for the current situation. These global trends are also significant in the South African context as crime and trafficking in children and drugs are increasingly taking on a transnational form. Social development policies and programmes need to take cognisance of these changes.

The above demonstrates how the globalisation process impacts on the lives of people. The personal security of individuals, families and their communities are being threatened by the growing interdependence of people and nations, impacting on their ability to live long, healthy, creative and fulfilling lives. The real wealth of nations is said to lie in its people (UNDP 2003). The purpose of development is to create an enabling environment for people to achieve human security and personal and social well-being. Responses to globalisation have been largely of an economic nature and the UNDP in successive Human Development Reports has drawn attention to the need for a social and human response to globalisation (UNDP 2003; 2002; 2000; 1999). A fuller understanding of the social aspects of globalisation is needed. However, the implications of globalisation for the welfare state have been commented on by different authors, especially in relation to the contraction of the welfare state in the era of globalisation (Midgley, Tracy, Livermore 2000; Mishra 1998).

Social welfare systems across the globe have been shaped by the complex social, cultural, economic and political histories of countries and regions. There is therefore considerable variation in the vision, purposes, principles and types of social welfare policies and programmes in different societies. Welfare systems also differ in how the relations between the state, the voluntary sector and the market are conceptualised. Different beliefs and assumptions about what social welfare is, exist in contemporary societies.

'Social welfare systems across the globe have been shaped by the complex social, cultural, economic and political histories of countries and regions.'

What is social welfare?

The idea of organised social welfare emerged in the late 19th century to address social problems and meet human needs arising from industrialisation. The latter process involved the re-organisation of productive activity and gave rise to the factory system, urbanisation, the separation of church and state and scientific and technological innovation. This period, which is also referred to as the rise of modernity, was marked by the development of new forms of government and the increasing bureaucratisation of societies. The nation-state exercised power in a defined geographic area and played a critical role in the economy, in the exercise of social control and in the regulation of access to societal goods and services based on citizenship rights.

Initially, social welfare services were provided by religious and voluntary organisations. Gradually governments, the voluntary sector and other social actors in society became involved with meeting needs, managing social problems and providing social benefits and social programmes. From this perspective social welfare can broadly be defined as:

> *'A nation's system of programs, benefits, and services that help people meet those social, economic, education, and health needs that are fundamental to the maintenance of society' (Zastrow 1995:5).*

This definition identifies what people can expect from society and is a yardstick by which a society can measure how well it is meeting the needs of its people, both rich and poor (Kirst-Ashman 2003; Zastrow 2000). Social welfare is also understood to be not only about meeting needs; it is also about the management of social problems or conditions and the maximisation of opportunities to promote the common good (Midgley 1997). Social welfare policies and programmes serve to promote social inclusion, social cohesion and integration in a society. The idea of social welfare also encompasses the social goals and the guiding principles of a society and what it hopes to achieve for its citizens. A state of human well-being is considered to be the goal of social welfare (Midgley 1997). The concept social welfare, according to Giddens (1998), is essentially a non-economic one and is of a psychosocial nature. He argues that the achievement of human well-being and human security – a state of positive social welfare – is a worthy societal goal to pursue. When social goals are combined with economic objectives and investments in human capital, a 'welfare society' can be achieved.

In liberal democratic societies, the state gains legitimacy through social welfare provision and has to obtain the consent or support of the people for its social welfare programmes that are publicly funded. The social welfare policies that are actually adopted are often highly contested by interest groups and are generally the outcome of negotiations. The meaning of social welfare and the assumptions underpinning social welfare are intensely political and ideological and continue to shape the debate about what the direction of social welfare should be in a society. In an interconnected and interdependent global world, the nature and meaning of social welfare continues to be contested. In many developed and developing countries, social welfare policies and programmes have been in retreat. This has led to a narrow definition of social welfare, which emphasises interventions by charitable and voluntary organisations. Instead of being seen as a positive contribution, social welfare has been viewed negatively as a drain on societal resources and has been criticised for promoting the dependency of welfare recipients on the state. Moral values also shape how welfare systems are viewed.

'The meaning of social welfare and the assumptions underpinning social welfare are intensely political and ideological and continue to shape the debate about what the direction of social welfare should be in a society.'

For the purpose of this book, social welfare is broadly defined as an integrated system of social policies, social services, benefits, programmes and social security to promote social development, social justice and social functioning in a caring and enabling environment (Department of Welfare 1997). The goal of social welfare is to achieve the wider societal and global goal of human well-being and human security. Welfare policies and programmes are considered to have the following dimensions: the meeting of needs, the management of social problems, the maximisation of opportunities, and the promotion of human empowerment and social inclusion.

Social welfare focuses on, inter alia, income protection, attaining autonomous livelihoods and minimum living standards, and the meeting of needs of populations at risk such as children, youth, women and families, the elderly, people with physical and mental disabilities and chronic illnesses including HIV/AIDS. The management of contemporary social problems such as mass poverty, joblessness, substance misuse, crime and violence, urban decay, rural underdevelopment and the protection of children, youth and those who are vulnerable, are some of the social conditions that are receiving public attention in the South African context.

The welfare system is made up of various professionals and paraprofessionals in health, education and the social services. Social work and other social service professions such as auxiliary social workers, community development workers, child and youth care workers, probation officers, social security personnel and social care workers are also an integral part of the welfare system.

Theoretical perspectives on social welfare

'The dominant theoretical approaches to social welfare are: philanthropy, institutional, conservative, critical and social development perspectives.'

The thrust of the argument is that political, ideological, economic, social and cultural beliefs have a direct bearing on how social welfare is conceptualised and characterised. Other factors play a role: the history of a country and region and its level of development have a bearing on the way social welfare arrangements evolve. The dominant theoretical approaches to social welfare are: philanthropy, institutional, conservative, critical and social development perspectives (Midgley, Tracy, Livermore 2000; Midgley 1995). The different approaches to social welfare are discussed with reference to their implications for what kind of social welfare system is most desirable in a changing national and global world.

Social philanthropy

Through the ages private citizens and philanthropic organisations have met human needs through encouraging the provision of private goods and services to the needy. Philanthropy and charitable giving has ancient roots and is often prescribed by religious beliefs. Most religions, including Judaism, Christianity, Islam and Hinduism, prescribe charitable giving. In medieval times, the church played a significant role in caring for the needy. Philanthropy is also deeply rooted in the culture and traditions of societies. Oriental philosophy and tradition based on Confucianism and Buddhism has inspired people to engage in goodwill giving and the sharing of oneself for the benefit of others (Edna 2002). Individual and collective support for kinship groups and the community in traditional African societies found expression in the concept *Ubuntu*, which means humanity.

'The spirit of Ubuntu is one of mutual care and support and one's humanity is expressed through this.'

The social philanthropy approach to social welfare became firmly established in Europe and North America in the 19th century during the industrial revolution. Private philanthropic associations and religious aid pioneered the meeting of needs through alms giving to the poor, social relief, and taking care of the needy. During the colonial era, Christian philanthropy furthered by missionary activities formed part of organised philanthropy in countries that were under colonial rule. This approach to social provision was implemented in the colonies and, although it was of humanitarian value, it also undermined indigenous and traditional systems of giving and the provision of social support. According to Midgley (1995), missionary and secular philanthropy preceded government intervention.

In contemporary times, philanthropic voluntary organisations constitute a substantial sector in the overall system of meeting needs and have become more secular in their approach. Philanthropy is broadly defined as a love of mankind and the giving of practical benevolent assistance to people in need (Sykes 1982, The Concise Oxford Dictionary 1982). Philanthropy is also known as voluntary action for public good through voluntary action, voluntary association and voluntary giving. It also refers to monetary or non-monetary contributions by individuals, the corporate sector, foreign donors and international non-governmental organisations for humanitarian relief, developmental assistance, human rights, environmental protection, community development, educational, cultural and scientific development and peace and disarmament, to mention a few. The goals of philanthropy are to meet human and social needs. Philanthropic values such as charitable giving to the poor and humanitarianism are also emphasised. Social philanthropy exists in both developed and developing contexts and in different ideological systems, which may either encourage or inhibit its development. While philanthropic organisations rely largely on private donations and some support from governments, they are independent and organise services on a formal and/or informal basis.

Social welfare programmes delivered by philanthropic organisations have been inclined to be remedial, providing social relief and humanitarian aid, and have traditionally tended to view the beneficiaries of their services as passive receivers of goods and services. Eligibility was often based on selective access to services and benefits on account of religious affiliation or the notion of the 'worthy' poor. While the social philanthropy approach is traditionally associated with piecemeal and ameliorative interventions, social reformers operating within this framework have played a significant role in advocacy for social justice and in the promotion of social well-being.

International and transnational philanthropy is also expanding with the world-wide growth of civil society organisations over the last three decades. These organisations are becoming a significant force in promoting global networking, the pooling of resources and in effecting transnational co-operation in areas separate from those pursued by national governments. Iriye (2002) traced the historical development of international organisations over several decades and recorded the role that they have played and are playing in promoting international relations and human rights, and in humanitarian and social action aimed at steering globalisation in a more positive direction. In the changing global context, many national and international philanthropic organisations are dealing with the new challenges of accountability, more effective social partnerships and the redefinition of their relations with the state and multinational corporations. As they engage more with the state and the private sector, the question of their organisational autonomy and independence from the state and corporate interests continue to be of central concern (Patel 2003a; Iriye 2002).

Institutional approaches

'The institutional perspective conceives of social welfare as a normal 'first-line' function of modern industrial societies.'

Wilensky and Lebeaux (1965) identified two conceptions of social welfare: the residual or conservative and the institutional perspectives – both of which have been widely cited in the conceptualisation of welfare systems. The residual approach holds that social welfare institutions come into play when the market and the normal systems of support, such as the family and community networks, break down. It is associated with conservatism as a philosophy that upholds the idea of individual responsibility for meeting human needs. The institutional perspective conceives of social welfare as a normal 'first-line' function of modern industrial societies. This conception of social welfare (also referred to as the welfare state) is the opposite of the residual model.

Government involvement in social welfare can be traced to the enactment of the Elizabethan Poor Laws in the 16th century and to Bismarck's social insurance schemes in the 19th century, which were emulated across Europe and Britain in later years. Progressive liberalism and social democratic ideology have inspired institutional approaches to social welfare policy. Welfare states also emerged in countries with strong labour movements, which worked in close co-operation with governments and the private sector in developing and implementing social and active labour market policies, full employment and work-related social protection schemes such as social insurance.

Institutionalists are of the view that government agencies are the best deliverers of social policies and that access to social provision and social rights should be institutionalised through legislation, fiscal measures, statutory regulations and comprehensive services. The principle of universality is central to the institutional approach. It refers to the right of all citizens of a country to universal coverage and access to services and benefits such as income security, medical care, education and housing on an ongoing basis. Segal & Brzuzy (1998:13) define universality as the idea that social welfare should be equally available to 'all members of society, regardless of their income or their means'.

Other components of the institutional approach are full employment (or, at least very low rates of unemployment) and a set of social assistance programmes that are publicly funded, such as child and family support and social grants for the elderly and people with disabilities. The state's role in social welfare provision is substantial in the institutional approach, and state interventionism is seen as a necessary step in meeting needs in a modern industrial society.

Welfare states are perceived to ameliorate the negative effects of market failure in capitalist societies. Through the institutionalisation of services and benefits, liberal and social democratic regimes are able to retain their commitment to social goals. For institutional theorists, social rights are as important as civil and political rights. Values of altruism, social solidarity and collectivism underpin institutional thinking. Welfare states are characterised by extensive state spending and a weak non-profit sector that has been displaced by the strong service delivery role of the state. In spite of this, non-profit organisations do remain active but within a state-dominant mixed economy of social welfare.

Social welfare programmes in these types of political and social systems would tend to be more institutionalised in the form of public policy mandating and regulating such activities. For example, tax incentives and credits may exist to encourage individuals, families, voluntary organisations and businesses to become involved in social welfare and citizen action as an expression of altruism, a moral imperative of society and a public benefit. Social welfare programmes are also likely to be government-driven, but to be undertaken in collaboration with non-governmental organisations. Voluntary activities may be encouraged as an expression of collectivism and the personal development of the participants, and as a way of promoting social cohesion and stability in the society.

The institutional model has been implemented in most industrial nations in different ways, but those in Western Europe and particularly Scandinavia are considered to be the best examples of institutional ideals. Welfare states, and particularly the European and Scandinavian welfare states, have supported international humanitarian development and furthered human rights and peace initiatives. These programmes are also supported to promote social democratic ideas as solutions to society's ills.

Institutional approaches have been contested in the late 20th and early 21st centuries, and this has resulted in the restructuring and curtailment of social welfare policies and programmes due to reductions on social spending. Mishra (1999) argues that the globalisation process has adversely affected welfare states in that it has constrained the autonomous social policy choices of governments and has eroded institutionalised social rights. Other challenges facing welfare states are related to the adverse effects on national minimum standards, wages, working conditions, social protection schemes and full employment as public sector jobs have declined. These changes have exacerbated conflict in these societies, impacting negatively on social cohesion (Rodrik 1997).

The impact of institutional approaches on social welfare in the developing world has been limited. Some of the reasons cited are: the weakness of the state and democratic institutions, civil conflict and war, low levels of economic growth, fiscal constraints caused by the debt trap and the increasing marginalisation of poor countries and some regions in the global economy. Structural adjustment policies employed in many African countries in the 1980s and 1990s upon the advice of the International Monetary Fund and the World Bank also resulted in limiting social spending and the role of the state in social provision. Institutional approaches cannot be applied in their pure form in developing counties given the above scenario (Macpherson & Midgley 1987). However, what the nature and scope of the state and non-state actors should be in poor countries continues to be the subject of ongoing debate in the consideration of social welfare policy options.

Residual or Conservative approaches

'The residual approach to social welfare ... is associated with minimal state intervention in the provision and financing of social welfare services and social security.'

The residual approach to social welfare cited by Wilensky & Lebeaux (1965) is associated with minimal state intervention in the provision and financing of social welfare services and social security. It sees the family and the private market as the natural mechanisms for meeting needs. If there is a breakdown in these natural systems of support then a third mechanism in the form of social welfare comes into being. This proposition presumes that social welfare provision should be of a short-term, emergency nature and should tide people over a crisis period. Provision should cease once the crisis is over.

Eligibility for services and benefits is based on a means test, which uses a formula to set minimum criteria for determining a person's eligibility (New Dictionary for Social Work 1995). Instead of universal access to all citizens irrespective of income and need, the principle of selectivity involves the targeting of resources at selected groups who are considered to be most deserving. Selectivity is defined as the idea that social welfare benefits should be 'restricted to those who can demonstrate need through established eligibility criteria' (Segal & Brzuzy 1998:13). Critics of the principle of selectivity argue that it stigmatises those who are targeted to receive benefits and services and that it reinforces social divisions in the society.

The residual conception of social welfare is derived from conservative or neo-liberal approaches to social policy and has its origins in the laissez-faire economics of Adam Smith in the 18th century and Milton Friedman in the 20th century (Ginsberg 2000). During the post-World War II years, the institutional ideas of Keynes and Beveridge held greater sway and informed post-war reconstruction in Europe. Keynes argued for greater involvement of government in the economy to stimulate the demand for goods and services through full employment policies, cutting taxes or boosting welfare spending. These measures he said, would in the short-term address the problems arising from economic booms and slumps in capitalist economies. When the economy improved, government would be able to trim its spending and pay off its debts. However, these ideas were later challenged by proponents of neo-liberalism such as former President Ronald Reagan of the United States of America and former Prime Minister Margaret Thatcher in Britain in the 1980s. The ideas of the radical right were influential in international organisations at that time and helped to spread these views across the globe. As international economic competition grew, many welfare states struggled with the impact of globalisation on their economies as they faced increasing financial pressures and rising chronic unemployment. Other social and demographic changes also impacted on the viability of welfare states. It was against this background that conservative thinking began to hold greater sway: many governments began to make social policy adjustments, and this resulted in limiting or rolling back public social provision. In the contemporary global era, there has been a resurgence of conservative ideas about the economy and society.

The resurgence of free market ideas and reduced government involvement in social welfare is strongly associated with the conservative or neo-liberal thinking that has accompanied economic integration in the global context. Conservatives hold the view that governments should leave economies alone, as this is the best way to create wealth and development. They also argue for limited government intervention in human affairs, free markets, economic liberalisation and privatisation, individual responsibility for well-being and the creation of mediating structures between those in need and governments to address social problems and to defuse conflict between them.

Conservatives view government involvement in social welfare as an extension of big government into realms previously reserved for private non-profit activities. They tend to support local, community-based and community-run programmes as the best vehicles for addressing social problems rather than rely on public bureaucracies. For them, mediating institutions such as voluntary organisations also help to cushion the pressure on governments from grassroots groups. Social welfare from a conservative perspective tends to emphasise strong moral or religious principles, promote loyalty to the dominant ideology, emphasise individual responsibility, and target services and benefits at those in need and most deserving of social support. It also provides short-term crisis-intervention assistance delivered by non-governmental organisations. This approach conceives of social programmes as aiming to change the individual rather than the society.

The proponents of social welfare from a conservative point of view also advocate privatisation of social welfare through payment for services, private social insurance provision and the delivery of services by commercial enterprises, as these are considered more effective and efficient service-providers (Ginsberg 2000). They also argue that public resources spent on social welfare should be redirected to productive expenditure to promote economic growth and employment. Conservatives also hold that social welfare benefits create an underclass of poor people and dependency on welfare benefits – and tend to cause more problems than they actually solve. These ideas have challenged earlier notions of collective responsibility for social welfare and have resulted in considerable debate about the future of social welfare in the global era.

'The proponents of social welfare from a conservative point of view also advocate privatisation of social welfare...'

Critical approaches

Critical approaches are associated with feminist, neo-Marxist, post-modern and anti-discriminatory perspectives to social welfare, social policy and professional practice (Iatridis 2000; Robbins et al. 1998; Kincheloe & McLaren 1994.) These approaches denote an analysis of capitalist change and how capitalism's dominant institutions serve the interests of profit and an oppressive class. Critical analysts attempt to uncover the contradictions between capitalist notions of equality and race, class, gender and other forms of social discrimination and social divisions in society such as disability, age and sexual preference. Understanding power relations in order to create more humane and egalitarian societies through the promotion of social and economic justice is central to critical ideas. Public policy discourse tends to focus on social reformist community perspectives to social change, civil and human rights, the oppressive elements of the state and its bureaucracies and the power of professionals and experts in representing their interests.

Critical theorists challenge positivism which is a doctrine that claims that social life can be understood and studied in the same way that natural scientists study the world. Phenomena it is argued exist, in causal relations to one another and can be studied empirically and objectively. Positivism is associated with the rise of modernism which refers to massive technological, economic, political and social changes which occurred in the 18th and 19th centuries. Modernity saw the rise of capitalism and industrialisation, population changes and the rise of new forms of government. The Enlightenment movement of this period advocated new ideas about understanding the natural and social worlds, social progress based on reason, rationality and a world free of religious dogma (Bilton et al. 2001). The theoretical traditions of critical theory can be traced to the work of scholars of the Frankfurt School in Germany about seventy years ago. These perspectives gave rise later to critical social science associated with post-positivist social thinking and later to post-modernism (Iatridis 2000; Robbins et al. 1998). The assumptions under-girding social constructionism is that knowledge and social reality are relative concepts that are socially constructed on the basis of individuals' lived experiences, expressions and understandings of their world. This approach is essentially an interactive process involving analysis, reflection, questioning and monitoring of one's behaviour in relation to others. An important tenet of constructionist thinking is that human beings construct their worlds in a community rather than independently and they 'create knowledge from the interaction between their existing knowledge or beliefs and the new ideas they encounter' (Iatridis 2002:395–396).

Social welfare policies, programmes and professional practice in the social services from a critical perspective have found expression in the social justice approach and reflective practice which has been inspired by social constructionism. It is the process whereby human behaviour is mediated or negotiated through social processes such as social dialogue and human interaction. Human behaviour is thought to be socially constructed. These two approaches are discussed briefly with reference to social welfare policy and professional practice. It should be noted that these approaches do not spell out a vision of social welfare from a critical perspective. However, the idea of a humane and egalitarian society would be considered to be the most desirable.

Proponents of the social justice approach are likely to be engaged in advocacy to effect change in public policies, legislation and institutions in order to make them more responsive to the needs of disempowered and under-represented classes and social groups. Social and community action involving grassroots groups in issue-oriented campaigns for social change and forming local, national and global coalitions to effect change are other strategies that are also pursued. Activists in developed and developing countries that were involved with the mobilisation and organisation of poor people's movements have inspired social justice advocates. Paulo Freire worked with poor communities in Brazil in the 1970s and involved them in a critical reflection of their social reality. He developed the concept 'conscientisation', which referred to the process of awareness-raising through dialogue with people about the causes of

'Proponents of the social justice approach are likely to be engaged in advocacy to effect change in public policies, legislation and institutions in order to make them more responsive to the needs of disempowered and under-represented classes and social groups.'

their problems as they experienced them in everyday life (Freire 1970). His ideas are still considered relevant today and have been used by women's groups to develop awareness of gender oppression and an anti-discriminatory professional practice.

Critical theory has also informed social service practice with individuals, groups, communities and organisations and has found expression in the concept of reflective practice closely associated with the work of Donald Schön (1987; 1983). Thompson (2002:234) states that reflective practice is 'an approach to professional practice that emphasises the need for practitioners to avoid standardized, formula responses to the situations they encounter. It involves coming to terms with the complexity, variability and uncertainty associated with human service work'. Reflective practice requires an active and interactive process of understanding social situations and constructing solutions, and uses experience, knowledge and theoretical perspectives to guide and inform practice. These approaches are discussed further in Part 3, 'Social development practice'.

The goals and principles of this approach emphasise social and economic justice, democratisation, transformation of societal institutions and empowerment of the oppressed and marginalised. The social justice approach to social welfare policy favours universal access and coverage of social welfare provision, and promotes egalitarianism and the redistribution of resources in favour of the marginalised. In countries undergoing fundamental social change, policy and programme goals and interventions emphasise social transformation and renewal of education, health care and the social services. The choice of social goals is considered to be more important than the pursuit of rational technical means to achieve them. Beneficiaries of services are perceived to be active participants in a struggle for emancipation. Instead of viewing them as welfare clients, they are considered to be partners and collaborators in effecting personal and societal change. Practitioners also do not perceive themselves as detached and value-neutral about the social issues being addressed.

Finally, proponents of the social justice approach tend to value their independence from mainstream institutions and are likely to locate themselves outside the state and private sector organisations in order to maximise opportunities for critical engagement and expression. Often, alternative institutions are developed to promote a different vision to the status quo such as co-operatives and community-based independent living arrangements. In practice, there are many differences among social justice advocates about what the most effective tactics and strategies are. Whilst some proponents of the social justice approach may be more purist and exclusive in their actions, others may adopt a more active engagement stance – forming broad alliances with diverse actors to influence and shift opinion on a range of issues. These differences are also evident in their local and international activities.

'In practice, there are many differences among social justice advocates about what the most effective tactics and strategies are.'

In response to globalisation, there has been a resurgence of interest in critical perspectives in the field of social welfare, social research, social policy and professional practice. In a changing and complex world, critical theories provide important perspectives on power, inequality, social exclusion and social control in an increasingly interdependent but also fragmented world. These perspectives are also useful in interpreting the meaning of these changing conditions for people and in understanding how they are socially constructing aspects of the human experience (Robbins et al. 1998).

Social development

The social development approach to social policy was first introduced by the United Nations to address human development needs in the world's poorest nations following independence from colonial rule in the 1960s. In the late 20th century, the social development approach re-emerged as a response to unequal and distorted development and was endorsed by the United Nations World Summit for Social Development in 1995 (United Nations 1996).

The proponents of social development argue that social investments in social programmes that enhance people's welfare through their participation in the productive economy are the most effective ways of enhancing people's welfare and achieving economic development. Midgley (1995:250) defines social development as 'a process of planned social change designed to promote the well-being of the population as a whole in conjunction with a dynamic process of economic development'. The approach requires purposeful intervention from state and non-state actors and the 'creation of organisational and institutional arrangements at national level that harmonise economic and social policies within a comprehensive commitment to people-centred development' (Midgley & Tang 2001:246). Governmental action through policy and legislation of a protective and regulatory nature is needed, including the removal of barriers to the achievement of equity and the social advancement of individuals and groups.

Proponents of social development have countered the neo-liberal view that social welfare is a drain on national resources by positing the argument that it is a social investment in key social services that contribute to economic development. A key assumption underpinning this approach is that economic development does not automatically translate into social improvements and that the benefits of growth do not reach all people equally. For this reason social investments in human development are needed to address these inequalities and distortions in development outcomes. It is also argued that human well-being is about the development of people and that the achievement of human well-being is the goal of social development. The connection between economic and social development, it is argued, can best be achieved through macroeconomic policies that promote employment. Such policies should foster social inclusion of people in the development process through employment and self-employment and raise the standards of living of the poor and the unemployed. Investments in building the capacities of poor people to participate productively in the economy through human capital development (such as education and skill development), social capital development (such as social networks), micro enterprises and credit are also proposed. Social investment and the promotion of the productive capacities of people (also referred to as the 'productivist' approach), rather than the reliance on social welfare benefits only, are at the core of social development (Midgley & Tang 2001; Midgley 1999).

Another tenet of the approach is that it emphasises comprehensive and universalistic interventions and progressive social change. The approach has very strong leanings towards the institutional approach to social welfare, as it supports the principle of universalism, redistribution and strong governmental action in social welfare. It differs from institutionalism in that it does not see a separation between economic and social policy. It is also less focused on entitlement rights to social benefits and supports the targeting of development efforts at the poor and marginalised (Midgley & Tang 2001) and has also been referred to as neo-institutionalism.

Social development is essentially a people-centred approach to development that promotes citizen participation and strengthens the voice of poor people in decision-making and in building democratic and accountable institutions. Democratic participation is considered integral to the achievement of human development and is an end in itself.

'The social development approach is essentially a pluralist approach focusing on strong government action and partnership between individuals, groups, communities, civil society and the private sector.'

Social welfare policies and programmes from a social development perspective set goals that are likely to lead to tangible improvements in people's lives. Beverley and Sherraden (1997) argue that primary health care, primary education, nutrition, basic housing and skills training provide tangible social and economic returns. The principles informing the programmes are geared to promoting participation in development efforts, empowerment of the poor through productive employment, building the assets of the poor and strengthening local institutions and social capital. Social development policies and programmes are also of a cross-cutting nature, and focus on effecting improvements in, inter alia, community and preventative health care, basic education, and local economic and infrastructure development. The social development approach is essentially a pluralist approach focusing on strong government action and partnership between individuals, groups, communities, civil society and the private sector. Welfare beneficiaries are considered to be partners and development change agents working at local, national and international levels.

While recognition of the social development approach has grown internationally, it has been criticised at three levels. Firstly, it is considered to be a new and evolving approach and needs to be strengthened at a theoretical level and in its application in different contexts (Payne 1997; Beverly & Sherraden 1997). Secondly, the applicability of the approach in different societal contexts and different levels of social and economic development is being questioned. Although social development is being applied in emerging economies and in industrialising societies faced with rising poverty and chronic unemployment, its applicability in developed societies and mature welfare states is questioned (Dahl et al. 2001; Payne 1997). Cross-national studies of different models of social development are needed to assess how the approach is being applied in different social, cultural, economic and political contexts. It is also important to consider how social development is being conceived of in different regions around the world – such as, for example, the European Union (Imbrogno 1997) and the Southern African Development Community (SADC).

Thirdly, social development is further criticised for not paying sufficient attention to the development of models of action and for promoting a form of action to be incorporated into social work (Payne 1997). Its major weakness, according to Payne (1997), is that it works within existing social structures and does not approach social change from a critical perspective. Green also calls for 'combining analytical understanding of development processes with post-modern reflexivity in order to critically reflect on practice and contribute to its evolution and impact' (Green 2002:53).

The social development approach to social welfare in the South African Context is discussed in Part 2 of the book. It is an evolving approach in the South African context and whilst many achievements are noted, it is also faced with significant challenges and its future is uncertain. An exposition of a social development practice model and consideration is also given to local innovation and practice skills in Part 3.

'The social development approach to social welfare in the South African context is an evolving approach and whilst many achievements are noted, it is also faced with significant challenges and its future is uncertain.'

The table that follows summarises the basic tenets of the different approaches to social welfare in relation to key concepts such as its vision, goals, principles, types of social welfare programmes, access to services and benefits, auspices and their local, national and global activities. The conceptual representations of the approaches to social welfare are ideal types and do not necessarily exist in such a form in the real world. These concepts and propositions about social welfare are useful tools to guide and inform analysis of welfare systems. In different contexts, various permutations of these approaches are possible and can be combined around a new nucleus or a central principle or can co-exist in a contradictory or a complementary way.

Table 1.1: Approaches to Social Welfare

	Philanthropy	Institutional	Conservative/ Neo-liberal	Social Justice	Social development
Vision	service to humanity; social welfare is rendered by private citizens based on religious prescriptions, cultural traditions and secular philosophy	a state of well-being in society also referred to as 'a welfare society'. Social welfare is part of a comprehensive system of social services; market failure is considered to be the cause of declining social conditions	social welfare in a free market system; solutions are advocated to overcome government failure in meeting societal needs; limited government intervention; low spending on social services; voluntary sector is a mediating structure between state and people	humane and egalitarian society; critical analysis of class inequality and social divisions associated with social stratification and social exclusion	empowered, humane, just and democratic society; focused on pro-poor change; challenges the unequal and distorted economic, social and political development nationally, regionally and globally; proactive involvement of governments in developmental social welfare
Goals	meeting of basic and social needs	social and individual goals	individual change	social and economic justice; democratisation, and transformation of systems and institutions	promote social and economic development; participation of socially excluded in development efforts; achieve tangible improvements in the quality of life of the people
Principles	support for the needy and the poor	citizen rights, social solidarity, altruism, social justice, societal cohesion	religious, moral values, state loyalty, individual responsibility for meeting needs	social justice, social and human rights; empowerment, equality, distributive and liberation values	social and economic justice; empowerment; collective action to promote public benefit, distributive and liberatory values
Programme type	predominantly remedial, it may be focused on social reform; addresses diverse humanitarian needs	comprehensive services, social security and personal social services	remedial; short-term crisis and emergency actions; localised community-based activities	action to challenge social discrimination and marginalisation; support for social movements to promote access, equality, empowerment of the excluded	activities connected with human, social, economic and community development; building assets of the poor; local economic development; promote productive employment of the socially excluded; promotion of good governance and democracy

	Philanthropy	Institutional	Conservative/ Neo-liberal	Social Justice	Social Development
Access	selective access to services	universal access to enhance quality of life	selective and targeted programmes at 'deserving poor'	universal access to social services is advocated but with a special focus on the poor and socially excluded	universal coverage but with a focus on targeted interventions at the poor and socially excluded groups
Auspices	informal or formally organised by philanthropic organisations mainly independent; or part of a plurality of service actors	government-dominant model; weak civil society, space exists for non-state actors e.g. NGOs, philanthropy service is formal and institutionalised through legislation, fiscal and taxation measures; significant state spending on social services	voluntary sector-dominant model with minimal role for government	Auspices: independent of state; active in organisations outside the state; associated with alternative institutions	operates as part of a pluralist system – public, private and civil society; strong role for government in development action
View of providers and beneficiaries	paternalist view of beneficiaries but may be participatory if programmes are oriented to social reform	humanitarian view; may perceive beneficiaries as passive receivers of support	providers must facilitate movement off welfare and into work; punitive view of beneficiaries	both are change agents	both are active participants in development; change agents
Local and global activities	local, national, international, transnational focus	local focus coupled with significant international action	local action geared to promote individual responsibility; international and transnational focus could be humanitarian; but also oriented to strengthen the influence of conservative thinking globally	local, national, international, transnational in focus	local, national, regional and global focus on human and social development; active involvement of international state and non-state actors in development

Source: Adapted from Patel, L. (2003b).

Conclusions

This chapter has outlined the profound technological, economic, political, cultural, social and demographic changes associated with the process of globalisation. These changes present new risks to human security, and new needs and challenges to welfare systems in both rich and poor countries. What should the response of societies and their welfare systems be to the new challenges while they continue to grapple with past unmet needs? What is the future of social welfare in the global era?

Social scientists have highlighted the spread of neo-liberal ideas internationally and a continuing trend toward residual approaches to social welfare, a reversal of past social policies and/or adaptive responses to the pressures. Increasing human insecurity, continuing conflict and a 'world in crisis' is one possible future. McGrew (1992) and Bilton et al. (2002) are of the view that the future is not fixed and that different future scenarios are likely. Another scenario is that mature welfare states may be able to withstand the pressure to reform, adapt proactively to the changing situation and retain their commitment to the idea of the welfare state. A third future scenario is a 'transformed world' where there is an integrated global society and political system (McGrew 1992). This could include what Mishra (1999) refers to as the creation of supranational and regional social standards to protect people against these risks and the implementation of social rights across nations. A fourth scenario may give greater prominence to the role of social movements and non-state actors in shaping a global social agenda. This may ultimately lead to a new social contract to harmonise social and economic relations and achieve human development nationally, regionally and globally.

By drawing on the different perspectives to social welfare discussed in this chapter different possible futures could emerge and different combinations of approaches could be adopted towards the new global realities. Historically, societies fashioned their welfare systems on the unique needs, problems, histories, culture and political and economic contexts in which they found themselves. Their regional and global connections were also a factor in determining how their welfare systems evolved and responded. In the present global context, these factors may hinder or facilitate the renewal of social welfare systems. South Africa is a society in transition struggling with addressing the twin challenges of globalisation and its colonial and apartheid past. It is also part of the Southern African Development Community (SADC) and the New Partnership for Africa's Development (NEPAD), which is attempting to address these challenges regionally and continentally. Chapter 2, The Social dimensions of regionalism: A Southern African perspective, situates South Africa's efforts to pursue economic and social development in the SADC region.

CHAPTER SUMMARY

- Globalisation is a process whereby economic, political, cultural and social relations take on a global form. It has distinct features – among them new technological tools that are the driving force of the new information age. Global economic and social integration has far-reaching consequences for the achievement of human security. Globalisation also presents nations with new opportunities to address human needs, manage social problems and maximise opportunities to achieve human well-being and social development.
- Social welfare evolved in response to industrialisation. Different approaches to social welfare evolved on the basis of the unique history and political, ideological, economic, social and cultural contexts of particular societies and regions. The salient differences between the various conceptions of social welfare were outlined with reference to their basic tenets and character. These are ideal types and in the real world there are many variations between social welfare systems.
- The different conceptions of social welfare are a useful tool in considering what the future of social welfare is likely to be in an increasingly interconnected and interdependent world.

CRITICAL THINKING QUESTIONS

1. What are your experiences of globalisation?
2. Do you agree with the proposition that globalisation has created new needs and is a threat to human security? Give reasons for your answer.
   Which of the approaches to social welfare are most convincing to you, and why?
3. What do you think is the most likely future scenario of social welfare in an interdependent and interconnected world?

Bibliography

ALLEN, T. and EADE, J. (2000), The Politics of Identity. In Allen, T. and Thomas, A. (eds.), *Poverty and Development into the 21st Century* (485–508). United Kingdom: Open University in association with Oxford University Press.

ANHEIER, H.K. and SALAMON, L.M. (1999), Volunteering in cross-national perspective: initial comparisons. *Law and Contemporary Problems*, 62:4, 43–65.

BECKER, D. et al. (1987). *Post Imperialism*. Boulder, CO. Lynne Rienner.

BEVERLEY, S. G. and SHERRADEN, M. (1997), Investment in Human Development as a Social Development Strategy. *Journal of Social Development Issues*, 19:1, 1–15.

BILTON, T., BONNET, K., JONES, P., LAWSON, T., SKINNER, D., STANWORTH, M. and WEBSTER, A. (2002) *Introductory Sociology*. 4th ed. Houndmills, UK: Palgrave Macmillan.

BORJA, J. and CASTELLS, M. with BELIL, M. and BENNER, C.(1997), *Local and Global Management of Cities in the Information Age*. London: Earthscan.

CASTELLS, M. (2000), *The Information Age: Economy, Society and Culture. End of Millenium Vollume III.* Oxford: Blackwell Publishers.

DAHL, E., DRØPPING, J.A. and LODEMEL, I. (2001), Norway: relevance of the social development model for post-War welfare policy. *International Journal of Social Welfare*, 10:300–308.

DEPARTMENT OF WELFARE (1997), *White Paper for Social Welfare*. Government Gazette Notice 1108 of 1997. Pretoria: Ministry for Welfare and Population Development.

EDNA, E.A. CO. (2002), Civic Service in East Asia and the Pacific. Paper Presented at the International Conference on 'Towards a Global Research Agenda on Civic Service', Buenos Aires, Argentina September 3-4, 2002.

FISHER, J. (1998), *NGOs and the political development of the Third World*. Hartford Connecticut: Kumarian Press.

FOWLER, A. (1995), *Non-governmental Organizations in Africa: Achieving Comparative Advantage in Relief and Micro-Development*. Institute of Development Studies Discussion Paper. England: University of Sussex.

FREIRE, P. (1970), *The Pedagogy of the Oppressed*. Harmondsworth: Penguin Books.

FRIEDMAN, T.L. (2000), *The Lexus and the Olive Tree. Understanding Globalization*. New York: Anchor Books.

GELB, S. (2005), An overview of the South African economy. In Daniel, J., Southall, R. and Lutchman, J. (eds.), *State of the Nation 2004–2005* (367– 400). Pretoria: Human Sciences Research Council & East Lansing: Michigan State University Press.

GREEN, M. (2002), Social Development: Issues and Approaches. In Kothari, U. and Minogue, M. *Development Theory and Practice. Critical Perspectives* (52–77). Hampshire: Palgrave.

GIDDENS, A. (1998), *The Third Way. The Renewal of Social Democracy.* Malden MA: Blackwell Publishers.

GIDDENS, A. (2000), *Runaway World*. New York: Routledge.

GINSBERG, L. (2000), Conservative Approaches to Social Policy. In Midgley, J., Tracy, M.B. and Livermore, M. (eds.), *The Handbook of Social Policy* (377–392). Thousand Oaks, CA: Sage Publications, Inc.

IATRIDIS, D. S. (2000), Critical Social Policy. In Midgley, J., Tracy, M.B. and Livermore, M. (ed.), *The Handbook of Social Policy* (393–410). Thousand Oaks, CA: Sage Publications, Inc.

IMBROGNO, S. (1997), A European Concept of Social Development. *Journal of Social Development Issue,* 19:2/3, 1–16.

IRIYE, A. (2002), *Global Community. The role of international organizations in the making of the contemporary world*. Berkeley: University of California Press.

KINCHELOE, J.L. and MCLAREN, P.L. (1994), Rethinking critical theory and qualitative research. In K.H. Denzin and Y.S. Lincoln (eds.), *Handbook of qualitative research*. Thousand Oaks, CA: Sage.

KIRST-ASHMAN, K.K. (2003), *Introduction to Social Work and Social Welfare. Critical Thinking Perspectives*. United States: Thomson Brooks/Cole.

LEE, M.C. (2003), *The Political Economy of Regionalism in Southern Africa*. Cape Town: The University of Cape Town Press.

MACPHERSON, S. and MIDGLEY, J. (1987), *Comparative Social Policy and the Third World*. Sussex: Wheatsheaf Books.

MCGREW, A. (1992), A global society. In Hall, S., Held. D. and McGrew, T. (eds.), *Modernity and its Futures*, (61–116). Cambridge: Polity Press.

MIDGLEY, J. and TANG, K. (2001), Introduction: social policy, economic growth and developmental welfare. *International Journal of Social Welfare*, 10:4, 244–252.

MIDGLEY, J. (2000), Globalization, Capitalism and Social Welfare: A Social Development Perspective. *Canadian Social Work*, 2:1, 13–28.

MIDGLEY, J., TRACY, M.B. and LIVERMORE, M. (2000), *The Handbook of Social Policy.* Thousand Oaks, CA: Sage Publications, Inc.

MIDGLEY, J. (1999), Growth, Redistribution and Welfare: Towards Social Investment. *Social Service Review*, 77:1, 3–21.

MIDGLEY, J. (1997), *Social Welfare in Global Context*. Thousand Oaks: Sage Publications.

MIDGLEY, J. (1995), *Social Development. The Developmental Perspective in Social Welfare*. London: Sage Publications.

MISHRA, R. (1999), *Globalization and the Welfare State*. Cambridge: Edward Elgar Publishing.

MISHRA, R. (1999), *Globalization and the Welfare State*. Cheltenham: Edward Elgar Publishing Limited.

MOORE MCBRIDE, A., BENITEZ, M., SHERRADEN, M. and JOHNSON L. (2003), Civic Service Worldwide. An Assessment. *Journal of Service Enquiry*, First Edition (3–17).
NEW DICTIONARY FOR SOCIAL WORK (1995), Terminology Committee for Social Work.
PATEL, L. (2003a), Social development in a society in transition. *Social Development Issues*, 25, 150–161.
PATEL, L. (2003b), Theoretical Perspectives on the Political Economy of Civic Service. *Global Service Enquiry*, 1:87–100
PAYNE, M. (1997), *Modern Social Work Theory*. London: Macmillan Press Ltd.
POLANYI, K. (1973), *The Great Transformation*. New York: Octagon.
RODRIK, D. (1997), *Has Globalization Gone Too Far?*. Washington DC: Institute for International Economics.
ROBBINS, S.P., CHATTERJESS, P. and CANDA, E.R. (1998), *Contemporary Human Behaviour*. Boston: Allyn & Bacon.
SCHÖN, D.A. (1987), *Educating the Reflective Practitioner*. San Francisco: Jossey
SCHÖN, D.A. (1983), *The Reflective Practitioner*. New York; Basic Books.
SEGAL, E. AND BRZUZY, S. (1998), *Social welfare, policy, programs, and practice.* Itasca, IL: Peacock.
SHERRADEN, M.W., MOORE, A. and CHO, S. (2002), *Toward a Global Research Agenda on Civic Service: An International Conference.* St Louis: Global Service Institute and Washington University.
SINGH, A. (2000), *Global Economic Trends and Social Development.* United Nations Research Institute for Social Development. Occasional Paper 9. Geneva:UNRISD.
REPUBLIC OF SOUTH AFRICA (2003). *Towards Ten Years of Democracy. Progress in the First Decade of democracy – challenges of the Second Decade.*
SWILLING, M. and RUSSEL, B. (2002), *The size and scope of the non-profit sector in South Africa.* South Africa: Graduate School of Public and Development Management, University of the Witwatersrand, Johannesburg and the Centre for Civil Society, University of Natal.
SYKES, J.B. (ed.) (1982). *The Concise Oxford Dictionary*. Oxford: Oxford University Press.
TREVILLION, S. (1999), *Networking and Community Partnership.* 2nd ed. England: Ashgate Publishing
THOMPSON. N. (2002), *People Skills*. 2nd ed. New York: Palgrave Macmillan.
UNESCO (UNITED NATIONS EDUCATIONAL, SCIENTIFIC AND CULTURAL ORGANIZATION) (2000), *Culture, trade and globalization. Questions and Answers*. Paris: UNESCO Publishing.
UNDP (UNITED NATIONS DEVELOPMENT PROGRAMME) (1999), *Human Development Report*. Oxford: Oxford University Press.
UNDP (UNITED NATIONS DEVELOPMENT PROGRAMME) (2000), *Human Development Report*. New York: Oxford University Press.
UNDP (UNITED NATIONS DEVELOPMENT PROGRAMME) (2002), *Human Development Report*. Oxford: Oxford University Press.
UNDP (UNITED NATIONS DEVELOPMENT PROGRAMME) (2003), *Human Development Report*. Oxford: Oxford University Press.
UNITED NATIONS (1996), *Report of the World Summit for Social Development: Copenhagen*, 6–12 March 1995. New York.
WILENSKY, H.L. and LEBEAUX, W. (1965), *Industrial Society and Social Welfare* New York: The Free Press.
ZASTROW, C. (2000), *An Intoduction to Social Work and Social Welfare.* 7th ed. Belmont: Wadsworth Publishing Co.
ZASTROW, C. (1995), *An Introduction to Social Work and Social Welfare*. 5th ed. California: Brooks/Cole.

CHAPTER

2

The social dimensions of regionalism: a Southern African perspective

LEARNING OUTCOMES

After you have read this chapter you should be able to:

- Define the concepts of regionalism and regionalisation.
- Describe the Southern African region in terms of its history and its contemporary socio-economic and political context.
- Define and explain the social development framework and how it is evaluated.
- Discuss the social development situation in the Southern African Developemnt Community (SADC) with reference to its achievements and challenges.
- Discuss the implications of the regional social situation for regional action to promote social development in the SADC.
- Critically discuss the key social development questions that are relevant to the chapter.

The concepts of regionalism and regionalisation

Regionalism can be defined as 'the adoption of a regional project by a formal regional economic organisation designed to enhance the political, economic, social, cultural, and security integration and/or co-operation of member states' (Lee 2003:2). This type of regionalism is highly formalised through institutional co-operation and integration. Regionalism can also be of an informal nature and can involve state and non-state actors sometimes referred to as 'network regionalism'. *Regionalisation*, according to Lee (2003:8), refers to a process of interaction by 'state and non-state actors (seeking) to enhance their economic, political, cultural, social, and security interaction with societal forces within a region through formal and informal structures'. Regionalisation or the process of regional integration is a partnership between a group of countries to increase their levels of welfare through more efficient arrangements than unilateral or independent policy and action that each country could effect.

'Regionalism has become significant in the 1990s as part of the globalisation process and also in response to it.'

Regionalism has become significant in the 1990s as part of the globalisation process and also in response to it. On the one hand there has been a concern with the growing economic power and political influence in the world of the regional trading blocks in North America, Europe and Asia that are the main beneficiaries of globalisation, and on the other hand, the marginalisation of countries on the periphery. Globalisation is widely believed to have resulted in the inclusion of some countries and regions in the global economy and the exclusion of others. In this regard there is grave concern that these processes will lead to the further marginalisation of the African continent within the world economy and polity. It is these realities that prompted the formation of the New Partnership for Africa's Development (NEPAD) by African countries to reverse these trends and to promote democracy, peace, economic development and poverty eradication (NEPAD 2001).

Several economic regional groupings were established in Africa in the 1960s to promote the reconstruction and development of their economies and societies in the post-colonial period. Regional groupings existed in East, West and Southern Africa to free the continent from its external dependence and to provide the safeguards and benefits of interdependence through the achievement of economic integration. This approach was advocated as a vital element in the international strategy for development (Abegunrin 1990). However, these formations did not make significant strides in areas of human development. In most cases, integration was approached from a strictly economic angle. The export-oriented, lopsided, poor economic structures inherited from colonialism were in need of reconstruction. Integration was therefore seen as a means of helping to overcome the disadvantages of small size and making possible a greater rate of economic growth and development (Ezenwe 1983:12). Consequently, a number of regional groupings such as the East African Community (EAC) and the Economic Community of West African States (ECOWAS) were founded in order to advance the political and economic programmes of post-colonial African states. In 1980, the Southern African Development Co-ordinating Conference (SADCC) was also formed.

The poor performance of African economic blocs such as the EAC led to a re-think of the strategies for regionalism in the mid-1970s. Some sober lessons were learnt from the inadequacies of the EAC and African states began to realise that political independence was no longer the sole precursor of economic development. The 1973 oil crisis also added to the realisation that external factors had a bearing upon the performances of local economies and the volatility of international markets could no longer be ignored. Neither could the illegitimacy and undemocratic nature of governments in these regional formations be ignored. The political changes in Namibia and South Africa also resulted in a re-evaluation of the SADCC in the 1990s.

Regionalism and regionalisation have been pursued in the context of three theories of regional integration: market or economic integration, regional co-operation and regional development integration, which are outlined briefly (Lee 2003).

Market integration. It is a process of integration that progresses in a linear way and includes different forms and degrees of integration such as a free trade area, customs unions, common markets, economic unions and total economic integration. In each of these types of integration, different measures are designed to remove restrictions that exist between nations, and that hamper the economic development of the region. These include measures such as the removal of tariffs or the introduction of tariffs against non-member countries; the introduction of a common market and the free flow of money and labour between member states including the harmonisation of macro-economic policies. The final stage of integration is known as total economic integration, where monetary and fiscal policies are unified and where a supra-national authority has the power to make and enforce economic decisions leading to political integration or the creation of a regional union. Robson (1980:3) has cited a number of benefits that can be realised from market integration. These are increasing the production of goods based on the comparative advantage of a region, the optimisation of economies of scale, realising improvements in terms of trade of a group relative to other regions, increasing investments and technological advancements.

Regional co-operation. It consists of collaboration between two or more countries with similar interests, including economic, political, social, and cultural interests. Co-operation could be of a technical nature; it could also include the implementation of joint projects, policy harmonisation or collaboration in running a service or in environmental resource management. This is a less ambitious form of co-operation and some authors argue that it may be a more realistic option in the African context where there is such diversity between countries and disruptive elements like conflict and war (Lee 2003; McCarthy 1996). It has the benefit of building co-operation incrementally based on concrete projects and is less threatening as it does not encroach on the sovereignty of member states (Haarlov 1997).

Development integration. This approach to regionalism attempts to correct the weakness of the market integration model, which ignores social development. Stimulating productive capacity, increasing state intervention in the economy and in the promotion of regional co-operation, increasing political commitment to regionalism and to a more equitable distribution of the benefits realised from this process are some of the development integration strategies which have been proposed. The proponents of development integration also argue for redistributive and compensatory measures. Most of these are however of an economic nature. While a regional industrial development strategy is proposed, little is said about a regional social development strategy to harmonise social and economic development.

The African and Southern African region has been historically impoverished by the legacy of colonialism, the cold war, and international economic systems favouring rich and powerful nations in relation to trade and access to markets. Inadequate policies, limited implementation capacity, lack of skills coupled with the brain drain, dysfunctional economies, poor quality leadership, corruption and poor governance have been cited as some of the reasons for the slow pace of change in the post-independence period in Africa. Low economic growth rates have not allowed for the rebuilding of societies, and this has led to a vicious circle of economic decline, indebtedness, marginalisation and exclusion of the region from the new global information economy (Patel & Wilson 2004; NEPAD 2001; Castells 2000; UNDP 1999).

Against this background, national governments are beginning to recognise that the welfare and development of their societies are inextricably linked to regional and global realities. Poverty, the HIV/AIDS epidemic and seemingly intractable social problems can no longer only be addressed unilaterally. Regional co-operation is therefore critical to promoting national and regional social development. There is however a lack of understanding of the social dimensions of regionalism and its implications for social welfare and development at national and regional levels. There is a paucity of research on the subject and regional action to promote social development is still in its infancy. The aim of this chapter is to promote an understanding of the social dimensions of regionalism and to begin to locate social welfare and social development policy and action in South Africa in its regional and African context. The implications of the social situation for regional social development action are explored in relation to the SADC's social development strategy. To achieve this an understanding of the history and contemporary social and economic, and political context of the Southern African region and its impact on the human development standing of the region is needed. The Southern African Development Community (SADC) is a formal regional structure that was established to promote regional co-operation and integration. It is a significant institution through which regional social development may be achieved. However, regional action to promote social development may also be relevant if pursued through regional co-operation by state and non-state actors. These options are explored in the concluding section to this chapter.

'... national governments are beginning to recognise that the welfare and development of their societies are inextricably linked to regional and global realities.'

History of the Southern African region

The Southern African region has always had inter-linkages with other parts of the world, notably Asia, dating back to pre-colonial times. Even before the Arab slave routes were established there was already trade in this area, which was linked to the East Coast of Africa. Spices and other commodities from Asia were exchanged for local ones like gold. Thus, kingdoms like Zimbabwe flourished in the 15th century from these external ties. Slavery and colonial penetration only served to deeply embed Southern Africa in the global system. Trade was a major factor that allowed pre-colonial communities to transcend local boundaries and interact with other continents. The Southern African region has always been an open political and economic system that has been dealing with the effects of 'globalisation' for over 350 years (Swatuk 1996).

Different tribal communities that either co-existed with each other or were constantly engaged in feuds typified the pre-colonial Southern African landscape. The earliest inhabitants of the region were the San people, who were hunter-gatherers; but were driven off the land by the Bantu-speaking people in latter years who moved to other parts of the region. The Bantu were mainly pastoralists and kept livestock, and at times cultivated the land, as they were subsistence farmers. These tribes had met their needs through tight-knit family structures, which have remained important institutions in this part of the world for centuries. Despite the family being the primary unit of socialisation, the traditional set-up of the village also guaranteed human well-being with the clan and kinship ties being the most important systems. Thus, vulnerable members were catered for by the extended family. However, the indigenous people of Southern Africa were already facing two major threats: one was the arrival of the Portuguese explorers at the Cape in the fifteenth century; the second was the annexation of the Cape by the Dutch in 1652. The slave trade on the East Coast also represented a major turning point for the peoples of Southern Africa and had devastating consequences for community life, especially for the communities in the coastal areas.

Southern Africa has experienced numerous social and political upheavals in the last hundred years. Shaka's 19th century wars of conquest contributed to the dispersion of many tribes in the region. It is social turbulence of this nature that resulted in the diffusion of cultures and traditions in the region, which is still discernible even today. European colonial powers such as the Dutch, English, Germans, and Portuguese eventually carved up the region for their own benefit. However, this region has been described as the core of Anglo-Saxon Africa because it attracted the lion's share of British investments in Africa. It is here that two million white, English-speaking descendants of settlers created colonial communities and colonial-style states during the 19th and 20th centuries. Two older colonial traditions also survived alongside the Anglo-Saxon one, however. These were the Portuguese, who came from Europe and Asia to settle in the central and eastern parts of the region in the 16th and 19th century (Birmingham 1995), and the Dutch.

'Southern Africa has experienced numerous social and political upheavals in the last hundred years.'

Cecil John Rhodes, who dreamed of a highway from the Cape to Cairo, conceived of the first infrastructural interconnections of the Southern African region. Even though the idea did not materialise, a railway line that criss-crossed the Southern African region up to the Congo can be credited to Rhodes. He was at the helm of the British South African Company (BSA), which pursued British imperial interests – leading to the appropriation of large tracts of land (that were populated by different African nations) for commercial, mining and agricultural ventures. Many African communities were also decimated or displaced in the process of British colonial expansion. Later, the descendants of the Dutch, the Afrikaners, also appropriated indigenous land for commercial purposes. This situation rendered African people landless. The only recourse open to them was to work on the same land under appalling conditions or to work as contract migrant workers in neighbouring white settler states, particularly in South Africa and Zimbabwe. The majority of neighbouring states, such as Mozambique, Lesotho, Swaziland, Botswana and Malawi, were relegated to labour reserves. This occurred because of the way in which capitalist development took place in the nineteenth century: it relied on cheap labour supply from labour reserves in the region.

European populations became more concentrated in South Africa than in other Southern African countries due to the country's rich mineral wealth and vast commercial opportunities. Thus people of French, Belguim, German, Portuguese, and Italian origin found their way to South Africa because of the gold and diamond rush of the nineteenth century. There was also a large Asian community from India, Malaysia and China who either came as indentured labour or merchants. Southern Africa has drawn much of its present racial composition from its earlier descendants (Marais 1998).

Anti-colonial resistance movements were established in many Africa countries in the first part of the twentieth century, resulting in great social upheaval. However, when colonial rule became politically, economically and socially untenable after the Second World War, many African countries achieved independence in the 1960s. Social upheavals did not abate in the post-colonial period. In the last three decades, Southern African communities have witnessed further conflict and modern warfare in some countries. Wars of liberation were fought in Namibia and South Africa and these two countries were the last countries on the continent to achieve independence. The former Portuguese colonies of Angola and Mozambique did not gain self-rule via a negotiated settlement but from wars of liberation, which unfolded in the early 1960s up to the mid-1970s. Upon attaining political independence, these two countries were immediately plunged into civil wars that cost over a million lives. Most citizens of these two countries ended up as refugees in the neighbouring countries of Malawi, Zambia and Zimbabwe (Lowe 2002).

Today, Southern African countries have many commonalities that emanated from the social and political history of the region, although differences do exist between the countries. For instance, the linguistic patterns in the region allow for easy social mobility, communication as well as cultural similarities because of past influences. The peoples of

'Today, Southern African countries have many commonalities that emanate from the social and political history of the region, although differences do exist between the countries.'

'Regional differences that exist arose from the different approaches adopted by the various colonial rulers and their administrations.'

Botswana, Lesotho, South Africa, the Caprivi Strip in Namibia and the Lozi of Western Zambia all have a common understanding of the Sotho and Tswana languages due to the dispersions of their people in the nineteenth century. Regional differences that exist arose from the different approaches adopted by the various colonial rulers and their administrations. The two former Portuguese colonies of Angola and Mozambique have a distinct official language (Portuguese), while most Southern African countries that were former British colonies are English-speaking. The Democratic Republic of the Congo (DRC), Mauritius and the Seychelles are French-speaking countries.

Regionalism in the Southern African context

Three decades ago, Southern African countries identified regionalism and regional integration as a vehicle that could help to harness both the human potential as well as the natural resources of the region in order to spearhead both social and economic development. The general political climate at the time, which pitted independent African countries in the region against those that were still under white minority rule, served as an important incentive for regional co-operation. On 1 April 1980, leaders and representatives of the nine independent Southern African countries of Angola, Botswana, Lesotho, Malawi, Mozambique, Swaziland, Tanzania, Zambia and Zimbabwe assembled in Lusaka, Zambia, to sign the declaration entitled *Southern Africa: Towards Economic Liberation*. Accelerated economic development and regional self-reliance were the central objectives of the declaration (Achola 1987). The Southern African Development Co-ordinating Conference (SADCC) emerged out of this declaration. Even though the SADCC was initially conceived in 1978 and was later given content in 1979 at the Arusha Meeting of Ministers in Tanzania, the Lusaka Declaration legitimised the structure and got it off the ground. The objectives of the SADCC were as follows:

- The reduction of economic dependence, particularly, but not only, on the Republic of South Africa;
- The forging of links to create a genuine and equitable regional integration;
- The mobilisation of resources to promote the implementation of national, interstate and regional policies; and
- Concerted action to secure international co-operation within the framework of the SADCC's strategy for economic liberation (SADCC Secretariat 1984 in Achola 1987:40).

The SADCC emanated from regional political concerns, as most of its member states were also part of the *Frontline States,* which provided assistance to the liberation movements of Southern Africa fighting white minority rule. Julius Nyerere of Tanzania and Kenneth Kaunda of Zambia were the kingpins of this alliance that incorporated liberated countries into its fold to press for the emancipation of the entire region. Thus, the call to sever economic ties with South Africa, while perhaps not economically prudent, must be seen in this light. It would have been futile to champion Southern African self-determination while independent countries in the region survived on South African goods and services.

The independence of Namibia and South Africa as well as the changed political situation in the region in the 1990s necessitated a re-evaluation of the concept of regionalism in the context of the SADCC's *raison d'être*. In 1992, the SADCC broadened its concerns to facilitate regional economic integration and became the Southern African Development Community (SADC). The 1992 Windhoek Treaty laid out the SADC's aspirations for regional co-operation. Integration initiatives were also given content in a series of protocols that provided a framework for the negotiation of specific programmes for greater co-operation. The overarching aim was to build a community that could compete globally, with regional integration yielding balanced economic growth and development for the member states (Jenkins and Thomas 2002:390). The Treaty also mooted the creation of a Free Trade Area (FTA).

Lee (2001) is of the view that the successful implementation of an FTA in Southern Africa would mark a major turning point in the history of regionalism in Africa, since to date market integration has failed miserably on the continent. However, the FTA's main challenge remains the economic disparity that exists between South Africa and other SADC countries – as evidenced by that country's highly industrialised sector that generates 71 percent of the SADC's Gross National Product (GNP). The equitable distribution of the benefits of regionalisation is a major issue, as in most cases it is the regional giant that benefits from such integration (Lee 2001).

'The equitable distribution of the benefits of regionalisation is a major issue, as in most cases it is the regional giant that benefits from such integration.'

South Africa joined the SADC in 1994 and a year later membership increased with the inclusion of Mauritius and the Seychelles. By 1997, the DRC had joined the SADC – making it the latest member of the grouping. The SADC region is a formally constituted region made up of the following 14 countries: Angola, Botswana, the Democratic Republic of Congo (DRC), Lesotho, Malawi, Mauritius, Mozambique, Namibia, Seychelles, Swaziland, South Africa, Tanzania, Zambia and Zimbabwe. The Indian Ocean islands of Mauritius and the Seychelles are the only SADC countries not located on mainland Africa (SADC 2003).

In summary, Southern African regionalism has involved violent struggle. The legacy of the past has had a profound influence on today's regionalism. Furthermore, the standing of individual countries is inextricably bound up with this history. What transpires at a regional level has direct implications for South Africa, as it is interconnected to Southern African countries both formally and informally. Southern

'What transpires at a regional level has direct implications for South Africa, as it is interconnected to Southern African countries both formally and informally.'

African countries are also getting attuned to the wider global complexities that are impinging upon the standing of the region vis-à-vis other regional groupings in the world.

Southern African countries have not been able to escape the forces of globalisation, especially in the last decade. In Chapter 1, the nature and meaning of globalisation was discussed and it was argued that the process of economic, political and cultural integration on a world-wide scale has had both benefits and social costs for individuals and communities. Driven by a combination of technological advances and the liberalisation of trade and financial flows, which brought considerable benefits in terms of increased trade, investment and growth, it has also resulted in new challenges for governments. In particular, the developing world has experienced heightened vulnerability of domestic economies to external shocks (Jenkins & Thomas 2002). It has been argued that Southern Africa has had fewer gains from globalisation. Lipalile (2001) points out that globalisation has favoured the rich nations of Western Europe and North America. In this regard he states that for 'the debt-ridden and poverty-stricken developing economies of Southern Africa, however, globalisation represents a threat and not a promise as it ultimately endorses and perpetuates their relations of dependency and dominance, and the economic marginalisation and unfair terms of trade they face' (Lipalile 2001:296).

Global forces have always impacted on Southern Africa prior to colonialisation and, subsequently, after independence. Today, trade and Foreign Direct Investment (FDI), which have facilitated globalisation in fundamental ways, have influenced Southern African regionalism. Southern African regionalism has been understood from the point of view of the economic gains and advantages that could be derived from this process. Regionalism is also considered to provide good preparation for globalisation and multilateralism, and could present countries of the SADC with an opportunity to negotiate as a united, stronger front (Kubalasa 2003). Lipalile (2001) also indicates that it is not economically viable for any country or group of countries to ignore the potential benefits and attractions offered by integrated global markets without alienating themselves from the prospects for upward economic mobility. A cost–benefit analysis is proposed in order to come to grips with the effects of globalisation on the SADC in relation to the structure of regional economies. This analysis would include the impact of globalisation on the technological, political and social development of the region. Such an appraisal is important because the effects of globalisation on nations vary depending on the stage of economic development attained and how effectively member states of a given sub-region manage and harmonise their trade policy within the framework of regional integration (Lipalile 2001:295). Regionalism and regionalisation can also yield social gains through regional development integration and co-operation to improve the human development situation (SADC 2003).

Contemporary socio-economic and political context

Southern Africa is a huge landmass stretching from the rivers Congo, Zambezi, Limpopo to the Orange. It includes two of the world's largest man-made dams, namely the Kariba and the Cabora Bassa. It also borders on the shores of both the Indian and Atlantic Oceans, and stretches towards the sand dunes of the Kalahari and Namib deserts as well as the open spaces of the Karoo. The region also hosts some of the oldest inhabitants of the African continent, the San, who can still be found in certain parts of Angola, Botswana, Namibia and South Africa. The total landmass of the SADC region is estimated to be 906 million hectares, 147 million hectares of which is arable land. Consequently, agriculture plays a major part in the regional economy, contributing 35 percent to its Gross Domestic Product (GDP) (SADC 2003). About 70 percent of its people depend on agriculture for food, income and employment. The SADC is also richly endowed with abundant mineral and human resources. The region possesses a vast and highly diversified mineral resource-base, including precious and base metals, and industrial and precious stones. In 2001, the region had a combined population of 208 million people (SADC 2003). The majority of the people live in rural areas with about 70 percent of the population being directly dependent on agriculture. There is also a high rural urban migration rate in the region due to migration and the displacement of populations and refugees because of economic and social under-development, and regional conflict.

The contemporary political and socio-economic context of Southern Africa correlates directly with its human development profile. Civil war and political contestation in the region coupled with natural disasters have worsened the socio-economic and human development standing of the region. The on-going political and economic crises in Zimbabwe since 1997 have impacted negatively on human well-being. The eviction of white farmers from their land through imprudent and counter-productive land reform policies has not served the best interests of ordinary Zimbabweans. Political opposition is being suppressed and the economy has virtually collapsed. Political instability in both Angola and the Democratic Republic of the Congo (DRC) has also reached alarming levels. Despite being very resource-rich, these two countries are classified low-income countries and contain some of the worst poverty levels in Africa (Department of International Development 2002).

'The contemporary political and socio-economic context of Southern Africa correlates directly with its human development profile.'

Effective democratic governance is an important factor in achieving national stability and human development. Effective governance is about having free and democratic elections, respect for national constitutions, working democratic institutions and administrative systems and a set of principles and values that protect people from the arbitrary and unaccountable actions of governments, corporations and other

'Effective democratic governance is an important factor in achieving national stability and human development.'

forces more powerful than them. Southern Africa falls short in these areas as constitutions have been flouted deliberately by political actors so as to entrench the rule of certain leaders. There has also been a reversal of democracy and a return to authoritarian rule in some countries. For example, the Namibian president successfully ran for a third term after manipulating that country's constitution, while the Malawian presidency had also entertained the same thoughts amidst national disaffection with the leadership. In Swaziland the monarchy has been accused of human rights violations and not tolerating opposing views, especially from civil society. Lesotho emerged from a constitutional crisis that was created by the annulment of the 1998 elections after bloody protests and the military intervention of South Africa (Country Profiles 2004).

Despite these shortcomings and challenges, there are still some positive political developments in the region. Botswana is still believed to maintain one of the most sustainable democratic systems in the developing world. The indictment of the former Zambian leader Frederick Chiluba by the new administration on corruption and embezzlement of national funds may send a message to the rest of the African continent that national resources should not be used for personal gain. In South Africa, reconciliation, reconstruction and development still underpin the new democratic dispensation, highlighting the importance of negotiation rather than conflict. South Africa is widely cited as an example of a country that has achieved a peaceful transition to democracy and is also credited with playing a constructive role in raising the standing of the African continent in the changing global environment. South Africa and its leadership have also been praised for playing a constructive role in ending civil conflicts in the Southern African and Great Lakes Regions affected by civil conflict, war and ethnic genocide. Calls for an African Renaissance or its re-birth have been echoed in South Africa and on the African continent by the New Partnership for Africa's Development (NEPAD).

The regional political situation has impacted negatively on the internal economies of individual countries such as Angola, Zimbabwe and the DRC. After 27 years of civil war in Angola, the overall financial situation is very weak. Despite a booming oil sector that has resulted in a 15 percent growth in real Gross Domestic Product (GDP), poverty is widespread in both urban and rural areas (International Monetary Fund 2003). Likewise, the Zimbabwean economy has contracted over the past seven years due to inappropriate macro-economic policies, governance and a breakdown in law and order which has undermined investor confidence (African Research 2003).

SADC member states are at different stages of economic and social development with some countries achieving high growth rates and others attaining very low growth rates. In spite of the small size of the market, which is comparable to Belgium, in the African context the

SADC has the highest GDP per capita in Sub-Saharan Africa. Economic performance has improved since the mid-1990s because of the improved political situation and management of the economies. The overall economic situation remains fragile due to natural disasters, an increasing debt burden in most countries and the underdeveloped structure of the regional economies. The main challenge for the region is to create environments and measures to promote high economic growth rates, eradicate poverty, effect improvements in the delivery of social services and place the region on a sustainable development path (SADC 2003). Overcoming limitations in institutional capacities, macro-economic management and other fiscal policies are other challenges facing the region. Economic growth is important in achieving social development in the region as it directly reduces income poverty for many households, increases their savings and frees resources for investments in human development (UNDP 2003). However, economic growth by itself is meaningless if it does not lead to a better quality of life for the peoples of Southern Africa

The contemporary political and economic situation in the SADC region has resulted in declining human development indicators in many countries.

'The main challenge for the region is to create environments and measures to promote high economic growth rates, eradicate poverty, effect improvements in the delivery of social services and place the region on a sustainable development path.'

Defining and assessing social development

In the 1990s, the focus on the achievement of human well-being as a goal of development in both rich and poor countries re-emerged internationally to overcome the narrow focus of development on economic development. The quest to put people's needs, aspirations and capabilities at the centre of development efforts and to bring an end to social discrimination and social divisions in societies was advocated by the United Nations. Social development re-emerged to counteract market-oriented approaches and the curtailment of welfare expenditure by governments, and this process culminated in the adoption of the World Declaration on Social Development in 1995.

The United Nations Economic and Social Council use the concept social development whilst the United Nations Development Programme tends to use the term human development when defining and assessing the social situation in a country or region. This has resulted in conceptual confusion and in this chapter; human development is used interchangeably with social development (UNDP 1999; Beverley & Sherraden 1997). Midgley (1995:66) is of the view that 'human development is nothing more than a synonym for social development' perhaps 'to placate conservatives who have long denigrated the word *social* in social development'.

The value of the human development framework of the United Nations Development Programme is that it has been used to analyse national, regional and global human development situations with the view to influencing policy and to mobilise development action by governments, international agencies and donors. More recently, the mobilisation of civil society as partners in promoting social development is being acknowledged (United Nations Economic and Social Council 2002). Global goals have been agreed at international forums to inspire action and to assess progress (UNDP 2003). The human development framework provides for the measurement and assessment of human development through the use of standardised measurement indicators. While these efforts have generated positive action and global awareness of social development concerns, they have also been criticised for relying on narrow quantitative indicators to assess progress (UNDP 1999; UNDP 2003).

Social development according to the United Nations Development Programme could create an enabling environment for people to enjoy long, healthy, productive and creative lives (UNDP 1999). It could also lead to the widening of people's choices by creating opportunities for expanding their human capability and functioning. Through effecting improvements in health status, educational attainment and income, individuals are able to live longer, lead fulfilling lives and have access to resources to improve their standard of living. The Human Development Index (HDI) includes three measures: longevity, educational levels and income per head. The HDI is used to measure the human development situation across countries and to assess social progress. For Amartya Sen, the 1998 Nobel Laureate in Economics, the HDI provides an alternative measure of development to previously used narrow indicators of development such as Gross National Product (Sen 1999 cited in United Nations Development Programme 1999). Human development is also about valuing other choices such as democracy and human rights, cultural freedom and a sense of community, and provides opportunities to be creative and productive and to have dignity and self-respect (Streeten 1999).

'The human development framework addresses itself to the question of pervasive poverty in a manner that tilts development efforts in the direction of people.'

The human development framework addresses itself to the question of pervasive poverty in a manner that tilts development efforts in the direction of people. Conscious public policies will have to translate economic growth into concrete improvements in people's lives and in the restructuring of economic and political power (Haq 1995). Human development also involves a process of achieving these human capabilities in a way that is equitable, participatory, productive and sustainable. Since the creation of the HDI in 1990, three supplementary indices have been developed to highlight particular aspects of human development: the Human Poverty Index (HPI), the Gender-Related Development Index (GDI) and the Gender Empowerment Measure (GEM). The HPI measures human deprivation in relation to survival, exclusion from access to knowledge and deprivations in attaining a decent living standard. The GDI measures achievements in the same dimensions and uses the same indicators as the HDI, but captures inequality in achievement between women and men

(UNDP 2003). It is simply the HDI adjusted downward for gender inequality. The Gender Empowerment Measure (GEM) gauges whether women are taking an active part in economic and political life (UNDP 2003). In addition to these measures, the Millennium Development Goals and targets are also used as measures to assess national, regional and global progress in human development and to identify challenges for future action (UNDP 2003). The goals and targets focus on key human development issues such as income and poverty eradication, health, food and nutrition, education, children and women, and human security. However, this approach to assessing human development is considered to be too narrow and promotes a top-down approach that is seen to be unrealistic in some countries. The goals are not considered to adequately address the structural causes of the social situation in many countries, including institutional constraints and complexities. However, the value of the approach lies in its potential to assess progress, monitor changing global trends and inspire action by governments and non-governmental organisations to address pressing human concerns.

The social development situation and challenges in the SADC

The social development situation measured through the Human Development Index (HDI) for the region improved between 1995 and 1998 from 0.538 to 0.568, according to the SADC Human Development Report of 2000 (UNDP 2000). The assessment of the social situation is based on the best available data, which is not up-to-date for all countries as information systems are poorly developed due to resource and institutional limitations and skill shortages.

Seven of the countries fell within the medium human development range with an index value of 0.500 – 0.799, and six countries were in the low human development range with an index value below 0.500. The Gender-Related Development Index (GDI) also recorded a decline of 0.87 percent from the mid-1990s. This situation is considered to be due to the impact of the HIV/AIDS pandemic. Botswana and Zimbabwe have experienced the greatest reduction in life expectancy in Sub-Saharan Africa (World Bank 2003). This situation may be offset by an increased fertility rate from 4.9 in 1990 to 5.1 in 1997 (Development Policy Research Unit 2001). However, these demographic changes will have a far-reaching impact on the social and economic development prospects of the region because of the HIV/AIDS pandemic.

Poverty and income

Poverty remains one of the greatest challenges facing Southern African countries. The poverty situation in the region is reflected in low levels of

'Poverty remains one of the greatest challenges facing Southern African countries.'

income, and high levels of human deprivation. About 70 percent of the population in the region live below the international poverty line of US$2 per day. Approximately 40 percent of the region's population, or 76 million people, live in extreme poverty and have incomes of less than the international poverty line of US$1 per day (SADC 2003). Poverty also varies between countries, with half of the SADC member states having a poverty index below the regional average. While poverty was declining in the late 1990s, human poverty is increasing in some countries.

Poverty in Southern Africa is a consequence of economic, technical, environmental, social, political and exogenous factors. Low and unsustainable rates of economic growth in the wake of higher rates of population growth resulted in low incomes. Often, the poor lack adequate capital assets, which may be physical, financial, human, natural and social (SADC 2003). The poor also include people who are marginalised – such as children, people with disabilities, women, rural communities, youth and those who have been displaced. Southern Africa includes several countries referred to as Highly Indebted Poor Countries (HIPC) and confirms the underdeveloped status of the region. The term HIPC was developed by the World Bank and the International Monetary Fund (IMF) in 1996, with the aim of helping poor countries reduce their external debts. To qualify, countries had to meet certain conditions laid out by these multilateral organisations. Angola, the DRC, Mozambique, Tanzania and Zambia are all Highly Indebted Poor Countries.

The average Gross National Product (GNP) per capita for SADC is US$1,307.00. Higher-income countries in the region include Seychelles, Mauritius, Botswana and South Africa, with GNP per capita levels ranging from US$3,090.00 in South Africa to US$9,920.00 in the Seychelles. The low per capita income countries in the SADC region, with income levels below US$350, are the DRC, Malawi, Mozambique, Tanzania, Angola and Zambia (SADC 2003).

Health, food and nutrition

Health and food insecurity presents a further challenge to the region. Debilitating diseases such as cholera, HIV/AIDS, malaria and tuberculosis are impacting negatively on the welfare of the people. Southern African countries have the highest rates of HIV/AIDS infections in the world with many of them now experiencing rates of HIV infections of about 20 percent among adults, and in an increasing number of countries, in excess of 30 percent (SADC 2003). The country with the greatest HIV prevalence is Botswana, where one out of every three adults has contracted the virus (38.8 percent of people in the 15–49 age group). In Swaziland, Zimbabwe and Lesotho the infection rate is at least one out of every four adults (World Bank 2003). Furthermore, the United Nations Programme on AIDS (UNAIDS) estimates that 60 percent of today's 15-year-olds are likely to be infected with HIV/AIDS in countries such as

South Africa and Zambia (World Bank 2003). A regional scenario outlined by the Department of International Development (2002) is that over the next decade some 5–7 million people will die during their prime years as a result of the disease, leaving some 2 million orphans and transforming family structures and social norms. The capability of governments to provide services will also come under severe pressure, thus increasing the burden on the state and society as demand increases, and staff losses rise. HIV/AIDS will also affect the competitiveness of business (Department of International Development 2002).

Health issues form an integral part of social development as they are directly related to human resource development, which is critical in the realisation of the full potential of the people and their countries. Social development is highly dependent on a healthy and energetic populace and the HIV/AIDS pandemic (amidst a host of other incapacitating diseases) is reversing many of the socio-economic gains made by Southern African countries in past decades. Furthermore, HIV/AIDS impacts negatively on household productivity. Infection rates are also higher among women – 80 percent of whom are involved in food production in Sub-Saharan Africa (Ellis 2003). HIV/AIDS also erodes assets, aside from labour. Cash savings that might have been used on other productive ventures are spent on medical fees and drugs (Ellis 2003). Although the SADC region remains devastated by the pandemic, there is a positive outlook in certain countries. In Zambia, HIV prevalence among young women decreased by 4 percent between 1996 and 1999, offering hope that it would become the second country on the continent after Uganda to reverse the crisis (UNDP 2003).

'... The HIV/AIDS pandemic is reversing many of the socio-economic gains made by Southern African countries in past decades.'

Most of the countries in the region are faced with food insecurity that is also worsened by fluctuations in weather patterns. The drought of 2002 left almost 15 million people hungry. Inappropriate government policies also exacerbate food insecurity leading to nutritional deficits. In 2002, hunger in Southern Africa was tipped over the official 'famine' threshold after two consecutive years of bad harvests. Acute malnutrition increased in the same period, with 35 percent of the people in the famine region being undernourished.

Health indicators such as infant, child and maternal mortality rates vary between countries in the region. The poor health indicators are a reflection of the burden of disease experienced by many countries, especially in relation to communicable diseases. HIV/AIDS remains a major public health and development challenge in Southern Africa.

Education

Between 1980 and 1995, the gross combined enrolment ratio at primary, secondary and tertiary levels rose from 38 percent to 51.8 percent, but fell marginally in 1998. Among individual countries, the ratio declined in Angola, DRC, Mozambique and Tanzania. Enrolment rates

'This situation has negative implications for the attainment of universal coverage and access to education.'

for these countries for the year 1998 were 25 percent for Angola, 33 percent for DRC, 25 percent for Mozambique and 33 percent for Tanzania (Development Policy Research Unit 2001). The average adult literacy rate for the SADC rose from 48 percent in 1970 to 71 percent in 1995, but fell to 67.32 percent in 1998. Adult illiteracy was highest in Angola (58 percent), Mozambique (57.7 percent) and Malawi (41.8 percent) respectively (Development Policy Research Unit 2001). The majority of SADC countries have net enrolment rates at the primary level below the range of 80-100 percent. Inefficiency and ineffectiveness in the system also lead to poor retention rates. This situation has negative implications for the attainment of universal coverage and access to education. At the secondary level, only four SADC countries have net enrolment rates in the range of 80-90 percent (SADC 2003).

Children and women

The health and educational status of children varies across countries and whilst the region compares favourably with Sub-Saharan Africa, the human development situation of children is far behind that of other regions of the world. The situation of children in conflict-ridden and war-torn countries in the region is acute.

As a result of conflict, the region still hosts one of the largest numbers of child soldiers in the world. Angola and the DRC are countries where thousands of child soldiers are still being used in armed conflicts. Both government and rebel forces are responsible for the problem. Approximately 100 000 children were separated from their families during the twenty-year war in Angola and family tracing and reunification programmes are being implemented to reconcile the children with their families and communities. Many children have been injured because of landmines.

Lack of food has also negatively affected children. Owing to this situation, child malnutrition also increased between 1992 and 1998, with 23.5 percent of children under the age of 5 years suffering from the condition. The average infant mortality rates (per 1000 live births) in the SADC declined from 113 in 1970 to 110 in 1996 and then fell further in 1998. However, for some individual countries, infant mortality rates rose. South Africa's infant mortality rates increased from 50 in 1996 to 60 in 1998 and Zimbabwe's rate rose from 49 in 1996 to 59 in 1998 (Development Policy Research Unit 2001). The biggest challenge facing children in the region is the HIV/AIDS pandemic.

The Gender-related Human Development Index (GDI) measures longevity, knowledge and the standard of living of women. The GDI in the region in 1998 adjusted for income inequality was 0.501 in 1998 with Mauritius and South Africa having the highest values and Mozambique and Malawi faring the worst of the 12 countries for which data was available (SADC 2003). In comparison with 1995, the regional GDI declined by 0.87, with Zambia, Malawi and Botswana reflecting declining rates of GDI. This illustrates a declining life expectancy, educational access and attainment and standard of living for women in the region. Furthermore, the status of women in the SADC is low. According to the Gender Empowerment Measure (GEM), South Africa had the highest score in 1997 followed by Botswana, and Lesotho. Women's share of national income in Botswana is the highest in the SADC, while the GEM for Malawi is the lowest in the SADC, because women have a very small number of seats in parliament and in administrative, managerial, professional and technical jobs (Development Policy Research Unit 2001).

Security

There have been persistent calls for demilitarization of the region through a reduction of military establishments and the re-direction of resources from financing huge armies towards investment in social development (Goncalves 1999). The SADC's past is riddled with conflicts which reversed human development. Presently, regional security continues to be threatened by conflict despite mediation and ceasefire agreements in Angola and the DRC. In recent years, the SADC has also been affected by election-related conflicts and civil unrest in Mozambique (1999) and Tanzania (2000 after the Zanzibar election), Zambia (2001) and Zimbabwe (2002) (Mutukwa 2002).

The political crises experienced in the region have led to the unprecedented migration of refugees and displaced populations from Angola, the DRC and Zimbabwe to neighbouring countries such as South Africa, Tanzania and Zambia. Tanzania shoulders the largest burden of refugee populations – estimated at 43 percent of the SADC total – followed by the DRC (about 29 percent) and Zambia (about 23 percent) (United Nations Development Programme 2000). This in turn has also brought new challenges to the countries in the region and has strained already limited national resources.

Transnational crime, which includes car-jacking, fraud associated with money laundering, transfer pricing, small arms and drug trafficking, is a serious problem in the region. Among other things, crime has a negative influence on investor confidence, on production and other aspects of the economy, including social integration. Also, crime heightens insecurity in the region, contributes to the loss of human and physical capital and can lead to violence (UNDP 2000:25). There are governmental initiatives aimed at curbing criminality in the region. Various structures and processes exist to co-ordinate security: these include the SADC Regional Drug Control Programmes (SRDCP) and initiatives of the Southern African Regional Police Chiefs Co-ordination Organisation (SARPCCO).

Achievements

Whilst regional co-operation in human development has been limited, many countries have adopted national policies and programmes to promote human development. Despite the poor overall regional social and human development situation, some achievements in the human development situation are worth noting. In comparison with other African countries and the Least Developed Countries (LDCs), some SADC countries have received more Foreign Direct Investment (FDI) relative to Gross Domestic Product (GDP) than other developing countries. Furthermore, tourism is one of the fastest-growing industries in the SADC region with immense potential for further regional co-operation and economic development (SADC 2003).

In relation to progress in human development indicators, universal access to primary education and enrolment rates have increased markedly since independence. As a consequence, between 1970 and 1995, adult literacy in the region increased from 48 percent to 71 percent (UNDP 2000). Countries such as Zambia and Zimbabwe invested significantly in human resource development, especially in the areas of education. In relation to life expectancy, people in the region could expect to live 11 years longer than 35 years earlier and the infant mortality rate also fell from an average of 131 in 1970 to 105 per live births in 1996 (UNDP 2000). Although in some countries these positive indicators are being reversed due to the HIV/AIDS pandemic. While the Gender-Related Human Development Index shows improvements, the gap still remains wide and has in fact fallen in some countries.

'Concerted efforts are being made to bring about political stability in the region and to restore peace in some countries through mediation and negotiations.'

Concerted efforts are being made to bring about political stability in the region and to restore peace in some countries through mediation and negotiations. The ceasefire in Angola has created opportunities for progress and development to take root. Owing to the cessation of hostilities in Angola, many refugees are being repatriated to their home countries. There have also been substantive gains in infrastructure development – especially in transport and communication systems. The Maputo Corridor is an example of an infrastructure project benefiting social and economic development. It is a transport system that runs through Southern Africa's most industrialised and productive regions to fast track economic growth and employment creation in the region. Other examples are electricity and water projects such as the rehabilitation of the Cabora Bassa Power station.

Regional action towards human development

What are the implications of the current human development situation for action at a regional and sub-regional level? Initially, the SADC adopted a regional co-operation and development approach, which involved co-operation through joint projects. This was later replaced by a sectoral strategy co-ordinated and implemented by a country that was responsible for one or more sectors. Twenty-two sectors existed and human development projects were mainstreamed through existing sectors – but principally through the Health and Human Resource Development sectors, which were sub-divided into sub-sectors such as Education. The advantage of this approach was that it provided for country ownership and participation of member states. However, it was assumed that these countries had the skills and institutional capacity to provide leadership and management of the sectors at a regional level. All the sectoral programmes were highly dependent on foreign donor funds and their sustainability was questioned.

In 1992, the SADC was transformed into a development community based on the market integration approach. This approach focuses on trade integration, although this was only implemented in the latter part of the 1990s. This approach was a response to the regional, political and global economic context. A review of the SADC's Programme of Action in 1997 showed that 70 percent of the projects were donor-funded. In 2000 there were 378 regional projects (amounting to US$7.7 billion), most of which had a national rather than regional focus. Only 20 percent of the projects appeared to reflect regional SADC priorities (Lee 2003; SADC 2003). The new SADC structures and institutional arrangements resulted in the creation of four clusters which included Trade, Industry, Finance and Investment; Infrastructure Services; Food, Agriculture and Natural Resources; Social and Human Development and Special Programmes. All the clusters are co-ordinated by the SADC Secretariat under the auspices of the Council of Ministers. A Strategic Planning division was created in the Secretariat to address cross-cutting issues and to promote policy harmonisation.

The Social and Human Development and Special Programmes cluster's mandate is to harmonise policies, strategies and standards including labour standards in education, skills development and training, social welfare with a focus on vulnerable groups, health care, employment and labour standards. A co-ordinating role is envisaged for the cluster in combating the HIV/AIDS pandemic and other communicable diseases. The management of special programmes to combat illicit trafficking in drugs and small arms and to ensure the management of an SADC regional disaster centre was also envisaged. Social policies, guidelines and strategies based on the SADC's priorities have been developed including protocols to guide implementation (SADC 2003).

A SADC evaluation (2003:64) identified a range of shortcomings in policy co-ordination and integration within and between the Social and Human Development cluster and other sectoral programmes. Cross-sectoral co-ordination and integration of programmes is considered to be vital and involves connecting diverse efforts such as health and food security, sanitation, environment and safe water supply to improve health status, for example. The evaluation also suggests a tendency to address social needs at a regional level, rather than to devolve responsibilities to national levels or to non-state actors. Such devolution of responsibilities to the lowest level is considered to be more effective in meeting needs in keeping with the principle of subsidiarity.

The evaluation also highlighted the need to adopt appropriate human development goals and targets suited to regional realities and in keeping with institutional and management capacity, available human and financial resources and based on SADC-specific needs and challenges. The evaluation cautions against the uncritical adoption of internationally agreed human development goals and targets, especially in the areas of health and education. Policy and strategic challenges in key areas were identified by the SADC evaluation (SADC 2003) and selected challenges are outlined briefly.

The inadequacy of labour standards and regulations was emphasised, including the need to take account of the ILO labour standards, Draft Codes of Conduct on child labour and social security. Improved measures are needed to protect children against labour exploitation. The region has high unemployment rates and economic growth and employment creation remains a priority; this would include the harmonisation of social security and social protection for the unemployed.

In relation to health and HIV/AIDS, a future priority identified by the SADC is the need to implement the SADC Protocol on Health, which provides for comprehensive action in many critical areas of need. A long-term plan is needed to work towards achieving the Millennium Development Goals to reduce malnutrition, child and maternal mortality and to reverse HIV/AIDS prevalence in the region. A lack of resources, care infrastructure and services and trained health care personnel are other priorities that were identified.

'The educational challenges facing the SADC include the need to improve access, equity for disadvantaged groups and the quality and efficiency of the education systems.'

The educational challenges facing the SADC include the need to improve access, equity for disadvantaged groups (especially for women and people with disabilities) and the quality and efficiency of the education systems. The skills shortage in critical areas needs to be addressed, and there is a need for high-level training to overcome the mismatch between the supply and demand for skilled labour. In order to prepare students for self-employment, relevant technical and entrepreneurial skills training initiatives are also needed. Finally, the SADC has also identified the need to proactively address the impact of the HIV/AIDS pandemic on educational attainment and to address the loss of skills because of the brain drain, and the impact of the HIV/AIDS pandemic (SADC 2003:27).

The *Declaration on Gender and Development* (1997) and the *Declaration on the Prevention and Eradication of Violence Against Women and Children* (1998) were adopted by the SADC to promote gender equality and human rights at a regional level. These instruments are aligned with the international standard-setting instruments of the

United Nations. A *Plan of Action for Gender in SADC* was also adopted in 1999. The mainstreaming of gender efforts in sectoral programmes remains a major challenge, and includes the incorporation of the regional instruments into national laws and policies. The latest draft SADC Framework for Integration (2003) identifies regional priorities such as poverty eradication, combating the HIV/AIDS pandemic, achieving gender equality and development, and promoting food security; it also places human and social development high on its agenda.

The framework, however, does not focus specifically on social welfare provision and the protection of vulnerable groups. Constraints in implementing national and regional policies and human development programmes are a further challenge due to a lack of institutional capacity and fiscal constraints. In view of regional conflict, Lee (2003) questions whether there is the political will to improve human development through regional integration. Member states have also not implemented many of the protocols that have been adopted. This may be partly due to the way in which the organisation was conceived and constituted. The approach to policy implementation is a hierarchical, government-led integration model, which overlaps with intergovernmental organisations competing with lists of projects (Southern African Research and Democratic Centre 2001). Private sector and civil society in almost all the SADC countries were largely excluded from the preparation of regional strategies and programmes (Southern African Research and Democratic Centre 2001). Spaces have not been created for non-state actors to articulate an alternative regional agenda on social and human development. Non-governmental Organisations (NGOs), Community-Based Organisations (CBOs) and Faith-Based Organisations (FBOs) are involved in addressing key priority areas such as HIV/AIDS, promoting the needs and rights of women and children and in poverty reduction initiatives. In many countries in the region, these organisations are not perceived as social development partners but as threats to the existing political order. This is a significant weakness in current thinking about social development in the context of regional integration. There is considerable scope for national and regional co-operation between state and non-state partners in achieving human development. Regional integration frameworks need to give effect to this concept at institutional levels and to support such co-operation through funding, capacity building and active involvement in policy dialogue and implementation of programmes.

'Constraints in implementing national and regional policies and human development programmes are a further challenge due to a lack of institutional capacity and fiscal constraints.'

While the current SADC Framework for Integration (SADC 2003) acknowledges the need for the harmonisation of social security policy, there is a need to consider appropriate policy options in this field more vigorously. Some countries in the region have fairly well-developed social security systems, while others are underdeveloped. A common feature of social protection in the region is that the schemes focus on those who are employed in the formal sector. There is a heavy reliance on general tax revenue, and this strains government financing of publicly funded social assistance schemes. These are still in the embryonic stage, and beneficiary numbers are low (Olivier & Kalula 2003). Co-ordination of social security is almost non-existent in the region. Administrative inertia and institutional inefficiency in the area of social security delivery are, with notable exceptions, major obstacles. A future policy agenda needs to explore financially sustainable options for expanding the social security net to reduce poverty including complementary alternatives to social security and innovation.

Finally, the Southern African region is undergoing various changes both at the formal and informal levels. Regional integration will only be viable if member states and ordinary citizens are the beneficiaries. There is need for politicians, policy-makers, professionals, business people, non-governmental organisations and ordinary citizens in the region to come to grips with the social dimensions of regionalism and their implications for the social welfare of individual countries.

'Regional integration will only be viable if member states and ordinary citizens are the beneficiaries.'

South Africa is one of the strongest member states in the region and is a significant beneficiary of regionalism at an economic level through increased trade. In addition, South Africa has also benefited from the 'brain drain' suffered by other African countries. In relation to South Africa's role in the region, two arguments are advanced. On the one hand it has been argued that for South Africa, regional integration has been essentially an economic project with limited commitment to regional social development. On the other hand, South Africa is believed to have the potential to be an 'engine of growth' and recovery in the region (Lwanda 2004; Marais 2001). The challenge facing South Africa is to promote a form of regionalism and regional integration that is equitable, inclusive, democratic and sustainable, and that empowers ordinary citizens to lead creative, healthy and productive lives.

Since the opening of South Africa's borders, it has been faced with increasing economic migration in the region (Solomon 1996). The humane treatment of illegal immigrants and xenophobia are major public issues. Other growing social problems include the spread of HIV, the trafficking in children and drugs and cross border crime. Limited research has been conducted of the impact of regionalisation on health, education, social security and welfare services in South Africa. For instance, little is known about the impact of increasing migration, the flow of refugees and asylum seekers on the demand for welfare and development services. How might development actors respond to these new realities and challenges and what is the trade off between meeting the needs of South Africans and foreign migrants? How are social welfare organisations addressing social exclusion and discrimination of foreigners? To what extent are agencies and child and family welfare organisations able to give effect to the child protection provisions for refugee children contained in the United Nations Convention on the Rights of the Child and the African Children's Charter? These and many other issues remain unexplored.

South African development actors need to come to grips with the implications of regionalism for national social development in relation to macro social policy and planning, social development co-operation and development practice. Co-operation initiatives to address the wide range of human development challenges that cut across national boundaries remain under-explored. Monitoring of national and regional trends is critical to planning for the future and there is scope for research to inform regional action. In the search for solutions, South Africans also need to look to neighbouring countries as there is much that can be learnt from innovation and best practice in development efforts at a regional level. Regional co-operation and networking is one way of addressing the social development challenges at a regional level.

CHAPTER SUMMARY

- Regionalism has become more prominent as a result of the globalisation process and could lead to the exclusion of some countries and regions from the benefits of global economic and social integration.
- There are grave fears that globalisation will lead to the marginalisation of the African continent from global processes. Formal regional co-operation in Southern Africa was a response to the national development needs in the post-independence period. Market or trade integration has been prompted by global economics and its social implications for poor countries located on the periphery of world developments present opportunities and challenges that need to be addressed.
- The social dimensions of regionalism in the Southern African Development Community (SADC) were discussed and assessed with reference to the human development framework advocated by the United Nations Development Programme. The indicators used to assess human development were explained including their limitations in measuring the social dimensions of development. Although improvements have been noted in some dimensions such as adult literacy, the situation varies between countries with just under half of the countries in the SADC falling within the low human development range. Political instability and conflict, the HIV/AIDS pandemic and mass poverty and underdevelopment are some of the key features of the regional social situation.
- Social development has been placed high on the SADC agenda, although institutional, resource, socio-economic and political constraints hamper progress. The challenge for the SADC is to shift from a wholly government-led approach to one that forges social development partnerships and co-operation with non-state actors – the private sector and organisations of civil society – in its social development strategy.

CRITICAL THINKING QUESTIONS

1. Explain why it is important to study the social dimensions of regionalism in a changing global world.
2. Will regional integration lead to improvements in social and human development in the SADC region? Give reasons for your answer.
3. HIV/AIDS is the most important development challenge facing the SADC region. Do you agree with this statement? Motivate your answer.
4. Seventy per cent of the population in the region lives below US$2 per day. Why do you think this is so?
5. Can you think of a social issue that could be addressed through regional co-operation in a practice situation?

Bibliography

Abegunrin, O. (1990), *Economic dependence and regional cooperation in Southern Africa*. Lewiston, NY.: The Edwin Mellen Press.

Achola, P. (1987), Co-ordinating Tertiary Educational Programmes within SADCC Countries: A Strategy in Self-Reliance. In P. Achola and A. Msimuko (eds.). *Development Through Self-Reliance in the SADCC Region,* (39–53). New York, NY.: Professors World Peace Academy.

African Research, (2003), Annual Profile: Zimbabwe. www.sarpn.org.za (2 April 2004)

Beverley, S.G. and Sherraden, M. (1997). Investment in Human Development as a Social Development Strategy. *Social Development Issues*, 19:1, 1–18.

Birmingham, D. (1995), *The decolonization of Africa*. London: UCL Press Limited.

Cain, E.J. (1999), A World Free from Poverty: A Revitalized Framework for International Cooperation. *Social Development Issues*, 21:2, 4–10.

Castells, (2000), *The Information Age: Economy, Society and Culture Vol III.* 2nd ed. Oxford:Blackwell Publishers.

Country Profiles, (2004), *The Kingdom of Lesotho*. www.fco.gov.uk (8 March 2004)

Department for International Development (DFID) (2002), Southern Africa: Strategy Paper. Pretoria: DFID.

DPRU (Development Policy Research Unit) (2001), *Human Development Indicators in the SADC Region*. Cape Town: DPRU.

Ellis, F. (2003), Human Vulnerability and Food Insecurity: Policy Implications. (Unpublished Paper).

Ezenwe, U. (1983), *ECOWAS and the Economic integration of West Africa*. London: C. Hurst and Company.

IMF (International Monetary Fund) (2003), Globalization: Threat or Opportunity? Issues Briefs (Unpublished).

Goncalves, F. (1999), The Ideology of Militarism and Human Security. *SADC Today*, 3:06, 1–2.

Haarlov, J. (1997), *Regional Cooperation and Integration within Industry and Trade in Southern Africa: General Approaches, SADCC and the World Bank*. Aldershot:Averbury.

Haq, M.U. (1995), *Reflections on Human Development*. New York, N.Y.: Columbia University Press.

Jenkins, C. and Thomas, L. (2002), Creating a sustainable regional framework for development – The Southern African Development Community. In D. Belshaw and I. Livingstone (eds.). *Renewing Development in sub-Saharan Africa. Policy, performance and prospects*, (389–408). London: Routledge.

Kubalasa, D.K. (2003), *Review of Regional Strategies Addressing Poverty.* Paper presented at the MISA Conference, Dar-es-Salaam 10–12 September 2003.

Lee, M.C. (2001), SADC and the creation of a free trade area in Southern Africa. In E. Maloka (ed.) *A United States of Africa?* ,(255–275). Pretoria: Africa Institute of South Africa.

Lee, M.C. (2003), *The Political Economy of Regionalism in Southern Africa.* Cape Town: University of Cape Town Press.

Lipalile, M. (2001), Globalisation, Regional Integration and Development in Southern Africa. In E. Maloka (ed.) *A United States of Africa?*, (295–307). Pretoria: Africa Institute of South Africa.

Lowe, S. (2002), *The Price of Civil War* www.caa.org.au/world/africa/bigissues/conflict.html (8 March 2004)

Lwanda, G. C. (2004), Betrayal or Fulfilment: Is Post Apartheid South Africa Stalling Regional Integration? Paper presented at the South Africa Ten Years On Conference. London, 10–12 September.

Marais, H (1998), *South Africa – Limits to Change. The Political Economy of Transition.* Cape Town: University of Cape Town Press.

McCarthy, C. (1996), Regional Integration: Part of the solution or part of the problem? In Ellis, S. (ed.) *Africa Now: People, Policies, Institutions*. London: James Currey.
Midgley, J. (1995), *Social Development. The Developmental Perspective in Social Welfare*. London: Sage Publications.
Mutukwa, K. (2002), Parliament's role in conflict mediation/resolution. Paper presented at the Policy Dialogue on Legislative Development, 20–22 November 2002, Brussels.
Nepad (2001), *The new Partnership for Africa's Development* (NEPAD). http://www.dfa.gov.za/events/nepad.pdf. (5 August 2002)
Olivier M.P. and Kalula, E.R. (2003), Regional Social Security. In Olivier, M.P., Smit, N. and Kalula, E.R. (eds.). *Social Security: A legal Analysis*, (655–678). Durban: Lexis Nexis Butterworths.
Patel, L. and Wilson, T., (2004), Civic Service in Sub Saharan Africa. *Nonprofit and Voluntary Sector Quarterly,* 33:4, 22–38.
Robson, P. (1980), *The Economics of International Integration* 2nd ed. London: George Allen and Unwin.
Sadc (2003), *The Comparative advantage of the SADC region as an investment destination*. (10 October 2003)
Sadc (2003), *The SADC Framework For Integration.* (10 October 2003)
Sardc (The Southern African Research and Democratic Centre), (2001). *20 Years of Development in Southern Africa – A sectoral review of regional integration in SADC.* (4 February 2004)
Solomon, H. (2001), *Strategic perspectives on illegal immigrants.* www.iss.co.za/pubs/ASR/5NO4/Strategic perspectives.html (1 December 2004).
Streeten, P. (1999), Ten Years of Human Development. In UNDP (1999), *Human Development Report.* (17–18). New York, NY: Oxford University Press.
Swatuk, L.A. (1996), *Power and Water: The Coming Order in Southern Africa.* Bellville: University of the Western Cape.
Undp (United Nations Development Programme), (1999), *The Human Development Report.* New York, NY.: Oxford University Press.
Undp (United Nations Development Programme), (2000), *SADC Regional Human Development Report. Challenges and Opportunities for Regional Integration.* Harare: Southern African Regional Institute for Policy Studies (SARIP)
Undp (United Nations Development Programme), (2002), *The Human Development Report.* New York, NY: Oxford University Press.
Undp (United Nations Development Programme), (2003), *The Human Development Report.* New York, NY: Oxford University Press.
World Bank, (2003), *The World Development Report 2004,*. New York, NY.: Oxford University Press.
United Nations Economic and Social Council (2002), *Social and Economic Development.* www.un.org/esa/socdev.html (3 April 2004)
World Bank, (2003), *AIDS Regional Update: Africa.* http://web.worldbank.org/WBSITE/EXTERNAL/NEWS/0, contentMDK...:4607,00.ht (10 October 2003)

PART 2

Social development in South Africa

CHAPTER

3

History of social welfare in South Africa

LEARNING OUTCOMES

After you have read this chapter you should be able to:

- Describe the development of social welfare in the colonial period.
- Describe social welfare under apartheid.
- Discuss the challenges to the apartheid social welfare system and the beginning of a new approach to social welfare.
- Describe and discuss the issues, events and thinking that shaped the transition from apartheid to social welfare in a democracy.
- Critically assess and discuss how the specific events, ideas, values, policies and the practices of social welfare in the past have shaped the present and the future.

Early approaches to social welfare

'Both colonialism and apartheid shaped the evolution of the nature, form and the content of social welfare policy in South Africa.'

Both colonialism and apartheid shaped the evolution of the nature, form and the content of social welfare policy in South Africa. MacPherson & Midgley (1987) have argued that colonialism disrupted and denigrated most traditional forms of social welfare. In pre-colonial times, the welfare needs of individuals were met through the wider society, and communalism, co-operation and mutual aid and the social group were highly developed. However, the social relations that developed from the colonial economy and society came into conflict with these traditional modes of social provision.

South Africa was a Dutch colony from the mid–17th century to the early 18th century, when the British acquired sovereignty over the Cape colony in 1814. Colonial administrations adapted the socio-economic organisation of the colonies to their own interests, with the primary aim of establishing and sustaining the conditions necessary for economic activity. Indigenous inhabitants in the colonies had to adapt their technology, methods of production, forms of social organisation, culture, political, legal, and welfare systems to meet the demands and world views of the colonial powers.

The colonisers further aimed to 'civilise' the indigenous people and acted as the trustees of what they perceived to be civilisation (Mair 1987). The Dutch who settled in South Africa were Calvinists and their belief in predestination and of being the 'chosen people' gave religious sanction to their racial attitudes (McKendrick 1990). The exclusive group consciousness of the Dutch Settlers manifested itself in the expression of racial and social supremacy, and they judged the African people, their customs and their rich tradition of social organisation, to be inferior.

These concepts had a powerful effect on the eventual development of social welfare programmes and policies. The foundation of racial discrimination, denigration of indigenous ways, paternalism in social services and the distorted nature of social welfare policies favouring whites as the welfare elite, were laid during colonial times and permeated social welfare thinking for more than two centuries. Colonialism imposed enormous social changes on traditional societies, but no responsibility was taken for the social costs of such large-scale social disruption.

'Colonialism imposed enormous social changes on traditional societies, but no responsibility was taken for the social costs of such large-scale social disruption.'

The discovery of minerals in 1860 heralded the process of industrialisation in South Africa, transforming its social and political structures in a relatively short time from those characteristic of a predominantly agrarian society to those of a highly developed industrial society. The way in which industrialisation occurred impoverished blacks – and some whites – and laid the foundation of racial capitalism and racial differentiation in social welfare.

The mining industry, the engine of industrialisation, required a large labour force and thousands of black workers were employed on the mines. The peasantry and subsistence farmers were coerced into wage labour by hut and poll taxes, the Squatters Law of 1895 and the passing of the 1913 Land Act, which reserved less than 10 percent of the land for Africans, depriving them of their most important means of production. Migrant labourers lived in large compounds, earning low wages and working under extremely poor conditions. They were also not permitted to bring their families to the cities. They were forced to remain in the reserves, becoming increasingly impoverished.

The reserves in the rural areas fulfilled the role of social reproduction of the labour force, which supplied cheap labour to the mines. These labour reserves became repositories of women, the young and old, the sick and the disabled whose livelihoods depended on subsistence farming. Callinicos (1987) has pointed out that the system of migrant labour saved mine owners considerable amounts of money, as they were able to pay wages at the level of individual, rather than family reproduction. This contributed to rapid economic development, the benefits of which were not shared by black workers and their families.

Dependency theorists have argued that capitalist development occurred as a direct result of underdevelopment in the reserves, which in turn resulted in the system of labour coercion and the racial segregation of black workers (Legassick & Wolpe 1976; Wolpe 1972). Welfare programmes for black workers in urban areas were non-existent, as they were not considered to have political or welfare rights and their needs were assumed to be met by the subsistence economy of the reserves.

Wolpe (1972) and Legassick & Wolpe (1976) developed the cheap labour power thesis to account for the relationship between racial policies (and later apartheid), and the development of capitalism. They argued that capitalist expansion in the early years of industrialisation was dependent on the creation and the maintenance of a supply of cheap labour secured by preserving pre-capitalist forms of production and distribution. Workers were forced to maintain their links with the rural subsistence economy through the system of temporary migration. This, in turn, lowered the cost of reproducing African labour power, since wages paid had to be sufficient to cover the individual needs of migrant workers only. The balance necessary to ensure family reproduction was generated by pre-capitalist economic activities such as subsistence farming. Cheap labour made possible high rates of profits and exploitation. Thus, racial policies were explained in terms of their functional contribution to capitalist development (Hindson 1987; Wolpe & Legassick 1976; Wolpe 1972). Welfare functions were supposedly met through the subsistence economy and the kinship group, thereby allowing the state to ignore services for blacks. The subsistence economies declined rapidly over time due to extraneous factors and the migration of African labour to the cities, which diminished the self-sufficiency of the reserves and left many people desperately poor.

The processes of industrialisation and urbanisation resulted in large-scale poverty, housing and health problems. The needs of children, people with disabilities and poor relief received particular attention in the early years, and these needs were met mainly through institutional care for orphaned and vulnerable children by religious organisations, such as the Dutch Reformed Church. The first social legislation that was promulgated addressed the needs of these vulnerable groups. Potgieter (1973), the most noted historian on the development of social welfare in South Africa, has recorded welfare initiatives pertaining to social provisions for whites, which reflects the bias in South African welfare policy and in the recording of the history of social welfare. Whites received social support mainly through the church and the family, although voluntary welfare efforts, particularly by Afrikaner women's organisations, increasingly featured over time. The first two child welfare organisations in the Cape and in Johannesburg were established in 1908 and 1909 respectively. Potgieter (1973) showed that after the formation of the Union of South Africa in 1910, national welfare planning for whites became possible through co-ordination of church and voluntary welfare initiatives, and this laid the foundation of the partnership between the state and the voluntary sector in social welfare delivery.

In 1929, the Carnegie Commission of Enquiry conducted an investigation into the 'poor white problem', which had developed as more and more Afrikaners lost access to land. Subdivision of land into increasingly unviable small fragments, drought and cattle disease all brought hardship to small farmers, while commercial farming grew – with government encouragement – to feed the newly developing cities. *Bywoners*, tenants and squatters were forced off the land as commercial farming developed. Soon the towns were crowded with poor and hungry white families, most of whom had no skills suitable for industrial life.

Industrialisation proceeded apace after the First World War. Mining and agricultural production expanded and new industries started up. Soldiers returning from the war were faced with a lack of employment which added to the 'poor white problem'. The new government of the Union wanted to reconstruct white society and became increasingly involved in poverty relief through the creation of employment opportunities in the armed forces, railways, municipalities and agricultural settlements. The rationale for this was less than altruistic – it was designed to build a stable white society and to mitigate the tension between black and white workers caused by the competition between them for employment (McKendrick 1990).

According to Malherbe (1978), the Carnegie Commission was diagnostic rather than remedial, and represented the first attempt at a scientific and inter-disciplinary approach to the study of social problems in South Africa. One of the Commission's major recommendations was that a state welfare department be established to overcome the piecemeal approach of the various departments which dealt with welfare matters. As a result, the first state welfare department was instituted in 1937; this marked the beginning of organised state intervention in social welfare, and the professionalisation of social work. Concerted efforts were made in the 1940s to train social workers at universities and at religious colleges run by the Dutch Reformed Church and other churches that adhered almost entirely to European and North American models (Potgieter 1998; Winckler 1969). The social work profession, influenced by the growth of the psycho-analytic school in Europe and North America during the 1940s and the social treatment approach, began practising social case work which involves one-to-one relations and interventions as the dominant method of social work in welfare settings (Hare, Mckendrick & Hoffmann 1987). As Midgley (1981) has pointed out, social work in the Third World was influenced by Western industrial models, which resulted in the adoption of approaches inappropriate to the conditions in poor countries.

'... social work in the Third world was influenced by Western industrial models, which resulted in the adoption of approaches inappropriate to the conditions in poor countries.'

The main functions of the state welfare department were defined as 'rehabilitation of the socially maladjusted individual or family, the study and treatment of conditions giving rise to social maladjustment and the co-ordination of such services' (Brümmer 1964:20). At this early stage in the development of welfare policy, the principle of partnership or joint responsibility between the church, state and private initiative was emphasised. State financial support was given to voluntary welfare organisations, which were expected to deliver and co-ordinate services and raise professional standards of service delivery.

Both the Carnegie Commission and Afrikaner thinkers and politicians of that time conceptualised poverty as being caused by social and economic underdevelopment, and by the powerlessness of the

Afrikaner working class to effect changes in their lives (Le Roux 1978). The Carnegie Commission argued that poverty led to demoralisation, a loss of self-respect and sense of inferiority. At a conference on the 'poor white question' HF Verwoerd, later to become one of the key architects of apartheid and the National Party's third Prime Minister, called for a comprehensive economic, political and social strategy to deal with white poverty and its effects. This strategy included the creation of employment opportunities, extensive supportive social services and concerted state intervention (Le Roux 1978). This strategy was systematically implemented after the National Party came to power in 1948.

Social welfare policy in South Africa was also influenced by Darwin's theory on the evolution of human society, and the belief that a natural hierarchy of races existed on a scale from the primitive to the civilised (Chisholm 1990; Dubow 1987). According to Chisholm (1990: 110), two aspects of social Darwinist thought were influential in approaches to child welfare. Firstly, social conflict was interpreted as a struggle between 'superior' and 'inferior' races, and secondly, the 'inferior' races were perceived to have a negative and contaminating influence on the 'superior' race. These notions became powerful justifications for racially segregated welfare policies and programmes under apartheid.

Apartheid social welfare

Ideas, values, policies and practices

In 1948 the National Party came to power as a result of a class alliance of the Afrikaners and with a strong support base among white workers. The Nationalist government set about implementing its policy of apartheid, a system of institutionalised racial discrimination, and ruled the country for 46 years. The government argued that the integration of all races in a common society would not guarantee peace, freedom and prosperity for all, and that the solution lay in 'apart-ness' or separate development. Apartheid was enforced through a wide range of legislation, the Population Registration Act of 1950 being one of its cornerstones. This Act classified the population into four racial categories, which structured differential access to social welfare resources. Africans, Coloureds and Indians were denied both citizenship and welfare rights in a common society. Disenfranchised, they were unable to utilise legitimate institutional mechanisms to influence the flow of welfare resources in their direction. Thus, race became a primary factor in the access to services and benefits and in the allocation of welfare resources. Racial differentiation was an explicit principle of the South African welfare system (Department of Constitutional Development and Planning 1985).

'Racial differentiation was an explicit principle of the South African welfare system.'

Successive white governments secured the continued support of the electorate through both social investment programmes and large-scale employment in the civil service. Welfare state policies and programmes modelled on post-war institutional approaches to social welfare in Europe and North America were implemented and shielded white workers from the negative effects of the market economy. Public education, public health care, subsidised housing, rent control, employment, social benefits and social welfare services, which included poor relief, community services such as luncheon clubs for the elderly, residential care and rehabilitative social services were provided for those in need. The fruits of economic growth benefited whites disproportionately relative to other population groups and by the mid-1960s substantial improvements in the material conditions of whites were noted. Public welfare for whites also represented an important economic and political stabiliser in government efforts to maintain white support.

Table 3.1 sets out the percentages of state expenditure on welfare for the different population groups between 1950 and 1990. It should be noted that in 1990 whites made up 13 percent of the population in comparison with Africans (76 percent), Indians (3 percent) and Coloureds (9 percent) (SAIRR 1992).

Table 3.1: Welfare expenditure for the different population groups

Population Groups	1950	1976	1990
Whites	61%	56%	23%
Africans	25%	28%	52%
Coloureds/Indians	14%	16%	24%

Source: SAIRR 1992; Terblanche 1987.

This table shows that welfare expenditure was extremely high, given the small white population and their high standard of living relative to other groups. The proportion of government spending on social welfare for Africans almost doubled over a 14-year period, while white welfare expenditure decreased by 32,5 percent. This could be explained by the changed economic and political climate in the country, the changed social conditions of whites and the adoption of privatisation as a principle of state welfare policy in the 1980s. If equity is taken to mean the equitable allocation of welfare resources in proportion to population size, then Africans should have received 76 percent of the budget, and whites 13 percent.

'Black welfare needs were neglected during the apartheid era.'

Black welfare needs were neglected during the apartheid era. These, it was argued, were met through pre-capitalist or non-capitalist modes of production, which subsidised the social reproduction of migrant labourers and their families, thereby resulting in increased profitability for mining and manufacturing. Hindson (1987) argued that this held true for the period up to the mid-1950s, after which there was a rapid decline in subsistence production. This decline resulted in higher living costs in the rural areas. As a result, temporary migrants to the towns were faced with higher subsistence costs than their permanent urban counterparts as they had both to support themselves and provide for their families in the rural areas. It is against this background that the independent African trade union movement that emerged in the 1970s and 1980s pressed for higher wages to cover the full costs of the reproduction of migrant labour. 'Migrant labour, once a source of cheap labour power, now imposed an added burden on profitability' (Hindson, 1987:83).

Hindson (1987) also argued that the original justification for cheap labour did not account for the social costs of reproducing a permanent urban labour force, which increased rapidly after the Second World War. The urban social service infrastructure, which developed, was extremely residual. It provided controlled access to limited services such as education, housing, health and personal social services. At the same time, industrial decentralisation policies controlled African urbanisation by providing housing and employment close to the borders of the homelands in the rural areas, which – subsidised by the central government – increasingly took on a social welfare function. Social old age pensions, which were fully publicly funded, were also expanded for Africans in the homelands and provided an important safety net. These social benefits were racially differentiated for each of the population groups. In 1987, Africans received old age pensions amounting to R117; Coloureds R167, Indians R167 and Whites R218 per month (SAIRR 1987/1988). All social benefits and resources for social services were racially differentiated in this way.

This illustrates how the principle of racial differentiation in social welfare has been tied to the political and economic objectives of the ruling elite. Racial differentiation also operated through the wide network of separate structures and institutions created for the different population groups. There was a total of 18 state welfare departments, eight in the Republic of South Africa, six in the self-governing states (non-independent homelands), and four in the independent homelands. Yet the finance for all these departments came from the same exchequer (Department of Constitutional Development & Planning 1985). The welfare system was extremely fragmented, bureaucratic, inefficient and costly to implement. Racial differentiation entrenched inequalities between welfare beneficiaries, violating a fundamental principle of social justice and human rights, namely equal access to resources (Rowland 1984).

'The welfare system was extremely fragmented, bureaucratic, inefficient and costly to implement.'

The partnership between the state and the community-sponsored welfare initiatives emerged prior to 1948 and became an important feature of welfare services under apartheid, and over the years, a substantial number of agencies were formed. The Department of

National Health and Population Development (1990) estimated that 2 400 organisations with welfare objectives were registered under the Fundraising Act No 107 of 1978 on 31 March 1990, while 1641 community welfare organisations were operating under the National Welfare Act No 100 of 1978.

The community-sponsored welfare organisations, which included welfare services of religious organisations and services delivered by Afrikaner Women's organisations, were later co-ordinated by approximately 22 national councils operating in various fields such as child and family care, disability, mental health, corrections, chemical dependence and welfare for the aged. National organisations can be traced to the early activities of the Afrikaner Women's organisations that were formed in the late 19th century. The first two national bodies – the National Council for Mental Health (formed in 1920) and the National Council for Child and Family Welfare (formed in 1924) – were formed to promote and co-ordinate social welfare services in specialised fields. Later, national councils expanded and came to operate at local and regional levels, and formed ad hoc structures to liaise with the state about matters of general interest. The majority of the community-sponsored social welfare organisations rendered essentially rehabilitative social work services, and some statutory services were delivered on behalf of the state. The voluntary community-based welfare organisations were largely subsidised by government, and many organisations enjoyed a privileged relationship with government. Although the organisations were independent, their autonomy and integrity were compromised as they relied almost entirely on the government to finance their services.

In 1978 the government also enacted the Social and Associated Workers Act No 110 of 1978 which granted full professional status to the social work profession. However, this legislation was widely believed to be an attempt to control the political activities of social workers that were anti-apartheid activists. The legislation created much suspicion and affected the credibility of this body.

'In 1978 the government also enacted the Social and Associated Workers Act No 110 of 1978 which granted full professional status to the social work profession.'

Circular 66 of 1966 issued by the Department of Social Welfare and Pensions required welfare organisations to implement apartheid policies in the welfare field. These included the enforcement of legislation pertaining to the separation of race groups in terms of the use of amenities; the attendance of meetings; the creation of separate services for the different race groups and separate boards of management of welfare organisations. There was also the ruling that social workers should render services to persons of their own race group, and social work salaries were racially differentiated and unequal – because they were based on differentiated government subsidies. Circular 29 of 1966 and those issued subsequently (Circular No 65 of 1978 and No 6 of 1981) had a profound impact on voluntary welfare organisations. In every field of social welfare service delivery and social service practice, racial legislation had to be implemented, and this impacted negatively on human development. For instance, the adoption of children could often not be concluded if the race classification of the parents was not known; this meant that many children remained in institutions. While some organisations resisted these developments, the majority complied.

Extracts from Circular 29 of 1966

1. The Government's policy on welfare organisations is based on the principle that each population group should service its own community in the sphere of welfare.
2. The practice of certain welfare organisations maintaining multi-racial organisations having representatives of different races at council and committee meetings, is not only contrary to this policy, but represents other problems: ...
3. ... non-White welfare agencies should be established for the various racial groups and be given the opportunity to develop side by side with the corresponding White societies, and should be encouraged under the guidance and with the advice of White societies to unite, by affiliation, into fully independent national welfare organisations for each racial group...'

Source: Department of Social Welfare and Pensions, Pretoria. 21st June 1966 (pp. 1–2).

In a submission to the Truth and Reconciliation Commission in 1999, welfare organisations in the Gauteng region apologised to the people of South Africa for their implicit or explicit compliance with human rights violations in the welfare field. The submission also indicated that had organisations 'refused from the start to implement the policy, the course of social service history might have been changed' (Submission to the Truth and Reconciliation Commission by the Greater Johannesburg Social Services and Development Forum 1999:4).

McKendrick and Dudas (1987) identified other structures through which co-ordination and co-operation with the state was facilitated. Firstly, The National Welfare Act No 100 of 1978 provided for 24 regional welfare boards representing state and community interests charged with regulating, co-ordinating, promoting and planning welfare activity within their regions. These regional boards were structured along racial lines. There was also a multi-racial national welfare board that advised the government on social welfare concerns. In view of the racial structuring of the regional welfare boards, as well as their wide powers to register only welfare organisations, which are apolitical, these bodies were rejected by some sectors of the welfare community. Fundraising legislation adopted in 1978 was also criticised for curbing and controlling the foreign funding of progressive welfare groups.

A second structure which had a bearing on the implementation of welfare policy was the National Development Advisory Committee which advised the Cabinet on development needs. The country was divided into eight development regions, each with a multi-racial Regional Development Advisory Committee responsible for identifying priorities for social, physical, and constitutional development. These committees were represented at national levels.

Thirdly, there was the Population Development Programme launched in 1984 with the task of stimulating community development activities at local level, and improving the quality of life of the people. Private sector representation was also encouraged at local level. In the mid-1980s, the state embarked on a key shift in its policy direction and formulated a national community development strategy through which the welfare sector was urged to move away from remedial approaches to community development. However, this strategy was never implemented, as finance was not available for development activities, and there were suspicions at a local community level that state community development activities were a part of the state's campaign to win the 'hearts and minds' of the people for their reform initiatives (Lund 1985). Furthermore, welfare organisations were geared towards remedial approaches and no account was taken of how the change toward community development was to be managed and implemented.

Finally, the National Security Management System had covert structures operating in parallel to other social welfare structures. This system had regional and local configurations which operated at community level, and attempted to co-opt grassroots organisations and the personnel working in state social services, education and health care at local levels to advise and co-operate with the security establishment. The primary purpose of this security strategy was to restore administrative stability in contested urban townships, and to counter the 'revolutionary war' by winning support for government initiatives. During the latter part of the 1980s, the government began to concede grudgingly that poor living conditions contributed to political unrest. Thirty-four 'Oil spots' were identified as high-risk security areas and finance was provided through security structures to provide social and infrastructure services to them. A close relationship developed between the meeting of social welfare needs, and the political and military objectives of the state (Concerned Social Workers 1988; Swilling and Philips 1988).

'A close relationship developed between the meeting of social welfare needs, and the political and military objectives of the state.'

Social security and welfare services

Publicly funded social security programmes, known as social assistance, consisted of temporary emergency support for specific sectors of the population who qualified for such services. Services were selective and means-tested for all population groups. Non-contributory social pensions constituted the most expansive of these social assistance programmes. Other social grants that were available included maintenance, disability, foster care, and single care grants, for those caring for disabled persons. Family allowances were available to white, Coloured and Indian families only.

Through stringent eligibility requirements and racially determined eligibility criteria, social assistance excluded the majority of the people. The system of social benefits did not provide a comprehensive safety net and the unemployed were particularly affected. Bureaucratic inefficiency in the administration also made the system inaccessible. The programmes were generally of a paternalistic nature and distinguished between the 'worthy' and the 'unworthy' poor. This approach to social security showed the influence of 'The Poor Law Tradition' with its origins in the moral precepts of Luther, Calvin and their followers (Dolgoff & Fieldstone 1984). Other principles which underscored the social security arrangements involved adherence to the work ethic, the principle of individual responsibility, the acknowledgement of the nuclear family as the basic unit of society and, later, the privatisation of social welfare provision (Patel 1988).

However, a significant strength of the social assistance programme is that old age pensions and disability grants provided a significant safety net to rural households, even though lower payment levels existed for Africans (Ardington & Lund 1995). This will be discussed further in Chapter 5.

South African social security benefits were largely tied to employment through contributory social insurance schemes, which included retirement and medical benefits, workmen's compensation, unemployment and maternity benefits. These benefits were designed to protect people against the loss of income-earning capacity and constituted a risk-based social insurance approach. Because of the worsening plight of white pensioners in the 1940s, consideration was given to a national contributory pension scheme for all South Africans with contributions from indviduals levied on the basis of income and with equal contributions from government. These ideas were consistently rejected over the years. In the South African context, work-related benefits provided a form of social control of the workforce. Demands for worker rights often resulted in loss of employment and, consequently, social benefits. Furthermore, the poorest sectors of the population – rural people and the unemployed – had no access to unionisation or other forms of organisational expression. Since benefits were tied to employment, inequalities and divisions deepened between those who were employed and those who were not, with urban, unionised workers becoming a more privileged sector of the black working class (Patel 1988).

In addition, a fairly developed infrastructure of social welfare services existed within the formal welfare sector. This was made up of a state sector, community social services, and services rendered by religious organisations; in later years, social services were offered by large enterprises, especially the mining companies. Access to the latter was available only to employed workers, and residents of the communities where the enterprises were located were excluded. Welfare services had a strong urban and racial bias in favour of whites, which further contributed to divisions and social inequalities (Department of National Health and Population Development 1990; McKendrick 1990; De Villiers 1984).

Largely in response to the impact of the international economic crisis on the domestic economy in the 1980s, the South African government increasingly adopted a policy of privatisation of social welfare in line with international trends. The government attempted to cut back welfare expenditure and to limit wage increases in the state sector. Privatisation in education, health and social security was vigorously advocated, which gave rise to a substantial private sector in welfare, particularly in health care.

The government claimed that the privatisation of state enterprises, including welfare provision, would provide it with the finance to repay foreign debts, 'upgrade' townships and 'depoliticise' the social services. However, critical observers believed that the government came to realise that political change was inevitable and that privatisation would prevent a post-apartheid government from adopting radical redistributive social policies.

The principle of privatisation in social welfare implied limited state responsibility for social services in line with conservative welfare thinking. The government argued that South Africa was not a welfare state and that a partnership had always existed between the state, the private business sector, and voluntary religious and community initiatives to provide social welfare. The government encouraged community and individual responsibility for meeting needs through market mechanisms, emphasising volunteerism, mutual aid, and reciprocity between providers and consumers, fees for service and private social work practice. At the same time, the government also contended that it could no longer afford to finance services on the scale previously provided (Department of Constitutional Development & Planning 1985). Selective and residual policies were advocated and state subsidies – for example, for food – were systematically withdrawn.

The voluntary welfare sector, progressive professional organisations and critical academics warned against the folly of such policies in South Africa, where racial differentiation and privatisation in welfare would deepen mass poverty, social inequalities and political instability. In particular, they pointed to the fact that the majority of the population was simply too poor to afford such services (McKendrick 1990; Lund 1988).

The formal welfare system and the policies on which it rested were fundamentally undemocratic. The majority of the population had no say in the allocation of welfare resources or in identifying welfare priorities. Since the majority of the people had been disenfranchised, attempts by the government to promote participation in state social welfare structures and in social development were widely rejected at local community level – a rejection that presented the formal welfare sector with a serious legitimacy crisis.

'The formal welfare system and the policies on which it rested were fundamentally undemocratic.'

State welfare policy proposals developed during the mid-1980s met with widespread criticism by welfare groups who were not consulted about the policy alternatives (Patel 1989). In this regard, McKendrick (1988:17) had noted that:

> *The policy did not originate out of widespread and open consultation between the government and all sections of the community: it was created in camera by civil servants. Where limited consultation did take place with the private sector welfare community, key community requests were ignored ... Systems, if they are to be supported by the people, cannot be forced upon them in an authoritarian or paternalistic manner.*

Finally, the social welfare system was based on a First World model: it was curative, located largely in urban areas, specialised and required highly trained professional social workers to deliver remedial and statutory services. There was also an over-reliance on institutional care for children, the elderly and for people experiencing physical and mental disabilities. The services were incapable of meeting the needs of the majority and were orientated towards social control and influencing people to adapt to an unjust social system (McKendrick 1988). The methods of service delivery, fashioned on British and American models, were inappropriate to the political, economic and socio-cultural context of South Africa.

Submission to the Truth and Reconciliation Commission:
Greater Johannesburg Welfare, Social Services and Development Forum; South African National Council for Child and Family Welfare; National Coalition for Social Services and South African Interim Council for Social Work (1999).

The Forum mobilised its members to reflect on our painful past. This process involved coming to terms with the role played by welfare organisations, academic institutions and professional associations in the development, maintenance and implementation of apartheid. In its apology to the people of South Africa, members of the Forum acknowledged their failure to uphold the ethics and values of the social work profession.

The testimonies spoke of the hurt and anger caused by a welfare system which was racially discriminatory, inequitable, undemocratic and unresponsive to the needs and rights of the majority of the people. The submissions also pointed to the relationship between the welfare system and the security establishment, the phenomenon of 'state abuse' of children and youth during the 1980s, and the harassment of social workers and development workers opposed to government policy. It was also the first time in welfare circles that the role of the Afrikaner Broederbond was brought to light. They were members of governmental and non-governmental welfare organisations where they were not only the architects of apartheid welfare policy, but also the implementers of the system. In many organisations they also played a powerful ideological role in defending the system itself.

The system of social welfare had far reaching implications for the lives of all South Africans... Ultimately, individual social workers had to make the difficult choices for themselves... The social work profession lost many capable people to other professions. Many left the country. Nobody was unaffected by the context in which they lived and worked. Implicitly or explicitly we all complied in one way or another with an unjust social order. This could have taken the form of the placement of a child in racially segregated children's homes, or through the processing of a social grant for a person in need which was inequitable. It is vital that we reflect on what it meant to be a social worker in apartheid South Africa, and to take personal and organisational responsibility for one's own actions.

The submission by the Forum was a bold step in promoting reconciliation and healing in social welfare and is an important historical document.

Source: Extracts from the Foreword to the Submission, Leila Patel, June 1999.

Challenges to apartheid social welfare

The history of resistance in South Africa is characterised by the opposition of the indigenous people to colonialism and apartheid. Over many different generations, opposition grassroots organisations and social and political movements advocated the political, economic and human rights of all South Africans in a common society and drew attention to the effects of this deprivation on their well-being. Alternative social development initiatives emerged throughout the 20th century in response to the neglect of basic services by the state for the black population and as part of the general political activities of opposition movements to apartheid.

'Alternative social development initiatives emerged throughout the 20th century in response to the neglect of basic services by the state for the black population ...'

The African National Congress (formed in 1912) and the Communist Party of South Africa (formed in 1921) spearheaded political campaigns against the passing of legislation that restricted access to land and the freedom of movement of Africans as a result of the introduction of the pass laws. Trade unions emerged to organise African workers to respond to their declining conditions and to the introduction of job reservation restricting access to certain jobs for whites only. Grassroots actions such as strikes, defiance campaigns and protest actions were recorded throughout the 20th century.

Voluntary social welfare activities by community groups were also established independently of political and trade union organisations to address the needs of the disadvantaged. The Durban Indian Child Welfare Society was established in 1927, the Bloemfontein Bantu Child Welfare Society in 1945 and a number of child welfare organisations emerged in the Western Cape. The Johannesburg Indian Welfare Association formed in 1934 addressed the plight of poor and destitute Indian people after the great depression. The story of JISS is inextricably linked to the turbulent history of Indians in South Africa (Johannesburg Institute of Social Services 2004). Similar developments occurred to address the needs of other vulnerable groups: these included services for the blind, which were established for Indians and Coloureds in 1949. Many religious organisations also established social welfare activities. Independent social welfare activities by disadvantaged communities, including activities directly or indirectly related to resistance to apartheid, have not been well documented.

Grassroots mutual aid and self-help groups provided an important form of social support in urban areas. In the 1940s mineworkers formed 'home groups' and what Webster (1983) referred to as proto-voluntary associations; these played a vital role in worker solidarity and resistance. Some of the 'home groups' provided support to workers in times of illness and in meeting burial needs. Women were also active in community-based self-help and advocacy groups to address food scarcity during the Second World War; housing needs and permits to remain in urban areas were some of the other issues that concerned them (Walker 1982). Burial societies, *stokvels* and various savings schemes have their origins in mutual aid and community self-help efforts. Burial Societies were popularised in the 1930s to provide social support and assistance with the burial needs of migrant workers. While some of the societies were independent, many were also initiated by political leaders. The names of the *stokvels* reflected a spirit of togetherness, group identity and co-operation such as 'Itereleng' (do things for yourself) and 'Masibambane' (let us join together) and fulfilled important financial, moral and social purposes. Stokvels later became associated with parties and *shebeens*, but the *stokvel* subculture and informal savings schemes are nonetheless firmly established in African townships (Lukhele 1990).

What is a *stokvel*?

A *stokvel* is an informal group savings scheme whereby the members agree to contribute a fixed amount of money to a common pool on a regular basis. This money or some of it may be drawn by the members on a rotation basis or as needed. It is a member driven association, they set their own rules and define their purpose. Besides providing mutual financial assistance, they also provide valuable social networks, support and recreation (Lukhele 1990). Roughly 2 million people are members of a *stokvel* and contribute about R245 per month (Finscope SA 2004 Survey).

In response to the enactment and implementation of apartheid laws, the Congress Alliance and the Federation of South African Women mounted defiance campaigns to protest against unjust laws. Thousands of people participated in protest action against pass laws and Bantu Education. The Congress Alliance also spearheaded the adoption of the Freedom Charter, which called for a just, non-racial and democratic society. Some of the demands set out in the Freedom Charter were relevant to the achievement of a society that would promote human dignity and the well-being of all its citizens in areas such as health, education and social welfare (Patel 1991a; Patel 1988).

The 1950s were characterised by patterns of protest, government reaction, sporadic violence and the banning of individuals. This was followed by a state of emergency and the banning of political organisations such as the African National Congress (ANC), the Pan Africanist Congress (PAC) and the Communist Party of South Africa (CPSA). The leadership of the organisations was either banned or jailed, and others set up the resistance movements in exile. During the 1950s social development initiatives were a response to the social and political context and emerged as part of the general political resistance of that time.

Mass resistance to apartheid re-emerged in 1976, which provided the turning point in the opposition to apartheid. The country was faced with a deepening economic and political crisis. Oil prices increased and an international recession coupled with growing industrial, political and economic instability led to the crisis. Unemployment also increased and these conditions contributed to the uprisings at Soweto and elsewhere in the country, which were sparked by the introduction of Afrikaans in black schools and were against separate education for African children. These events had a profound politicising effect on the people. The Black Consciousness Movement, based on self-assertion, autonomy and the dignity of black people, also emerged in the 1970s and was especially influential among black students. The Black Consciousness Movement gave rise to widespread protests against apartheid education. Again many young people were jailed and others went into exile to join the armed wings of the ANC and the PAC. The Black Consciousness Movement also initiated many community-based development programmes founded on the principles of African self-help, communalism and community action. The Black Community Programmes were active in education, health and integrated rural development projects.

After 1976, protest became endemic and the Apartheid State's deepening economic, political and ideological crisis provided the impetus for continued mobilisation and organisation in all spheres of life. The 1980s saw the mushrooming of grassroots formations, which organised around the day-to-day needs and concerns of the people and articulated the demands of the Freedom Charter. Demands included social and economic rights such as the meeting of the basic needs of the people for housing, affordable rents, equal education, affordable health care and equal social welfare services and benefits. The labour movement grew throughout this period and articulated the demand for the extension of the social wage, such as increased work-related social benefits (maternity benefits, pensions, provident funds and medical aid). All of these anti-apartheid activities contributed to a vibrant, politicised environment and emphasised the principle of equality, and a participatory and rights-based approach. The prominent focus on the role of civil society organisations in social development can be traced to these demands and political struggles.

'The prominent focus on the role of civil society organisations in social development can be traced to these demands and political struggles.'

Protest action during the 1980s gave rise to civic associations, and student, youth, and women's organisations. Mass-based community organisations multiplied throughout this period. These organisations later formed the membership base of the United Democratic Front (UDF), which was launched in August 1983 to lead the campaign against the government's new constitutional dispensation, which provided for the participation of Coloureds, Indians and whites in a tri-cameral parliamentary system in which whites maintained the majority. These initiatives also provided for the participation of urban Africans in local government, while retaining the homelands system whereby Africans were to exercise their political rights. This new constitutional dispensation was widely rejected by the alliance of the UDF and the Congress of South African Trade Unions (COSATU) because it excluded the black majority from political decision-making

(Swilling 1988; UDF 1987). The UDF organised nationally and built a non-racial unity made up of 700 grassroots organisations. The depth and geographic extent of the actions of these popular organisations coalesced into an urban uprising and resulted in the declaration of two successive states of emergency. Grassroots organisations and their activists formed more localised organisational structures to respond to the effects of repression. The concept of 'people's power' also informed the creation of alternative formations such as people's courts, street committees and community development organisations, which were understood to be rudimentary forms of self-government (Seekings 1989). These organisations addressed social problems such as crime, drinking problems and social conflicts, but in some townships the excesses of the militant youth were widely believed to have marred the positive impact of people's power. By 1986, many of these alternative structures had broken down as a result of state repression.

The deepening economic recession, the state's financial constraints in meeting popular demands for basic needs, and the ongoing political challenge to the state as a result of the illegitimacy of state reforms resulted in urban revolt. This was also evident in other parts of the world such as Latin America, where urban movements took root in response to increasing pauperisation stemming from deteriorating economic conditions (Henry 1985; Castells 1979).

It was in this context that the social development initiatives of popular grassroots organisations began to emerge and take root. The social service and development programmes of grassroots organisations were conceived of as alternative or progressive welfare services (Patel & Taback 1989). These organisations provided services in areas that were neglected or not provided by government as a critical response and a challenge to the dominant apartheid welfare system. The progressive organisations differed fundamentally from the formal welfare system in their vision, goals, principles, conceptualisation and methods of service delivery. Patel (1991a) argued that two modalities of social welfare co-existed in the South African context at the time in a complementary and a contradictory relationship. Services not provided by the formal welfare sector were met through progressive organisations, while the formal welfare organisations continued to provide much-needed remedial services. However, the point of departure of the approaches adopted by the formal and progressive services differed significantly.

'The social service and development programmes of grassroots organisations were conceived of as alternative or progressive welfare services.'

Progressive social welfare and development organisations were funded by sympathetic foreign donors; many were aligned or sympathetic to the mass democratic movement and were people-centred and participatory in their approach to service delivery. The organisations experimented with alternative methods of service delivery, which were considered to be more legitimate and appropriate in meeting the needs of the people at local levels, and were community-based in their approach. The aims of the organisations ranged from meeting basic needs to the promotion of empowerment, social justice, human rights and the development of alternative models of welfare services which could inform social welfare policy and thinking in a post-apartheid society. Research conducted on the social service programmes of progressive organisations in the late 1980s also documented many organisational, managerial, administrative, financial and practical problems in the delivery of services. Difficulties in translating their social and political ideals into practical and viable projects and giving effect to principles such as non-racialism, democracy, empowerment and equality – especially in relation to gender equality – were also noted (Patel 1991a). The social welfare model that emerged from the activities of progressive organisations was strongly oriented toward a social development approach to social welfare, and a framework for developmental social welfare emerged from the research study (Patel 1991a; Patel 1991b; Patel 1991c).

'The social welfare model that emerged from the activities of progressive organisations was strongly orientated toward a social development approach to social welfare...'

The social service activities of progressive organisations were also closely connected with the activities of professionals who were active in anti-apartheid activities and the United Democratic Front and the Congress of South African Trade Unions. Alliances were forged and collaborative projects and campaigns were undertaken between professionals, professional associations, community organisations and social movement organisations. Campaigns supported by social service workers were pertinent to the areas of their work, as social service professionals were acutely aware of the psychosocial impact of political violence and repression on human well-being. A conference drawing attention to the detention of children in 1986 was attended by over 500 people and rallied support for the release of children from South Africa's jails. The delivery of alternative social services for individuals and families affected by state repression was another significant area of involvement. Academic institutions were challenged to review their uncritical adoption of First World modalities of social work education and to be more responsive to the local situation. The Golden Jubilee Conference of the School of Social Work at the University of the Witwatersrand in 1987, titled *The Contribution of Social Work in a Changing South Africa* , was an attempt to explore how traditional social work could begin to engage with the change agenda (McKendrick 1987).

An activist organisation of social workers – Concerned Social Workers – was formed during the state of emergency; it built alliances with other progressive social service organisations in its campaigns and conducted action research. Concerned Social Workers and the School of Social Work at the University of the Witwatersrand sponsored a research study on *Social Welfare Policy Options for South Africa* in 1988 from which several publications emerged to inform policy debate and advocacy. The Organisation of Alternative Social Services of South Africa (OASSA) published a journal and delivered counselling and support services to detainees and their families. Professional organisations such as the

South African Black Social Workers Association, the Society for Social Workers in the Transvaal, the Social Workers Forum and the Durban Welfare Policy Group convened a national conference in 1989 titled *Toward a Democratic Welfare System: Options and Strategies* (Patel 1989). By this time, it was clear to many role-players in the formal welfare sector that apartheid in social welfare was unworkable. Some of the most influential national, regional and local bodies came out in support of the conference resolutions. The aim of the conference was to protest against government policies, privatisation in social welfare and state repression. A new social welfare dispensation in a democratic society promoting a just social welfare dispensation was articulated by the conference and the resolutions were presented at a government conference, which was held at the same time.

The efforts in the social welfare field were matched by similar activities on an even larger scale in the health and education sectors. This was a time of vibrant debate about 'people's education' and 'health care for all' and focused on joint action by community and progressive professionals in health and education. Policy research centres mushroomed at universities and research on the actual workings of the apartheid system in the different fields, including policy options for the future, featured high on the research agendas of these research groups.

Of particular relevance to the search for alternatives was the publication of the *Report of the Second Carnegie Inquiry into Poverty and Development in Southern Africa* in 1988. The first study focused on poor white poverty in the 1920s and 1930s, while the second study set about uncovering the truth about poverty, inequality and underdevelopment in Southern Africa. The focus of the second study was on poverty as it affected the black majority. Research was conducted, a national conference was convened, all people involved with work with the poor contributed their knowledge and experiences, photographic exhibitions and film festivals were hosted – all of which documented the conditions of the poor. The study was led by Francis Wilson and Ramphele Mamphela – two noted South African scholars. The Inquiry documented the nature and extent of poverty and all its related manifestations in the Southern African context. The causes of poverty were located in past and present factors, which in turn were deeply rooted in the unequal and distorted nature of development in the countries in the region. Recommendations for transformation in key areas such as health, education, social welfare, employment and a greater social investment role for the state in addressing the legacy of the past were proposed (Wilson & Mamphela 1989).

While policy research on a post-apartheid society was being conducted, it took place against the background of great political upheaval and struggle. Policy research was also an important advocacy tool and for many researchers, practitioners, activists and communities the idea that apartheid could actually end was 'beyond our wildest dreams' (van Kessel

2000). The policy alternatives were inspirational and of an ideational nature, and this informed future constitutional and policy debate in the transition period in the 1990s and in a post-apartheid society.

The 1980s provided post-apartheid South Africa with an important legacy. In a study of the UDF between 1983 and 1991, Seekings (2000:322) expressed the view that the UDF 'bequeathed a lasting legacy to post-apartheid politics'. The UDF and popular grassroots action, supported by other strata and classes in the society, brought a particular character to South Africa's democracy. It also gave rise to the efficacy of civil society, a plural democracy and the salience of rights and political and economic alternatives based on these rights.

'The UDF and popular grassroots action brought a special character to South Africa's democracy: it gave rise to the efficacy of civil society, a plural democracy and the salience of rights.'

Social welfare in transition

In February 1990, the National Party government announced the unbanning of political organisations and the opening of negotiations to arrive at a peaceful settlement of the intractable conflict that had plagued South Africa for over 300 years. The announcement was met with joy and great trepidation about the future. The crisis of apartheid could no longer be contained and all parties came together to search for a settlement to establish a non-racial democracy.

However, this process was complex and fraught with many obstacles and challenges. Political violence reached unprecedented levels and created instability, confusion and grave concern that the social consquences of the conflict and destabilisation would further erode the already poor living standards and conditions of the majority of the population, placing even greater pressure on a post-apartheid government. The social situation in the early 1990s was characterised by political and social instability, low projected economic growth rates and risingexpectations by the people that a future government would meet the great backlog in basic needs. The new government was inheriting a country with a wealth distribution that ranked among the most unequal in the world, poor human development indicators, rising unemployment, increasing urbanisation and an economy in crisis. Increasing social disintegration in the society was evident in relation to growing domestic violence, crime, delinquency, addiction and trauma. The need to reconcile and heal the wounds of the past was considered to be vital, as were the inclusion of the formerly excluded and the reintegration of political exiles and prisoners.

In order for social welfare to effectively address the challenges of the unfolding social situation, a re-orientation in welfare thinking was needed which would break fundamentally with some of the old conceptions and paradigms. A new path needed to be charted for social welfare as an instrument in the promotion of national reconstruction and social development. Debate about the country's future policies and programmes created opportunities for many different organisations to shape that future. Some of these will be reflected on below, but this should not detract from the expansive efforts of communities, welfare organisations, professional associations, and forums that contributed to shaping a just and democratic welfare dispensation.

The first conference to engage in dialogue between the ANC and health and welfare role-players took place in Maputo in 1990 and a *Declaration of health and welfare in Southern Africa* was adopted. The conference committed itself to transforming health and social services, promoting a new vision, and devising an appropriate welfare policy and the prioritisation of primary health care as a basis for the provision of health and welfare services (Conference Organising Group 1990). The ANC political structures were established internally and policy units were created to develop public policy in all spheres of governance. Consultation and involvement of internal organisations was uneven between the ANC's policy units and there were concerns between 1990 and 1994 that not all of the local knowledge and experience was being harnessed in preparing for governance.

Alongside these developments, conferences, research and policy alternatives remained high on the agenda of organisations. Some of these included a *Regional Conference on National Reconstruction and Social Development* in 1991 convened by Concerned Social Workers and the School of Social Work at the University of the Witwatersrand (Patel 1991c). A research study was conducted by the National Children's Rights Committee and UNICEF on the *Situation of Children and Women in South Africa* (UNICEF & NCRC 1993). The NCRC advocated children's rights, which were later enshrined in the interim and final constitutions of the country and in the Bill of Rights.

In order to influence public policy developments in the transitional period, a range of national sectoral forums emerged in housing, local government and education. Drawing on this experience of participatory policy discourse in other social, economic and political sectors in society, welfare leaders formed an alliance of national organisations and launched the National Welfare Forum at a National Welfare Summit attended by 700 delegates at the end of 1993. This was the largest non-racial gathering of welfare and development organisations in South Africa. The purpose of the Welfare Forum was to be a voice for the welfare sector and to engage with government about the transformation and restructuring of social welfare. The Forum also responded to the policy initiatives emanating from the National Party government, which was still in power between 1990 and 1994. At that time, the government was still bent on implementing privatisation of social welfare.

The Welfare Forum set up national and regional structures and, in spite of funding and organisational difficulties, remained an effective voice and watchdog for the sector. As it was a broad alliance of organisations, it operated on a consensus model of decision-making, which helped to build welfare consensus. It could be argued that this may have compromised the Forum in leading more radical positions, but the climate in the country was one of building national unity, given the social divisions of the past. The Forum functioned effectively until 1999, when it was disbanded in many parts of the country because of financial problems and a possible inability to reposition itself in the changed post-apartheid context. Some commentators felt that it had perhaps outlived its significance but the absence of a welfare voice in the post-apartheid era was a major setback for the sector. There are however initiatives to re-establish this body.

Prior to the elections of 1994, the ANC published its election manifesto and programme for the new South Africa – the Reconstruction and Development Programme (RDP): A Policy Framework (1994). The RDP was widely consulted in the ANC and comments were received from the public. The RDP policy framework was to inform economic, political and social development in a post-apartheid society. The RDP advocated a developmental approach to social security and social welfare, a focus on basic needs, social welfare rights, a review of policy and legislation and the creation of a single national social welfare and development department and provincial departments. The need for a safety net was articulated and there was a focus on the needs of vulnerable groups. This framework was to guide the dismantling of apartheid welfare and the institution of a just and democratic welfare system for all South Africans.

CHAPTER SUMMARY

- This chapter described the events, ideas, values and principles that under-girded and shaped welfare policy and practice through different stages in the development of South African society. It showed how the social, cultural, economic and political context influenced the nature and the character of the welfare system. While South Africa's social welfare development followed a similar path to other countries where social welfare emerged in response to industrialisation, in the African and South African context, colonialism and apartheid had a distinctive influence on social provision. State welfare policy was the cause of many of the social problems in the society and not the solution.
- The chapter illustrated how apartheid ideology was translated into action through the way in which the society was governed and administered. The social work and social service professions were torn apart. Individuals and organisations became willing and unwilling partners of the apartheid state.
- The evolution of a 'society of positive social welfare' evolved from a struggle for national liberation over many generations. The vision for a new welfare system unfolded through the struggle for social justice in communities and through their organisations and social movements, and this process was widely supported by different strata in the society such as professionals and academics. This demonstrates the role that social movements played in bringing about a just social welfare system. Similar processes occurred in other parts of the developed and developing world and continue today.

CRITICAL THINKING QUESTIONS

1. Kirst-Ashman (41–44: 2003) argues that, as professionals, social workers have ethical responsibilities to their clients, to their profession and to the broader society. Apartheid social welfare presented social workers and social service professionals with major ethical dilemmas. If you were a social worker in a child welfare agency in 1966 where you were expected to implement Circular 29 of 1966, how would you have resolved those ethical dilemmas?
2. What are the ideas, values and principles that emerged during the mass struggles for social justice during the 1980s and early 1990s? How do these ideas and values connect with your own perspective on social welfare in South Africa today?

Bibliography

ANC (African National Congress) (1994), *The Reconstruction and Development Programme. A policy framework.* Johannesburg: Umanyano Publications.

Ardington, E. M. and Lund. F.J. (1995), Pensions and development: social security as complementary to programmes of reconstruction and development. *Journal of Development Studies Southern Africa,* 12:4, 557–577.

Callinicos, L. (1987), *Working Life 1886–1940.* Vol. 2. Johannesburg: Ravan Press in Association with the University of the Witwatersrand History Workshop.

Brümmer, F. (1964), *The Structure and Policy of Welfare Services in South Africa with Particular Reference to the Role of the State.* Pretoria: The Government Printer.

Castells, M. (1979), The Class Struggle and Urban Contradictions. In Cowley, J., Kaye, A., Mayo, M. and Thompson, M. *Community or Class Struggle?* (40–46). Great Britain: Whitstable.

Concerned Social Workers (1988), *Welfare in the South African Context – The Challenge to the Social Work Profession. Proceedings of the Annual General Meeting of Concerned Social Workers.* Johannesburg: University of the Witwatersrand.

Chisholm, L. (1990), Class, Colour and Gender in Child Welfare in South Africa, 1902–1918. *South African Historical Journal,* 23: 100–121.

Conference Organising Group (1990), Declaration on health and welfare in Southern Africa. *Journal of Critical Health*, 31:32, 4–5.

Department of National Health and Population Development (1990), *Voluntary Welfare Initiative and the Financing of the Welfare System, Draft Proposal.* Working Committee of the South African Welfare Council and the Interdepartmental Committee on Social Welfare.

Department of Constitutional Development and Planning (1985), *Report on an Investigation into the Present Welfare Policy in the Republic of South Africa.* Pretoria: Government Printer.

De Villiers, J.C. (1984), *Report and Recommendations of the Committee of Enquiry on Possible Further Facilities for Medical and Dental Training.* Pretoria: Government Printer.

Dolgoff, R. and Feldstein, D. (1984), *Understanding Social Welfare.* 2nd ed. New York: Longman.

Dubow, S. (1987), Race, Civilisation and Culture: The Elaboration of Segregationist Discourse in the Inter-War Years. In Marks, S. and Trapido, S. (eds.), *The Politics of Race, Class and Nationalism in Twentieth Century South Africa* (120–132). London: Longman.

Finscope (2004), Finscope SA 2004 Survey.http://www.finscope.co.za

Greater Johannesburg Welfare, Social Services and Development Forum (1999), *Submissions from the welfare sector to the Truth and Reconciliation Commission.* Johannesburg: Greater Johannesburg Welfare, Social Services and Development Forum.

HARE, I., MCKENDRICK B.W. AND HOFFMANN, W. (1987), *Social Work Education at Wits 1937–1987*. School of Social Work. Johannesburg: University of the Witwatersrand.

HENRY, E. (1985). Urban Social Movements in Latin America – Towards a Critical Understanding. In Slater, D. (ed.), *New Social Movements and the State in Latin America*, (114–136). USA: Forms Publications.

HINDSON, D. (1987), *Pass Controls and the Urban African Proletariat*. Johannesburg: Ravan Press.

JOHANNESBURG INSTITUTE OF SOCIAL SERVICES (2004), Jiss 1934, 70th Anniversary. Johannesburg: Johannesburg Institute of Social Services.

KIRST-ASHMAN, K. K. (2003), *Introduction to Social Work and Social Welfare. Critical Thinking Perspectives.* United States: Thomson Brooks/Cole.

LEGASSICK, M. and WOLPE., H. (1976), The Bantustans and Capital Accumulation in South Africa. *Journal of Review of African Political Economy*, 7, 87–107.

LE ROUX, P. (1978), The Poor White Problem – An Economist's Perspective. *Social Work/Maatskaplike Werk*, 14, 8–20.

LUKHELE, A.K. (1990), *Stokvels in South Africa. Informal Savings Schemes by Blacks for the Black Community*. Johannesburg: Amagi Books.

LUND, F. J. (1988), *Will Private Hands do Public Tasks? Privatisation and Welfare in South Africa*. Paper presented at the 19th Congress of the Association of Sociologists of Southern Africa. (ASSA).

LUND, F.J. (1985), *A Description and Preliminary Assessment of South Africa's National Community Development Strategy*. Centre for Applied Social Sciences. Durban: University of Natal.

MACPHERSON.S, and MIDGLEY, J. (1987), *Comparative Social Policy and the Third World*. Sussex: Wheatsheaf Books

MALHERBE, E.G. (1978), The Carnegie Poor White Investigation: Its Origin and Sequels. *Journal of Maatskaplike Werk/Social Work*, 9, 81–90

MAIR, L. (1987), *Anthropology and Development*. London: Macmillan.

MCKENDRICK, B.W. (1990), The South African Social Welfare System. In McKendrick, B.W. (ed.), *Introduction to Social Work*, (30–43). Pretoria: Haum Tertiary.

MCKENDRICK, B.W. (1988), What is happening in welfare in South Africa? In Concerned Social Workers. *Welfare in the South African Context – The Challenge to the Social Work Profession*. In Touch. Special AGM edition, proceedings of the Annual General Meeting.

MCKENDRICK, B.W. and DUDAS, E. (1987), South Africa. In Dixon, J. (ed.), *Social Welfare in Africa*, (184–217). London: Croon Helm.

MCKENDRICK, B.W. (1987), *The Contribution of Social Work in a Changing South Africa*. Proceedings of the Golden Jubilee Conference, 6–7 July. School of Social Work, Johannesburg: University of the Witwatersrand.

MIDGLEY, J. (1981), *Professional Imperialism: Social Work in the Third World*. London: Heinemann.

PATEL, L. (1991a), Social Welfare Options for South Africa. Unpublished Ph.D. Thesis. Johannesburg: University of the Witwatersrand.

PATEL, L. (1991b), The Evolution of a Democratic Welfare Policy for a Post-apartheid South Africa. *Journal of Maatskaplike Werk/Social Work*, 27:2, 154–164.

PATEL, L. (1991c), *Principles, Guidelines and Recommendations for Developmental Social Welfare Policies and Programmes in a Democratic South Africa*. Regional Consultative Conference on Social Welfare Policy in National Reconstruction and Development, 21–22 June, Johannesburg: University of the Witwatersrand.

PATEL, L. (1989), *Towards a Democratic Welfare System Options and Strategies.* Proceedings of the National Social Welfare Policy Conference. Johannesburg: University of the Witwatersrand.

PATEL, L. (1988), Towards People's Welfare. *In Touch.* Occasional Paper 1. Johannesburg: Concerned Social Workers.

PATEL, L. AND TABACK, R. (1989), A Survey of Progressive Social Services. *In Touch.* Occasional Paper 2. Johannesburg: Concerned Social Workers.

POTGIETER, M.C. (1998), *The Social Work Process.* South Africa: Prentice-Hall (Pty) Ltd.

POTGIETER, M.L. (1973), *Maatskaplike Sorg in Suid Afrika.* Stellenbosch/ Grahamstown:Univsersiteits Uitgewers en Boekanderlaars.

ROWLAND, W.P. (1984), Being Blind in the World. A Phenomenological Analysis of Blindness and a Formulation of New Objectives in Rehabilitation. Unpublished Ph.D. Thesis. Cape Town: University of Cape Town.

SAIRR (1992), *South African Race Relations Survey (1991/1992).* Johannesburg: South African Institute of Race Relations.

SAIRR (1988), *South African Race Relations Survey (1987/1988).* Johannesburg: South African Institute of Race Relations.

SEEKINGS, J. (2000), *The UDF. A History of the United Democratic Front in South Africa 1983–1991,* Cape Town: David Phillip.

SEEKINGS, J. (1989), People's Courts and Popular Politics. In Moss, G. and Obery, I.(eds.), *South African Review Five* (119–135). Johannesburg: Ravan Press.

SWILLING, M. and PHILLIPS, M. (1988), Reform, Security and the Significance of the Municipal Elections. In Concerned Social Workers (1988). *Welfare in the South African Context – The Challenge to the Social Work Profession. Proceedings of the Annual General Meeting of Concerned Social Workers.* Johannesburg: University of the Witwatersrand.

SWILLING, M. (1988), The United Democratic Front and Township Revolt. In Cobbet, W. and Cohen, R. (eds.), *Popular Struggles in South Africa* (pp.90–113). London: Africa World Press.

TERBLANCHE, S.J. (1987), *A New Fiscal Policy and Economic Philosophy for South Africa in Transition.* Department of Economics: University of Stellenbosch.

UNITED DEMOCRATIC FRONT (UDF) (1987), *National Working Committee Conference Report* 29–30 May.

UNITED NATIONS CHILDREN'S FUND (UNICEF) & NATIONAL CHILDREN'S RIGHTS COMMITTEE (NCRC)(1993). *Children and Women in South Africa: A Situation Analysis.* Johannesburg: UNICEF & NCRC.

VAN KESSEL, I. (2000), *Beyond Our Wildest Dreams. The United Democratic Front and the Transformation of South Africa.* Charlottesville: University Press of Virginia.

WALKER, C. (1982), *Women and Resistance in South Africa.* London: Onyx Press.

WEBSTER, E. (1983), Black Industrial Protest on the Witwatersrand 1901–1902. In Webster, E. (ed.), *Essays in Southern African Labour History.* Johannesburg: Ravan Press.

WINCKLER, A.T. (1969), *Volkswelsynsbeleid.* Stellenbosch: Kosmo.

WILSON, F. AND MAMPHELA, R. (1989), *Uprooting Poverty. The South African Challenge.* Cape Town: David Phillip.

WOLPE, H. (1972), Capitalism and Cheap Labour-Power in South Africa: From Segregation to Apartheid. *Journal of Economy and Society.* 1,1–33.

CHAPTER

4 Social welfare in a democratic society

LEARNING OUTCOMES

After you have read this chapter you should be able to:

- Describe the new context within which social welfare is located.
- Discuss the South African conception of developmental social welfare with reference to social rights, the inter-relationship between economic and social development, democracy and participation, social development partnerships and bridging the micro/macro divide in intervention.
- Discuss the institutionalisation of developmental social welfare in relation to the structure and functions of government, legislation and financial and fiscal arrangements.
- Reflect critically on the achievements and challenges of social welfare in a democratic society.

Dismantling the old and constructing the new

After the unbanning of political organisations in 1990, the parties embarked on a protracted and difficult process of constitutional negotiations, which culminated in the adoption of the interim constitution known as The Constitution of the Republic of South Africa Act 200 of 1993. The constitutional negotiations took place against the backdrop of escalating and unprecedented levels of violence in the country as political parties struggled to reach compromises on the nature and direction of a new democratic nation. That such compromises could be reached and a relatively peaceful transition to democracy achieved after the injustices of the past remains the miracle of the new South Africa. The South African example of achieving a democracy through negotiations is highly regarded internationally as a model of what is possible in a conflict-ridden and divided world.

The 1993 Constitution laid the foundation of the new society and paved the way for the first democratic elections held in April 1994, which resulted in an electoral victory for the African National Congress (ANC). The new democratically elected government led by former President Nelson Mandela was inaugurated on 27th April 1994 and a Government of National Unity was formed by the ANC, the National Party (NP) and the Inkatha Freedom Party (IFP). The promotion of national unity and reconciliation was one of the distinguishing features of the Mandela government. The post-1994 period saw the formation of a Constituent Assembly made up of all political parties and, after a nationwide consultative process, *The Constitution of the Republic of South Africa* (Act 108 of 1996) was adopted (this is also referred to as the final Constitution).

The Constitution in its founding provisions recognises a common South African citizenship, universal adult suffrage, a multi-party democracy, a free press and judicial review of government and legislation to ensure that government operates within the framework of the Constitution and a Bill of Rights. The Bill of Rights guarantees civil and political rights, language and cultural rights, the right to social security, children's rights and social and economic rights of all citizens. The Constitution followed the lead of international human rights instruments, which informed many of the demands of opposition movements for a just, democratic and peaceful society committed to human rights. Some of the international instruments that were particularly pertinent to Constitution-making in South Africa were: the Universal Declaration of Human Rights (1948); the European Convention on Human Rights (1950); The United Nations Educational, Scientific, and Cultural Organisation (UNESCO) Convention against Discrimination in Education (1960); United Nations Covenant on Economic, Social and Cultural Rights (1966); the Convention on the Elimination of All Forms of Racial Discrimination against Women (1979); the African Charter on Human and People Rights (1981); the Convention on the Rights of the Child (1989); and the United Nations World Declaration on Education for All (1990). Provision was made for a Constitutional Court to protect and interpret the Constitution and for judicial review. Other independent institutions were created to promote human rights and gender equality and an Independent Electoral Commission was set up.

The Constitution also made provision for a move to a federal structure of governance. Schedule 6 of the Constitution sets out the areas of governmental responsibility for services. Schedule 4 outlines concurrent responsibilities between national and provincial governments for social service delivery such as health, education and social welfare. These provisions provide for a complex system of service delivery, which is discussed further in this chapter.

'The RDP advocated the idea of developmental social welfare and set out preliminary proposals, which were widely supported by the social welfare sector.'

The Reconstruction and Development Programme (RDP), the political programme of the ANC, was adopted by the new democratic government. The *White Paper on Reconstruction and Development* (1994) set out the government's strategy for transformation which included five key policy objectives: the provision of basic needs, developing human resources, building the economy, the democratisation of the state and society and the implementation of the RDP. The RDP advocated the idea of developmental social welfare and set out preliminary proposals, which were widely supported by the social welfare sector. It also paved the way for the further development of social welfare policy in South Africa (Sewpaul 1997; Triegaardt 1996).

A special Cabinet Committee on the RDP, co-ordinated by the Minister without Portfolio, was responsible for RDP policies and programmes, co-operation, funding, change management and monitoring and evaluation of programmes. For the first two years of the new government, the

Minister without Portfolio, Jay Naidoo, played a critical role in facilitating the adoption and implementation of RDP goals, priorities and targets by government departments. Key projects were identified, and targets were set for these projects in health, primary school nutrition, land reform and restitution, housing, infrastructure development, small and medium enterprise development and public works programmes to create employment. An RDP fund was established and R2.5 billion was allocated in 1994/1995. The funds came from savings that were effected by government departments. The fund was intended to grow and was to be supplemented by international donor funds. In addition, government departments were required to effect savings within their existing budgets, to reprioritise their programmes in line with the RDP and to fund new priorities from savings.

The targets for many of the programmes were extremely ambitious given the inadequate institutional delivery systems, lack of capacity in government, limited funding, an over-loaded transformation agenda coupled with the simultaneous restructuring of the public sector and high expectations of the new government to deliver on its promises. These realities and constraints impacted on the successful roll-out of RDP programmes within the short timeframes that were set. In addition, the RDP was to be implemented through government departments whilst the RDP office was to play a facilitating and co-ordinating role and ensure the effective management of the transformation process. Government departments were required to develop transformation policies and plans which would constitute one of the main vehicles for the transformation of government programmes. This was an extremely complex endeavour given the way in which government administration and Ministries were organised and given their accountability to the executive and parliament. Competition between the RDP office and Ministries and departments ensued, coupled with the complex political dynamics of operating within a coalition government. The inability of the RDP to meet its targets also led to waning public confidence. This situation, coupled with political and public management difficulties, eventually resulted in the closure of the RDP Ministry and office in 1997. In future, the RDP was to be mainstreamed through government departments led by Ministers responsible for their portfolios and the government reaffirmed its commitment to the policy framework and intentions of the RDP. The RDP achieved great visibility for government's social goals and it was widely supported as the beacon of what the government sought to achieve 'without which it would lose all legitimacy' (President Mandela, Parliament of the Republic of South Africa 1994). In the years following the closure of the RDP Ministry and office, the government's commitment to its social goals has constantly been in question.

'The RDP achieved greater visibility for government's social goals and it was widely supported as the beacon of what the government sought to achieve without which it would lose all legitimacy.'

The closure of the RDP coincided with the subsequent adoption in 1996 of the government's macro-economic policy – the *Growth,*

Employment and Redistribution (GEAR) policy. The GEAR strategy was intended to stabilise the economy and to integrate the economy into the regional and global economic system. GEAR has been described as a voluntary structural adjustment programme that embraced economic liberalisation and led to the opening of the economy to foreign investment and competition (Mhone & Edigheji 2003). The strategy aimed to generate an economic growth rate of 6 percent, employment through a market-based approach, the reduction of inflation and the budget deficit, and to contain fiscal expenditure and achieve a macroeconomic balance. The government argued that this was necessary given the long-term structural economic crisis that faced the South African economy, international isolation of the economy, the need to restructure the economy and to promote investor confidence. The strategy was well received by the private sector and internationally but high economic growth rates and improved living conditions have not been realised over the past decade.

'The challenge remains to promote equitable and sustainable human development that is inclusive and that addresses the twin challenges of the country's apartheid past, and the demands of an industrialising society and an emerging economy and democracy in the global era.'

Critics on the left argued that GEAR represented a shift away from the government's commitment to its social goals and that the government embraced a neo-liberal paradigm in response to pressures from big business and economic globalisation (Sewpaul 2001; Bond 2000). This implied a shifting of responsibility for social welfare from government to individuals, families and the private sector, and resulted in the abrogation of state responsibility for meeting needs. It was also argued that the intractable problems of poverty, inequality, unemployment and large-scale social disintegration in the society could not be adequately addressed because of the tension between GEAR and the RDP in the post-apartheid period between 1996 and 2004 (Mhone & Edigheji 2003). The challenge remains to promote equitable and sustainable human development that is inclusive and that addresses the twin challenges of the country's apartheid past, and the demands of an industrialising society and an emerging economy and democracy in the global era. These issues will be revisited in the concluding section to this chapter.

Establishing a developmental path for social welfare

It is against this background that the *Ministry for Social Welfare and Population Development* was established in 1994 and welfare policy and strategy was developed and implemented. For the first time in South Africa's history a separate Ministry for social welfare was created, as social welfare was historically part of the health portfolio. This was viewed positively as reflecting the government's commitment to the promotion of social well-being, poverty-reduction and support for the most vulnerable. The social welfare sector welcomed this initiative but grave concerns were expressed when the Mandela government appointed a National Party Minister, Abie Williams, to head the welfare portfolio. At provincial level, Members of the Executive Councils (MECs) were responsible for the social welfare function or combined social welfare with other functions such as health, sport and recreation and culture. Two of the MECs were National Party representatives, one was from the Inkatha Freedom Party and the remaining MECs were ANC representatives in the provincial governments. The Government of National Unity (GNU) was created to build national consensus and to include diverse political perspectives in the leadership and management of the new social welfare portfolios. Since the provincial governments had concurrent powers with the national government for social welfare, there was political contestation between them about their respective powers and functions and the political direction of the welfare portfolio. In the early years of the GNU, political leaders struggled to find a way forward because of their different perspectives on social welfare.

Restructuring and Transformation Committees were established at provincial level in 1994. The members of these committees were appointed by the MECs and consisted of specialists and practitioners from the voluntary sector, government and academia. Most of the restructuring committees conducted situation analyses of the welfare function and social security and made recommendations on the strategy, functions and new structures of social welfare departments in the provinces. New senior management teams were appointed in keeping with the provisions of Chapter B Special of the Interim Constitution of 1993 to create a representative public service. A key challenge that the restructuring committees and the new leadership addressed was rationalising and amalgamating the different racially-based administrations from 14 down to 9 provincial departments and one national department. The amalgamation of the different social security systems remained an enormous challenge in relation to policy, legislation, management, administration and information technology systems (this is discussed in Chapter 5).

Whilst the pace of change in the provinces progressed, albeit slowly, there was considerable political contestation between the National Minister and the ANC Members of the Executive Councils over the leadership and direction of change in social welfare. In December 1994 the national Minister and the MECs convened a meeting in Cape Town and it was agreed that a national consultative process was needed to develop a new national consensus for social welfare. It was also hoped that such a process would build co-operation and understanding between the parties and would break the impasse that had been reached. The terms of reference of the process of developing a White Paper through a democratic consultative process was agreed. In view of the political dynamics described above, the process of consensus-building and restructuring in social welfare commenced much later than in other government departments and accounted for the slow pace of change in the early years of the transition.

The National Strategic Management Committee mandated by the Ministers Committee for Social Welfare and supported by the national Department of Social Welfare and Population Development had the task of building national consensus. Six technical committees were established: these consisted of representatives from governmental and non-governmental organisations, practitioners, interest groups representing different populations at risk and service user groups. The National Welfare Social Services and Development Forum, which had established itself as a national organisation with membership across all the provinces, represented organised social welfare and development organisations. This forum conducted its own research and consultative processes to develop its positions and to inform its contributions and mandates (Mazibuko 1996). The technical reports were collated into a Discussion Document that was widely consulted. A national consultative conference held in Bloemfontein in June 1995 and attended by over 400 national organisations debated the policy framework and finally endorsed the developmental model of social welfare. The document was then published for comment; again, extensive comments were received and integrated. The Portfolio Committee on Social Welfare and Population Development in the National Assembly also held public hearings and many organised groups and individuals made formal submissions. After a two-year consultative process the *White Paper for Social Welfare* was extensively debated in Parliament and adopted by all political parties in 1997. By this time the National Party had withdrawn from the GNU and the first ANC Minister for Social Welfare, Geraldine Fraser-Moleketi, was appointed in 1996.

The process of developing national policy was a complex one as it involved the mediation of divergent sentiments, histories, philosophies and paradigmatic perspectives, and professional, organisational and sectoral interests of various kinds. Fiscal resource constraints loomed large in the debate as the parties hoped for increased fiscal allocations in order to expand service provision to the majority of the population. The new developmental model was extensively debated as the current remedial model of service delivery, coupled with residential institution al care and the delivery of services to specialised groups of clients, was not only costly but considered to be of limited impact. The challenge was to address service needs in an integrated fashion with maximum developmental impact; however, service providers and practitioners were cautious in their support as this approach required a fundamental shift away from old methods of practice and the balancing of micro and macro interventions. The need to renew the financing policies of social welfare services and to address the rising costs of implementing welfare legislation was also highlighted. The government faced a particular challenge to expand its financing of progressive development organisations, which were not previously funded by the former government. In relation to social security, the trade unions called for a

'The process of developing national policy was a complex one as it involoved the mediation of divergent sentiments, histories, philosophies and paradigmatic perspectives...'

review of the social security system and for the development of a comprehensive system of social security. The particular contribution of social assistance to poverty reduction was reaffirmed and the research toward developing the policy also brought to light the inequity of the child maintenance grant system and the cost implications of the expansion of child support grants to all South Africans (Lund Committee on Child and Family Support 1996).

It remains a phenomenal achievement that such a consensus was forged. There were a number of factors that made this possible. Firstly, the birth of the new nation was a powerful unifying force. For many professionals in the social services, the adoption of a Bill of Rights and Constitution that resonated with the values and mission of the social work profession was a strong catalyst to promote a convergence of ideas. Secondly, the Reconstruction and Development Programme (RDP) of the Mandela government provided a national integrated policy framework that sought to reconcile economic growth and social development. Thirdly, the social development vision itself for social welfare was compelling and was shaped from the bottom up. In addition, it received global endorsement by governments around the world at the United Nations World Summit for Social Development, which was held in Copenhagen in 1995. Fourthly, the policy formulation process was explicitly designed to promote participation, draw on the extensive knowledge of service providers and users and build consensus based on the people's willingness to make compromises in the broader national interest.

In relation to the policy development process, Mazibuko (1996) points out that, previously, bureaucrats and government officials made decisions that were undemocratic. The policy formulation process afforded the welfare sector the opportunity to participate fully in the process and to gain first-hand knowledge and experience of the policymaking process, policy advocacy, negotiation and compromise and in identifying issues pertinent to policy implementation. Letsebe (1997:87) said that 'the principles of participation, transparency and accountability were espoused as ideals in the process, but in practice they were not easy to realise. For example, decisions on who participated in the process were largely the prerogative of welfare departments'. The tight timeframes did not allow for adequate preparation of participants and for comment on the documents. Across the nine provinces there was uneven preparation and input into the process. For some critics the compromises achieved favoured the formal voluntary welfare organisations in the early stages of the process. They also argued that the emerging policy framework advocated social reform and was not sufficiently oriented to social transformation (Sewpaul 1997; Asmal 1995). Finally, for some participants, the policy did not go far enough and for others it went too far. It was, however, the beginning of dismantling the old and constructing the new.

'The policy formulation process afforded the welfare sector the opportunity to participate fully in the process and to gain first-hand knowledge and experience of the policymaking process.'

South Africa's conception of developmental social welfare

'South Africa's developmental approach to social welfare evolved from the country's unique history of inequality and the violation of human rights as a result of colonialism and apartheid.'

South Africa's developmental approach to social welfare evolved from the country's unique history of inequality and the violation of human rights as a result of colonialism and apartheid. This history, experience and meaning of oppression for the majority of South Africans together with a long tradition of human agency and social action to change these conditions shaped the construction of the new society. Consequently, social welfare thinking and practice were infused with notions of transformation and human emancipation and an acknowledgement that reconciliation and healing the divisions of the past were critical to building a united South Africa based on democratic values, social justice and human rights. These ideas are enshrined in the Constitution of the Republic of South Africa Act 108 of 1996 and a rights-based approach is the first theme in the conception of developmental social welfare in the South African context. The other four themes informing the policy framework of the White Paper for Social Welfare are, firstly, the inter-relations between social and economic development to overcome the distorted and unequal nature and form of development; secondly, democracy and participation in development; thirdly, social welfare pluralism with particular reference to the role of the state and civil society in social development. A fourth theme relates to reconciling the micro-macro divide in developmental social welfare theory and practice.

A rights-based approach

The developmental perspective to social welfare in South Africa is firmly rooted in a rights-based approach. Its goals include achieving social justice, a minimum standard of living, equitable access and equal opportunity to services and benefits, and a commitment to meeting the needs of all South Africans with a special emphasis on the needs of the most disadvantaged in the society. These ideas are firmly embedded in the Constitution of the Republic of South Africa (1996), which guarantees to all citizens the right to dignity as one of its central values and 'connotes the inherent worth of the human being and his or her humanity' (Davis, Cheadle & Haysom 1997:73). The Bill of Rights and the Constitution also make provision for legally enforceable economic and social rights such as the right to housing (Section 26), the right to health care, food, water and social security (Section 27) and the right to education (Section 29). These rights are judicially enforceable and the Constitutional Court has in a number of cases, such as the *Grootboom* and *Treatment Action Campaign*, affirmed the interconnectedness and indivisibility of social and economic rights, and civil and political rights. The Constitution also obligates the state to give effect to these rights within its available resources and to achieve progressively the full realisation of these rights (South African Human Rights Commission 2003).

Developmental social welfare approached from a social rights and social justice perspective proceeds from the assumption that social justice is 'definable, desirable and possible' (Longres & Scanlon 2001:448). The philosophical ideas of T. H. Marshall (1950) and John Rawls (1971) are useful in the theoretical study of social rights and social justice. These ideas have influenced international social welfare thinking in the post-World War II period.

Marshall's views on citizenship are based on a progression of civil, political and social rights. For him, civil rights assure the individual the rights to freedom of action and dissent whilst political rights assure the individual the opportunity to influence political decisions and political power. Social rights are considered to be substantive and necessary to afford the individual the opportunity to achieve a minimum social status in society. They also include the achievement of economic welfare and security and the 'right to share fully in the social heritage and to live the life of a civilised being according to the standards prevailing in the society' (Marshall 1963:10). These rights, according to Marshall, are guaranteed to the individual as a right of citizenship and are founded on the principle of equality. Marshall's conception of social citizenship and the social rights derived from it legitimate the inequalities produced by capitalism – inequalities that gave rise to 'welfare state capitalism', notions of equal opportunity and the right of access to education, health care and social services (Drover 2000).

Drover criticises Marshall's view of social citizenship as fostering a passive notion of social citizenship based on the state's obligations to individuals rather than a deep social citizenship grounded in active citizen participation, relational reciprocity, care and civic virtue. Citizenship, according to Drover (2000), needs to be reconceptualised to be more active and should not only address inequalities derived from class, but should also include other social divisions in society derived from race, gender, age, disability and sexual preference. In this regard Drover (2000:31–32) states the following:

> *'Unlike passive citizenship, which relies on political representation and delegation of authority through electoral processes, deep citizenship implies a set of civic virtues and participation. Hence, deep citizenship values the struggles for identity claims, and the importance of institutional checks and balances as well as responsible personal life-style decisions in which expectations about entitlement are backed by co-operation and self-restraint'.*

The principles under-girding the *White Paper for Social Welfare* (1997) reaffirm the government's commitment to securing basic welfare and human rights and active citizen participation in promoting human well-being. Section 30 of the National Developmental Welfare Strategy states that the 'promotion of social development is a collective responsibility and the co-operation of civil society will be promoted' (Department of Welfare 1997:19). In the policy debate, the policymakers embraced a broadernotion of social citizenship and social welfare rights: they saw these phenomena as active, reciprocal and participatory, and their approach resonated with Drover's thinking about active social citizenship.

The social welfare policy framework also embraces the principle of equity, which refers to the equitable distribution of services and benefits to overcome past disparities of race, gender, geography, the urban/rural divide and sectoral disparities. The policy states explicitly that services and benefits should benefit the least advantaged. This principle is central to upholding social rights and achieving social justice as it refers to the way in which economic and social goods and services are distributed in a society. John Rawls's Theory of Justice (1971) acknowledged the importance of the equal distribution of material and non-material goods and services. He argued that such primary social goods – liberty and opportunity, income and wealth and the bases of self-respect – should be fairly and equally distributed and that such distribution was just if it benefited the least advantaged. Rawls claimed that a just society can allow for differences in the distribution of resources as long as the result accrues to the benefit of the least advantaged and there is equal opportunity for access to resources. Rawls's work has been influenced by the social contract theories of Locke and Rousseau and gave rise to the notion of minimum protection for the least advantaged. His theory combines libertarianism and egalitarianism and is also referred to as a *liberal egalitarian* view of social justice. For libertarians, the core value is liberty or freedom and such thinkers focus on individual rights, from which all other rights are derived. Libertarian ideas go back to the social thought of Herbert Spencer and John Locke, who advocated individual liberty. Egalitarianism can be traced to Jean-Jacques Rousseau and Karl Marx and their emphasis on the distribution of social advantage. 'Liberal egalitarianism combines the features of libertarianism and egalitarianism' (Fleurbaey 2002:2). In this regard, it can be argued that the South African Bill of Rights and the Constitution embodies both liberal and egalitarian ideas and that the new constitutional dispensation envisaged 'not only ... a political transformation of South Africa society, but also its social and economic transformation' (Albertyn & Boldblatt 1998:272).

Liberal egalitarian:

The core values of the liberal egalitarian view of justice is firstly individual rights and freedom where liberty is considered to be a basic human right from which other rights are derived. A second value is to achieve genuine equality in economic conditions by giving priority to the least advantaged.

Closely related but distinct from Rawls's theory of justice is the notion of relational or processual or procedural justice, which is particularly meaningful in the field of social development and social work practice (Young 1990). Relational justice refers to the need for fair decision-making processes about the distribution of goods and services and whether institutions are organised in a manner that achieves a fair and just distribution. This takes us into the realm of the just administration of social welfare services and benefits and ethical decision-making in direct and indirect practice (Longres & Scanlon 2001). Section 33 of the South African Constitution provides for administrative action that is just, reasonable and procedurally fair. It also states that citizens have the right to demand reasons for decisions taken, review of administrative action by a court and the promotion of efficient administration.

These approaches to social rights, which are derived from social citizenship and theories of distributive justice, are *normative theories*, which are especially useful in the applied social sciences to formulate principles to inform social policy, research and practice. Normative theories provide criteria by which societies are able to evaluate their performance in realising civil, political, social, cultural and economic rights.

There has been much debate about whether universal principles of this nature could provide a meaningful understanding of 'the rich texture of moral experience or the varied demands of justice' (McCormick 2003:22). Different models of justice focusing on feminist, pluralist or theological notions of justice have been posited as alternative models of social justice (McCormick 2003).

Normative theory:

Normative theory is evaluative in nature and consists of principles or criteria to evaluate whether social interventions achieve their goals.

In the post-World War II period, universal principles, norms and standards advancing human rights have been widely institutionalised through the United Nations system and have also influenced the formulation and adoption of national constitutions and regional charters in different parts of the world. This gave rise to the development of modern international human rights law, which was needed for the protection of human rights. The United Nations Universal Declaration of Human Rights adopted in 1948 was the first comprehensive international human rights instrument to be proclaimed. It has enjoyed high moral, legal and political status over the years. The Universal Declaration of Human Rights provides for two broad categories of rights: civil and political rights, on the one hand, and economic, social and cultural rights, on the other hand. The declaration is based on the proposition that everyone is entitled to the realisation of economic, social and cultural rights within the limits of the resources of the state. It is also proposed that the realisation of such rights is fundamental to the achievement of human dignity and the free development of the individual personality.

In relation to social and economic rights, the United Nations Declaration proclaims the right to social security, to work and to 'protection against unemployment', to 'equal pay for equal work' and to 'just and favourable remuneration ensuring for himself and his family an existence worthy of human dignity, and supplemented, if necessary by other means of social protection' (United Nations Declaration of Human Rights Articles 24). Article 25 also states that everyone has a right to a standard of living adequate for the health and well-being of himself and of his family. It also recognises the right to security in the event of loss of income due to circumstances beyond the individual's control such as unemployment, sickness, disability, age or lack of livelihood. The United Nations Human Rights system has evolved over the years and many new instruments were adopted that have been outlined previously and that influenced the drafting of the Constitution of the Republic of South Africa. In addition to the rights mentioned previously, the rights of children are established in Section 28 of the Constitution and are in line with the United Nations Convention on the Rights of the Child adopted in 1989. The Constitution provides special safeguards for children in view of their vulnerability and due to particular social conditions that may not be in the best interests of the child – such as situations of armed conflict, exploitation, hunger and disability. The rights of children are considered further in Chapter 6.

'In summary, social welfare in the South African context is firmly rooted in a rights-based approach to social development policy and practice.'

In summary, social welfare in the South African context is firmly rooted in a rights-based approach to social development policy and practice. The Constitutional Court in its judgments over the past decade has affirmed the obligation of the state in giving effect to social rights but subject to the limitation of available resources. However, in its judgement the Court indicated that the state must take reasonable steps to realise these rights and is required to use all the appropriate means at its disposable and to work expeditiously towards the full realisation of these rights. The Constitution and the social development policy framework envisages an expanded role for the state in social welfare including the horizontal application of these rights in civil society and partly in the private sphere to achieve social justice. According to Klare (1998), the South African constitution can be characterised as 'post-liberal' in that it promotes social redistribution and a caring, positive, participatory, multicultural society that is geared to social transformation of the society.

Economic and social development

A second theme under-girding the policy framework set by the *White Paper for Social Welfare* (1997) relates to the inter-relation between economic and social development. It states that the welfare of the population will not automatically be enhanced by economic growth only. Development must be accompanied by redistribution through social investments in key social sectors that can make a significant contribution to human and social capital and can improve the human development status of the majority of the population. Economic growth and redistribution are mutually reinforcing, and social investment is not considered to be a drain on national resources, but contributes positively to economic development.

These ideas are based on the *theory of developmental social welfare*, which have been advanced by Midgley and his colleagues in a series of publications (Midgley 2001; Midgley & Sherraden 2000; Midgley & Livermore 1998; Midgley 1999; 1996; 1995). The central tenet on which the theory is based is the need to integrate economic and social policy, as these are considered to be equally important components of the development process: one cannot replace the other. The integration of social and economic development can enhance the welfare of all in the society. Through harmonising national macro-economic and social policies within a comprehensive commitment to sustainable and people-centred development, the problems of mass poverty and inequality caused by distorted and unequal development could be addressed. The bifurcation of economic and social development leads to what Midgley refers to as distorted development. For Midgley, this goal can be achieved through three primary axioms (2001:246–247).

'The integration of social and economic development can enhance the welfare of all in the society.'

Firstly, *organisational and institutional arrangements* are needed at national governmental level to give effect to integrating economic and social development. Social service and economic development agencies must work closely together within a unified framework. Secondly, *macro-economic policies* are needed to promote employment and attain people-centred economic development outcomes. Thirdly, this approach is also known as a *productivist* approach to social welfare in that it promotes economic participation in the economy, which in turn leads to positive economic returns. Social investment programmes that contribute to economic growth and social progress are therefore selected. These programmes address material needs, invest in what Amartya Sen (1985; 1999) refers to as human capabilities and promote participation and social inclusion in the economy and society. Beverly and Sherraden (1997) also argue that investments in basic needs and human capital will yield social returns in the form of increased participation, connectedness and social stability, whilst economic returns include increased productivity, economic growth and reduced income and asset inequality. These types of social investments are favoured over an excessive focus on the provision of social benefits such as social grants and remedial and maintenance-oriented social services. Strategies advocated include: employment programmes, skills development, public works, self-employment for the poor and marginalised, micro-enterprises, fostering asset accumulation through subsidised savings schemes and ensuring cost-effective services with a high impact.

The inter-relation between economic and social development is explained further in relation to two key concepts: human capital and social capital. *Human capital investments* in, inter alia, education, housing, health care and nutrition are widely recognised to yield positive returns for the beneficiaries and also for society. Human capital investments in developmental welfare programmes also refer more specifically to capacity-building programmes; vocational training matched with employment opportunities; investments in educational development and support for children such as primary school nutrition, fostering social skills and competencies of school-going children, entrepreneurial training for youth, and learnership and internship programmes. Midgley (2001) also advocates investing in *social capital formation* as a direct association has been established between social capital in a community and its economic well-being. Social capital refers to social networks that encourage trust and co-operative social interaction for the benefit of the community in order to promote social integration (Midgley 2001; Putnam1995). Communities that have a high degree of social capital are more likely to be economically prosperous (Diaz, Drumm, Ramirez-Johnson & Oidjarv 2002). It is self-evident that communities that have a high degree of social disintegration due to crime and violence, alcohol and drug misuse tend to have low levels of economic development (Midgley 2001). Strengthening community networks, trust and co-operation, participation and community care and support are important goals in themselves, but such networks when combined with local economic development strategies have improved the financial situation and the level of self-sufficiency of communities (Diaz, Drumm, Ramirez-Johnson & & Oidjarv 2002; Midgley & Livermore 1998). *Asset-based* policies are growing in importance in many countries for people living in poverty. In the United States, asset-based policies are being implemented through the matching of the savings of poor people by the state in entities known as Individual Development Accounts (IDAs). These are policies that attempt to build the financial and tangible assets of poor people through household savings and asset accumulation, which could yield positive economic and social returns (Sherraden 2003).

Developmental social welfare is beginning to be implemented in the South African context through the policies and programmes of the Department of Social Development but also as part of an overall inter-sectoral strategy across all government departments. Similar policies have been developed in both the economic and social sectors in keeping with the Reconstruction and Development Programme, which provided the overall national policy framework to integrate social and economic development. After the closure of the RDP, government departments were required to implement the policy framework. Without a central national agency to facilitate and integrate social and economic development, the impetus was lost although the central co-ordination function for social and economic policy shifted to the President's office. The goal of the macro-economic policy (GEAR) was to promote economic growth and redistribution. Economic growth over the past decade and job-creation has not kept pace with the increased number of people seeking employment. A situation of mass unemployment and poverty exists in the country: the unemployment rate is between 30 percent and 40 percent depending on how employment is defined. This remains an urgent challenge for macro-economic policy. Expanding economic opportunities have been created through small business development, skills development policies and programmes through Sector Education and Training Authorities (SETA) for each of the economic and social sectors. Each sector is 'taxed' a skills levy on its payroll from which it can claim back funds for investment in skills development to improve human capabilities. These initiatives have been slow in meeting their objectives. Labour laws have been enacted to promote greater protection for workers and the Employment Equity Act 55 of 1998 has instituted active labour market policies to remove discrimination based on race, gender and disability and to create opportunities and access to employment.

Democracy and participation

Democracy and participation in social and economic development is a key premise of the developmental approach to social welfare in South Africa. The concept democracy has its origin in the Greek term *demokratia*, which means rule by the people. Democracy broadly means a striving for political equality, the protection of liberty and freedom and the defence of the interests of the people of a society. This idea is embodied in the demand that the 'People Shall Govern', which is contained in the *Freedom Charter* adopted at the Congress of the People in 1955. The Constitution echoes this idea in its preamble when it states that the people of South Africa commit themselves to laying the 'foundations for a democratic and open society in which government is based on the will of the people'. Whilst the Constitution makes provision for democracy in the political sphere (i.e. electoral democracy), it also takes a broader view of democracy by referring to the social sphere or broader social life – workplace, school, community, family and other institutions of society. The Reconstruction and Development Programme (RDP) aimed to democratise the state and society. The RDP and the *White Paper for Social Welfare* also introduced the notion of participatory democracy to promote social development. Social welfare policy states that welfare and development constituencies must be consulted in decisions that affect them and that citizen participation in development is critical to ensure accountability by government and civil society for their actions. It also incorporates the concept of citizen participation in service delivery as partners in meeting human needs.

'Democracy and participation in social and economic development is a key premise of the developmental approach to social welfare in South Africa.'

'The UNDP (2002) argues that improved human capabilities through education, health and a decent standard of living, coupled with human action to improve social life, can only benefit democracy, as these are mutually reinforcing capabilities.'

Participatory democracy is a more direct form of decision-making involving those affected by decisions taken; it also includes direct consultation (Giddens 2001). Proponents of participatory democracy are critical of liberal or representative democracy in that it is considered to be a more passive form of democracy whereby elected representatives take decisions affecting the society. In the field of social development, participatory democracy rests on three axioms. Firstly, through participation and active involvement in social and community life, personal responsibility to act as a responsible citizen is fostered. It emphasises character-building and the fostering of a democratic ethos based on active citizenship. Examples include volunteerism, paying taxes, donating blood and acting responsibly in one's community to benefit the common good of society. Secondly, participation also involves consultation about decisions with those affected and the fostering of active involvement of citizens in their communities and organisations to care for those in need; the promotion of economic and social development; the solving of social problems; and the improvement of the quality of life of the people. Thirdly, participation also rests on the notion of active or 'deep' citizenship that incorporates rights and obligations, emphasises the interests of the disadvantaged and is critical in that it attempts to uncover the causes of social, economic and political injustice. The social justice approach to democracy and participation is concerned with effecting structural change in society through participation, open and informed social dialogue, the contestation of power and by ensuring the accountability of the powerful (UNDP 2002). Whilst some theorists classify these approaches to citizen participation and participatory democracy into conservative, liberal and social justice perspectives (Westheimer & Khan 2002), all of these notions are pertinent to a broader formulation of democracy in the South African context, which emphasises both representative and participatory democracy and people-centred development. The policy documents also make the link between democracy, participation and human development more explicit. These ideas are based on the assumption that democracy in itself is a public good, fosters social integration and is more likely to lead to equitable development. South Africa is a new and emerging democracy and the desire for democracy is deeply rooted in the people's struggle for a democratic and just society. However, democracy could be built through active participation of the people in the wider social sphere of the society. This in turn will strengthen democracy in the political sphere. The UNDP (2002) argues that improved human capabilities through education, health and a decent standard of living, coupled with human action to improve social life, can only benefit democracy, as these are mutually reinforcing capabilities.

Social Development Partnerships

A prominent role for the state in social development and a mixed economy of social welfare or *welfare pluralism* is envisaged by national social welfare policy. The meeting of human needs is a national collective responsibility and the policy states that, in view of resource constraints and the neglect of basic needs over many years, government, civil society, corporate social investment and occupational social service programmes should be provided through a collaborative partnership. Private social service practice for social workers and psychologists is envisaged for those people in need who are able to pay for services.

Welfare pluralism:

Welfare pluralism refers to the way in which social welfare provision is structured, organised and delivered including the roles of the four sectors in service delivery.

A mixed economy of social welfare or welfare pluralism consists of four sectors – government, voluntary (e.g. non-governmental organisations), informal (e.g. informal support by family, friendship and other social networks) and commercial sectors – through which social provision could be financed and delivered (Gilbert 2000). In the *public domain* welfare resources are allocated via government through grants or subsidies, indirect spending through special tax subsidies and tax exemptions and through the regulatory power of government. The *private* sector refers to informal networks of family and friends that provide social support and mutual aid, and the voluntary sector, which is made up of non-profit voluntary welfare and development organisations. Finally, there is the commercial sector made up of profit-oriented firms that are involved in social welfare. Gilbert (2000) points out that the boundaries between these sectors are often blurred and can overlap.

Although a commercial sector is developing, the public-private mix (also known as state-voluntary or civil society relations) remains the dominant approach in the South African context, with the state continuing to be the major financier of social assistance and services for the poor and marginalised. Social welfare services are delivered by voluntary and faith-based organisations in fields of service such as child and family welfare, mental health, disabilities, substance abuse, crime prevention, rehabilitation and restorative justice, and chronic illnesses. Voluntary organisations operate as public service contractors, on the one hand, and also raise funds independently and operate autonomously from government, on the other hand. South Africa has a substantial voluntary sector (estimated to consist of 98 820 organisation) with an operating budget of R9.3 billion (representing 1.2 percent of gross domestic product in 1998) and providing employment

'Volunteerism is also significant, with an estimated 1.5 million volunteers actively engaged in culture, recreation, advocacy, politics, faith-based initiatives, and the social services.'

equivalent to 645 316 full-time employees. Volunteerism is also significant, with an estimated 1.5 million volunteers actively engaged in culture, recreation, advocacy, politics, faith-based initiatives, and the social services. The volunteer labour that volunteerism makes up is worth R5.1 billion (Swilling & Russell 2002).

Close to a quarter of voluntary organisations focus specifically on social services, and have expertise, infrastructure and other resources that could complement public provision. In order to recognise the progressive non-profit organisations that were not previously funded by the former government, policy and enabling legislation was developed to promote an inclusive partnership. The Welfare Laws Amendment Act 106 of 1997 authorised financial awards to non-profit organisations rendering developmental social welfare services and broadened the range of activities to be funded. In addition, the Non-profit Organisations Act No 71 of 1997 created an administrative and regulatory framework within which relations between the state and civil society could be funded and managed. The Taxation Amendment Act of 2000 also provided for a more favourable tax regime to support non-profit organisations. Voluntary organisations contribute in excess of R1 billion to the social development sector. The new policy also recognised partnerships with less formal and community-based organisations. These organisations are considered to have a comparative advantage over formal welfare organisations, as they are believed to be more accessible at the local level and are better able to target the poor. At least half of the total number of voluntary organisations were localised, less formalised and community-based and could play an important role in poverty-alleviation, providing indigenous support networks, savings schemes, income-generation and HIV/AIDS care and support. Further research is needed to assess the developmental potential of these organisations.

Government non-profit relations are generally classified into different models based on two distinguishing activities: the financing and authorisation of services, on the one hand, and the actual delivery of services, on the other. Gidron et al (1992) identified three types of government non-profit models to describe the complex relations between the parties. The government-dominant model refers to government financing and direct provision of services, whereas the third sector-dominant model is characterised by voluntary financing and delivery of services. A hybrid of the two types is referred to as a dual or parallel-track model, where non-profits could either supplement or complement public provision.

The South African collaborative partnership model has features of state dominance in financing and third-sector dominance in relation to delivery of services. A hybrid relationship also exists in relation to the delivery of specific types of services. An analysis of government expenditure over the past three years indicates that the government allocates 62 percent of its budget for welfare services to voluntary organisations involved in the welfare field. The remaining 38 percent of the welfare service budget is allocated to services that are publicly funded and delivered. In some provinces, this division between public and voluntary financial support is less favourable to the voluntary sector, especially in the more rural provinces with limited voluntary organisations. Voluntary organisations have also protested about the lack of increase in the funding for developmental welfare services.

A new trend emerging in the voluntary sector is towards income-generation strategies and entrepreneurial initiatives to achieve sustainability, cross-subsidisation of social programmes, and the diversification of programme-funding bases while increasing these organisations' independence from the government. For example, organisations in the disability field have formed empowerment partnerships with other commercial consortia bidding for large public contracts and the licensing of public services. Another institution caring for mentally disabled children won a contract to bake bread for one of the local prisons. Twenty three non-governmental organisations involved in development activities have formed a Black Economic Empowerment group called Ditikeni which is now a shareholder in a major Black Economic Empowerment consortium. The intention of Ditikeni is to redirect income from investments to community based development programmes.

These are important innovations as organisations begin to embark on economic development initiatives. However, the question should be posed as to whether such entrepreneurial activities divert organisations from their core services or whether these distort the goals of voluntary organisations. Do voluntary organisations compromise their comparative advantage when they engage in public service contracting or Black Economic Empowerment? Should public funds earmarked for basic needs be used to generate commercial ventures to cross-subsidise services? (Patel 2003).

Finally, voluntary organisations play a vital role in complementing government efforts in meeting human needs and in strengthening democracy. South Africa's collaborative approach to social development partnership is also a viable option in middle-income countries faced with resource constraints and a limited institutional capacity to meet human needs. However, the state has a primary responsibility for meeting needs and voluntary sector partnerships should not lead to the abrogation of state responsibility for meeting human needs.

'However, the state has a primary responsibility for meeting needs and voluntary sector partnerships should not lead to the abrogation of state responsibility for meeting human needs.'

Macro and micro divide

The national policy attempts to bridge the divide that has existed historically in the social work and social service professions between micro interventions, on the one hand, and mezzo and macro interventions, on the other hand. This dichotomy between micro interventions aimed at individuals and families and macro interventions aimed at changing the structures and institutions of society that caused social economic injustice, is a long-standing debate in social work. Social development must transcend this dichotomy and enhance individual, family, community empowerment and development. It must build on the strengths of all those it purports to serve and meet their needs in a contextually appropriate manner – one, in other words, that recognises the diversity and dignity of all people. The point of departure of the social development approach is that social welfare users of services and those who seek help are not passive recipients of services but are active partners in solving problems in human relations and social conditions which impede people's functioning. In addition, its intersectoral focus emphasises collaboration with social service professionals and sectors to solve real-life social problems and promote citizen participation, community development and deliver community-based services within an integrated and generalist model of social work and social service practice. Instead of delivering casework services only, it needs to expand its methods to include group, organisational, community, and research and policy interventions, which balance rehabilitation, prevention, promotion and social and economic development goals. Interventions should be selected that have a greater developmental impact and that are cost-effective and use resources in a sustainable manner for the benefit of future generations. A focus on the poor, and on those who are socially, economically and politically excluded, should be placed at the centre of interventions. An understanding of economic issues and how to infuse economic development strategies into social work and social service intervention processes is critical. The policy breaks with the traditional micro/macro social work and social service dichotomies. It requires an integration of methods and levels of intervention to address the complex dynamics of change in the changing local and global scenario.

'A focus on the poor, and on those who are socially, economically and politically excluded, should be placed at the centre of interventions.'

Institutionalisation of social development

National policies are institutionalised through legislation and the adherence to rules and procedures that should be inclusive and fair and that operate within clearly defined institutional arrangements governing social interactions, which define the roles and relations between the parties. Rules and procedures must also be transparent and the people should be able to hold decision-makers accountable for their actions. These are some of the principles of good governance, which is considered to be one of the most important critical success factors in eradicating poverty and promoting social development (UNDP

2002). The achievement of social development requires sound institutions, as many problems in delivery are caused by institutional and organisational failures.

Structure and functions of government

Government refers to the 'regular enactment of policies, decisions and matters of state on the part of the officials within a political apparatus' (Giddens 2001:420). *Governance* is the activity or manner of governing a society or particular functions of government. How is the social development function governed in South Africa? What are the basic principles, structures and mechanisms to ensure that government policies are developed and implemented?

The Constitution is the supreme law of the country and all other laws and policies are derived from it. It also makes provision for a form of governance known as *Co-operative Governance*. According to the Constitution, there are three spheres of governance, which are distinctive, interdependent and inter-related. These are national, provincial and local government. All spheres of government must observe and adhere to the principles of co-operative governance. Some of the pertinent principles of co-operative governance include:

- Securing the well-being of the people.
- Providing effective, transparent, accountable and coherent government.
- Respecting the constitutional status, institutions, powers of government in other spheres.
- Assuming only the powers and functions conferred on them.
- Co-operating in mutual trust and good faith through fostering friendly relations, assisting and supporting one another, informing one another, consulting one another on matters of common interest, co-ordinating actions and legislation, adhering to agreed procedures, avoiding legal action against one another.
- Establishing structures to promote and facilitate inter-governmental relations and the settlement of disputes.

The structure and functions of the South African government are embodied by Parliament (also known as the National Assembly), which is made up of 350–400 members. Parliament acts as the Legislative Authority and has Parliamentary Portfolio Committees consisting of members representing different political parties; these are known as 'multi-party committees'. The functions of the Portfolio Committee for Social Development are to exercise oversight of government and to consult with government and constituencies in civil society in the development and implementation of legislation. Much of the legislative deliberations are conducted in these committees. It also has a monitoring function and may call a Minister or any official of government to account to it on any matter of its choice in relation to social development. The National Council of Provinces is made up of 90 delegates and also considers national laws that have provincial effect. Should there be disagreement on such laws, a mediating Committee is appointed to negotiate agreements between the National Council of Provinces and the National Assembly.

The Executive Authority of government is vested in the Cabinet, consisting of the President, Deputy President and Ministers who are responsible for government decisions. Judicial Authority rests with the Constitutional Court, a Supreme Court of Appeal, High Courts and Magistrates' Courts.

'The social development function operates within the overall structure and functions of government.'

There are provincial governments in each of the nine provinces. Each provincial government has a Legislative Authority and an Executive Authority that is made up of the Executive Council headed by a Premier and Members of the Executive Council (MEC). The nine provincial governments have the authority to decide if there will be a single social development portfolio or a combination of this portfolio with other portfolios. Social development issues have a higher visibility and political standing when they fall under a single portfolio and constitute a formal function of government at national and provincial levels. Finally, there is the third sphere of government known as local government, which is made up of six metropolitan municipalities, 231 local municipalities and 47 district municipalities. The Constitution and the Local Government: Municipal Structures Act, 1998 contain criteria for determining the three types of municipalities, which were rationalised and restructured in 2000.

The social development function operates within the overall structure and functions of government. A National Ministry and Department of Social Development is responsible for national functions, which include national policy, planning, information management, policy monitoring and evaluation of inputs and outcomes; national laws; national programmes; social development finance and human resource development. It is also responsible for the population and development function for government as a whole including the administration of the National Development Agency (NDA), which is responsible for the financing of non-governmental organisations involved with the delivery of social and developmental services. The provincial governments share these powers and functions concurrently with the national government. According to Schedule 4 Part A of the Constitution, welfare services are shared functions between national and provincial governments along with health, education (except tertiary education), urban and rural development and housing. The provinces are responsible for the delivery of welfare services. Since social security has become a national function since the passing of the National Social Security Agency Act of 2003, this function will be transferred to the national government. The Provincial Executive Councils are responsible for ensuring that national legislation is implemented. This responsibility is limited to the extent that the province has the administrative capacity to assume effective responsibility. The national government has an obligation to build the capacity of provincial governments to assume these responsibilities. This principle also applies to the responsibility of provincial governments in relation to building capacity at local government level.

Local governments have limited social welfare responsibilities and provinces may delegate responsibilities to local authorities. Except for the Gauteng province, none of the other provinces has to date enacted legislation or delegated functions to the local level, although some local authorities do perform a limited social development function. Schedule 4 Part B of the Constitution specifies other functions of local government, such as childcare, municipal health services and municipal public works. *The Local Government White Paper* (1998) makes provision for the establishment of developmental local government responsible for the mobilisation of capacity to deliver services to meet the basic needs of its communities and to promote local social and economic development among other things. Considerable scope exists for the further decentralisation of developmental welfare functions in order for them to be more accessible to people at local level and to promote social and economic development.

Legislation

The term legislation refers to Acts of Parliament and Provincial Legislatures, and includes subordinate legislation such as Regulations issued to guide the implementation of legislation. Prior to 1994, the Former Department of Social Welfare and Population Development and the tri-cameral welfare departments administered nine Acts of Parliament. These Acts pertained to children, the elderly, criminal justice, substance abuse, social assistance and legislation regulating the profession of social work and welfare services. The former Independent Homelands also administered legislation on social pensions, children and national social welfare provision. In addition, the welfare departments administered a range of laws in co-operation with other government departments such as health, justice and correctional services, and there were also many other laws that had a direct bearing on the protection and enhancement of social functioning. The legislation was fragmented, and there was considerable duplication and a lack of co-ordination in the administration of the legislation.

The approach adopted by the *White Paper for Welfare* (1997) was to amend legislation in the short term to align it with the Constitution and the new policy directions of the democratically elected government after 1994. In the medium to longer term a review of legislation was required to develop comprehensive legislation. Between 1994 and 2001, approximately 27 laws administered by the Departments of Social

Development were amended or repealed, and new laws were adopted by the National Assembly and Provincial Legislatures.

The Department of Social Development is responsible for the drafting of legislation, the management and facilitation of participatory processes with constituencies and the management of the adoption of legislation by Parliament and Provincial Legislatures in keeping with parliamentary rules and procedures. The Departments of Social Development are also responsible for the execution and monitoring and evaluation of legislation, which includes setting up the administrative and management systems, and building the capacity of personnel to implement the legislation and funding. Norms and standards set in legislation should be appropriate to the local social and cultural context, should be in line with the level of development of the country, should be feasible in terms of implementation and should be financially viable. Parliamentary rules and procedures also provide for mechanisms of public participation in the process of law-making. Social workers, social service and development workers should be acquainted with these processes in order to participate effectively in the formulation, adoption, monitoring and review of policy and legislation. Professional social service workers can also provide technical support and advice and advocacy for policies and legislation to reflect the interests of client groups and communities. In order to contribute effectively, human service and development professionals, agencies and communities should keep abreast of legislative developments, Bills that are tabled, and policies and subordinate legislation published by the Government Printers for public comment, or give oral evidence at public hearings.

Financial and fiscal arrangements

Financial and fiscal reforms have been implemented since 1994 to realign budgets and the financing of the social services with the principle of co-operation between different spheres of government and the new policy directions and priorities of government. Budget reforms have also been effected to improve planning, transparency, accountability and improving public service delivery. The government moved away from annualised budgeting to multi-year budgets and the implementation of the Public Finance Management Act 1 of 1999 has resulted in improved accountability for managing budgets and for results and outputs. In the early years of the transition, the provinces overspent on the budgets that were not aligned with departmental strategic plans and inadequate financial statements and annual reporting existed. However, since April 2003, provincial departments are required to develop strategic and performance plans based on uniform budget formats for each of the social service sectors. They are also required to publish annual reports; however, the quality of these reports needs to be improved (Republic of South Africa, National Treasury 2003).

Government budgets are the main tools to steer social and economic development. The Minister's Committee for Social Development is made up of the national minister and provincial ministers who decide on the priorities. In order to set priorities, choices are made between some services, benefits and social programmes. This has led to a trade-off between them and where some programmes cannot be funded or are funded at a lower level. Budgets are also drawn up within set parameters, which fix the limits of what can be spent. The budgets of the national and provincial governments determine what the departments may spend on the various programmes. Cabinet and the Provincial Executive Councils make the most critical decisions on the allocation of resources, which is the culmination of a long budgetary process that involves all the spending agencies and the relevant intergovernmental structures. The Financial and Fiscal Commission (FFC) is a key party in the budget process. It advises the government on the equitable division of revenue between the national, provincial and local spheres of government in order to ensure that provincial and local governments have sufficient resources to deliver basic services for which they are responsible. The public and the beneficiaries of development agencies can play a role by monitoring budgetary trends in social development and by participating in the public debates by raising questions as to whether the expenditure is likely to contribute to social and economic development.

'The public and the beneficiaries of development agencies can play a role by monitoring budgetary trends in social development and by participating in the public debates by raising questions as to whether the expenditure is likely to contribute to social and economic development.'

Approximately 89 percent of provincial spending goes to the delivery of services based on shared responsibilities between the national and provincial governments. These include services such as primary schooling, health care, social grants, welfare services and housing, provincial roads and agricultural support. The provinces receive transfers from the national government; in 2002/2003 these amounted to 96.1 percent of total provincial income. National government revenue raised from taxes is shared between the provinces based on a system of intergovernmental grants. These grants are based on a formula to equitably distribute revenue between the provinces. The more populous and under-developed provinces also receive proportionately more revenue in order to overcome the past racially-based system of resource allocation and to address the historical disparities between the provinces. The equitable share of the revenue that a province receives also includes a conditional grant that may only be used for specified programmes and to achieve minimum standards. Provinces raise very limited funds themselves from provincial taxes – about 4 percent. Legislation was passed in 2001 to promote the growth of provincial revenue but most provinces projected declines in their ability to generate their own revenue in the short term.

Unlike provincial governments that are totally dependent on national government grants for the financing of social services, 66 percent of municipal activities are self-funded, as municipalities raise their own revenue from user charges for basic services. Income is also generated from property rates and taxes.

Municipalities also receive national governmental transfers, comprising on average about 17 percent of local government revenue. However, poorer and more rural municipalities received up to 60 percent of their funds from national revenue in 2002/2003. The grant formula enables local authorities to provide basic services and to perform functions that are assigned to them. Municipalities receive an equitable share of national revenue to provide basic services to the poor. The provision of free basic services to the poor is a key priority. Households with expenditure of less than R1 100 per month are targeted to receive free basic services such as water, electricity, and sanitation and refuse removal. This is estimated to amount to R300 per person on average and, since households are targeted, the amount increases to R1 200 per annum per household. This implies that an even larger allocation is made per poor household of R3 700. The challenge remains to ensure that these services are effectively targeted at the poor. Other challenges are related to revenue collection and the need for improved financial management. National allocations for free basic services to the poor are set to increase in real terms by 18.3 percent in 2005/2006. However, this is inadequate to address the backlogs in local government infrastructure – estimated to be R52 billion (Republic of South Africa, National Treasury 2002; 2003).

The social development departments in the provinces are responsible for social security programmes and welfare services. In the early to mid-1990s the overall social welfare budget increased significantly to address the racial disparity in social grants. It was the largest increase in social spending and health and education expenditure remained constant over this period. In 1995/1996, expenditure for social welfare was 8.7 percent of the national budget and 2.7 percent of Gross Domestic Product. However, in the previous three-year budget cycle between 1998/1999 to 2000/2001 real expenditure declined by an average annual rate of 0.5 percent. Over the next three years social development expenditure is set to grow by 2.6 percent in real terms. These increases are driven largely by projected increases in social grants especially for children, which have been expanded considerably. Expenditure on social assistance makes up 91 percent of the overall welfare budget, and contributes significantly to poverty reduction. Welfare services only account for 9 percent of the budgets and in some provinces expenditure drops to 5 percent. The welfare services component of the budget is severely under-funded, and will not be able to meet the Constitutional, legislative and new developmental welfare policy mandate. Increased social security expenditure has resulted in the 'crowding-out' of welfare services, and this has hampered progress in the achievement of the government's developmental welfare service goals.'

'Increased social security expenditure has resulted in the 'crowding-out' of welfare services, and this has hampered progress in the achievement of the government's developmental welfare service goals.'

The transformation of social welfare services is guided by the Financing Policy (Department of Welfare 1999) which sets out the priorities and paradigm shifts that are needed from a social treatment to a developmental social welfare service delivery model. In view of the financing constraints – including capacity and institutional difficulties – limited progress was made in the transformation of welfare services. The current financing policy does not comply with government's cost-based approach to allocating nationally raised revenue. This approach requires that costs be calculated on the basis of an agreement as to what the basic package of welfare services should be in each province, as costs will vary depending on infrastructure, human resources, access and other key variables. Further, the policy also does not address the financing of minimum standards set in current policy and legislation. This has had a negative impact on the delivery of developmental welfare service. Sewpaul & Hölscher (2004) critique the Financing Policy from a neo-liberal and postmodern stance and argue that the financing policy worked against the transformation goals of social welfare. Its use of business terminology such as accountability, efficiency and monitoring and reporting mechanisms of government funded programmes resonate with managerial and market discourses that have emerged in the First World. The lack of available funding for welfare services is both 'coercive and disempowering to both the social work profession and its client systems (Sewpaul & Hölscher 2004:940).

Social development expenditure trends should be located within the context of overall social spending by the government on health, education, social security and welfare services and housing and other services. Social spending between 1990/1991 and 2002/2003 is nearly half of total government expenditure and increased from 46 percent to 49 percent over the past decade. Education receives the largest share of total expenditure on the social service sector, followed by health and welfare. The proportional increase in the allocation to social security has been the greatest, while housing and other social services, including land reform, water and sanitation, have declined (Gelb 2003). Social security increases represent the single-largest increase in the social service sector, whilst health and education's expenditure remained fairly constant over the same period.

Finally, social investment spending is reaching the poorest households. Expenditure has increased three-fold in rural areas of the country and the coverage of social assistance has increased from R2.6 million in 1994 to R5.1 million in 2003. Meth & Dias's research (2004:83) indicates that the intensity of poverty appears to have decreased because of social welfare expenditure while the number of people falling below the poverty line increased between 1999 and 2002.

The global diffusion of neo-liberalism is associated with the retreat of the state from social welfare in many industrial societies. Scholars and advocates of social rights have argued that the South African

'A tension is perceived to exist between the social and economic goals of the state and the macro-economic vision of the country, which favours growth over social development.'

government's GEAR policy is a conservative neo-liberal economic policy that has resulted in increased privatisation and liberalisation of the economy, leading to cuts in social expenditure and a weakening of labour rights. A tension is perceived to exist between the social and economic goals of the state and the macro-economic vision of the country, which favours growth over social development.

The review of social spending however indicates that a contraction in overall social spending did not occur and neither have labour rights been eroded. Much progress has been made in effecting improvements in access to education, health care, nutrition for primary school children, water, electricity and housing through state financing, subsidisation and the provision of services and benefits in partnerships with communities and voluntary organisations. Social grants for children have in fact expanded and have not been reduced. Taxation policies, regulation and active labour market policies for women, people with disabilities and black people, which are designed to overcome economic inequality but also to promote social equality in the society, have been enacted. However, low economic growth rates – averaging 1.7 percent per annum over the past decade – coupled with rising poverty levels due to increasing unemployment (especially for the least skilled and those trapped in rural areas) and institutional inefficiencies are impeding the realisation of social and economic rights.

Bold social development policies are needed to address persistent unemployment, poverty and inequality in South African society. Such policies and social programmes are needed to prevent the development of a mass 'underclass' of poor people who are living on the margins of the society and trapped in poverty with no means or capability of escaping from it. What kind of social policies and how best to achieve social justice continues to be the subject of much debate. For some advocates, more public assistance through social grants is the answer to achieve income protection, whilst the government is arguing for employment creation strategies and a productivist approach. Unlike advanced industrial societies, South Africa does not have extensive public assistance programmes for the unemployed and so the question of moving people off welfare and into work does not arise. The real issue for South Africa is how to combine social assistance with developmental strategies that will promote economic and social development through employment and social investment programmes that will build human capabilities to promote social and economic inclusion and reduce poverty. Can this be done on an accelerated scale that will absorb the critical mass of unemployed people? What adjustments should be made to macro-economic policies to promote employment through market and social market mechanisms? Can a balance be found between striving for global competitiveness, on the one hand, and building a strong domestic economy that can create jobs for the least skilled in the society, on the other hand? What institutional capacity and effective institutional arrangements are needed to achieve these social and economic goals?

CHAPTER SUMMARY

- The dismantling of the apartheid welfare system and the development and institutionalisation of the new developmental approach to social welfare was informed by the overall transformation and restructuring of South African society. The Bill of Rights and the Constitution of the Republic of South Africa (1996; 1993) together with key policies such as the Reconstruction and Development Programme (RDP) set the agenda for change.
- A two-year consultative process led to the adoption of the *White Paper for Social Welfare* by Parliament in 1997. This policy framework informed the redesign of social security and social welfare services in keeping with the social development perspective to social welfare.
- South Africa's conception of developmental social welfare is based on a rights-based approach promoting social justice and favouring the meeting of the needs of the most disadvantaged. A second feature emphasises the inter-relation between economic and social development based on Midgley's theory of developmental social welfare. Democracy and participation involving both representative and participatory democracy is a third feature. Social development partnerships based on welfare pluralism, in which the state plays a leading role in development together with civil society and the private sector, is a fourth feature. Bridging the micro/macro dichotomy in the theory and practice of social development constitutes a fifth feature of the South African approach to social development.
- The institutionalisation of social development was explained in relation to the structure and functions of government within the Constitutional framework of co-operative governance.
- The approach to legislative reform and the legislative mandate of the social development function were outlined.
- The chapter also reviewed financial and fiscal reforms to promote the efficiency, effectiveness and accountability of government. Expenditure trends in the social service sector and more specifically in relation to social development were outlined.
- Throughout the chapter, the achievements in the dismantling of apartheid welfare were considered, including challenges in the overall development, implementation and review of social policies. Institutional constraints and challenges were discussed and debates on macro-economic policies were considered.

CRITICAL THINKING QUESTIONS

1. What do you think the achievements and challenges are in dismantling the apartheid welfare system and in developing and institutionalising developmental social welfare?
2. Discuss Midgley's theory of developmental social welfare and comment on its applicability in the South African context.
3. Do you agree with the view that the South African government has adopted a neo-liberal approach to economic and social policy? Motivate your answer.

Bibliography

ALBERTYN, K and GOLDBLATT, B (1998), Facing the challenge of transformation: difficulties in the development of an indigenous jurisprudence of equality. *South African Journal Human Rights,* 248, 249–272.

ASMAL, K. (1995), Keynote address at the National Welfare Summit. Unpublished Keynote address at the National Consultative Conference on the White Paper for Social Welfare. Bloemfontein.

BEVERLY, S.G., and SHERRADEN, M. (1997), Investment in human development as a social development strategy. *Social Development Issues,* 19, 1–18.

BOND, P. (2000), *Transition: From Apartheid to Neoliberalism in South Africa.* London: Pluto and Pietermaritzburg: University of Natal Press.

BUERGENTHAL, T. (1988), *International Human Rights.* St. Paul, Minn.: West Publishing Co.

DAVIS, D., CHEADLE, H., and HAYSOM, N. (1997), *Fundamental rights in the constitution: commentary and cases.* Cape Town, South Africa: Juta and Co Ltd.

DIAZ, H.L., DRUMM, R.D., RAMIREZ-JOHNSON, J., and OIDJARV. (2002), Social capital, economic development and food security in Peru's mountain region. *International Social Work*, 45, 481–495.

DEPARTMENT OF WELFARE (1997), *White Paper for Social Welfare* (Government Gazette Notice 1108 of 1997). Pretoria, South Africa: Ministry for welfare and population development.

DROVER, G. (2000), Redefining social citizenship in a global era. Special issue. Social work and globalization, 29–47. *Canadian social work. Special issue 2 & Canadian Social Work Review 17.*

FLEURBAEY, M (2000) *Normative economics and theories of distributive justice,* from www.univ-pau.fr/scfleurbae/papiers/toj6.pdi (15 December, 2002).

GELB S. (2003), Inequality in South Africa: Nature, causes and responses. DFID Policy Initiative on Addressing Inequality in Middle-Income Countries. Johanneburg: The EDGE Institute (unpublished research report).

GIDDENS, A. (2001), *Sociology* 4th ed. Cambridge: Polity Press in association with Oxford: Blackwell Publishers.

GILBERT, N. (2000), Welfare pluralism and social policy. In Midgley, J., Tracy, M.B. and Livermore, M.(ed.), *The Handbook of Social Policy.* (411–434). Thousand Oaks CA: Sage Publications.

GIDRON, B., KRAMER, R.M., and SALAMON (1992), Government and the third sector in comparative perspective: Allies or adversaries. In Gidron, B. Kramer, R.M. and Salamon, (eds). *Government and the third sector. Emerging relations in welfare states* (1–30). San Franscisco: Jossey Bass.

KLARE, J. (1998), Legal Culture and Transformative Constitutionalism. *South African Journal of Human Rights,* 146: 154–155.

LETSEBE, M.A. (1997), Social welfare in transition in South Africa: structures and processes. *International Social Work,* 40, 75–88.

LONGRES, J.F., and SCANLON, E. (2001), Social justice and the research curriculum. *Journal of Social Work Education*, 37, 447–463.

LUND COMMITTEE ON CHILD AND FAMILY SUPPORT (1996), Report of the Lund Committee on Child and Family Support.

MARSHALL, T.H. (1950), *Citizenship and social class and other essays.* Cambridge: Cambridge University Press.

MARSHALL, T.H. (1963), *Sociology at the crossroads.* London: Heinemann.

MAZIBUKO, F.N.B. (1996), Policy analysis as a strategy of welfare policy development: The White Paper process. *Social Work/Maatskaplike Werk,* 32, 234–241.

MCCORMICK, P.T. (2003), Whose justice? An examination of nine models of justice. In Stretch, J.J., Burkemper, E.M., Hutchinson, W.J. and Wilson J. (ed). *Practicing social justice* (7–25). New York: Haworth Press Inc.

METH, C. and DIAS, R. (2004), Increases in poverty in South Africa, 1999–2002. *Development Southern Africa*, 21:1, 59–85.

MHONE, G. and EDIGHEJI, O. (ed) (2003), Globalisation and the challenges of governance in the new South Africa: Introduction. *Governance in the new South Africa: The challenges of globalization* (1–15). Cape Town: University of Cape Town Press.

MIDGLEY, J. (1995), *Social development. The developmental perspective in social welfare.* London: Sage.

MIDGLEY, J. (1996), Involving social work in economic development, *International Social Work*, 39, 13–27.

Midgley, J. and Livermore, M. (1998), Social capital and local economic development: Implications for community social work practice. *Journal of Community Practice*, 5, 29–40.
Midgley, J. (1999), Growth, redistribution and welfare: Toward social investment. *Social Service Review,* 77, 3–21.
Midgley, J. and Sherraden, M. (2000), The social development perspective in social policy. In Midgley, J., Tracey, M.B. and Livermore, M. (ed). *The handbook of social policy* (435-446). Thousand Oaks CA: Sage Publications, Inc.
Midgley, J. (2001), South Africa: The challenge of social development. *International Social Welfare,* 10, 267–275.
Patel, L. (2003), Social development in a society in transition. *Social Development Issues,* 25, 150–161.
Putnam, R.D. (1995), Bowling alone: America's declining social capital. *Journal of Democracy,* 6, 65–78.
Rawls, J. (1971), *A theory of justice.* Cambridge, MA: Harvard University Press.
Republic of South Africa National Treasury. (2003), *Intergovernmental Fiscal Review.* Pretoria: South Africa.
Republic of South Africa (2003), *Towards Ten Years of Freedom. Progress in the First Decade – Challenges of the Second Decade.*
Sen, A. (1999), *Commodities and capabilities.* Amsterdam: North Holland.
Sen, A. (1985), *Development as Freedom.* New York: Knopf.
Sherraden, M. (2003), Introduction. Alternative Approaches to Global Needs. *Social Development Issues,* 25, Numbers 1 & 2, 1–11.
Sewpaul, V. and Hölscher, D. (2004), *Social Work in Times of Neoliberalism A postmodern discourse.* Pretoria: Van Schaik Publishers.
Sewpaul, V. (2001), Economic globalisation and social policy reform: Social work curricula in the South African context. *Social Work/Maatskaplike Werk,* 37, 309–323.
Sewpaul, V. (1997), The RDP: Implications for social work practice and social welfare policy development in South Africa. *Social Work/Maatskaplike Werk,* 33:1,1–9.
South African Human Rights Commission. (2002–2003), 4th Economic & Social Rights Report. Johannesburg: SA Human Rights Commission.
Swilling, M. and Russell, B. (2002), *The size and scope of the non-profit sector in South Africa.* Graduate School of Public and Development Management Johannesburg: University of the Witwatersrand and Centre for Civil Society. Durban, South Africa: University of Natal.
Triegaardt, J.D. (1996), The reconstruction and development programme: a beginning discussion and analysis for social work policy. *Social Work/Maatskaplike Werk,* 32, 142–147.
UNDP (United Nations Development Programme) (2002), *Human Development Report. Deepening democracy in a fragmented world.* New York: Oxford University Press.
Westheimer, J. and Khan, J. (2002), What Kind of Citizen? The Politics of Educating for Democracy. Paper presented at the annual meeting of the American Political Science Association, Boston, MA.
Young, I.M. (1990), *Justice and the politics of difference.* Princeton, NJ: Princeton University Press.

CHAPTER

5 Social security

LEARNING OUTCOMES

After you have read this chapter you should be able to:

- Define social security.
- Explain the different social security strategies – namely, social assistance, social insurance and indigenous, informal systems.
- Discuss the nature and scope of social security provision in South Africa.
- Describe the successes and challenges of social security in South Africa.
- Explain the developmental approach to social security.
- Identify the roles of social service practitioners in relation to social security.

Introduction

There is general agreement in developed and developing countries about the importance of social security for poverty reduction, in ensuring a basic minimum standard of living for the people and in achieving a more equitable income distribution in a society. Social security programmes expanded in developing countries after World War II following the de-colonisation process. Social security programmes in many developing countries were influenced by European and British social security systems (Midgley & Kaseke 1996:103). South Africa incorporated many of these elements into its social security system, which was fashioned on social provision in advanced industrial societies. The local system was, however, adapted to suit the racially discriminatory apartheid welfare policy (Lund 2002:178). Today, it is widely acknowledged that South Africa has a fairly well-developed social security system and, in particular, a social assistance programme for a middle-income developing country (Van der Berg & Bredenkamp 2002). A global ranking of national social security systems indicated that Australia had the best-designed social security system in the world (Dixon 2000:113). South Africa was ranked 64 out of 172 countries with the USA ranked 62, just slightly ahead of South Africa.

'Social security systems are under pressure internationally, and this has resulted in the restructuring and redesign of the systems.'

Social security systems are under pressure internationally, and this has resulted in the restructuring and redesign of the systems. In South Africa, the new democratic government initiated a review and restructuring of the social security system after 1994. The Committee of Inquiry into a Comprehensive Social Security System for South Africa (2002) – the Taylor Committee – was established and made recommendations on the restructuring and redesign of the system. The Taylor Committee concurred with earlier findings that the assumptions under-girding social security were based on European conceptions of social security which were not entirely appropriate in local environments. The Taylor Committee highlighted the gaps in social provision for the unemployed and the limited coverage for children. Greater income security for the poor and unemployed was advocated through a Basic Income Grant and the expansion of benefits to children. In addition, an expansion of public works programmes was recommended and consideration was given to health, retirement, disability, and constitutional and legal requirements – including the institutional organisation and financing of the system. In 2003 the government accepted the recommendation to expand benefits to children and in 2004 the president announced the extension of employment through the expansion of public works programmes and small business development (Presidential Speech in Parliament, Business Day 24th May 2004). A national coalition of organisations in civil society are continuing to campaign for the expansion of publicly funded social assistance to include a universal Basic Income Grant (BIG) and the extension of the age limit for eligibility to social grants for children up to the age of 18 years.

Conceptualisation of social security

There is a range of definitions on social security, and these vary according to ideological and contextual interpretations. Lord William Beveridge, Britain's most notable social security expert, provided a simple but perhaps provocative definition of social security. He said: 'Social security is a job when you can work and an income when you can't' (deSchweinitz in Ball 1978:3). The most widely accepted definition of social security throughout the developing and developed world is that of the International Labour Organisation (ILO). The ILO states that social security is:

> *the protection which society provides for its members through a series of public measures, against the economic and social distress that otherwise would be caused by the stoppage or substantial reduction of earnings resulting from sickness, maternity, employment injury, unemployment, invalidity, old age and death; the provision of medical care; and the provision of subsidies for families with children (International Labour Organisation 1989:29).*

The above definition makes provision for social security by both *government* and the *private sector* as a mechanism to ensure the protection of individuals who have been exposed to contingencies beyond their control, and who are unable to mobilise resources to take care of themselves. The resources, which have been mobilised for social protection, will presumably ensure that individuals do not fall below an acceptable standard of living.

Social security has been defined in South Africa as covering:

> *a wide range of public and private measures that provide cash or in-kind benefits both, first, in the event of an individual's earning power permanently ceasing, being interrupted, never developing, or being exercised only at unacceptable social cost and when such person is unable to avoid poverty and secondly, in order to maintain children. The* domain *of social security is: poverty prevention, poverty alleviation, social compensation and income distribution (Department of Welfare and Population Development 1997:48).*

'The South African Constitution (1996) makes provision for social assistance to people without any means.'

The South African Constitution (1996) makes provision for social assistance to people without any means. Section 27 (1c) protects the rights of everyone to access to social security and appropriate social assistance if they are unable to support themselves and their dependants. The *White Paper for Social Welfare* (1997) advocated a comprehensive and integrated social security system which would include social assistance and social insurance and where there would be co-responsibility between employers, employees, citizens and the state to ensure universal access and coverage of social security. It also promoted the idea of creating new models of social security, which combined social security with community and social development strategies and employment programmes such as public works programmes (Department of Welfare & Population Development 1997:53).

South African social security strategies consist of social assistance, which includes social relief, social insurance and private savings. *Social assistance* is the most significant social security strategy and refers to a range of benefits in cash or in kind intended to provide protection for the most needy in a society. These social benefits are also known as *non-contributory schemes* in that they are publicly funded and are given to an individual or a household according to their income level or their ability to earn an income (Subbarao et al. 1997:35). A distinction is also made between *chronic incapacity* to work and earn and *transient incapacity* to earn a living. Social assistance strategies are generally designed to address either chronic poverty or transient poverty caused by life–cycle events and economic, social and environmental conditions that affect an individual or a household's earning capacity. *Social relief* forms part of social assistance that is of a short-term nature to tide people over crises in cases of transient poverty. It is a non-contributory scheme that is needs-tested and that provides support to individuals or communities in emergency situations such as floods, fires or other natural disasters. Social assistance and social relief programmes are also referred to as *safety nets*, although for some authors the safety net includes social assistance and social insurance.

It has been noted that *indigenous informal* or *semi-formal systems* of social security exist alongside the formal social security systems in developing countries (Mukaka, Kalikiti & Musenge 2002; Subbarao et al. 1997; Ardington & Lund 1995). While some remnants of traditional systems have survived modernisation and colonialism, others have evolved due to the lack of access to formal systems of social provision. Examples of traditional and informal systems of social security are credit and savings schemes, burial societies, co-operative arrangements, and remittances of migrant workers to relatives in rural areas, in-kind support, family and friendship networks and mutual aid and self-help groups. These informal systems are based on personal reciprocity, social solidarity, social networks of trust and direct face-to-face interaction between individuals, households and communities and are pertinent in poverty alleviation – especially in rural areas.

Social insurance is defined as benefits organised by the *state* through specified contributions by employers and employees and is also referred to as *contributory schemes* to cover specific risks. These include benefits such as unemployment, retirement, sickness and maternity benefits. *Private savings* refer to the voluntary savings by individuals for unexpected contingencies and risks.

There is no agreement on how comprehensive social security should be. This is particularly pertinent in developing countries in view of fiscal resource constraints, limited formal employment, and inadequate institutional capacity and administrative systems to deliver the services efficiently and effectively. Conceptions of social security organised around the formal wage economy are considered inappropriate in addressing needs in developing countries (Olivier 2003; Committee for Inquiry into a Comprehensive Social Security System 2002; Kaseke 2000; Midgley & Kaseke 1996). Internationally, social security systems have been based on a traditional notion of the nuclear family where the male was the head of the household and the main breadwinner. The system was also organised around full employment policies in advanced industrial societies, which resulted in limited social assistance coverage in these societies as most people had employment and work-related social benefits. This situation does not exist in the South African context where mass unemployment and income poverty prevails, where increasing numbers of people are employed in the informal sector and where family structures and forms have evolved very differently (Lund 2002; Lund Committee on Child and Family Support 1996). In addition, the country is faced with a growing HIV/AIDS pandemic, which continues to have devastating economic and social consequences for the society.

'Conceptions of social security organised around the formal wage economy are considered inappropriate in addressing needs in developing countries.'

It is against this background that the Committee for Inquiry into a Comprehensive System of Social Security adopted a broader view of social security. The Taylor Committee argued that 'there is a growing need for a platform of general social protection that supports both the unemployed and the working poor' (Committee of Inquiry into a Comprehensive Social Security System 2002:39). The policy approach to social security adopted by the Taylor Committee broadens the vision of social security to integrate those people who are currently marginalized and excluded from coverage of the present social security system and to accommodate the realities of developing countries. The Committee for Inquiry into a Comprehensive Social Security System (2002:41) favoured the term Comprehensive Social Protection (CSP) and defined it as follows:

> *Comprehensive social protection ... incorporates developmental strategies and programmes designed to ensure, collectively, at least a minimum acceptable living standard for all citizens. It embraces the traditional measures of social insurance, social assistance and social services, but goes beyond that to focus on causality through an integrated policy approach including many of the developmental initiatives undertaken by the state.*

The Taylor Committee also located social security within a *human development* and a *social justice* perspective, emphasising the relationship between social and economic development in line with the formulation of the United Nations Commission on Social Development (United Nations 2000).

Payment of social grant in Gauteng. 'Social Assistance is one of South Africa's most effective poverty reduction programmes.'

The nature and scope of social security

Social Assistance

Social assistance programmes for families and children, war veterans, the elderly and people with disabilities evolved over many decades. Child and family support programmes were introduced after the formation of the Union of South Africa. The Children's Protection Act of 1913 made provision for the payment of maintenance grants for children and family support was introduced to protect white families living in poverty in 1921. These family support measures were gradually extended to coloured and Indian families, while Africans who had rights to live in urban areas were included initially. However, after the nationalist government came to power and independent states and self-governing territories were formed, eligibility to some of these grants was restricted for Africans. Modern social assistance emerged in South Africa in the form of military pensions in 1919 to meet the needs of war veterans as a result of World War 1.

Social pensions were granted to whites and coloureds in 1928 subject to age criteria and these were means-tested to ensure that only the needy were targeted (Van der Berg 2001:189). Race was a determining factor in assessing eligibility in terms of the Old Age Pensions Act of 1928. In addition, white people received a larger pension than coloured people. Social pensions provided the government with a support base and represented a critical economic and political stabilising factor for the country. The rationale for not providing African people with pensions was that traditional sources of social security were still effective in the rural areas, and that social welfare for Africans would be incompatible with segregationist policies and the viability of the migrant labour system (Van der Berg 2001; Sagner 2000).

To address the 'poor white problem' in the 1930s, resources were mobilised to develop and implement employment programmes amounting to close to 16 percent of Gross National Product (GNP). Most unemployed white people were provided with work on road, railway and irrigation works. Further social security reforms enacted included the institution of a pension for blind persons in 1936 and disability grants in 1937. However, these grants were allocated to whites and coloureds only and were later extended to other race groups in 1946. Blind and old age pensions were only expanded to Africans and Indians in 1944 by the Smuts government.

'To address the 'poor white problem' in the 1930s, resources were mobilised to develop and implement employment programmes.'

In the 1940s, war veterans' pensions were introduced and family allowances for large low-income families were enacted around the same time. The State Maintenance Grant (SMG) system was also implemented during this period and targeted single-parent families. This grant was initially available to white families only, but later the government extended these to coloured and Indian families (Community

Agency for Social Enquiry 2000:7). The administration of maintenance grants and foster-care grants continued to be discriminatory and, at times, were inaccessible in the former black independent homelands. During the 1970s and 1980s, there was a sharp increase in the number of grants awarded to coloured and Indian families, while African people remained excluded from child and family grants (Lund Committee on Child and Family Support 1996:11–12). Since white standards of living had increased fewer white people qualified for the grant.

During the period 1948 to 1961, the gap in the amounts paid to white and African pensioners widened considerably. In spite of the widening gap between white and African pensions, with the United Party government prior to 1948 under Smuts, and later when the Nationalist Party was in power, old age pensions for African people were used as a propaganda tool for the outside world. Sagner (2000:540) commented that 'given the uniqueness of the South African state pension system in Sub-Saharan Africa, the scheme was a means to make South African "native policy" look rather more respectable in the eyes of the outside world'. The Native Trust managed the disbursement of black pensions, and only half of its pension revenue was distributed. Pension payments were geographically differentiated with eleven different pension rates until 1960, and eight pension rates thereafter. The introduction of old age pensions to many poor South Africans was to have a major impact on the history of poverty in this country since this grant was a significant factor in the survival of poor households. Sagner (2000:547) noted further that 'old-age pensions were not only of direct economic value but also of eminent social and symbolic significance'. Parity of pensions was introduced in 1993 following the unbanning of political organisations and, by this time, 81 percent of social old-age pensioners were black (Van der Berg 1998:6).

Contemporary social assistance

'In South Africa, the nature and scope of state-funded cash transfers that are non-contributory and means-tested may be considered to be an exception in comparison with other countries of the same level of development.'

Targeted social assistance to reduce poverty through cash transfers is limited in most developing countries and in developed countries it forms part of a safety net that includes social insurance (Subbarao et al. 1997). In South Africa, the nature and scope of state-funded cash transfers that are non-contributory and means-tested – commonly referred to as social grants – may be considered to be an exception in comparison with other countries of the same level of development (Seekings 2002). Approximately 5.8 million impoverished people were receiving social grants at the end of April 2003 and this figure is expected to increase to 7.5 million by the end of 2004 (Republic of South Africa, National Treasury 2004). The actual increases have been much higher than expected and are contained in Table 5.1. The government is expanding income support through social assistance, which provides an invaluable safety net to poor people (Department of Social

Development Annual Report 2003:39). Safety nets of this kind protect a person or a household against chronic and transient poverty.

Currently, there are different types of *social assistance or social grants.* These social grants are paid to older persons, people with disabilities, caregivers of children with disabilities known as the care dependency grant. Social grants are also paid to the caregivers of children up to age 14 years (Child Support Grant), foster care, war veterans and social relief of distress. All the social grants are means-tested and target the poor and vulnerable – except for social relief of distress, which is needs-tested. In order to qualify, all beneficiaries should be South African citizens, should be resident in South Africa at the time of the application and should have the relevant identification documents. Each of the grants has particular requirements such as a qualifying age; in the case of disabilities, evidence is required confirming the nature of the disability. The grants are also aimed at caring for the older persons, war veterans, people with disabilities and children in communities. There is a requirement that the beneficiary should not be maintained or cared for in an institution. In this way the grants provide for *support and care in the community*. In the case of Child Support Grants, the grant is paid to a caregiver who does not have to be the biological parent of the child. This approach is innovative, as there is recognition that large numbers of South African children are cared for apart from their parents due to the migrant labour system and historical factors. It is also responsive to the situation of orphaned and vulnerable children affected by the HIV/AIDS pandemic.

State Old Age Pensions. The best-known form of social assistance or social grant is the State Old Age Pension (SOAP). Social pensions are gender-sensitive, reach far into rural areas, and support extended families in impoverished circumstances. Research has demonstrated that social pensions contribute significantly to supporting poverty-stricken households, and in particular rural households (Moller & Sotshongaye 1996; Ardington & Lund 1995). Without the contribution of social pensions, poor people, particularly in rural areas, will simply not survive. Households with pensioners are not as poor as households that have no pensioners. By 1998, social pensions reached about 75–80 percent of the population who were eligible in terms of age – women from age 60 years, and men from age 65 years (Van der Berg 1998:6). Currently, just over 2 million elderly people receive social pensions (Department of Social Development 2004:39). SOAP is the largest social assistance programme in rand terms, but the Child Support Grant (CSG) has the largest number of beneficiaries.

'Social pensions are gender-sensitive, reach far into rural areas, and support extended families in impoverished circumstances.'

Disability grants. Disability grants are the second-largest social assistance programme in rand terms. The number of grants has increased from April 2000 to April 2003 by 57 percent. About 3.5 percent of the

'... the largest proportion of people with disabilities is in the lowest income households with the lowest education levels.'

population between 17 and 66 years received disability grants (Republic of South Africa 2003:103). In November 2004, the number of disability grants increased significantly and beneficiary numbers reached 1 292 426 (Department of Social Development 2004). This growth may be attributed to rising numbers of people who are HIV positive and who now qualify for the grant. Data was not available to confirm this. Research conducted by the Community Agency for Social Enquiry (CASE 1998:29) revealed that the largest proportion of people with disabilities is in the lowest income households with the lowest education levels. The implications of this research finding are that developmental welfare and community-based development, including skills development programmes, are needed to address the socio-economic conditions of people with disabilities in poor households. This is discussed further in Chapter 6.

Care Dependency Grants are paid to family members who take care of a child with severe mental impairment and/or severe physical disability. Growth in the number of Care Dependency Grants has been rapid. This growth may be ascribed to the number of people infected and affected by HIV/AIDS, and will continue to impact on the increase in these grants. The number of care dependency beneficiaries has expanded fivefold between 1998 and 2003 (Republic of South Africa 2003:103).

Child Support Grants. The new democratic government, faced with racial inequity in State Maintenance Grants (SMGs) (which were accessed mainly by coloureds, Indians and a small percentage of white single parents), did not comply with the equality provisions of the Constitution of the Republic of South Africa No 200 of 1996. Consequently, the programme needed to be redesigned or abolished. The policy options open to the government were to expand the existing programme to include African single-parent families and to equalise the amounts paid to all population groups or to consider alternative policy options. The government appointed the Lund Committee on Child and Family Support in 1996 to make recommendations on the redesign of the system, taking into account the government's concerns about affordability and sustainability. The Lund Committee noted that the assumptions underpinning State Maintenance Grants were based on a traditional notion of the structure and form of the family – the nuclear family. Internationally, family forms have changed and many different family forms exist in South Africa with rising numbers of single-parent families and women-headed households living in poverty. The Lund Committee also noted that parents have the primary responsibility for ensuring the support of their children and that many children were also vulnerable because of failures in the judicial or private maintenance system. Consequently, women turned to the state maintenance system for support. The Lund Committee recommended the policy option of enacting a

Child Support Grant, which would be integrated with the promotion of the financial responsibility of parents for children. Recommendations were made to reform the parental maintenance system.

In 1997, the Cabinet adopted the recommendations of the Lund Committee. State Maintenance Grants (SMGs), which had existed since 1921, were phased out over a three-year period. The continued existence of the SMG would have been an anomaly in the context of an emerging democracy and its pursuit of equity and social justice (Triegaardt In Press). This was however a politically controversial step and the new government was severely criticised for taking benefits away from poor single parents, many of whom were denied access to benefits under the system of apartheid. The Child Support Grant (CSG) was received with a mixed reaction because it heralded the phasing out of the SMG on which many single-parent families in the Western Cape, and particularly coloured women, depended (Vorster & Rossouw 1997:318). Another concern raised with the new grant was that the amount paid by the grant was so low that it would have a limited impact on poverty and that the age limit excluded access to benefits by older children in need. The CSG was launched amidst a great deal of controversy on 1 April 1998.

This social grant was earmarked for the poorest children in South Africa aged 0–6 years of age and was considered to be most beneficial in the poorest provinces. In 2002, poor children were concentrated in KwaZulu-Natal (23 percent), Eastern Cape (21 percent), and Limpopo (17 percent), with Free State and Northern Cape not far behind. Poverty data analyses indicate that there are racial, geographic and gender dimensions to child poverty in South Africa. Child poverty in South Africa is most severe among children up to 14 years and in African households and, to a lesser extent, among children in the coloured population (Dieden & Gustafsson 2003:330; Van der Berg & Bredenkamp 2002). Many women, particularly single heads of households, are affected by poverty. Almost two-fifths of South Africa's children live in female-headed households. In addition, child malnutrition remains one of the biggest contributors to child morbidity and mortality in South Africa (The Committee for Inquiry into a Comprehensive Social Security System 2002:29). Furthermore, Martin (2003:37) has indicated that in 2001 approximately 14.3 million children (75 percent) lived in poverty. Of the total number of children living in poverty, approximately 11 million (76 percent) live in extreme poverty. Children living in rural areas are more likely to be poor than those in urban areas, as seven out of ten poor people in South Africa live in rural areas (Statistics South Africa 1997).

'Children living in rural areas are more likely to be poor than those in urban areas, as seven out of ten poor people in South Africa live in rural areas.'

The Child Support Grant (CSG) is an institutionalised social grant in South Africa and its benefits are being widely recognised. Since its inception, the age limit has been raised for the poorest children up to the age of 11 years, and in 2003 the government announced a further age extension up to 14 years (Department of Social Development Fact Sheet

2003:2). However, this age extension will be effected in phases. At the end of November 2004, there were 5.4 million children in receipt of the CSG. There are 416 532 nine- and ten-year-old children on the SOCPEN system, which is the payment system for social grants (Personal Communication 8th December 2004, Department of Social Development 2004). Uptake of the grant has increased significantly for this cohort. It is estimated that 6.5 million children will eventually qualify for this grant (Republic of South Africa, National Treasury 2004:495). Many advocacy groups continue to press for extending the grant to children up to age 18 years, which was also supported by the Taylor Committee.

Research findings revealed that the CSG has had a significant impact on poor children and poverty-stricken families. The CSG was used mainly for food, clothes and education (CASE 2000:43). In addition to the CSG being paid as a cash transfer to the primary caregiver of the child, the safety net also includes free health care for children under 6 years and feeding programmes for children. The purpose of the Integrated Nutrition Programme is to provide an inter-sectoral and co-ordinated programme for nutritional deficiencies among women and children, through health and community-based nutrition services.

Lloyd (2000:50) has argued that the benefits of the Child Support Grant should be noted in four areas. Firstly, the CSG ensures greater access for poor children to an integrated and sustainable social security system in the country. Secondly, it provides a grant on an equitable basis to those children in need regardless of their family structure, form, tradition or race. Thirdly, it prevents children from unnecessarily entering statutory substitute care; and, lastly, it keeps children off the streets and out of juvenile detention centres. The grant, although small, supplements household income and provides the poorest children with resources to meet basic survival needs.

Other social grants. Another social grant, which has increased steadily since 2000, is that of *foster-care grants.* The provinces of Limpopo and KwaZulu-Natal have experienced significant increases in the number of foster-care grants. This rise in the number of grants may be attributed to the impact of the HIV/AIDS pandemic that has been greatest in these provinces. About 18 percent of the estimated number of orphans received the foster-care grant and the number of foster-care beneficiaries expanded more than threefold between 1998 and 2003 (Republic of South Africa 2003:103). Foster-care grants are intended to provide some financial support to non-related caregivers that are willing to provide a child with a secure and nurturing home environment. The award is subject to a means test and a full investigation conducted by a social worker. This may lead to the placement of the child in foster care and a Children's Court makes the award. Once the court makes the award, ongoing supervision and reconstruction services are supposed to be provided to the foster family and the natural family of the child by a social worker. In the absence of other forms of alternative care for children affected by HIV/AIDS, foster care is increasingly seen as a means of caring for orphaned and vulnerable children. However, the current design of the programme is extremely resource-intensive and expanding the reach of the programme will require more social workers and judicial officers in the Children's Courts – and an increase in financial resources. A more sustainable foster-care model is needed to meet the challenges of the HIV/AIDS pandemic. The search for solutions should be linked to other proposed home and community care interventions that are discussed in Chapter 6.

'A more sustainable foster-care model is needed to meet the challenges of the HIV/AIDS pandemic.'

A comprehensive *food relief programme* was introduced in 2002. The aim of the programme was to mitigate the food crisis, which developed as a result of rising food prices. Food parcels are distributed to vulnerable and needy persons by provincial governments through a Conditional Grant to the provinces for Food Relief that amounted to R388 million per year over the medium-term expenditure framework (Republic of South Africa Estimates of National Expenditure 2004). Social relief policy is in the process of being developed. *War veterans' grants* have declined over the past few years and will gradually phase out over time.

Summary. Table 5.1 summarises the different types of social assistance programmes, the target groups served and the number of beneficiaries and the amounts paid in 2004. These amounts increase annually and, depending on available resources, the levels of the grants are adjusted for inflation; sometimes increases in real terms are made. The Minister of Finance or the Minister for Social Development announces these increases in Parliament when the annual national budgets are debated.

In November 2004, a total of 9 118 236 beneficiaries were in receipt of social grants and beneficiary numbers increased exponentially over the past year. In general, the three poorest provinces – the Eastern Cape, KwaZulu-Natal and Limpopo – have the highest proportion of social grant beneficiaries – 55.5 percent. KwaZulu-Natal has the largest proportion of social grants nationally – 23.3 percent (Department of Social Development Annual Report 2003). Social grants are, therefore, key elements of a safety net to lift people out of chronic and transient poverty. They also contribute significantly to poverty reduction and social inequality. They are an integral part of the new developmental welfare strategy.

Table 5.1: Social assistance: type, target group, amount paid and number of beneficiaries

Social Assistance	Target Group	Amount of Grant (2004)	Number of beneficiaries
Social Pensions	Women over the age of 60 years; men over the age of 65 years	R 740	2 084 244
Disability Grants	Persons medically-diagnosed disabled over the age of 18 years	R 740	1 292 426
Care Dependency Grants	Parents, the primary caregiver or foster parent of a disabled child who requires permanent care or support at home by another person	R 740	85 250
Child Support Grant	Paid to the primary caregiver of a child/children up to 14 years	R 170	5 404 684
Foster-care Grant	Foster families caring for children under 18 years old	R 530	234 436
War Veterans' Grant	Veterans of the two world wars and the Anglo-Boer War	R 758	3 489
Grants-in-Aid	A Person with a physical or mental condition requiring regular attendance by another person	R160	13 707

Source: Figures supplied as at 8th December 2004 by the Department of Social Development.

Social policies promoting social protection. There are other social policies that contribute to the safety net, that protect the population against risk and that promote human development, some of which are outlined briefly. These public policies are not generally considered to be part of social security but they play a vital role in providing social protection and in complementing existing social assistance arrangements.

The *Road Accident Fund* (RAF) provides social protection against risks arising from motor vehicle accidents, which is a major cause of mortality and disability in South Africa. The RAF makes provision for compensation to victims who have suffered loss or damage as a result of motor vehicle accidents. The RAF fund is financed through a levy on fuel sales, which is a unique system of financing internationally (Committee of Inquiry into a Comprehensive Social Security System 2002:109). The Fund has been criticised for poor administration, for the length of time it takes to compensate victims and the limited payments received that do not cover the high medical expenses of those affected.

Other social policies that have a direct bearing on social security and the achievement of human development include *health care provision and the reform of the private maintenance system.* The *primary school nutrition scheme* also provides nutritional support to children in need. Legal aid is also provided for those who cannot afford to pay for legal representation. The national government also allocates grants to local authorities to subsidise basic *municipal services for the poor* such as electricity, water, and sanitation and refuse removal. Although these programmes are not formally classified as social assistance, they do contribute to the safety net and overall social expenditure and do not include those services and programmes administered by other government departments. There is a need to assess the total contribution of governmental programmes to promote human development and the impact of these programmes on the reduction of poverty.

'There is a need to assess the total contribution of governmental programmes to promote human development and the impact of these programmes on the reduction of poverty.'

Access to health care is vital to ensuring social development including the promotion of parental support through the private maintenance system. Prior to 1994, the health care system developed as a twin system consisting of private and public provision. Those who have the means and/or have occupational insurance have access to private health care. People who do not have the means have access to free primary health care services and means-tested health care in the public sector. Destitute persons have access to free health care at public facilities. The range of internationally accepted primary health care services include the promotion of proper nutrition, an adequate supply of safe water and basic sanitation services. Other primary health care services include maternal and child care, reproductive health services; immunisation against major infectious diseases; prevention and control of locally endemic diseases; promotive and preventive health education and appropriate treatment for common diseases and injuries (ILO 1989:33). In South Africa many of these services are provided in varying degrees at primary care facilities. The needs of children under six years and pregnant women have been prioritised in primary health care delivery, and these services are without cost. Health care has not traditionally been considered as a component of social security (Van der Berg 2001:204).

With regard to *private maintenance*, the Lund Committee (1996:48) drew public attention to the importance of increasing parental financial support and responsibility for children through the private maintenance system. Administrative ineffectiveness of the private maintenance system administered by the Department of Justice made it extremely difficult for claimants to obtain maintenance from the parents of their children. Many gave up the struggle and were left with little or no support. Following further recommendations by the Law Commission, the Maintenance Act No 99 of 1998 was passed and implemented in 1999. The new legislation was made more stringent and provided for the attachment of property and wages and mandated the establishment of investigators to trace and find respondents. If a respondent defaulted on payments and disregarded court summonses, the courts could make orders by default. Many difficulties continue to hinder progress in the implementation of the new legislation; these include delays, which are costly for claimants. A proper implementation of the legislation is vital to address the hardships experienced by maintenance complainants. On the basis of research on the implementation of the new legislation, Wamhoff and Burman (2002) made some important recommendations for further improvements to the law and in the administration of the system – such as finding cheaper and quicker ways of responding and avoiding litigation through mediation or arbitration. Procedural amendments and administrative improvements to the system were also recommended including the education of claimants as to their rights. The authors also point out that, in a country with high unemployment and where it is difficult to trace respondents and where resources are constrained, remedies will have to be found in making the current system more effective.

Social insurance

Social insurance and occupational insurance expanded in the 1920s and included predominantly white, skilled employees. The Unemployment Benefit Act of 1937 made provision for the payment of unemployment benefits and when the Act was passed it covered only about 88 000 workers, and excluded all black workers in mining, agricultural and domestic service. In 1956, the Pensions Act was passed to regulate retirement funds and protect the interests of their members. Occupational retirement was widened in the 1960s and early 1970s to include less skilled workers (Van der Berg 1998:4). At the same time, rapid economic growth and industrialisation attracted many more workers into formal employment, which impacted on both occupational and private retirement funds. Membership of both of these funds grew from 923 000 in 1958 to 9 309 000 in 1993 – a growth rate of almost 7 percent per annum over three and half decades (Van der Berg 2001:188; Smith Committee 1995). Since the 1980s, trade union movements have taken a more active interest in retirement funds. Many provident funds, rather than pension funds, were established. The difference between provident and pension funds is that the former can be withdrawn at anytime whilst pension funds are only paid out on retirement. Low-income workers preferred to collect the lump-sum benefit of provident funds at retirement, rather than receive a third of pension funds on retirement, and thereafter a monthly payment for the balance of the pension. Also provident funds allowed workers to draw from their funds to meet the cost of contingencies.

As indicated previously, *social insurance* (also referred to as occupational insurance) is provided to protect employees and their dependants: this takes the form of insurance against contingencies which interrupt income. These schemes are contributory for both employers and employees. The contributions are wage-related and the employees and the employers agree upon a percentage to be paid by each of the parties. Social insurance covers contingencies such as pensions or provident funds, medical benefits, maternity benefits, illness, disability, unemployment, employment injury, family benefits and survivor's benefits.

Occupational retirement insurance in South Africa is not available to those outside paid employment and those who are in informal employment or what is sometimes referred to as 'piece work' or casual labour. Therefore, many unskilled labourers are not covered by this particular safety net. South Africa's private pension and insurance sectors are estimated to be the largest in the world relative to the gross national product (GNP) (Committee for Inquiry into a Comprehensive Social Security System 2002:93). Pension fund contributions are recorded to be about R54.3 billion a year – 14 percent of total personal remuneration. According to Van der Berg and Bredenkamp (2002), about 73 percent of formally employed persons were covered by various retirement schemes in the mid-1990s and 45 percent of the labour force was covered (Van der Berg & Bredenkamp 2002; Smith Committee 1995). This low level of coverage of the labour force was due to widespread unemployment and the lack of coverage in informal sector employment. Coverage also varies between economic sectors, with low coverage in trade, catering, agriculture and domestic service which is estimated to be about 20 percent of the labour force (Van der Berg & Bredenkamp 2002). In addition, workers who may have worked all their lives and earned a low income and who have saved consistently through a retirement scheme may only receive about 40 percent of their final salary, which is a disincentive to save for retirement. Occupational retirement benefits may be small for this group; they are, however, eligible for means-tested social old age pensions. In this regard Kaseke (2000:5) points out that, in many African countries, low wages paid to workers makes it extremely burdensome for them to contribute to any social insurance scheme because the contributions take away income that could contribute to meeting immediate needs. Therefore, the working poor tend to consider insurance against future risk as futile and a drain on limited resources.

'Occupational retirement insurance in South Africa is not available to those outside paid employment and those who are in informal employment.'

South Africa has experienced rising *unemployment* alongside poverty and inequality for several decades. The present unemployment rate, based on the expanded definition of unemployment, is 41.6 percent (Statistics South Africa 2003). Unemployment insurance coverage has been instituted for the protection of workers in the event of temporary unemployment related to illness, maternity, adoption and termination of employment. The purpose of unemployment insurance is to safeguard the individual from financial catastrophe during periods of involuntary short-term unemployment. The Unemployment Insurance Fund (UIF) established in terms of the Unemployment Insurance Act of 2001 is financed by contributions from employers, employees and the government. Employers and employees contribute one percent of the employee's monthly earnings and, if the employee has accumulated sufficient credits, benefits are paid on a sliding scale for 34 weeks. The government extended its safety net to the unemployed by making provision for domestic workers in 2003 in the statutory unemployment insurance scheme.

'Approximately 45 percent of the labour force is covered by UIF. Informal sector employees, independent contractors, the self-employed and the unemployed are not included in coverage.'

Van der Berg and Bredenkamp (2002) have indicated that the reform of unemployment insurance has made the system more progressive in that low-income workers benefit more than other categories and benefits are paid up to 58 percent of prior earnings. Approximately 45 percent of the labour force is covered by UIF. Informal sector employees, independent contractors, the self-employed and the unemployed are not included in coverage. The fund has been made more sustainable by including higher income earners in paying contributions, but its role in providing income maintenance for this group is limited.

Compensation for injuries and diseases at work is covered by the Compensation for Occupational Injuries and Diseases Act (COIDA) 130 of 1993. This Act replaces the former Workmen's Compensation Act of 1941. The COIDA makes provision for no-fault compensation of employees who are injured in accidents which arise out of and in the course of their duties. Domestic workers, those employed in the informal sector and self-employed contractors are excluded from COIDA. Mineworkers are covered by the Occupational Diseases in Mines and Works Act (ODMWA, Act 78 of 1973 as amended by Act 208 of 1993). This scheme provides compensation to miners for occupational diseases, which are common to work in the mines.

Informal and indigenous systems of social security

Traditional and semi-formal systems of social security have arisen mainly in developing countries. These communal and co-operative forms of self-help assistance developed in response to economic and social hardships. Research in Zambia (Mukuka, Kalikiti & Musenge 2002:97) has identified an informal savings scheme assisting those who are unable to raise money required for business or buying household items. *Chilimba* (which means strengthening) began as an informal rotating credit and savings (without interest) scheme that provided mutual assistance among poor migrant miners on the Copperbelt of Zambia during the colonial period as a means of coping with the perennial problem of lack of money. Patel (1992:34) contends that 'the social relations which developed from the colonial economy came into conflict with these traditional modes' and undermined indigenous forms of social provision. As noted earlier in the history of social assistance, these traditional modes of mutual assistance were used as an excuse by the South African government not to award social pensions to African people in the rural areas, and this was done to support the government's segregationist policy.

Over decades, informal and indigenous systems have existed alongside the formal social security systems. These systems have developed in response to the inaccessibility of formal social security systems. They have also developed as a consequence of economic and social hardships. Researchers have referred to the critical role played by these informal systems in providing a safety net, particularly in rural areas (Mukuka, Kalikiti & Musenge 2002; Ardington & Lund 1995). People employed in the urban areas send cash or in-kind remittances home to relatives in the rural areas. Informal and traditional forms of mutual aid include those of *stokvels* or savings schemes, and burial societies. Valuable empirical information is now available demonstrating the importance of personal reciprocity and informal safety nets in developing countries and in some economies in transition (Subbarao et al. 1997:4–5).

Indigenous systems of social security have a tendency to exploit women for the benefit of other members of the extended family, with no guarantee of women's own social protection (Kasente 2000:39). There is a tendency to depend heavily on women's reproductive work of caring for the children, the sick and other members of the household, a role which has been loaded with more responsibility as more women have been drawn into productive work in the economy. With the number of orphaned and vulnerable children increasing due to the HIV/AIDS pandemic, the burden of care has fallen heavily on women as community and home-based carers and kinship groups that are already strained. This situation has placed increased pressure on indigenous and informal systems of care and has been described as a 'safety net with holes'.

Despite these limitations, indigenous and informal modes of reciprocity have been the bulwark against social and economic insecurity. Kaseke (1998) has noted that 'In Africa, the extended family was an important social security institution, providing support to its members based upon culturally determined patterns of mutual assistance'. However, with increasing industrialisation and urbanisation, the role of the extended family system as a social security institution has been seriously eroded. This paved the way for the development of mutual aid societies, which includes savings clubs, food co-operatives and other semi-formal systems. Burial societies and *stokvels* are more common in urban areas (Molefe 1996:177–178). These informal social security arrangements have ensured the survival of people in adverse conditions. Semi-formal systems of social security, which by their very nature are flexible and oriented towards meeting both immediate and future needs, seem to offer the best possibilities for women and most men (Kasente 2000:39). Their suitability for women lies in the fact that they are able to enjoy some autonomy in building social networks that suit their interest and social situation and that would not marginalise them.

'Despite these limitations, indigenous and informal modes of reciprocity have been the bulwark against social and economic insecurity.'

However, there is always the risk of loss of membership of these networks if they are unable to pay their dues. Indigenous and informal social security need to be strengthened as complementary to the formal safety net. The design of safety net programmes should build on the strengths of the formal and informal systems and should not undermine their efficacy.

Table 5.2: Summary table of social security

Social Assistance	Social Insurance	Informal and Indigenous forms of social security
Social grants – state funded cash transfers that are non-contributory.	Insurance against contingencies that interrupt income, contributory.	Communal and co-operative forms of self-help and assistance.
e.g. SOAP	e.g. UIF	e.g. *Stokvels*

Successes and challenges of social security

Social security in South Africa evolved over several decades and the country inherited a fairly well-developed social assistance programme, social insurance, social legislation and an administrative infrastructure to administer social benefits, especially pertaining to social grants. A major success in the post-1994 period has been in securing constitutional safeguards for the right to social security and social assistance for those in need. Section 27c of Chapter 2 of the Constitution of the Republic of South Africa No 108 of 1996 states that 'everyone has the right to access to social security, including, if they are unable to support themselves and their dependants, appropriate social assistance'. Other successes are the achievement of social equity through the equalisation of social grants for the different race groups, the amalgamation of the 14 different administrative systems inherited from the apartheid era and in the expansion of benefits to children. Good coverage exists for the elderly and fair coverage also exists for people with disabilities – accurate prevalence rates are not known and it is not possible to assess coverage accurately. Social security and especially social assistance has received widespread popular endorsement by the public in the 2004 campaign for the national general election. In the main, the programme has a high level of visibility through the publicising by government of social assistance. Civil society advocacy groups have also mushroomed. Not only have they achieved greater visibility and legitimacy for the safety net, but they have also played a critical role in drawing public attention to poverty reduction through expanded social assistance strategies. The Alliance for Children's Entitlement to Social Security (ACESS) advocates raising the age limit for access to Child Support Grants to 18 years of age. The Basic Income Grant (BIG) Coalition, which is made up of NGOs, faith-based organisations, human rights groups and organised labour, has also campaigned for the introduction of a universal Basic Income Grant to reduce poverty and promote greater equality in the society.

A critical gap in the social security system is its lack of coverage of the unemployed and a lack of social insurance coverage for people employed in the informal sector, independent contractors and those who are self-employed (Lund 2002). Many people are also unemployed because of structural, cyclical and to some extent seasonal unemployment. Unfortunately, the Unemployment Insurance Fund (UIF) only caters for people affected by cyclical unemployment. People who are unemployed due to structural factors do not have an adequate safety net. Since the phasing out of State Maintenance Grants for single parents, there is no social assistance targeted specifically are women.

'A critical gap in the social security system is its lack of coverage of the unemployed and a lack of social insurance coverage for people employed in the informal sector, independent contractors and those who are self-employed.'

Whilst current social assistance strategies make a significant contribution to the reduction of poverty, a vast percentage of the poor who are unemployed and have no visible means of making a livelihood continue to remain poor. Women and out-of-school youth up to age 35 years are particularly vulnerable to unemployment and poverty and people living in rural areas where there is limited access to opportunities to earn a livelihood. Unemployment in South Africa is caused by both cyclical factors – such as sudden changes in the economy (which is of a short-term nature) – or is seasonal, where work opportunities are available at certain times only (such as in the agricultural sector). Another cause of unemployment pertains to structural factors, which includes a mix of socio-political, demographic and economic forces. The historical economic crisis and apartheid economic and social policies such as a lack of educational opportunities are cited as causal factors of unemployment. Furthermore, the negative effects of globalisation on the domestic economy have also resulted in rising unemployment that could be considered to be of a structural nature. Job losses at the lower end of the labour market, where people have limited skills, have increased the vulnerability to poverty of the lower-income groups. This situation has been especially prevalent in the mining and manufacturing sectors, which have been hardest hit by job losses. According to the Committee of Inquiry for a Comprehensive Social Security System (2002:70), there were 2.6 million unemployed individuals who lived in households where there was no one employed and where the monthly total expenditure of the households was less than R800 per month. Of this total, 1.4 million were women and 96 percent were African. There are also gender, age and racial dimensions to unemployment, especially in households where there is likely to be chronic poverty.

Basic primary and secondary education, adult basic education and further education and training are vital to address the skills problems related to unemployment and poverty. But labour supply strategies –

such as job placement, skills development and on-the-job training through learnership programmes – need to be complemented with *job creation programmes* through market-based approaches promoting economic growth, and also through governmental job creation programmes. In this regard, the government's newly announced Expanded Public Works Programme due to be rolled out in the course of 2004 is aiming at creating labour-intensive public works employment for one million people. A National Youth Service is also expected to be implemented that will place over 20 000 youth in public and community service agencies over the next three years. The youth will be expected to perform a service, and they will receive basic skills and mentoring. Appropriate exit strategies will need to be developed to link them with other employment and or educational opportunities after they have completed a year of service. Very little is known about the programme design and implementation strategies to assess the job creation potential and impact of these programmes. Small business development and livelihood strategies are also receiving increasing prominence in governmental efforts to address poverty and to create opportunities for greater social and economic inclusion.

The government's approach has been to expand the safety net for children and to combine this with a productivist approach, which includes employment strategies such as public works and other programmes outlined above, instead of expanding the safety net through a Basic Income Grant. The Taylor Committee (2002:31) recommended the expansion of the safety net through the introduction of BIG as it argued that cash transfers or social grants cover only 40 percent of all the poor. The reason for rejecting the recommendation for a BIG was that it was unaffordable and that it was a universal grant available to all citizens. The Taylor Committee and others (Martin 2003; Samson 2002) argued that the Basic Income Grant (BIG) would give effect to the right to social security, it would successfully reduce poverty and 6.3 million people would benefit directly. There appears to be no agreement as to the gross cost estimates for the grant. Samson et al. (2003:33) pegged the cost at R43.8 billion, based on 2001 figures, while Bhorat, using 1999 figures, estimated that an additional R61 billion in revenue would be needed (Bhorat 2003:99). From a social perspective, proponents of BIG have argued that a universal grant, which does not involve a means test, would remove the stigma and labelling of grant recipients as the 'undeserving poor'. They also argue that the grant would have other benefits beyond income protection and could have other positive human development impacts. At the economic level it is anticipated that it would stimulate the overall level of aggregate demand in the economy and it could also stimulate economic growth. The impact could also be positive in raising the Gini-coefficient and it could promote political and social stability. Research commissioned by the ILO on a Research Review on Social Security Reform and the Basic Income Grant concluded that BIG is feasible, affordable, and supportive of poverty reduction, economic growth and job creation (Samson et al. 2002:32). Van der Berg and Bredenkamp (2002:40) were cautious in their approach and indicated that the fiscal and administrative constraints limited the potential for grand schemes such as the Basic Income Grant.

With regard to children, a need exists to develop strategies to increase the uptake of children to the Child Support Grant, especially for those children above 6 years of age who qualify. Improvements in the child maintenance system are needed to support claimants to access parental support and the principle of parental support for children must continue to be fostered as a social policy principle. Addressing the social security needs of individuals and families infected with and affected by HIV/AIDS remains a critical priority for government, civil society, employers and the private sector. Disability grants and foster-care grants have increased exponentially with significant cost implications for the state. Budgets for community-care and support are still small and policy and infrastructure to facilitate home and community care are underdeveloped. Some pilot programmes are being implemented. Foster care is an important family-centred and community-based strategy to provide for the needs of orphaned and vulnerable children. However, there is scope to remodel this programme to be less resource-intensive and more suited to the local context whilst bearing in mind some of the limitations of over-extending women, kinship and social networks of support that are already strained. Social policy to guide and structure social relief is also a vital mechanism to address transient poverty and distress caused by short-term contingencies.

Policy changes, demographic factors, poverty and income levels, increasing access to benefits, and the progression of the HIV/AIDS epidemic are some of the factors that have a bearing on the growth and sustainability of social assistance programmes in the future. There is an urgent need for an effective monitoring and evaluation system of social assistance to assess the social and economic impact of the programme on poverty and inequality and to monitor changing trends and unintended consequences.

'There is an urgent need for an effective monitoring and evaluation system of social assistance to assess the social and economic impact of the programme on poverty and inequality and to monitor changing trends and unintended consequences.'

It is acknowledged that social policies also have unintended consequences – that is, outcomes that were not intended when the policy was developed. Unintended consequences of social policies are politically sensitive and could also be used as ideological justifications for why certain policies should not be pursued. For these reasons there is often a reluctance to confront such issues. The government has, for instance, expressed concern that a Basic Income Grant could have a negative effect on work incentives and that it could foster a culture of 'hand-outs' and dependency. Some social workers have provided anecdotal reports that the Child Support Grant has had pro-natal consequences in that some women are choosing to have more children in order to secure an income (Personal Communication 2004). These types of anecdotal reports remain untested. Other types of unintended consequences of social policies may be that social policies may heighten existing social divisions or could create new social divisions of a racial, gender, age or geographic nature. Whatever the nature of such unintended consequences, qualitative research from an interpretivist perspective could assist with deconstructing the meaning of social assistance for beneficiaries and its implications for social action.

'The challenge for South Africa is to deliver efficient social security services and to progressively expand coverage to the poor in a sustainable manner.'

In conclusion, the delivery of social security services has been hampered by ineffective and inefficient administration, lack of institutional support, human resources and fraud and corruption. The government has made a concerted effort to stamp out corruption by re-registering beneficiaries in order to root out the 'ghost' beneficiaries. The newly created National Social Security Agency will be responsible for the delivery of social assistance nationally and is an attempt to address the gap between policy and implementation. As social assistance coverage is expanding, social spending on social grants is rising exponentially and is fast approaching 4 percent of Gross Domestic Product (Financial Mail 2004). In this respect South Africa is an exception in comparison with other countries at similar levels of development. Although the government has relaxed its budget deficit targets to meet these social goals, spending on social grants is probably reaching its upper limit of what is fiscally feasible at current economic growth rates. There is the danger that other social service spending on health, education and welfare services may be curtailed. The challenge for South Africa is to deliver efficient social security services and to progressively expand coverage to the poor in a sustainable manner. Social assistance is focused only on income maintenance strategies and other creative innovations should be explored such as savings schemes, asset building and other complimentary social development strategies to reduce poverty.

A developmental approach to social security

There appears to be agreement that South Africa needs a comprehensive social security system that would reduce poverty and inequality and that would secure a minimum living level for all people. A further consensus exists that the social security system inherited from the past was not fashioned on local realities and was based on European models that were rooted in traditional notions of family structure (namely the nuclear family), and the organisation of social security in the form of social insurance linked to employment.

A comparative analysis between European and United States social security systems was conducted by Esping-Anderson (1990) and a typology was developed to illustrate the salient differences between the different types of welfare and social security systems. It will be demonstrated that this typology cannot be usefully applied in the South African context. Some of the salient features of the developmental approach to social security in South Africa will be identified on the basis of constitutional provisions, existing social policies, and new initiatives and ideas emerging in the course of the debates that were discussed above.

Esping-Anderson in the *Three Worlds of Welfare Capitalism* (1990), cited in Giddens (2001:333), compared Western welfare systems on the basis of whether or not they adopted market-based strategies to social welfare – and, if so, to what extent. In other words, the criterion used to classify welfare systems was the extent to which welfare services were free from the market, which he called welfare *decommodification*. Esping-Anderson (1990) identified three types of welfare systems: social democratic, conservative-corporatist and liberal systems. The *social democratic* and the conservative-corporatist systems are highly decommodified – that is, free of the market. Extensive social security benefits outside the market are provided, although full employment and publicly engineered social insurance is the preferred social security strategy. Limited social assistance is provided except for those who cannot be accommodated in formal employment. The Scandinavian systems were classified as social democratic: they had universal benefits, which covered the entire population, and their social programmes were state subsidised. France and Germany were considered to be examples of the *conservative-corporatist systems*: while highly decommodified, these were selective in their targeting of those in need of services and benefits. They tended to have a high regard for strong families and the purpose of social security was to achieve social stability and legitimacy. A strong alliance exists between labour and capital and agreements are reached between them on employment, wages and social benefits. Then there is the *liberal welfare system* of which the United States was the best example. This system was highly commodified: that is, there is a high degree of reliance on the market to meet needs, benefits were selective, means-tested and stigmatised and strong family values were emphasised.

The above countries are all advanced industrial societies and have been developing social security systems since the 1800s. In the present global context these countries are faced with the negative effects of economic globalisation, especially in relation to employment. However, unemployment levels are low in comparison with South Africa and they are still able to address risk and vulnerability through a highly decommodified approach. Many of the Western countries have renewed their social security programmes to varying degrees but fundamentally their social security systems have remained reasonably intact (Pierson 1994). Productivist elements, which refer to the role of work in social welfare, have been reintroduced in the Nordic countries. In Norway this has also been coupled with a greater emphasis on self-help efforts and reciprocity, social investment and labour market activation (Dahl et al. 2001). Western industrial countries also face further challenges like demographic changes, as they have large ageing populations, changing family structures, costly bureaucracies, economic recession and instability caused by their integration into the global economy and fiscal constraints. The idea that generous social benefits foster *dependence* on social support rather than promote self-sufficiency also became a justification for the 'rolling-back' of social benefits by conservative governments. Supporters of the welfare state have contested these ideas (Walker 1994). Despite arguments defending social security systems, significant welfare reforms have been implemented, such as welfare-to-work programmes to move beneficiaries off social welfare and into paid employment in the United Kingdom and the United States. Advocates of welfare reform have also promoted the use of dynamic labour market policies to create employment and move people off social benefits and into productive employment.

Despite the shortcomings in the South African social security system, it could be argued that the social security system with its large social assistance programme leans more to a decommodified system exhibiting some features of corporatism and selectivity of benefits targeting the poor. Given the low levels of economic growth that have been attained, social spending will probably not increase significantly in the short to medium term. GDP growth grew by 1.7 percent per annum between 1990 and 2001 – less than the population growth rate. This means that GDP growth per capita as well as the human development index in fact declined during this period largely due to increased morbidity and mortality as a result of the HIV/AIDS epidemic (Gelb 2003:3). Almost half of social spending goes to social services – that is, health, education and social welfare – and there has been a three percent increase in spending since the beginning of the 1990s (Gelb 2003:15). The largest increases have been in education spending and social security, while housing and other services have declined.

'The Esping-Anderson typology is not a useful classification for South Africa as the country does not fit neatly into any of its models.'

The Esping-Anderson typology is not a useful classification for South Africa as the country does not fit neatly into any of its models. South Africa is considered a middle-income country exhibiting vast disparities in wealth between rich and poor and which coincide with other social inequalities related to race, gender, disability and geography. It has mass unemployment and poverty, and has experienced slow economic growth following years of economic crisis and structural unemployment. The social fabric of the society is fragmented, social and kinship networks are strained due to economic pressures and the impact of the HIV/AIDS epidemic will be felt for years to come. Social insurance coverage is limited to just under half of the labour force and vast numbers of people – almost a third of the economically active population – have opted for informal and non-standardised employment, which is becoming a permanent way of working (Lund 2002). Given this background, it can be argued that South Africa's developmental approach to social security is probably the most appropriate approach to the provision of social protection.

The developmental approach to social security in South Africa

Some features of the developmental approach are:

- Everyone has the *right to access to social security*, including appropriate social assistance for those who are unable to support themselves and their dependants. Social security should be provided within the available resources of the state and will be realised progressively (Constitution of the Republic of South Africa No 108 of 1996 Sections 27 c and 27 (2).
- The government is responsible for the development and provision of a comprehensive national social security system based on two primary pillars: social assistance and social insurance (Department of Welfare & Population Development 1997).
- An approach to social insurance is needed which expands coverage of the informal sector and non-standardised workers. Lund (2002:177) argues that economically active people should be placed on a continuum of formal to informal employment, and this would also take account of gender and sectoral differences in access to coverage. Such inclusion of employees should involve multiple stakeholders – principally employers and the private sector.
- The two pillars of the safety net should be complemented by wider social and community developmental activities and should build on indigenous and informal systems of care. The design of the programmes should be such that it strengthens these different strategies and ensures that the overall scheme or layout of the system has a good structural fit between the different strategies so that gaps can be filled as far as possible.
- Other social policies that are not usually considered to be social security provide a much-needed safety net. These refer to other governmental programmes that are complementary to the existing safety net, and include health, nutrition, basic and further education, land reform, housing, justice, labour-intensive public works and micro enterprises.
- The Financial Sector Charter adopted by financial institutions to promote the transformation of the economy commits these institutions to, among other things, expanding access to social insurance to those who are under-served by the current system (Financial Sector Charter 2003). This is a new development, and it could have a significant impact on access to social insurance in South Africa.
- The above measures point to a *pluralist model* of social security provision involving government as the main provider of social assistance, government facilitation and regulation of social insurance, private savings, the private sector, the social insurance industry and complementary individual, social and community development strategies.
- The introduction of productivist ideas into the approach to safety nets is beginning to emerge through public employment creation (Expanded Public Works Programme, National Youth Service, job placement and skills development strategies) and a market-based approach to promote job creation through increased economic growth.
- Strengthening indigenous and family-centred and community-based care, support and development strategies to increase informal and semi-formal systems of care and social solidarity in such a way that burdens and costs of care are spread more equitably.
- Support for the principle of parental responsibility for the care and support of children. To give effect to this principle, improvements are necessary in the private maintenance system. Building and strengthening family and community life is also necessary, and this would include enhancing the capacity of households to provide support and nurture children.
- Acknowledgement that the causes of the problems leading to the need for social support and safety nets often lie in the inadequate workings of other systems in society, and these need to be addressed.

- Focus of social security on mass poverty, unemployment and social exclusion of vulnerable groups in society should be the main focus of the social security system.
- Selective and targeted strategies for those who do not have the means of social support are considered to be more redistributive and equitable than universal benefits. There does not appear to be a stigma attached to those who access public benefits and services in South Africa, as there is an almost 90% uptake of old age pensions. This may, however, become an issue when the society becomes more stratified in terms of social class in the future.
- A combination of cash and in-kind benefits are provided including opportunities for the development of human capabilities.
- Pilot flagship programmes on unemployed women and children and other livelihood-development programmes could inform best practice models to improve the nexus between social security, community development, individual and group empowerment interventions.

Roles of social workers and social service practitioners

The focus in social work has always been on how social security is used optimally for the benefit of individuals and families. What are the different types of programmes available to the poor and vulnerable and how can these people access these services and benefits? This chapter has provided an overview of the nature and scope of the different types of programmes, eligibility criteria, their impact and some of the policy issues. The roles of practitioners will be discussed with reference to Kirst-Ashman & Hull's generalist practice framework (2002).

Social workers in different settings spend much of their professional time in helping clients apply for social grants and access social relief. Many social workers feel that this could be done effectively by paraprofessionals such as auxiliary social workers. This role could be described as the *broker role*, where the social worker or social service practitioner links the client with different resources. Many community organisations and faith-based organisations perform this role effectively at local level, which is vital as people struggle to make their way through bureaucracies that are inaccessible to the public. In assisting clients to access much-needed resources to which they are entitled, the practitioner may also act as a *mediator* between various branches of government. For instance, the Department of Home Affairs is responsible for issuing identity documents, while the District Surgeon in the Department of Health conducts the assessment of whether a claimant qualifies for a disability grant. The Department of Social Development is responsible for the overall management of the process from assessment of eligibility through to the actual payment of the benefit. In working with all these different departments clients may need a mediator or a go-between between these different entities.

Practitioners also perform the role of *educator*: they inform client systems about their needs and rights and *counsel* them about their choices and options in addressing their social and economic needs. In working with populations at risk and in group and community settings, the practitioner may also be a *facilitator* and may *mobilise groups and communities* to take action in relation to their needs. Should there be large numbers of people in a community who have not received their grants or who have had their grants discontinued, the worker may help to mobilise the community to take action and to assist them in representing their concerns to the authorities.

In other instances, where there is high unemployment and limited opportunities to earn a livelihood in a community, the worker may assist the community in linking with public works programmes, social relief efforts and in community development activities. The Flagship programmes for unemployed women with children under 5 years initiated by the Department of Social Development were launched in July 1996. The first project was launched in partnership with the Babinachuene Women's Multi-purpose project in a deep rural area in Bochum/My darling, a district of the Limpopo province. The women developed a very successful agricultural project in the community and sold their vegetables to schools and clinics in the surrounding areas. Other similar programmes are operating in every province across the country involving activities such as vegetable gardening, sewing projects, a car wash, overnight establishments, an eating-house, bread-baking and fabric printing. These programmes have supplemented household income for people living on social grants or for those who had no income. Through these programmes the women have provided much-needed social support and have built social capital in the community.

Other roles that practitioners have performed include the *advocacy role* where practitioners have lobbied on behalf of their clients. Many organisations have also joined coalitions such as the BIG coalition that campaigned for increased access to services and benefits and that monitored existing safety net programmes. *Community action research* has also been critical in studying the needs of people for safety nets and in assessing impact, which in turn has helped to inform advocacy initiatives. Social service practitioners have also acted as *social planners* where they have studied local needs and have devised poverty-reduction strategies and developed business plans, which were presented to government and donor agencies for the funding of projects. In view of the first-hand knowledge and experience of social service practitioners in working at grassroots level, they have made valuable contributions to the formulation of social security policy since 1994.

Social security *innovation and experimentation* with new programmes is growing around the world. South Africa has its own innovations such as micro finance to finance micro-enterprises, although this is progressing slowly. Individual and co-operative savings schemes have a long history in South Africa through *stokvels* and burial societies that have provided much-needed funds to finance schooling, home improvements, funerals and livelihood projects. In the United States, independent development assets accounts known as IDAs have developed as saving schemes for poor people. This creative and unique development involves contributions by both the recipient and the government to an individual's savings account. These savings enable poor people to save to buy a home or possibly send a child to college for an education. In the case of Native Americans, they have opted to have a communal savings scheme since they favour more communal forms of savings. This creates the opportunity for poor people to build up assets or to grow their existing assets (Sherraden 2003).

'There is great potential for a more synergistic and innovative relationship between social security and developmental social welfare services.'

Social workers and social service practitioners often do not see the connections between their social work roles and social safety nets. Since welfare services are under-funded, social workers are of the view that social security is a drain on the overall social development budget, which means that there is less money available for welfare services. There is great potential for a more synergistic and innovative relationship between social security and developmental social welfare services, and this is discussed further in Chapter 6.

CHAPTER SUMMARY

- Pre-1994 social security provision was discussed in terms of the philosophy of social welfare within which it was conceived and evolved. Post-1994, social security was reformulated in relation to the social development perspective and aligned with the country's new constitution.
- Social security is defined as public and private measures that provide both cash and in-kind benefits to individuals whose earning power is permanently or temporally disrupted due to circumstances beyond their control. The purpose of social security is to reduce poverty and ensure a basic minimum standard of living for all people.
- Social security is also approached from a social justice and a human development perspective and includes the following strategies: social assistance, social insurance, private savings, indigenous and informal systems of support – including many of the development initiatives undertaken by the state.
- In its use of cash transfers, South Africa has a fairly well-developed social assistance system for a middle-income developing country. It has very good coverage for the elderly with an expanding safety net for children and fair coverage for people with disabilities.
- Other government departments provide services and benefits that complement the existing safety net, the actual cost of which has not been assessed.
- Less than half of the labour force is covered by social insurance, and workers in the informal sectors and non-standard employment do not have access to social insurance.
- Structural unemployment is estimated to be around 40% (expanded definition) of the labour force and for those not formally employed there is no coverage. Expanded employment opportunities are to be created by government and market-based strategies including skills development strategies. The government is increasingly adopting a productivist approach. However, the question remains as to whether these strategies can absorb the large numbers of people affected and whether the government has the administrative capacity to create employment on such a large scale. Indications are that the economy will grow slowly, and this will impact on the rate of job creation. Capital-intensive growth has also limited job creation for the less skilled people.

CHAPTER SUMMARY

- Other systems also need to be improved to meet the social security challenge: these include the private maintenance system to promote parental support for children, the mobilisation of the private sector and the strengthening of indigenous networks and informal systems of support. In all of these a gender-sensitive perspective is vital. The existing safety net also needs to be complemented by local social and economic development programmes.
- The features of the developmental approach to social security were outlined – namely, social security rights, the role of the state in ensuring a safety net including the responsibilities of the private sector, other non-state parties, individuals and social networks. This was referred to as a pluralist approach to social security.
- Building research capacity to monitor and evaluate programmes and to assess impact is critical: it enables practitioners to learn from best practice.
- Social service practitioner roles were discussed: these included the roles of broker, mediator, educator, facilitator, mobilisation of groups and communities, advocacy, community action research, social policy and planning and innovation.

CRITICAL THINKING QUESTIONS

1. How can social security be reformulated to progressively provide a minimum standard of living for all people? Motivate your answer.
2. What are the essential components of a comprehensive social security system from a social development perspective?
3. Do you think that expenditure on social assistance compromises economic growth and prosperity? Give reasons for your answer.
4. Do you agree with the view that social security provision leads to dependency? Motivate your position.
5. Discuss the roles of the social service practitioner in securing the safety net.

Bibliography

ARDINGTON, E and LUND, F. (1995), Pensions and development: Social security as complementary to programmes of reconstruction and development. *Development Southern Africa,* 12, 557–578.

BALL, R.M. (1978), *Social Security. Today and Tomorrow.* New York: Columbia University Press.

BHORAT, H. (2003), A universal income grant scheme for South Africa: An empirical assessment. In Standing, G. and Samson, M. (2003). *A basic income grant for South Africa* (107–123). Cape Town: University of Cape Town Press.

COMMITTEE OF INQUIRY INTO A COMPREHENSIVE SOCIAL SECURITY SYSTEM FOR SOUTH AFRICA (2002), *Transforming the Present – Protecting the Future. Draft Consolidated Report.*

CASE (COMMUNITY AGENCY FOR SOCIAL ENQUIRY) (1998), *Social Security for People with Disabilities.* Researched for the Department of Welfare. Johannesburg: CASE.

CASE (COMMUNITY AGENCY FOR SOCIAL ENQUIRY) (2000), *Phasing in the Child Support Grant. A social impact study.* Researched for the Department of Welfare. Johannesburg: CASE.

DAHL, E., ANDERS, J., DRÕPPING, and LODEMEL, I. (2001), Norway: relevance of the social development model for post-war welfare policy. *International Social Welfare,* 10,300–308.

DEPARTMENT OF SOCIAL DEVELOPMENT (2003), *Annual Report, 2002–2003.* Pretoria: Department of Social Development.

DEPARTMENT OF SOCIAL DEVELOPMENT FACT SHEET. (2003), *Fact Sheet: Extension of the Child Support Grant* Press Briefing by Minister Zola Skweyiya.

DEPARTMENT OF WELFARE AND POPULATION DEVELOPMENT (1997), *The White Paper for Social Welfare.* General Notice 1108 of 1997. Pretoria: Government Printers.

LUND COMMITTEE (1996), *Report of the Lund Committee on Child and Family Support.* Pretoria: Department of Welfare.

DIEDEN, S. and GUSTAFSSON, B. (2003), Child poverty in South Africa: an assessment based on microdata for 1995. *International Journal of Social Welfare* 12, 326–338.

DIXON, J. (2000), A global ranking of national social security systems. *International Social Security Review*, 53, 109–122.

ESPING-ANDERSON, G. (1990), *The Three Worlds of Welfare Capitalism.* Cambridge: Polity.

FINANCIAL MAIL (2004), *Chains of poverty*. October 2004.

GELB, S. *(2003),* Inequality in South Africa: Nature, causes and responses. Unpublished Research Report. Johannesburg: The EDGE.

GIDDENS, A. (2001), *Sociology* (4th ed.) Oxford: Blackwell Publishing.

INTERNATIONAL LABOUR OFFICE (1989), *World Labour Report.* Geneva, International Labour Office.

KASEKE, E. (2000), The challenges of extending social security to the poor: an African perspective. Unpublished paper. International Council on Social Welfare Biennial Conference, Cape Town, South Africa; 23–27 October- 16 pp.

KASEKE, E. (1998), Introduction. In Kaseke, E. (ed.), *Social security systems in rural Zimbabwe*. (v-ix). Harare, Zimbabwe: Friederich Ebert Stiftung.

KASENTE, D. (2000), Gender and social security reform in Africa. *International Social Security Review.* 53, 27–41.

KIRST-ASHMAN, K. and HULL, G. H. (2002), *Understanding Generalist Practice.* California: Brooks/Cole Thomson Learning.

LLOYD, I. (2000), Policy Performance of the Child Support Grant. 1 April 1998 to 30 June 1999. Unpublished M.M. dissertation. University of the Witwatersrand, Johannesburg.

LUND, F. (2002), Social Security and the Changing Labour Market. *Journal of Social Dynamics* 28, 177–206.

MARTIN, P. (2003), Vigilance and participation key to improvements. *Children First.* Alliance for Children's Entitlement to Social Security (ACESS). Special Edition: 37–41.

MIDGLEY, J. and KASEKE, E. (1996), Challenges to Social Security in Developing Countries: Coverage and Poverty in Zimbabwe. In Midgley, J and Tracy, M.B. *Challenges to Social Security. An International Exploration*. (103–122). Westport, Connecticut: Greenwood Publishing Company.

MOLEFE, S.P. (1996), An overview of characteristics of self-help organisations amongst Blacks in South Africa – A historical perspective. *Social Work/Maatskaplike Werk,* 32, 173–178.

MOLLER, V. and SOTSHONGAYE, A. (1996), "My family eat this money too": Pension sharing and self-respect among Zulu grandmothers. *Southern African Journal of Gerontology*, 5, 9–19.

MUKUKA, L., KALIKITI, W and MUSENGE, D. (2002), Social Security Systems in Zambia. *Journal of Social Development in Africa.* 17, 65–96.

OLIVIER, M.P. (2003a), The concept of social security. In Olivier, M. P., Smit, N. Kalula, E.R. (eds.), *Social Security: A Legal Analysis.* (23–47). Durban, LexisNexis, Butterworths.

PATEL, L. (1992), *Restructuring Social Welfare. Options for South Africa.* Braamfontein, Johannesburg: Ravan Press.

PIERSON, C. (1994), *Dismantling the Welfare State? Reagan, Thatcher and the Politics of Retrenchment.* Cambridge: Cambridge University Press

Republic of South Africa National Treasury (2004), *Estimates of National Expenditure 2004.* Pretoria: National Treasury.

Republic of South Africa National Treasury (2003), *Intergovernmental Fiscal Review.* Pretoria: National Treasury.

Republic of South Africa (2001), National Treasury. Minister of Finance, *Budget Speech*. 21 February. Pretoria.

Republic of South Africa (1996), *The Constitution of the Republic of South Africa.* Act 108 of 1996. Pretoria: Government Printers.

Sagner, A. (2000), Ageing and Social Policy in South Africa: Historical Perspectives with Particular Reference to the Eastern Cape. *Journal of Southern African Studies,* 26, 523–553.

Samson, M., Haarman, C., Haarman, D., MacQuene, van Niekerk, I., Khthi, G., Babson, O. and Stevens, A. (2003), The social, economic, and fiscal impact of a basic income grant for South Africa. In Standing, G. and Sampson, M. (2003). *A basic income grant for South Africa.* (19–38). Cape Town: University of Cape Town Press.

Samson, M. (2002), The Social, Economic and Fiscal Impact of Comprehensive Social Security Reform for South Africa. *Social Dynamics,* 28, 69–97.

Seekings, J. (2002), The Broader Importance of Welfare Reform in South Africa. *Journal of Social Dynamics*, 28, 1–38.

Sherraden, M. (2003), Alternative approaches to meeting global needs: Introduction. *Journal of Social Development Issues,* 25, 1–11.

Smith Committee (1995), *Report of the committee on strategy and policy review of retirement provision in South Africa.* Pretoria: Department of Finance.

Statistics South Africa (2003), *Census 2001*: Pretoria.

Statistics South Africa (1997), *Income and Expenditure Survey 1995,* Pretoria.

Subbarao, K., Bonnerjee, A., Braithwaite, J., Carvalho, S., Ezemenari, K., Graham, C and Thompson, A. (1997), *Safety Net Programs and Poverty Reduction. Lessons from Cross-Country Experience.* Washington DC: The World Bank

Triegaardt, J. (In press). The Child Support Grant in South Africa: a social policy for poverty alleviation? *International Journal of Social Welfare.*

Van der Berg, S. (1998), Ageing, public finance and social security in South Africa. *Southern African Journal of Gerontology,* 7, 3–9.

Van der Berg, S. (2001), Social Policy to address Poverty. In Bhorat, H., Leibbrandt, M., Maziya, M., Van der Berg, S. and Woolard, I. *Fighting Poverty. Labour Markets and Inequality in South Africa,* (171–204). Lansdowne:UCT Press.

Van der Berg, S. and Bredenkamp, C. (2002), Devising Social Security Interventions for Maximum Poverty Impact. *Social Dynamics,* 28, 39–68.

Vorster, J. and Rossouw, H. (1997), Transforming state support for children and families in South Africa: Single mother households footing the bill? *Social Work/Maatskaplike Werk.* 33, 315–327.

United Nations (2000), *Enhancing Social Protection and Reducing Vulnerability in a Globalising World: Report of the Secretary-General.* 39th session of the Commission for Social Development. New York: Commission for Social Development.

Wamhoff, S. and Burman,S. (2002), Parental Maintenance for Children: How the Private Maintenance System might be Improved. *Journal of Social Dynamics,* 28, 146–176.

Walker, C. (1994), Managing poverty. *Sociology Review*, April.

CHAPTER

6 Developmental social welfare services

LEARNING OUTCOMES

After you have read this chapter you should be able to:

- Explain the paradigm shift from a social treatment model of welfare service delivery to developmental welfare services.
- Identify the policy and legislative foundations for service provision.
- Provide an overview of the nature and scope of development services with reference to services for:
  - Children, youth and families
  - Older persons
  - People with disabilities
  - People infected and affected by HIV/AIDS
  - People affected by crime and violence
  - People affected by substance abuse.
- Critically discuss the achievements and challenges in the implementation of developmental welfare services.

The paradigm shift in service delivery

The new direction for developmental welfare services requires a *shift in the paradigm* of welfare service delivery from a social treatment model to a developmental service delivery model. A *paradigm* refers to a set of issues, interests, practices and institutional arrangements that characterise professional welfare service delivery in a particular historical period. A paradigm also refers to the knowledge base and values that inform a particular approach – in this case to welfare services (Bilton et al 2002). The evolution of social welfare from colonialism and apartheid to a welfare system in a democratic society was described in Chapters 3 and 4. This shift from an apartheid and remedial welfare model required a dramatic break with past policies and practices.

Social treatment model of welfare services

The welfare service delivery model inherited from the past was based on a *social treatment approach* to service delivery that was informed by the medical model with its sole emphasis on remediation, social pathology and individual clinical practice. This approach relied increasingly on psychological theories to explain human behaviour and social conditions. It was based on an understanding of deficits, which needed to be diagnosed and treated. The values and attitudes underpinning this approach were paternalistic, and the approach was piecemeal in its interventions; this tended to disempower and isolate individuals from the mainstream of society (Bilton et al 2002).

There was also an over-reliance on institutional care of vulnerable populations; welfare policy and services were racially discriminatory and favoured the white population with limited services provided for black and disadvantaged people. In 1995, close to 87 percent of the welfare services budget was spent on residential care for the elderly, children, persons with disabilities and treatment and care for substance misuse. This extremely costly model involved the provision of welfare facilities and services that were largely subsidised by the state and delivered by voluntary welfare organisations. A small proportion of services and facilities were provided directly by the state. The cost per person for institutional care at that time ranged between R11 000 and R22 000 per annum (van der Berg 1998). Around 6 680 residential and non-residential facilities provided services to 325 471 people, which demonstrates the limited reach and small number of beneficiaries served nationally (Department of Welfare and Population Development 1997).

Racial disparities were most prevalent in the provision of welfare services, which were unevenly and unequally distributed between the different provinces when the new government was elected in 1994 (Department of Welfare 1997). At that time, the Western Cape Province spent almost four times more on welfare services than the Eastern Cape, which had the least developed service infrastructure. Provinces that had the largest white and coloured population groups, such as the Western Cape, Northern Cape and Gauteng, were better served (van der Berg 1998:13).

A small percentage of the total welfare budget was spent on professional social work services and capital expenditure projects amounting to 13 percent of total welfare expenditure in 1994/1995. The number of social work posts that were subsidised by the state in the voluntary welfare sector was 2 079 at the end of 1994. The funding formula provided almost exclusively for the delivery of casework and statutory services delivered to individuals and families based on social worker caseload ratios. There were also differences in allocations to services for vulnerable populations, with children and family services receiving the largest allocation of 41 percent followed by the elderly, who received 39 percent of the total budget allocation of R1.1 billion in 1995/1996. People with disabilities received 12 percent of the total allocation, followed by substance misuse (4 percent) and services to offenders (3 percent). Community centres were allocated less than one percent of the budget, which reflected the low priority given to community-based services.

In sum, the welfare service delivery model inherited from the past was inequitable and discriminatory. It was also dominated by institutional care, and services delivered were primarily of a therapeutic and rehabilitative nature with statutory services being provided largely in relation to child protection and juvenile justice. Welfare services were also delivered to specialised client groups by specialised agencies which evolved over the years to deliver services to children and families, services for the elderly, people with disabilities, substance misuse and the rehabilitation of

'....the welfare service delivery model inherited from the past was inequitable and discriminatory.'

offenders among others. These organisations have a significant service delivery infrastructure and have built up valuable knowledge in serving particular client populations. The service delivery model inherited from the past was limited in its reach and impact and addressed needs in a fragmented way. It is also an expensive model in that it requires large numbers of professionally trained social workers to implement it as the principal professional actors in the delivery of services. The primary method of service delivery was one-to-one interventions that had a limited reach in terms of the numbers of beneficiaries who could be served. In 1995 there were around 8 000 social workers registered with the South African Council for Social and Associated Workers who were located mainly in urban areas where welfare services were most developed. This model of service delivery was considered to be inappropriate and unsustainable and could not address the challenges of service provision in a post-apartheid society.

Developmental model of welfare services

The new *developmental model of welfare services* breaks significantly with the remedial service delivery model of the past and posits a completely new paradigm and path for welfare services in a democratic society. The character of the developmental model of welfare services encompasses the overall conception of social development outlined in Chapters 1 and 4. The themes of the new paradigm are: a rights-based approach, economic and social development, participation, welfare pluralism (also referred to as social development partnerships) and bridging the micro-macro divide in the conceptualisation of social problems and social service practice. The following features distinguish the developmental welfare service delivery model:

- rights-based approach to service delivery;
- integrated family-centred and community-based services;
- generalist approach to service delivery; and
- community development and developmental welfare services.

Rights-based approach to service delivery

The founding values and beliefs of the Constitution of the Republic of South Africa No 108 of 1996, the international instruments and conventions to which South Africa subscribes, and the country's policies and legislation provide the over-arching framework for the delivery of developmental welfare services. The rights-based approach to social development was explained in Chapter 4.

Human rights are the foundation of social development and meeting needs is not sufficient: the promotion, protection and defence of the rights of those who are vulnerable and at risk are an integral part of sustainable human development. This means that services delivered to populations at risk should *focus on both needs and rights*, as rights cannot be realised if the needs of people are not met. Service delivery approached from this point of view operates at two levels: the *culture of the organisation*, and the *strategies of service delivery*. A human rights culture in a developmental welfare organisation refers to the values, beliefs, assumptions and expectations that underlie the workings and ethos of the organisation. Many social service organisations in South Africa are still working within an older cultural frame of reference. The transformation of welfare services requires the adoption of new principles and values that are pertinent to organisational change and development in the new context and the skills of effecting organisational change and building a rights-based culture in the organisation (discussed in Chapter 9).

The second level of operation of the rights-based approach refers to the infusion of human rights values and principles into service delivery strategies. It relates to what kind of developmental services are delivered and how these services can be delivered. Consider the delivery of developmental welfare services to populations at risk. Populations at risk are defined as 'groups of people with some identified characteristics who are at greater risk of social and economic deprivation than those in the mainstream. (Kirst-Ashman 2003:21). Whilst the needs and rights of all people in the society are of concern to developmental welfare, its focus is on those who are most disadvantaged. Developmental welfare service agencies provide services to populations at risk, which may include some or all of the following types of services that play a vital role in enforcing rights. These are services that:

'Populations at risk are defined as groups of people with some identified characteristics who are at greater risk of social and economic deprivation than those in the mainstream.'

- *Protect* the rights of different client populations through the implementation of national legislation for children, juveniles, the elderly, and rehabilitation services for people abusing substances and those affected by domestic violence. Social service professionals are directly involved in implementing legislation to protect the rights of those who are likely to be exploited, neglected, violated and discriminated against because of vulnerability or who are at risk of exposure to such situations. These types of services are also commonly referred to as statutory services in South Africa.
- *Promote rights* through educating people about their rights and duties.
- *Facilitate access* to rights and optimally use opportunities, including educational opportunities, health care services and applications for social assistance, to give effect to such rights.
- *Challenge* policies and practices that do not uphold rights.
- *Advocate* policies and social programmes that promote rights and that meet needs.

Finally, individuals and client populations are *subjects of rights*. This means that they are not the passive receivers of rights – they are active partners with those working for the realisation of rights and together they have a shared interest. Client groups should therefore be involved in decisions that affect them, in realising their rights and in honouring their responsibilities. Developmental welfare organisations that adopt a rights-based approach will need to align their policies and programmes with human rights. This will present service agencies with many value and ethical dilemmas, especially for those agencies that are actively engaged with government in the delivery of services and that are advocates for the rights of populations at risk. Values and ethical dilemmas that confront practitioners working from a rights-based perspective are discussed in Chapter 7 and anti-discriminatory theory and practice to promote equality and prevent unfair discrimination on grounds of race, sex, gender, marital status, colour, sexual orientation, ethnic or social origin, age, disability, religion, belief, culture, language and birth is discussed in Chapter 9.

Integrated family-centred and community-based social welfare services

Internationally, the limitations of the social treatment model of service delivery are being recognised, and this has resulted in the search for new models of social service delivery. In the United Kingdom, community care policies have been adopted to help people lead more integrated lives in local communities rather than be separated from them. There is a renewed interest in community-oriented social work and social services that are integrated, generic, decentralised and more accessible, and in those that have a quicker response and are focused not only on social treatment but also early intervention and prevention (Hadley & Leidy 1996).

As early as 1988, the United Nations advocated family-centred and community-based strategies as a guiding principle of developmental social welfare (United Nations 1988). Community-oriented social services have been adapted to local and cultural conditions in many African countries as a more appropriate way of addressing the intractable social problems and limited resources in developing countries. It is in these contexts that family-centred and community-based strategies are being pioneered through innovative strategies such as home-based and community care and development. In Uganda, Malawi and Zambia, community mobilisation strategies are being employed to address needs through different models such as home- and community-care strategies, volunteerism, capacity-building of community members and the mobilisation of grassroots groups to address the needs of people infected and affected by HIV/AIDS (Donahue & Williamson 1999). In South Africa, similar community-based approaches to meeting needs and promoting well-being are being widely advocated by many different government departments. These include the promotion of community and primary health care; community mental health; safety and security; national youth service; literacy and culture; and sport and recreation. Social policies stress the importance of the community as the context and the locus within which services and development are

'Social policies stress the importance of the community as the context and the locus within which services and development are promoted.'

promoted. In the context of the new policy, a family-centred approach is based on the assumption that various family forms and structures exist and that a broader conception of the family is envisaged which includes, extended families, single-parent families, same sex partnerships, foster families and nuclear families. South African households are therefore made up of many different family forms and all these are recognised when reference is made to family-centred or household centred approaches.

The *White Paper for Social Welfare* (Department of Welfare 1997) advocated individual, family and community empowerment through integrated services or 'one-stop' services that would be multi-purpose in nature and locally accessible. In this way, developmental welfare services were to be sustained and expanded to under-serviced communities. Family- and community-based services directed specifically at populations at risk were advocated as part of a network of integrated community-based developmental welfare services.

These services were to be established in collaboration with families, community and faith-based organisations and indigenous social and community networks to provide care and social support and promote community well-being. This approach is based on the idea that the local sphere of action and interaction is the most appropriate way to build organisational linkages between different role-players who are able to pool their resources, knowledge and experience of local conditions to meet needs. The local sphere is also the space where the day-to-day lives of people are lived, where there is the direct interface between the personal, household, family, neighbourhood, community and where social and economic and political processes take place. This approach builds on South Africa's rich tradition of formal welfare, faith-based organisations and informal community-based groups that are already involved in the provision of support and social care, a safety net in times of need and volunteerism. However, caution should be exercised in how family-centred and community based strategies are designed so that these do not reinforce the disproportionate responsibility that women and poor households have to bear in providing social and community care to populations at risk. The challenge is to design and implement programmes that promote gender equality and that attempt to shift the burdens and costs of care more equally between men and women and between the state, the family, community and the market.

Generalist approach to service delivery

Social development embraces the generalist approach to social service delivery and social work practice. Drawing on the dimensions of generalist practice identified by Landon (1995:1102) and the formulation of Kirst-Ashman & Hull (2002:6–8), the *generalist approach to social service delivery* incorporates multiple levels of intervention – including work with individuals, families, groups, organisations and communities. Generalist service delivery is based on the planned change model (Kirst-Ahsman & Hull 2002), which is designed to work with client systems of *different sizes* and a *diversity of client populations* and *contexts* in an integrated manner. A broad, eclectic knowledge base informing the approach is essential in that it draws on social science, human behaviour and developmental theories of social welfare. The central philosophical concepts under-girding the approach draw from both private issues and social justice concerns (Landon 1995:1103). Theories and conceptual frameworks informing practice should be compatible with the ideas, philosophy and practice modalities of the developmental approach to social welfare services. The appropriate selection of knowledge to inform practice is discussed further in Chapter 7.

Kirst-Ashman & Hull (2002:7-8) identify *four related processes of generalist social work practice* that are pertinent to the generalist approach to service delivery. Firstly, developmental services are delivered by a variety of *state and non-state organisations* that are structured differently but provide the framework within which services are delivered, evaluated and monitored. Professionals, paraprofessionals and associated social service professionals are employed in social service organisations; their peers also supervise them and informal community organisations are accountable to the people being served and the sponsors of the services. Social service and social work practitioners are also guided by the *values and ethics* of the social work and service professions set by the South African Council for Social Service Professions. Secondly, those employed in social service organisations assume a wide range of *roles* and require a variety of *skills* to work with all client systems and in a *variety of practice fields*. Instead of using only one skill, such as social work with individuals, and working with specialised client populations such as children only, generalist services and practitioners work with diverse needs and problems and require skills to work with client systems of different sizes. Thirdly, generalist social services and practitioners employ *critical reflective skills* to appropriately apply knowledge and practice to different contexts. Finally, developmental welfare services emphasise the empowerment of individuals, families, groups and communities to manage human relations, social problems and needs optimally whilst building on the strengths of client systems.

'Finally, developmental welfare services emphasise the empowerment of individuals, families, groups and communities to manage human relations, social problems and needs optimally whilst building on the strengths of client systems.'

The concept of *empowerment* is central to the ethos of generalist services in that it focuses not on individual pathology and inadequacies but draws instead on people's strengths, also referred to as assets. The strengths perspective for Saleebey (1997) focuses on challenges and opportunities presented by situations, the achievement of goals and aspirations, collaboration with client systems and the full utilisation of environmental resources and opportunities. Empowerment is also concerned with addressing the social and economic inequalities inherent in the way in which society is structured and organised, which lead to social and economic exclusion and experiences of marginalisation.

Social divisions based on race, gender, sexual preference, religion, language, ethnicity, disability and geographic location or any other socially constructed characteristics that differentiate people in a society may also lead to social and political exclusion and interpersonal isolation and alienation from the mainstream of the society.

'The concept of empowerment is central to the ethos of generalist services in that it focuses not on individual pathology and inadequacies but draws instead on people's strengths, also referred to as assets.'

Community development and developmental welfare services

Community development is widely recognised in social work and the social service professions as the intervention strategy most suited to addressing poverty, community participation and empowerment and social and economic development (Maritz & Coughlan 2004; Lombard 1996; Gray 1996). The developmental welfare policy proposed that the community development approach be used to re-orient service delivery from a treatment model to a developmental welfare service model. This was to be achieved through the application of a range of community development interventions such as the planning and development of community-based services and community care, self-help and mutual aid, community education, building of local institutions, economic development, civic engagement through participation in volunteerism and community service, social relief and advocacy (Department of Welfare 1997).

From the perspective of the new policy, the term *community development* is conceptualised broadly as an umbrella concept referring to different intervention strategies that combine the efforts of the people themselves with government to improve the economic, social, cultural and environmental conditions of communities. The interventions outlined above can be categorised into different practice models, which resonate to some extent with widely accepted models of community development practice such as: locality development or self help; and social planning also referred to as technical assistance and advocacy (Green & Haines 2002; Rothman 1995). Other practice models have also been identified such as community education and social marketing (Weyers 2001). An additional practice model that has emerged from the new policy on developmental welfare relates to the relationship between social and economic development and the need for community development interventions to contribute to poverty reduction. The Sustainable Livelihoods Framework has been widely advocated as a means of improving the livelihood outcomes of the poor through increasing income, reducing vulnerability, strengthening of social networks, improving the utilisation of resources and opportunities and promoting a more sustainable environment. This approach has been promoted by development agencies in the developing world but has not been successfully integrated with community development. Brocklesby and Fisher (2003) argue for a stronger link between achieving sustainable livelihoods and community development, which could be considered to be an additional practice mode that could inform interventions in poverty-reduction programmes.

Community development is multi-disciplinary in nature and evolved in developing countries to promote social development, especially in the colonial era. The United Nations later adopted it in the 1960s to denote economic and social development – although this was of a conservative nature based on modernisation theory and the economic growth models. In the 1990s, social development re-emerged after the failure of the economic growth models to improve the quality of people's lives. Community development has become associated with social development, participation and empowerment and people-centred human development. South African welfare policy acknowledges the special role that community development interventions can make in achieving the goals of social development. Social workers and social service professionals also contribute to community development along with other disciplines and social sectors such as health and education. Traditionally, the terms community work and community organisation have been used to refer to community work as a method of social work practice. However, the community development practice models referred to above are compatible with developmental social work and social services and refer to different modes of intervention.

'Community development has become associated with social development, participation and empowerment and people-centred human development.'

In summary, the features of the developmental approach to social welfare service delivery include the rights-based approach, integrated family-centred and community-based services and generalist service delivery and social work practice. Community development strategies and practice modalities are considered to be appropriate interventions to address poverty and underdevelopment in communities.

Table 6.1: Summary of two approaches to service delivery

Social treatment approach to service delivery	Developmental welfare approach to service delivery
• Inequitable and discriminatory. • Informed by the medical model. • Focus is on remediation, social pathology, client deficits, individual clinical practice and institutional care. • Paternalistic and piecemeal interventions. • Relies on social worker as principal professional actor. • Low impact and expensive.	• Informed by rights based approach to development. • Focus on social and economic development; empowerment; participation, pro-poor and populations at risk; partnerships. • Generalist practice combines macro and micro strategies; denotes interventions at different levels and with client groups of different sizes. • Integrated family-centred and community based social welfare services. • Collaborative involvement of a range of professions and non-professionals in service delivery. • High impact and cost effective.

Policy and legislation

Since 1994, policy and legislation have been formulated to bring these in line with the new constitutional and policy directions of the country. Some of the key policies and legislation that the Department of Social Development is mandated to implement are summarised in Table 6.2 below. Other relevant laws are referred to in the following chapters where appropriate. Social workers also implement legislation that is administered by other government departments such as the Departments of Justice, Health, Correctional Services and the South African Police Services. Furthermore, policy and legislation are also being aligned with international standard-setting instruments of the United Nations System and they now form part of international law. South Africa is accountable for promoting and protecting these rights both domestically and internationally. Many different international human rights treaties are applicable to the vulnerable populations for whom welfare services are being provided in South Africa. The overall human rights framework for welfare services is set by the *International Covenant on Economic, Social and Cultural Rights*, which was signed by the South African government in 1994 but has not yet been ratified. The *International Covenant on Civil and Political Rights* was ratified by the South African government in 1998.

Table 6.2: Policy and Legislative Mandates for Developmental Welfare Services

Policy and Legislation	Policy Intentions
White Paper for Social Welfare, Notice 1108 of 1997	The *White Paper* set out the principles, guidelines, proposed policies and programmes for developmental social welfare in South Africa. As the primary policy document, the White Paper serves as the foundation for social welfare in a post-apartheid era.
Financing Policy Notice 463 of 1999	The *Financing Policy* sought to transform welfare services; to promote universal access to services that are differentiated and integrated; it identified service levels, namely: prevention, early intervention, statutory processes and a continuum of care and developmental services. The policy was to be an instrument in achieving the paradigm shift in welfare service delivery and provided for Developmental Quality Assurance to promote effective and efficient delivery of services.
Aged Persons Act No 81 of 1967; Aged Persons Amendment Act 44 of 1994	The Act regulates the provision of services for the elderly, and the registration of homes for the elderly. The amendments in 1994 provided for the repeal of certain discriminatory provisions in the Act and other administrative matters. The Act is being redrafted and the Older Persons Bill has been presented to parliament. The Bill provides for the protection, well-being and empowerment of older persons; registration of facilities, accommodation and care; and for programmes for the development of older persons.

Policy and Legislation	Policy Intentions
Child Care Act No 74 of 1983 as amended Act No 96 of 1996	This Act was passed to protect children against neglect and abuse and to provide for the placement of children in alternative care. The amendments in 1996: • shifted the focus of the Act from the unable or unfit parent to the child in need of care; • protected children at risk through the creation of a National Child Protection Register; • extended the inspection of children's homes and places of care; • provided for the registration of street shelters; • extended the application of the Act to the whole of the Republic of South Africa; • provided a broader definition of marriage to include customary marriages; and • provided for legal representation of children in Children's Court proceedings. Further amendments were enacted in 1999, which provided for the establishment of secure care facilities and for the prohibition against the commercial exploitation of children. The South African law Commission was mandated to work with state and non-state partners to draft a new children's Bill for South Africa. The Bill has been presented to parliament. The new children's Bill addresses certain key aspects to promote the rights and well-being of children. These include: the definition of the rights and responsibilities of children; the definition of parental responsibilities and rights; the establishment of principles and guidelines for the protection of children and the promotion of their well-being; the regulation of matters concerning the protection of children and the well-being of children, especially those who are most vulnerable.
Prevention and Treatment of Drug Dependency Act No 20 of 1992	The Act provides for the establishment and implementation of a Central Drug Authority, the establishment of programmes for the prevention and treatment of drug dependency, the establishment of treatment centres and hostels and committal of persons to detention, treatment and training in such treatment centres. The Act was amended in 1996 to extend the application of the Act to the whole of South Africa and to establish a Central Drug Authority.
Probation Service Act No 116 of 1991	The Act provides for the establishment and implementation of programmes aimed at combating crime and for the rendering of assistance to and treatment of certain persons involved in crime. The Child Justice Bill has been introduced to parliament and makes provision for the institutionalisation of the restorative justice approach to juvenile justice.
Domestic Violence Act 116 of 1998	The Act provides for the protection of individuals against physical, sexual, emotional, verbal, psychological and economic abuse and for the prevention of violence and the provision of supportive services. Provision is made in the Act for protection orders prohibiting abuse.

Source: Department of Social Development. http://www.socdev.gov.za/Legislation/Legal.htm.

Client populations and the nature and scope of developmental services

The nature and scope of services for selected client populations are discussed with reference to children, youth and families; older persons; people with physical and mental disabilities; and those infected and affected by HIV/AIDS. Crime prevention and restorative justice and substance abuse will also be addressed. In each section a brief overview of the context will be provided, and this will be followed by the major thrusts and selected new directions for developmental social services.

Social services for children, youth and families

Context. Poverty, a lack of employment and access to social services, food insecurity, the fragmentation of the family and alienation from kinship and the community are some of the factors contributing to the declining quality of family life in South Africa. In addition, families are also faced with special needs and problems due to the HIV/AIDS pandemic, which has resulted in the loss of caregivers, increasing numbers of orphaned and vulnerable children and rising numbers of child-headed households. This situation is also compounded by other social problems such as substance abuse, family violence, problems in human relations and a lack of family and community support systems. Social changes in the society have also resulted in the changing structure of families such as changing national and regional migration patterns and changes in the traditional roles of women and men. The effects of past policies and current economic and social stresses contribute to feelings of powerlessness and frustration and hamper the capacity of families to function optimally. The traditional notion of the family as a nuclear family is contested and is evolving as reflected in a 2004 Court ruling that acknowledged marriages between same sex partners.

'Social changes in the society have also resulted in the changing structure of families such as changing national and regional migration patterns and changes in the traditional roles of women and men.'

Large numbers of South Africans do not find themselves in traditional nuclear or extended families. Households may be made up of different generations of families and may be bound by kinship, social and economic ties and/or marriage. Single-parent households, especially female-headed households, are a common family form, and these households are most vulnerable to poverty. A diversity of families exists: some are made up of gay and lesbian families. South African families are also beginning to reflect the racial, religious and cultural diversity of the society.

The Human Development Index and the Human Poverty Index, measured in terms of indices for life expectancy, education and income, declined between 1995 and 2002. Unemployment and the effects of AIDS on life expectancy are the main reasons cited for the declining human development situation. About half of the country's population has an income that falls below the poverty line of R533 per adult per month, and

10.5 percent of the population is estimated to earn less than US $1 per day (UNDP 2004). In 2002, poverty among Africans was eight times greater than that of whites and single-parent families and 'couples with children' are over-represented among the poor. Just over a quarter of the poor are single-parent families, with the Eastern Cape having the highest proportion of poor people in the country (UNDP 2004).

A lack of food results in malnutrition, stunting, child morbidity and mortality. South Africa's national infant mortality rate was reported as 45 per 1000 live births, with under-five-year mortality rates rising steadily – most likely due to the HIV/AIDS pandemic. The National Food Consumption Survey cited in UNDP Report (2004) found that 23 percent of children suffered from nutritional disorders and about 22 percent of households reported that they were experiencing hunger. The Service Deprivation Index (SDI) is a measure used to assess the extent to which households have access to basic services such as housing, energy, water, sanitation facilities and refuse removal services. Approximately 7.2 million (65 percent) of households were found to be deprived of access to these basic services and the situation was found to be most severe in the KwaZulu-Natal, Eastern Cape and Limpopo provinces (UNDP 2004). A significant achievement has been in increasing access to education, with 90 percent of all children between seven and fifteen years attending school. However, the quality of education and poor infrastructure remain major challenges.

Poverty levels for young children (0–6 years), older children (7–14 years) and female-headed households is much worse than that of the general population (van der Berg & Bredenkamp 2002). With regard to orphans and vulnerable children and those living in exceptionally difficult circumstances, the impact of HIV/AIDS on the protection, growth and development of children is a major public issue. Consider the following statistics based on a National Household HIV Prevalence and Risk Survey of South African children (Human Sciences Research Council 2004)

- The HIV prevalence rate among children 2 to 18 years of age is 5.4 percent and the maternal orphan rate is estimated to be 3.3 percent.
- A tenth of children are estimated to have lost a parent/caregiver by 9 years of age and 15 percent have lost a parent or a caregiver by age 14.
- Children of African descent, children in poor households and children living in informal settlements are most affected.
- 3 percent of children between 12 and 18 years indicated that they were heads of households.

Youth in the 18-35 year age group are more likely to be unemployed, with more women being unemployed than men. Youth are estimated to constitute 70 percent of the unemployed nationally if a broader definition is used, which includes discouraged and passive unemployment. Although significant numbers of youth have a secondary education, they lack appropriate vocational skills and employment opportunities. The psychosocial impact of unemployment can lead to a loss of self-esteem, confidence and a lack of recognised social status and identity in the family and community. Chronically unemployed youth are also at risk of engaging in high-risk behaviours such as substance abuse, crime and violence, and 10 percent of youth aged 15–24 years are HIV positive.

Major thrusts of services. The social development approach to welfare services for children, youth and families is based on the following major thrusts of services

- **Family as the basic unit of society.** This recognises that the family is the basic unit of society and plays a key role in the survival, protection and development of children under 18 years of age. Families should be supported and their capability should be strengthened to meet the needs of their members. Family and community support of youth is vital in making the transition from childhood to adulthood, from school to work and to becoming productive, proactive and responsible citizens of the society.
- **Continuum of services**. Families require a range of supportive services to promote family survival and development. At the one end of the continuum, financial and material resources are needed: for example, employment and a means to earn a livelihood, social security and food security. Other basic services that are essential to the social development of the family are housing, health, education, energy, and water and sanitation services. These basic services are essential to the protection of the family unit, the physical and emotional well-being of the family and building the human capabilities of its members. Beyond these services, some families may require additional supportive services to solve problems in human relations such as conflict, communication, parenting concerns, substance abuse, family violence and addressing problems arising from life changes and events. The required supportive social services may be limited, moderate or extensive in nature. Services may also include child protection services and substitute care of children through foster care and institutional care.
- **Multiple service strategies**. A range of methods of service delivery are possible – from counselling and peer counselling; to mutual aid and self-help; to family-centred, home and community-based care; to support and community development interventions. These services are the least restrictive and most flexible, whilst child protective services and substitute care are more restrictive and may require more specialised interventions.
- **Balance of intervention strategies**. An approach to service delivery that balances rehabilitative, preventative and developmental interventions is needed. The Financing Policy (1998) identifies the following service delivery levels: prevention, early intervention, statutory processes and a continuum of care and developmental

'Families should be supported and their capability should be strengthened to meet the needs of their members.'

services. Over time, it is the intention of the policy that a paradigm shift will take place in the approach to service delivery from a social treatment perspective to an integrated developmental social welfare approach.

- **Shifting focus to redress**. This means that services should be more accessible and relevant to the basic needs of children and families within the context of the family and community (National Council for Child and Family Welfare 2002). Prevention and early intervention services and more family- and community-based development strategies to meet needs that have a high developmental impact and reach should be employed.
- **Diversity & gender sensitive social work** and social services should also be rendered. For instance, services will need to be sensitive to changing family structures and forms and will be provided in a form and language that are acceptable to the communities served (South African National Council for Child and Family Welfare 2002). An understanding of different cultural practices and how these impact on children and families is vital to the implementation of culturally sensitive projects and strategies. Gender-sensitive social work practice promotes equality between men and women and strives to address social attitudes and behaviours that are sexist, discriminatory and that stereotype the roles that men and women play in the society. The generalist approach to social work practice provides a sound intervention framework spanning micro, mezzo and macro practice including advocacy for change by placing women's needs, experiences, realities and choices at the centre of interventions (Kirst-Ashman & Hull 2002). This does not exclude interventions with men and these are discussed in the section on gender-based violence. A gender-sensitive social work practice and social services in South Africa needs to take account of the reality that women are poorer than men, have less access to land and agriculture, have less access to jobs and are more vulnerable to HIV/AIDS infection. The sexual division of labour in the home also results in women carrying a heavier load of household responsibilities. Lack of access to services such as walking great distances to collect water, illiteracy and experiences of disempowerment are barriers to access to services and opportunities (Goldblatt 2004). These common circumstances that women face impact negatively on women's health and emotional well being.
- **Rights and advocacy**. This entails the protection, promotion, facilitation of access to rights and advocacy. Innovative community-based strategies to reduce child vulnerability and protect rights are being implemented by child welfare organisations. Coalitions of child rights organisations are involved in advocacy for policy and legislation and increased access to resources to give effect to children's rights.

Protecting children in the community

Child welfare agencies deal with more than 20 000 abused children a year. A National Child Protection Programme was developed to promote the well-being of children in their communities through the delivery of accessible services and to mobilise communities to become partners in the creation of safe communities for children. One-stop 24-hour services for abused children and families are being piloted in the provinces in partnership with voluntary agencies, the South African Police Service and the Department of Justice. This programme has expanded access to community services.

'Isolobantwana – Eye on the Children Project, is a community-based programme to prevent child abuse and neglect that was started by the Cape Town Child Welfare Society. It is part of a national community mobilisation programme that enlists the support of volunteers to be the eye of the children in the community. Community child protection committees are established with the help of volunteers who work with the one-stop service. Fifteen communities that had a high incidence of child abuse were selected nationally. The pilot programmes are being implemented in these communities. The programme has trained staff, developed training materials, solicited the support of 455 volunteers and built partnerships with communities and government agencies.

Case example:

Fifteen-year-old 'Janet' was severely beaten with a hose-pipe by her drunk father because she refused to go to the *shebeen* to buy more alcohol for him. A neighbour called an *Isolobantwana* volunteer, who acted immediately. The volunteer took the child to hospital, as she was bleeding profusely from wounds to her upper body and head. The South African Police Services was called in to assist the volunteer. The child was diagnosed with concussion and hospitalised for the night. The next day the volunteer took 'Janet' to the supervising social worker, who began the child protection assessment and investigation.

Source: SA National Council for Child and Family Welfare; Cape Town Child Welfare Society.

8

- **Mainstreaming of youth development policies and programmes into existing developmental welfare interventions.** This involves collaboration with governmental and non-governmental agencies and the private sector in developing skills and employment programmes for youth at risk of becoming chronically unemployable through facilitating access to public works programmes, National Youth Service initiatives, learnerships, and micro-economic development and livelihood strategies. Psychosocial support to youth and families with conflict resolution and mediation, building self-esteem and responsibility, poverty alleviation and treatment with problems arising from the misuse of substances, teenage pregnancies and personal protection against HIV/AIDS should form part of a range of integrated and multi-pronged youth development services.

Tulethu and Thandeka – mentor and mentee with the Big Brother Big Sister organization and their mentorship programme for children at risk.

Young people learning computer skills.

Social services for older persons

Context. Due to declining fertility and increased life-expectancy, the ageing population is increasing rapidly on a global scale. It is estimated that the world population over 60 years of age will increase from 10 percent in 2002 to 22 percent over the next fifty years. The majority of the world's populations of older people (60 percent) live in the less developed countries. Poverty and social exclusion remain the main stumbling blocks to the realisation of the human rights of older people worldwide. The implications of these demographic changes are an increased demand for health care, social security, affordable housing and other basic social and welfare services. As people live longer, there are fewer young people working and paying taxes on their earnings, with fewer resources available for social programmes. How to address the needs and rights of a growing ageing population remains a major challenge – especially in the Southern African region, which has the largest number of older persons on the continent.

> *'How to address the needs and rights of a growing ageing population remains a major challenge – especially in the Southern African region, which has the largest number of older persons on the continent.'*

Consider the following statistics on ageing in the local context.

- In 2000, persons older than 60 years made up 2.8 million (7 percent) of the South African population. This number will increase to 4.6 million (11 percent) by 2025 and 6.5 million (14 percent) by 2050 (Department of Social Development 2002:4).

- In view of increased life expectancy, the white population is significantly older than the rest of the population. The majority of the elderly are African (67 percent) and whites make up 23 percent of the population over 60 years.
- The ageing structure varies across provinces. Most elderly people live in KwaZulu-Natal, Eastern Cape, Gauteng and Limpopo. The populations of the Eastern Cape, Western Cape and Limpopo provinces appear to have a larger number of older persons over the age of 80 years than other provinces (Noumbisi & Zuberi 2003). The rural population remains older than its urban counterpart. The Eastern Cape, KwaZulu-Natal, Limpopo, North West and Free State provinces have the largest number of people living below the national poverty line, with the first three provinces having the least access to basic services (United Nations Development Programme (UNDP 2003).
- The elderly are more likely to reside in extended households, which vary across racial groups. More white older persons live in nuclear households, whilst the elderly from other race groups tend to live in extended families and households (Noumbissi & Zuberi 2003:1).
- In South Africa, the ageing population differs not only by geographic location, household structure and racial and poverty profile, but also by sex. There are more women than men among the elderly – with 43 percent of women aged 65 or more being widowed compared with about 12 percent of older men (Noumbissi & Zuberi 2003).

Inadequate retirement provision, poverty, social exclusion, lack of access to basic services, health care, food insecurity and a lack of affordable accommodation are some of the challenges facing older persons. The growing HIV/AIDS pandemic has resulted in the loss of the middle generation, leaving the elderly more vulnerable to a lack of care. Older persons are also caring for children and grandchildren and many have limited knowledge of the epidemic. The abuse of the elderly is rising as a result of family pressures, poverty, overcrowding and inadequate accommodation. Older persons are also faced with negative perceptions and attitudes: this is known as ageism, which is similar to sexism and racism. *Ageism* also involves stereotyping and myths about the capabilities of elderly persons that may be experienced as disempowering and could lead to the social exclusion of the elderly.

'Older persons are also faced with negative perceptions and attitudes: this is known as ageism, which is similar to sexism and racism.'

Gender and ageing

The proportion of elderly women is expected to grow significantly in the future. Older women who are the least skilled continue to be excluded from economic participation in the society. Old age pensions reach three times more women, reflecting higher poverty levels among elderly women. Older women provide much-needed childcare and family support. This contribution is often not economically recognised because it is considered to be 'domestic' and an extension of their normal responsibilities (HelpAge 1999).

In many African countries, superstition has resulted in the homicide of older persons. HelpAge (1999) reports that in Tanzania 500 women are murdered every year after being accused of witchcraft. In Limpopo, an older person's hut was set ablaze because of accusations of superstition and a police task team was created to deal with such cases.

Widowhood has also led to disputes over inheritance of property and possessions. These situations have resulted in older women being driven from their homes and communities, leaving them destitute.

Major thrusts of services. The United Nations World Assembly on Ageing held in 2002 in Madrid in response to population ageing adopted a plan of action promoting the development of societies for all ages (United Nations 2002). Some of the key new directions for national and global action are:

- Promoting the human rights of older persons.
- Eradicating poverty and increasing access to services and to social protection.
- Facilitating participation in decision-making, in employment for those who want to work, optimising life-long learning opportunities and engagement in civic service and volunteering.
- Strengthening of solidarity through equity and reciprocity between generations.
- Facilitating the provision of a continuum of care and services for older persons from various sources. Family-centred and community-based care is proposed as the primary focus of support.
- Supporting the care-giving role of older persons, especially older women.

'Intergenerational approaches to tackling poverty and strengthening the livelihoods of the elderly constitute other new directions for service delivery.'

The new philosophy underpinning the care of older persons in post-1994 is in line with the transformation of welfare services and national and global strategies to enable older persons to live active, healthy and independent lives for as long as possible. The development of community-based support and caring models of service delivery with the family as the core support system is considered to be paramount. The mainstreaming of services for the elderly into developmental welfare service programmes is slowly taking root. Intergenerational approaches to tackling poverty and strengthening the livelihoods of the elderly constitute other new directions for service delivery. The 'Bread for thy neighbour' programme in Limpopo Province encourages children to provide care for older persons. An eight-year-old girl takes bread to the granny next door before she goes to school every day. Income-generation programmes that include children and the elderly are other examples of promoting intergenerational approaches to a lack of resources. These links are also evident in an income-generation programme run by elderly persons in Limpopo Province where they make school uniforms at reasonable costs. For those children who cannot afford uniforms, a free uniform is provided.

Grandmother (also known as Gogo in Zulu) caring for children in the community.

Aged persons who can no longer function in the community owing to physical and/or mental frailty or inadequate social circumstances are accommodated and looked after in care facilities such as homes for the aged. Non-governmental organisations (NGOs) and faith-based organisations that are government funded provide institutional care for the elderly, especially frail care services. These services are subsidised and are provided for those who qualify according to a means test. In 2001, there were 27 626 beds in old age homes run by NGOs (data supplied by the Department of Social Development 2001). Most of the elderly in these facilities are located in the Western Cape and Gauteng provinces. Past occupancy patterns continue into the present where the white elderly largely uses institutional care. However, in the more rural provinces, where poverty rates are high and where services are limited, community-based care and development programmes are increasingly being used to address the needs of the elderly – 17 459 NGO community projects were funded by government. These approaches are a viable way of providing services to older persons in the community at lower costs and of reaching more people; they are more appropriate in building an age-integrated society.

Reaching out

Aged-in-Action is expanding its outreach to under-served rural and peri-urban areas. The organisation has established over a 1 000 clubs for the elderly that reach out to about 10 000 people. The services include nutrition, livelihood projects, recreation, volunteering and a lending depot where assistive devices can be obtained. The elderly are trained as peer counsellors and render home-care and other services. Micro income-generation projects are also implemented and training programmes are planned to increase knowledge and understanding of HIV/AIDS and to provide care and support to families. For Aged-in-Action, these programmes posit a positive view of ageing that engages the elderly in productive activities that build intergenerational reciprocity and solidarity.

Source: Age-in-Action. (2002–2003). *Annual Review*. The SA Council for the aged.

Services for people with disabilities

'A disability refers to a physical or mental impairment that limits that person's capacity to perform one or more major life activities.'

Context. The World Health Organisation has estimated that 10 percent of the world's population is disabled (Green 1997:343). A disability refers to a physical or mental impairment that limits that person's capacity to perform one or more major life activities. Physical disabilities that limit life activities are 'seeing, hearing, speaking, walking, breathing, performing manual tasks, learning, caring for oneself and working' (United States: Equal Employment Opportunity Commission 1997:1). These impairments vary in severity and may occur at any time in the life-cycle or may have an early onset and may last over the entire life-cycle (Kirst-Ashman 2003:299).

About 450 million people worldwide suffer from mental or neurological disorders or from psychosocial problems related to alcohol and drug abuse. Major depression is now the leading cause of disability globally and is predicted to increase substantially. Mental health problems account for 16 percent of total disability in sub-Saharan Africa. Factors leading to the onset of mental disorders are varied and include poverty, sex, age, major physical diseases, family and social environment and conflict, war and disasters (World Health Organisation 2001).

Estimates of disability in South Africa vary between 4.7 percent (CASE 1998:26) and 8.5 percent of the total population (Department of Welfare and Population Development 1997). The most common physical disabilities are quadriplegia, deafness and blindness - blindness accounts for a third of all physical disabilities. Many people also experience multiple disabilities. A range of factors contribute to impaired physical functioning, including unhealthy lifestyles, failed medical services, accidents, violence and war, poverty, inadequate information and poor social and environmental conditions (White Paper on an Integrated Disability Strategy 1997). Race, class, gender and geographic factors have a bearing on disabilities, with Africans experiencing the highest percentage of people with disabilities. More than 80 percent of children with disabilities live in extreme poverty and the largest concentrations of people with disabilities are in the lowest income-earning households with the lowest education levels (CASE 1998:29). Women with disabilities, especially black women, experience discrimination arising from culture and tradition based on the patriarchal division of labour. Women with disabilities are more likely to be poor, malnourished and illiterate, and have less chance of founding a family (White Paper on an Integrated National Disability Strategy 1997).

People with disabilities are faced with unemployment and a lack of employment in the open labour market. A lack of skills and access to education are some of the reasons for a lack of employment, including social discrimination in employment. Social services are mainly urban-based and health and other services for people with disabilities continue to lag behind the need (Leshilo 2004; Thejane & Muthukrishna 2000). A lack of services exists for children with disabilities, especially in rural areas. Inaccessible public facilities, social stigma and negative perceptions about the capabilities of people with disabilities still hamper their integration into the mainstream of the society. At the National Speak Out on Poverty Hearings in 1998, Manthipi Molamu of the Disabled People's Organisation called for the inclusion of people with disabilities. He said:

'Social services are mainly urban-based and health and other services for people with disabilities continue to lag behind the need.'

> *'Don't make us special. Don't look at my disability. Me, I am a person in a wheelchair. That is not my disability. Nor my paraplegia. My disability is the stairs at [the Departments of] Health and Welfare. That disables me. Just give me an accessible environment. That will make me part of South Africa.' (The People's Voices 1998:68)*

Major thrusts of services. The medical model of disability emphasises physical deficits; it views disability as a medical condition requiring treatment by professionals; and it focuses on inabilities and views patients as passive recipients of care (Bilton et al 2002:91). The social development approach to disability stresses a comprehensive approach, inclusion of the populations who have been marginalised from the mainstream, strengths and empowerment, human rights and full participation in economic, social and political life. Developmental social work and social services in the field of disability draw on empowerment theory and practice, strengths-based approaches and generalist social work practice to meet the needs and promote the rights of people with disabilities. Non-discriminatory practice and empowerment of service-users are paramount.

Social work services may involve micro-, mezzo- and macro-level interventions. At a micro level, individuals and families may need counselling and support whilst mezzo interventions could involve work with self-help groups such as the Disabled People's Organisation of South Africa (DPSA) that is involved with advocacy, public education and awareness-raising and livelihood strategies to promote independent living. The DPSA and related civil society organisations are new *social movements* that emerged to challenge the social arrangements in society that exclude them from full participation.

The above approach is aligned with policy and legislation and international instruments. Of particular importance are the *United Nations Standard Rules on the Equalisation of Opportunities for Persons with Disabilities* (1993) and the United Nations resolution 46/119 providing for the *Protection of Persons with Mental Illness and the Improvement of*

Mental Health Care (1991). These are important human-rights and standard-setting instruments that guide social service professionals in their work with people with disabilities.

Enabling legislation to overcome discrimination in employment led to the Employment Equity Act of 1998, which provides for the affirmative employment of black people, women and the disabled. Targets have been set for the employment of people with disabilities, and employers are required to report to government on an annual basis about the progress made. Because of the imperatives of the Employment Equity Act, many private sector organisations are piloting innovative employment programmes. For instance, a partnership between the National Council for the Deaf and Woolworths has resulted in the training of young deaf people who have completed their schooling to work as cashiers in Woolworths stores in Johannesburg. Community-based strategies to strengthen the livelihood capacities of people with disabilities are being implemented in developing countries. In the Philippines, government and the International Labour Organisation developed a community-based rehabilitation programme that is home-based. In Kenya, informal sector and self-employment for disabled micro-entrepreneurs have proved equally successful (Metts & Oleson 1995). The best example of entrepreneurship in South Africa is the training, financial and business support model developed by the MODE organisation for people with disabilities which is discussed in Chapter 8. These types of programmes may not be suitable for people with different kinds of disabilities. They work for people who do not need medical care and for those who have recovered from mental illness (International Labour Office undated).

Care in the community for people with mental illness has been found to be better than institutional treatment in relation to the outcome and quality of life of individuals with chronic mental disorders. Community care is cost-effective and respects the human rights of the patients, and community-based services can also lead to early intervention and limit stigma. However, this can only work effectively if community services are provided with backup crisis support services, appropriate accommodation and employment. Community care options also need to be accompanied by access to primary health care, the availability of psychotropic drugs, the involvement of families and consumers and public education and awareness campaigns about mental health and care.

'Community care is cost-effective and respects the human rights of the patients, and community-based services can also lead to early intervention and limit stigma.'

Services for people affected by HIV/AIDS

Context: HIV/AIDS has reached pandemic proportions in Africa, and especially in sub-Saharan Africa, and this has had grave social and economic consequences for individuals, families and communities. In sub-Saharan Africa, 25 million people are estimated to have HIV/AIDS.

Young people less than 25 years and women have the highest infection rates, with women in the 15 to 24-year age group being 3.4 times more vulnerable to HIV infection than men (UNAIDS 2004). Neighbouring countries such as Botswana has the highest infection rates in the world, with almost 39 percent of all adults there living with HIV. The pandemic is placing great pressure on systems of care and support, including health and family and community systems of care. Consider the statistics on HIV/AIDS in South Africa:

- Approximately 5 million people are infected by HIV. According to the AIDS Review (2001:10), nearly 3 million of those infected are women and 250 000 are below the age of 15 years. The number of orphans is expected to increase from 2.2 million (12 percent of all children) to 3.1 million (18 percent of all children) by 2010 (UNAIDS 2004:61).
- KwaZulu-Natal, Mpumalanga and Gauteng provinces continue to show an increasing trend in HIV prevalence (South African Epidemiological Fact Sheet 2002 in AIDS Review 2003). It is estimated that 30 percent of the mining workforce is HIV positive. Infection rates are highest among people living in urban areas and in informal settlements (Human Sciences Research Council 2002).

'The pandemic is placing great pressure on systems of care and support, including health and family and community systems of care.'

HIV/AIDS is having a negative impact on all facets of economic and social life. Vulnerable groups that are affected by and infected with HIV/AIDS are youth, children, the elderly, people with disabilities, women, homosexual men, migrants and single parents (Department of Welfare 1997:89). UNAIDS reports, that as the epidemic spreads throughout the world, young people are at greatest risk of infection. In view of regional migration, HIV/AIDS presents a particular challenge to countries in the SADC region. The cost of caring for people with AIDS in Africa has been rising: it has been estimated that about US $3 billion was needed in 2002 to provide the most basic care and prevention programmes (AIDS Review 2003:17).

Major thrust of services. In view of the grave consequences of HIV/AIDS for the society, the developmental approach to social welfare services and social work practice is the most appropriate means of intervention. HIV/AIDS services should be *mainstreamed* through all welfare programmes. This means that all social services should have a HIV/AIDS service component, which encompasses the range of services identified in the continuum of care (Department of Welfare, Financing Policy 1999). Specialist agencies are focusing on HIV/AIDS services for particular client populations, and these services need to be provided in a holistic and integrated manner. Women, youth, children, the elderly, people with disabilities and those abusing substances and offenders and victims of violence are infected and affected by the epidemic. They are also part of families, households, communities and the workplace, and an integrated response is needed that combines different intervention strategies that would effectively address the pandemic. Interdisciplinary collaboration between different social service sectors is a critical component of integrated practice involving collaboration between professionals in different settings such as health care, education, legal and occupational settings.

The main thrust of developmental welfare service programmes in responding to the HIV/AIDS pandemic is outlined below.

- **Care and social support.** This involves providing psychosocial support to individuals, groups and families who are infected and affected by HIV/AIDS. Counselling interventions may include pre-test and post-test counselling; providing ongoing supportive counselling; advice and guidance about critical life decisions; issues of disclosure and personal protection and care. Counselling is generally reality-based and attempts to address the here and now (Crowley 1995). Short-term crisis intervention care and support modes are used that may be delivered by social workers, lay counsellors, community carers, help lines, peer group support, self-help groups and volunteers.
- **Community mobilisation & mitigation of impact**. In African countries that are heavily infected and affected by HIV/AIDS, strategies targeted at strengthening the capacities of families and communities in geographic areas most affected through community-based programmes have proved to be the most effective and sustainable way to address the crisis (Donahue & Williamson 1999). Community mobilisation programmes have the potential to be scaled up and to reach larger numbers of people at lower cost. This approach uses participatory community development methods and techniques to mobilise communities to identify their needs and to act on their concerns. Community-action initiatives are varied and may include: building local neighbourhood and village level structures to respond to local needs; providing support for child-headed households and orphans; developing and implementing livelihood programmes to strengthen household economic resources; facilitating access to social relief such as food security; social assistance, capacity-building and linking care and prevention. They also involve strengthening existing indigenous community mechanisms to address needs through faith-based organisations, and working with traditional healers, leaders and structures. The challenges of community mobilisation are about how to scale up the programmes to match the scope of the epidemic and to sustain community action over a long period of time (Donahue & Williamson 1999).
- **Home and community-based care**. Home-based care is defined 'as the provision of health and social services by formal and informal caregivers in the home in order to promote, restore and maintain a person's maximum level of comfort, function and health

including care toward a dignified death' (Kganakga 2003). Home-care services may be preventative, promotive, therapeutic or rehabilitative, and may involve long-term palliative care and be an integral part of community-based care. Community-based care and support is described as care that consumers can access nearest to their homes; that encourages participation by the people; that encourages a sharing of responsibilities for caring and that is responsive to their needs (Department of Social Development, National Guidelines on Home Based and Community Based Care 2002; National Guidelines for Social Services to Children Infected and Affected by HIV/AIDS 2002).

'Community-based care and support is described as care that consumers can access nearest to their homes; that encourages participation by the people.'

The Departments of Health and Social Development are jointly responsible for the development and implementation of the Home- and Community-based Care Programme (HCBC). Volunteers are trained to conduct home visits to those who are ill. An assessment of the needs of the patient and the family is made; support is provided through the distribution of medicines and nutritional supplements; referrals for services are made and children in need of care are identified. The volunteer home-carers work closely with community-based and faith-based organisations and act as brokers to link the families with services and networks. They may also identify areas for community mobilisation and action.

The HCBC experimental programme of the Department of Social Development has had significant achievements. In 2000, around 314 HCBC sites were being supported by government and over 1 000 caregivers received stipends of between R225 and R500 each. Additional children in need of care were identified through the programme. Services rendered to children included the distribution of food parcels, clothing, counselling, placements in day care and after school centres/drop in centres, the placement of children in foster care and residential care, and the education and health needs of the children. In total, 20 695 families received support in the form of food parcels, assistance with funerals, and linking families with income-generating projects. The HCBC programme has also been a catalyst for the building of civil society through the recruitment and training of 1 604 volunteers and the establishment of 41 ChildCare Forums countrywide. Support groups for People Living with AIDS (PLWAs) were provided with both financial and professional support (Department of Social Development Progress Report 2003:11).

Many successful home- and community-based care and support programmes have been developed in African countries such as Uganda, Malawi, Zimbabawe and Zambia. These models could be adapted and replicated elsewhere. In South Africa, Hospice is an NGO that provides terminal care and combines institutional and home care effectively. Hospice care is valuable for people whose families are not able and or willing to provide care.

- **Education and prevention**. Forms of behaviour that increase the risk of HIV infection are unprotected sex; engaging in sex with one or more partners or with risky sex partners; mother to child transmission; having sex while under the influence of alcohol or other drugs; and needle-sharing. A lack of HIV/AIDS-related knowledge such as the modes of transmission and proper condom use, misconceptions, faulty beliefs and attitudes and peer pressure are other factors that increase the risk of contracting HIV. Close to half of the respondents in a national study reported that they had not used condoms in their last sexual encounter, with young people and women reporting higher levels of failure to use condoms (Patel, Noyoo & Lofell 2004).

  Public education and prevention provided by NGOs and supported by government and donors is proving to be successful in reaching large numbers of people. *loveLife* provides high-profile campaign-style programming to impart AIDS-related knowledge that is directed at youth, while *Soul City* programmes are broadcast on national television and are popular educational interventions. Social service agencies and practitioners also provide one-to-one educational interventions, group and community education and prevention programmes aimed at populations at risk. The programmes should be well designed and should provide quality AIDS-related knowledge and information to populations at risk and should meet the education and information needs of such groups. Successful prevention programmes, according to Malherbe (2002), should include sex health education, behaviour change interventions, voluntary HIV counselling and testing, promotion of the condom and female condom, and screening and testing for sexually transmitted infections and tuberculosis.
- **Poverty reduction and livelihoods strategies.** HIV/AIDS can lead to the impoverishment of families due to loss of income caused by illness. It may lead to the loss of employment, the loss of income of a breadwinner or member of the household, or it may compromise the capacity of a household to earn a livelihood. Caring for a sick person places additional financial stresses on families such as the cost of nutritious food, transport and medicines. Poverty-alleviation programmes and economic development strategies are vital in helping households to cope with economic hardship.
- **Gender-sensitive and non-discriminatory practice**. Unequal gender relations and social, economic and cultural factors are directly connected to the high infection rates among women (Malherbe 2002:339). For instance, some women have been hesitant to seek HIV testing or have failed to return for their results because they fear that disclosure of their HIV-positive status may result in physical violence, expulsion from their home or social ostracism (UNAIDS 2004:40). Interventions are needed that empower women to make decisions related to their sexuality and that ensure women's

access to HIV prevention, AIDS care and related services, including sexual and reproductive health (UNAIDS 2004:152). Strategies should also involve men in promoting women's empowerment.

People living with AIDS experience discrimination at the individual, institutional and societal levels (Francis 2004:70; Legido-Quigley 2003). Stigmatisation of and discrimination against people with HIV/AIDS are prevalent in South African society. AIDS-related stigma and discrimination could lead to the social isolation of people who are infected. These attitudes hamper progress in treatment and care, and in preventing the spread of the disease. It is important for practitioners to recognise gender and other forms of discrimination and to understand the consequences for those affected. Education and awareness programmes should also counteract oppressive attitudes and behaviour and organisations should be encouraged to adopt non-discriminatory policies and practices.

'People living with AIDS experience discrimination at the individual, institutional and societal levels.'

- **Social planning.** Development social service programmes require applied and community-based research to design programmes that are appropriate, effective and sustainable. Needs assessments are important in informing programme development; the monitoring and evaluation of programmes are also important to assess social impact. Community mobilisation also involves rapid appraisal studies and community involvement in surveillance systems and monitoring and assessment needs.
- **Social policy, legislation guidelines and advocacy.** Policy and legislation needs to be responsive to the needs and rights of populations at risk such as children, the elderly and in relation to access to services. Policy and legislation also ensures the rights of people with regard to informed consent, voluntary testing, and the prohibition of pre-employment HIV testing and on-the-job testing. National guidelines have been formulated to guide quality and ethical service delivery of HIV/AIDS-related services.

  Advocacy for legislative and policy reform is critical, and practitioners and service providers need to bring their knowledge and experience to the policy formulation agenda. Participation in public hearings convened by the legislature is vital.

HIV/AIDS advocacy and lobbying for children's rights

The following are some of the key points highlighted for advocacy to promote the rights of children growing up in child-headed households identified by Julia Sloth-Nielson of the Community Law Centre at the University of the Western Cape (Sloth-Nielson 2004:37).

- The monitoring of the implementation of the Promotion of the Equality and Unfair Discrimination Act No 4 of 2000 to ensure that discrimination against children affected by HIV/AIDS is challenged.
- Lobbying government to change the law that will prevent children heading households who are under 16 years from receiving the child support grant on behalf of younger siblings.
- Lobby government to develop a food security policy.
- Lobby for the legal requirement that consent for the treatment of orphans be revised and simplified.

- The Children's Bill process should be closely followed to make sure that the legal status of child-headed households is properly accommodated.
- Provision should be made for the appointment of household mentors with legal capacity for child-headed households.

- **HIV/AIDS in the workplace.** Many South African companies have introduced policies and programmes on HIV/AIDS in order to curtail the spread of the disease. Prouty (2002:16) notes that South Africa's economic fate in the 21st century depends on the willingness of corporations to implement proactive and compassionate HIV/AIDS workplace policies and programmes. Some companies have signed agreements with trade unions to provide anti-retroviral treatment and the co-funding of medication to boost the immune system of employees. Anti-discriminatory policies have been adopted by other companies (Merten 2003:28) and many employers are implementing HIV/AIDS care in-house or at clinics (Business Day 2004:11). Some pharmaceutical companies are also responding to the call for anti-retroviral medicines at preferential pricing to governments, non-governmental organisations and international aid groups.

Crime prevention and restorative justice services

Context. Escalating crime and violence continues to mark South Africa's transition to democracy. Concern with public and community safety and security is being expressed by all sectors of the society. Serious crimes such as robbery with aggravating circumstances, rape, child abuse, common assault, assault with the intent to inflict grievous bodily harm, culpable homicide and attempted murder have shown an increase in incidence over previous years. There has been a decrease in the number of homicides over the same period (South African Police Services Crime Statistics 2003). Young people are over-represented among victims and perpetrators of crime. The majority of offenders and victims of lethal violence are young men, particularly young black men between the ages of 18 and 30 years (offenders) and 16 and 35 years (victims) (Economic Development Unit 2003:97). Youth as perpetrators of crime between the ages of 18 and 25 years made up 39.05 percent of the total national prison population at the end of January 2004. Of this group, 38.02 percent were awaiting trial and/or sentenced and the balance was serving sentences. They were overwhelming male, with women making up a very small percentage (NICRO Gauteng 2004). Other challenges are rising domestic violence and gender-based violence. Crime and violence is inextricably linked with poverty, underdevelopment and the history of repression and associated violence in South Africa. The impact of past and continuing experiences of marginalisation and alienation in the society are considered to be contributing factors to crime and violence in the society.

'Crime and violence is inextricably linked with poverty, underdevelopment and the history of repression and associated violence in South Africa.'

The National Crime Prevention Strategy (NCPS) (1996) is a comprehensive policy framework for crime prevention and control. The NCPS rests on four pillars, which represent 16 programmes that cut across government departments. These programmes range from re-engineering the criminal justice system to rebuilding respect for the rule of law and curtailing the impact of international and regional crime. The focus of developmental social services in the criminal justice field is on *community-based strategies* to promote social crime prevention, crime reduction and rehabilitation of offenders from a restorative and a social and economic justice perspective. Community-based corrections are probation and parole services that monitor the behaviour of offenders while living in the community.

Main thrusts of service.

- **Restorative justice** is an approach to criminal justice 'which rejects punitive measures in favour of community-based sentences that attempt to raise awareness among offenders of the effects of their actions' (Giddens 2001:697). This approach informs national criminal justice thinking and attempts to shift away from the punitive justice approach of the past, which relied heavily on incarceration. This new direction acknowledges the complex causes and structural societal conditions that contribute to crime. Whilst imprisonment and rehabilitation are part of the new directions, restorative justice provides alternatives to imprisonment and diversion away from the criminal justice system as far as this is possible.

  The restorative justice approach to policy and legislation is currently most developed in addressing the needs of juvenile offenders and in victim empowerment programmes. It seeks to encourage full rehabilitation where treatment is aimed at enabling the offender, and more particularly the minor offender, to avoid a life of crime (NCPS 1996:6–7). The *White Paper for Social Welfare* (1997) provides a framework for principles, guidelines and recommendations for developmental social welfare programmes for offenders, victims of crime and their families. Restorative justice, diversion programmes, prevention and early intervention programmes are some of the programmes that are identified as governmental strategy (Department of Welfare 1997:84–85).
- **Victim empowerment.** The criminal justice system has focused in the past on the offender, while the needs of the victim have been neglected. The nationally driven Victim Empowerment Programme (VEP) has prioritised crimes against women and children and roughly 52 one-stop service centres were established that provide a wide range of services involving both professionals and volunteers. The services include support groups for victims; counselling; awareness campaigns; volunteer training; accommodation; crisis intervention; and economic empowerment programmes. The aim of the services is to reduce re-victimisation of victims of crime and

violence by ensuring that their welfare, health, psychological needs and legal needs are addressed.

- **Youth and crime.** The reform of the juvenile justice system from one that is based on a punitive philosophy to one that uses a restorative approach is founded on the idea that juveniles should be treated differently to adults who commit crimes. The Child Justice Bill proposes far-reaching changes in the management of children in conflict with the law. The Bill makes provision for the protection of children's rights, the responsibilities of probation officers, the assessment of children and their diversion away from formal court procedures and the entrenchment of restorative justice. The Bill defines restorative justice as the 'promotion of the reconciliation, restitution and responsibility through the involvement of a child, the child's parent, family members, victims and communities' (Juvenile Justice Bill xxvi).

'The juvenile is encouraged to take responsibility for his/her actions, to be accountable for his/her actions, and where possible to make amends to the victim.'

The Interim Policy Recommendations of the Inter-Ministerial Committee (IMC) on Young People at Risk (1996) provides a restorative justice framework to inform practice with young people who have transgressed the law. The focus is rather on the young person making amends, that is, putting the wrongs right, rather than punishment. The juvenile is encouraged to take responsibility for his/her actions, to be accountable for his/her actions, and where possible to make amends to the victim (Interministerial Committee 1996:17).

In order to divert children in conflict with the law away from formal court procedures with or without conditions, the Bill proposes an assessment process and, where diversion is appropriate, a range of diversion options should be considered and a special programme developed and implemented for the child. The rationale for a special perspective on juveniles is that they are minors whose parents are supposed to care for them, supervise and protect them (Kirst-Ashman 2003). Diversion options may include a family group conference, victim-offender mediation, counselling, and referrals to attend special programmes – all of which need to take into account the circumstances of the child, the nature of the offence and the interests of society.

Other diversionary measures of a preventative nature have been adopted to prevent children from sinking deeper into the criminal justice system. One such initiative was *Project Go* which is a national programme that involves an assessment of every child entering the criminal justice system and seeks to prevent the movement of children deeper into the system (Department of Welfare Annual Report 1999–2000:15). An estimated 18 063 children were assessed by the year 2000: this involved case reviews and the diversion of children away from the criminal justice system in collaboration with public agencies and community-based and non-governmental organisations. Children who were awaiting trial were diverted out of correctional facilities and places of safety and placed with their families where appropriate. Family preservation programmes were also provided. 'One Stop' integrated Justice Centres are also being established to provide accessible legal assistance, diversion programmes, family finding and children's courts that are supported by different governmental agencies involved in criminal justice (Department of Social Development Progress Report 2003:17).

Diversion programmes, family group conferencing and alternative sentencing (for example, home-based supervision programmes) as opposed to prison sentences for youth have become part and parcel of the criminal justice system. The Probation Services Act 116 of 1991 and the new Child Justice Bill make provision for the development of alternate programmes which includes diversion, family group conferencing and house arrest programmes for young people. These alternate forms of sentencing are congruent with a rights-based approach to service delivery in the new welfare paradigm. For children who have committed more serious crimes, secure care facilities have been provided in lieu of prisons. These secure care centres accommodate an average of 2 000 children and young people per month (Department of Social Development Progress Report 2003:17).

- **Domestic violence and gender-based violence.** The Domestic Violence Act 116 of 1998 affords victims of domestic violence protection in keeping with the Constitution and governmental commitments under the United Nations Convention on the Elimination of All Forms of Discrimination Against Women (CEDAW). Whilst it is acknowledged that women do abuse men and that abuse also occurs in same-sex partnerships, the reality is that internationally and locally domestic violence is carried out mainly by men against women (Giddens 2001; NCPS 1996).

  Domestic violence takes place in a wide variety of domestic relationships and takes on many different forms that may cause harm to the safety, health and well-being of the person affected. Domestic violence is defined in the Act as including acts of physical, sexual, emotional, verbal, psychological and economic abuse; acts of intimidation, harassment, stalking, damage to property and entry into a person's home without their consent. The Act provides for the issuing of protection orders prohibiting the respondent from committing any act of domestic violence and the order may prohibit the person from entering the residence of the complainant. It also provides for the seizure of weapons and for a warrant of arrest when a protection order is made.

  Public agencies, voluntary welfare organisations and non-governmental women's organisations provide a wide range of psychosocial support services, advocacy, women's empowerment programmes and services to women and children affected by domestic violence. Social service practitioners assist with the implementation of the Domestic Violence Act. Educational and information programmes for men and women are also provided by some organisations. There is a growing awareness that gender-based violence cannot be addressed without an understanding being gained as to the experiences of men and the *meaning of masculinity* within the context of gender relations in the local context. Programmes are beginning to involve men in promoting gender equity, preventing violence and in conversations promoting reproductive health and overcoming HIV/AIDS risk.

- **'Crisis of masculinity'** is a concept used by Connel (1995) to describe the fundamental changes that men are experiencing in modern societies due to changing roles between men and women in the family and community, in the labour market and in the political realm. These changes have threatened the social dominance of men in a gender hierarchy that is culturally sanctioned and that operates in private and social life. Gender violence and aggression are explained in terms of masculine identity and the crisis facing men in a changing environment. Other studies are beginning to draw the link between male unemployment and crime and violence (Giddens 2001:226).
- **Community reintegration of offenders.** The National Institute for Crime Prevention and Rehabilitation of Offenders (NICRO) assists

Reshaping gender attitudes in South Africa

Since 1997, thousands of South African men have participated in a national conversation in urban, semi-urban and rural areas to talk about gender issues. The workshops have also been conducted with mixed-sex audiences and have been conducted at schools, community centres, churches, workplaces and prisons. These workshops explore gender attitudes and behaviour that can compromise reproductive health and expose men to HIV/AIDS risk. Dialogues about partner communication, relationships, power and violence are discussed and are directly related to men's experiences and the social context in which they find themselves.

The initiative is part of the Hope Worldwide Men As Partners (MAP) programme delivered in collaboration with Planned Parenthood South Africa. The programme grew out of the need for constructive male involvement to address the twin epidemics of HIV/AIDS and violence against women.

Source: http://www.engenderhealth.org/itf/south_africa.html. Retrieved 23/7/2004

people affected by crime and violence through participatory, restorative and developmental interventions. Services to reintegrate offenders into the community and facilitate access to economic opportunities are two key national programmes. The target group of the programme is former prisoners, those who are serving community-based sentences, youth and members of the communities who are discouraged work-seekers. The Employment Opportunities Programme provides financial and non-financial support services through the provision of training, micro loans and access to revolving credit. NICRO formed a non-profit company through which financial support is provided. It has involved key strategic partners in government, the private sector, tertiary institutions and the International Labour Organisation to train their social development workers to implement the programme.

- **Preventing crime and violence**. Crime prevention is about addressing the causes of crime and violence. Crime prevention programmes attempt to address risk factors that lead to crime and violence in the society, such as poor socio-economic conditions, poverty and unemployment and a lack of economic, educational and social opportunities. Family and community breakdown and exposure and experience of a culture of violence in the society and peer group influences are some of the other risk factors that are cited. Social service agencies and non-governmental organisations are engaged in a variety of prevention and early intervention programmes. Some programmes target large populations based on a public health approach or are aimed at vulnerable and at risk groups such as youth in conflict with the law, children of school going age, ex-offenders and unemployed persons. Common preventative interventions include work in the school system, psychosocial support to youth and their families, poverty alleviation, employment and skills-building.

  School-based interventions are widely used by non-governmental organisations involved in the development and implementation of innovative crime prevention programmes such as life skills relevant to reducing crime – for example, conflict management, the promotion of self-esteem, communication skills and learning respect. The integration of crime prevention into English lessons using stories and exercises (known as curriculum-based and interactive learning experiences) is another innovation. The Life Orientation Learning Area of the new curriculum provides scope for integrating social competency skills into the school curriculum. Many school-based prevention programmes also include peer counselling and mediation, trauma counselling, mentoring, and programmes to create safer schools. The whole-school approach, which targets all stakeholders (learners, educators, parents and school administrators) to create non-punitive and safe learning environments, is the favoured best-practice intervention. School–community partnerships to promote community development are another example emerging from a good-practice study of crime-prevention programmes in South African schools (Griggs 2002).

'Many school-based prevention programmes also include peer counselling and mediation, trauma counselling, mentoring, and programmes to create safer schools.'

Substance abuse services

Context. With the advent of globalisation, national boundaries have become more permeable, and this has led to the increased international trade of illegal substances such as drugs. Alcohol and tobacco are the most commonly abused substances in South Africa, followed by cannabis and the combined use of cannabis and Mandrax ('white pipe') (South African National Drug Master Plan 1999:6). About half of the adult population in South Africa use alcohol, a third of these engage in risky drinking and many habitually drink to intoxication (Parry 2000). Fifty percent of people who die from non-natural causes have alcohol blood levels above the legal limit. Women are at a more serious risk than men with regard to their health and face the added risk of foetal alcohol syndrome. A research project on substance abuse among first-year university students (Peltzer, Malaka & Phaswana 2002) revealed that alcohol is the most commonly used substance, followed by tobacco, cannabis and then other opiate-type drugs. With regard to tobacco, the National Cancer Registry estimates that about 89 000 premature deaths per year can be expected in South Africa as a result of current smoking patterns (South African National Drug Master Plan 1999:6).

The term 'drugs' refers to the use of illicit drugs defined in the Drugs and Drug Trafficking Act 140 of 1992, and the abuse of illicit medicines. Alcohol, tobacco and volatile solvents are not included in this category of illicit drugs. The misuse of substances has negative consequences for productivity and economic growth, health and family life. In 1998, the economic cost of alcohol abuse in South Africa was estimated to be R1.7 billion per annum, or 2 percent of GNP – about thrice the amount generated by government through excise taxes (Parry and Bennets 1998). Health problems associated with the abuse of drugs like alcohol, tobacco and cannabis include chemical dependency, diabetes, cirrhosis of the liver, kidney failure, cardiac and lung complications, foetal anomalies, injuries from accidents and homicide (Peltzer, Malaka & Phaswana 2002:67).

There is a strong correlation between the abuse of drugs and crime, violence and HIV/AIDS. South African Police Services (SAPS) crime statistics (2:2003) reveal that drug-related crimes have increased from 1994 to 2003, while there has been a slight decrease in the statistics on driving under the influence of alcohol or drugs. During the first 6 months of 1998, over 5 percent of sentenced prisoners in South Africa were incarcerated for drug-related offences (Drug Statistics in South Africa 2003). Furthermore, a study of sentenced male prisoners in 1996 showed that 76 percent of inmates were taking alcohol and/or drugs immediately before or at the time of committing the offence for which they were imprisoned.

Major thrust of services. The SA National Drug Master Plan (NDMP) which was approved by Cabinet in 1999 was South Africa's response to the problems of drug abuse and trafficking, and set out the policies and priorities in the campaign against substance abuse. The purpose of this plan is to bring about the reduction of substance abuse and its related harmful consequences (National Drug Master Plan 1999:10).

Specialist NGOs such as the South African National Council for Alcohol and Drug Abuse (SANCA) provide substance abuse and related services nationally which consist of in-patient and outpatient facilities. The majority of the services are located in the major metropolitan areas and urban centres with some services in the hinterland. The Northern Cape and

North West have the fewest facilities with Gauteng and the Western Cape being well serviced. Poor areas with high alcohol risk, especially rural areas, need to be targeted for services. The Department of Social Development is responsible for regulating and monitoring drug-related services (Department of Social Development Annual Report 2002–2003:55). Drug-related services and facilities were upgraded in disadvantaged communities in Mpumalanga, Western Cape, North West, Free State and Limpopo provinces with a partnership between the Department of Social Development and the United Nations for Drugs and Crime.

'Poor areas with high alcohol risk, especially rural areas, need to be targeted for services.'

The main focus areas for the National Drug Master Plan (NDMP 1999) are crime, youth, community health and welfare, research, communication and information dissemination, and international involvement. The objectives of the NDMP (1999:10–11) cover a range of services such as educational programmes, awareness raising, national and public education, counselling, treatment, rehabilitation and after-care services. The target groups are students, teachers, governing bodies of schools; parents, and communities for prevention services. Services for people abusing substances include advice, counselling, treatment, rehabilitation and after-care services, while their families have access to advice, counselling and support services. Prevention and treatment and training programmes are aimed at health and welfare workers, law-enforcement officials and law students, human resource personnel and teachers, and any other role-players.

Community-based services as well as treatment programmes and services for high-risk groups are very limited and should be expanded (Peltzer, Malaka & Phaswana 2002). South Africa does not have sufficient treatment facilities, trained personnel and financial resources to deal with the rapid increase in drug victims. There is a need for community awareness and cooperation and partnerships in service delivery to counteract the far-reaching effects of widespread drug abuse. Comprehensive substance abuse prevention programmes at tertiary and school levels are needed that integrate substance abuse, HIV/AIDS primary prevention, gender-based violence and crime prevention programmes. Early intervention strategies are needed with school-going youth who are engaging in experimental and risky behaviour (Malaka 2003).

Ahanang (Let us build each other)

The South African National Council for Alcohol and Drug Abuse (SANCA) is partnering with the Department of Correctional Services to provide HIV/AIDS and substance abuse information, education, life skills and peer counselling services for youth in conflict with the law. The programme also provides training to pre-release prisoners who were judged to have the ability to be peer-counsellors in the field of substance abuse, crime prevention, HIV/AIDS and victim empowerment. Crime prevention programmes were provided to young offenders at eight prisons and detention centres in four provinces. The programme was funded by the National Lottery.

Source: SANCA (2004). Ahanang Correctional Services Project. Launch of Second Phase. Johannesburg: SANCA.

Achievements and challenges

There has been a significant shift in commitment to social welfare with a focus on pro-poor developmental welfare policies, legislation and social development programmes which were discussed in Chapters 4, 5 and 6. Significant achievements have been noted in the policy and legislative domain. Race as a criterion in determining access to services has been removed through legislation and services are being expanded to under-serviced communities. Family-centred and community-based generalist approaches, which are decentralized to local levels, are gradually being implemented. The new thrust of services for populations at risk demonstrates significant innovation in the implementation of developmental welfare strategies. The case examples and new directions in service delivery and innovation also indicate significant changes in the general thrust of services.

However, systematic monitoring of the implementation of the new directions has not been conducted. Patel & Wilson (2003a) conducted a review of welfare services in 2002. Progress was benchmarked against the data contained in the *White Paper for Social Welfare*. This review highlighted the paucity of data due to inadequate national and provincial management information systems and a lack of skills in the management of information. There is an urgent need for research to monitor and evaluate the implementation of policy to learn from best practice and to inform policy and programme review. The findings of this review are summarised below with reference to the new policy directions for developmental welfare services (Patel & Wilson 2003a; Patel 2003b).

'...systematic monitoring of the implementation of the new directions has not been conducted.'

Increased access. Legislative amendments and policy changes were enacted and implemented to ensure equal access to resources such as the Aged Persons Amendment Act 44 of 1994; the Social Work Amendment Act 52 of 1995 and the Welfare Laws Amendment Act No 106 of 1998. More specifically, the racially discriminatory means test determining access to residential facilities for older persons was abolished and uniform eligibility criteria were introduced to promote access to all residential and non-residential facilities. However, no audit has been conducted to determine the effectiveness of these measures in reaching the needy elderly.

Empirical data is not available on the extent to which welfare services are accessible to previously disadvantaged groups and whether services are more developmental in their approach. Some national and local organisations are recording significant changes in the demographic profile of welfare service beneficiaries whilst others have made limited progress. The South African National Council for Child and Family Welfare (2002) reported that 81 percent of beneficiaries of services are now black, which is a complete reversal of the organisation's previous beneficiary profile. Whether this is the case across all publicly funded voluntary organisations is not known. There has also been limited success in addressing the geographic disparities in the distribution of social service personnel, which impacts negatively on increasing access to services. In March 2004, there were 9 649 social workers registered with the South African Council for Social Service Professions. The majority of social workers (74 percent), were in Gauteng, the Western Cape and KwaZulu Natal with the remaining 26 percent in the poorest rural provinces of the country. There is clearly a need for more social service personnel in the poorer regions of the country. The backlog in needs and service provision in disadvantaged communities especially rural areas, remains a major challenge.

Community-based services. The shift from institutional care to community based services has been complex and limited. Again no audit of institutions has been conducted, but there appears to have been a small reduction in the number of funded beds between 1995 and 2001 (Department of Social Development 2001). This means that over 80 percent of total welfare resources are still tied up in residential care especially for the elderly. The pace of change from institutional to community based services has been slow and complex. The rural provinces such as the Eastern Cape where limited services exist have recorded increased community development programmes delivered by voluntary organisations although they have been hampered by limited capacity. At the same time the more urban provinces with more developed residential and specialized services including casework and statutory services, have made slower progress. The restructuring of the more developed provinces was therefore more complex. Interviews with Gauteng officials indicated that while means testing was instituted in old age homes, deinstitutionalisation was unsuccessful with clients who had no family or community support systems, which increased their vulnerability. Deinstitutionalisation was also challenged on grounds of reverse discrimination since the majority of the elderly in old age homes are white.

Whilst progress has been made in developing guidelines for HIV/AIDS home and community care services and home-based care supervision, there is no data on the extent of coverage of community care services, no national policy and financing to support community based interventions and a lack of human resources to implement the programmes. If community care is to provide quality care, the care-giving efforts of extended families and kinship networks need to be supported and strengthened. The assumption underlying community care is that there are families or capable women, who are willing and able to provide care. However, this is not always the case. There are clear indications that in some instances where community and family care fails, institutional care is needed. One example is the large number of HIV positive abandoned children who cannot optimally be cared for in the community due to stigma and where institutional care may be the only option. If community care is not to turn into community neglect, appropriate systems and procedures are needed to monitor the quality of care provided, and to intervene where necessary. Furthermore, foster care is a family-centred and community based way of caring for orphaned and vulnerable children. The number of children in foster care is growing, but here again, the statutory processes and monitoring systems mandated by legislation requires large numbers of social workers to implement the programme. Given the limited number of social workers in the rural provinces such as the Eastern Cape, Northern Cape and Mpumalanga which is under 5 percent of the total number of social workers nationally, foster care is more likely to be concentrated mainly in the more urban and developed provinces. The limitations of community based services need to be acknowledged and finding the balance between institutional and community care needs to be found. Policy and legislation also need to be reviewed, as these need to be based on appropriate and workable norms and standards suitable to local realities and should not be fashioned on North American and British models. It is vital that this be addressed if South Africa is to meet the needs of populations at risk especially in view of the growing impact of HIV/AIDS on families and communities. Governmental, non-governmental organisations and social work researchers have not grappled sufficiently with the gender implications of community based development strategies. The design and implementation of community based care and support needs to strive to promote gender equality and a more equitable distribution of the costs and burdens of care.

'The design and implementation of community based care and support needs to strive to promote gender equality and a more equitable distribution of the costs and burdens of care.'

Generalist services. The new policy envisaged a shift from specialist to generic services also referred to in this book as generalist services. Generalist welfare services were to be encouraged as these would be more holistic and could increase access to services in disadvantaged communities. Generalist services were envisaged to form part of multi-purpose community oriented services integrated and decentralized to local or district level. A balance had to be struck between rehabilitative, protective, preventive and developmental interventions through the delivery of generalist services and practice. To what extent have services become more generalist in their approach?

Models of multi-purpose centres are being piloted in some provinces although the lessons learnt from these have not been documented. Most voluntary welfare organisations deliver statutory services in partnership with government and in the urban provinces, considerable expertise has been built up to deliver specialist statutory services. These services also constitute roughly 60 percent of the workloads of social workers especially in child welfare services. Research is needed to inform feasible and sustainable policy options for statutory services particularly in relation to child protection, juvenile justice and the protection of women against abuse. There is no accurate estimate of the scope of statutory work, its cost implications and the extent to which it hinders the shift to generalist services and practice. Loffell (2001) called on the welfare sector to develop policy options to find a balance between generalist and specialist services. These policy options would need to be based on regionally specific conditions in view of the variation in service levels between the provinces and she warned against a 'one size fits all' approach. The policy options would also need to take account of multi-purpose community centres or 'one stop shop' concept as well as the division of roles and responsibilities between provincial and local governments. Statutory services are considered to be a governmental responsibility and voluntary organisations are inadequately funded to deliver the services (Loffell 2001).

Poverty alleviation. Since 1997, additional funds have been allocated annually by Parliament for poverty alleviation programmes across government departments. In 2000/2003 this amounted to R100 million. The programmes were targeted at women, youth and people with disabilities. Over the same period, a total of 416 programmes were funded including 51 additional food security projects, which were spent in the poor rural provinces. The programmes focused mainly on micro-enterprise development and even though some successes were noted, it appears that many projects were unsuccessful. Capacity building in micro-economic development is critical to ensure a successful outcome. Some of these issues are examined in Chapters 8 and 9.

A second channel through which government intends to promote poverty reduction is through the National Development Agency (NDA) established in 2000. The NDA is a statutory body that was created under the National Development Agency Act 108 of 1998. It is a financing body to promote a strong civil society through development funding of poverty reduction programmes, capacity building, research and policy development and dialogue. In 2003, a total of R290.8 million was allocated to the NDA and resources were in turn allocated to the respective provinces for social development projects, emerging farmers, cross-cutting health and HIV/AIDS initiatives (NDA 2004). Since its inception, the NDA has received almost R550 million in funding of which R400 million was committed to various projects (The Star 23/6/2004). The organisation has been bedeviled by gross inefficiency, mismanagement of funds, persistent staffing problems and a high turnover of staff and in its senior leadership. Other problems abound such as the mismanagement of funds, allegations of corruption, nepotism and misappropriation of funds by senior officials which has hampered the organisation in meeting government's poverty targets (The Star 23/6/2004). Welfare organisations have reported frustration in accessing funding for projects from the NDA, however, the number of applications do exceed the available funding.

Partnerships & institutional issues. In Chapter 4, the collaborative partnership approach in social development was discussed and some of the challenges identified. The full potential of the partnership approach has not been realised especially in relation to both informal Community Based Organisations (CBOs) and formal welfare agencies that have had a long standing relationship with government.

The Not-for-Profit Organisation's Act of 1997 intended encouraging smaller community based organisations to formalise their governance structures and procedures to access government financing for their programmes. The legislation created an administrative and enabling environment for the non-profit sector and it also structured the relations between the state and civil society. The Taxation Amendment Act of 2000 created a more favourable tax regime to support non-profits. In March 2002, approximately 5 064 non-profit organisations were registered indicating some success with the implementation of the legislation. It is not known how many community based organisations were able to access government or donor funding for their projects. These organisations are widely believed to play an important role in social development and future policies should build on their strengths and not compromise their uniqueness and comparative advantage (Patel 2003c). Capacity building of CBOs is vital to manage their programmes more efficiently and government funding criteria and application and reporting procedures should be more user friendly and suited to the realities of the way CBOs are structured and organised.

The collaborative partnership between government and the formal welfare service providers is faced with a range of challenges, which need to be addressed if the full potential of the partnership is to be realised. Solly Mokgata (2004) of the National Coalition of Social Services (NACOSS) which represents 4 000 service providers in the welfare and development field is of the view that there is an urgent need to address the funding crisis pertaining to welfare services and the lack of human resources. A disparity in funding between government and voluntary service providers especially in relation to the salaries of social service personnel was a pressing issue. There is an urgent need to define the roles and responsibilities of the parties and the levels of funding that will be provided. Conflicting roles, demands and priorities between national and provincial governments and many practical problems in the management of subsidised services were other concerns that were identified, all of which impact negatively on service delivery. A more enabling environment is needed to promote the partnership.

Progress in the implementation of the new policy has been hampered by a lack of financial resources to fund developmental welfare services coupled with institutional constraints. Limited human resource capacity, management and administrative problems and resistance to change by the key partners are some of the factors hampering a successful outcome. Leadership, management and staff mobility has also resulted in instability and loss of institutional memory that impacted on the nature and pace of change. Social workers have also grappled with understanding and implementing the theory and practice of developmental social welfare. Some training programmes were provided to facilitate the changes. Extensive re-orienting of social service professionals from a social treatment model to social development remains an urgent priority. The integration of social development theory and practice including gender into professional education and curricula is also needed. Social development needs to be placed at the centre of the curriculum if a major social transformation in social work education is to be effected. In order to meet the backlog in human needs, human resource capacity should be increased especially in the poorest regions of the country. The training and appointment of auxiliary social workers and paraprofessionals in the social services has been limited. There is scope to expand human resource capacity through complementing social workers with auxiliary social workers and paraprofessionals in a range of fields such as child and youth care workers, community development workers, community care workers and volunteering.

'Social development needs to be placed at the centre of the curriculum if a major social transformation in social work education is to be effected.'

In conclusion, this review of the achievements and challenges indicates that whilst much has been achieved in facilitating the paradigm shift, developmental welfare services is not yet a reality. The restructuring of social security to promote a more efficient and effective delivery system may have far reaching implications for welfare services as social security will in future be delivered by a national social security agency. This will mean that provincial governments will only be responsible for welfare services, which is a small component of the overall budget. There are grave concerns that the changed policy environment could lead to decreased funding for welfare services and a waning political commitment to welfare services. The expansion of social security and the reorganisation of social security delivery as a national government competency should not compromise the efficacy of welfare services.

CHAPTER SUMMARY

- Two approaches to the delivery of social welfare services were discussed. The key features of the social treatment approach are remediation, a focus on social pathology and deficits and on individual clinical practice. This social treatment model was informed and shaped by apartheid ideology, which shaped the character of welfare services in the local context.
- The developmental welfare service delivery model has the following key features: a rights-based approach to service provision, integrated family-centred and community-based services, generalist services and the re-orientation of services through the use of community development. The paradigm

CHAPTER SUMMARY

shift from social treatment to a developmental approach also involved the dismantling of past structures and institutions and the adoption of enabling policies and legislation to shift service delivery to a developmental perspective.

- Key policy and legislative initiatives were described which provide the mandate for developmental welfare services.
- The context and new thrust of services for specific populations were explained. Practice examples were used to illustrate these new directions and local and global standard instruments were discussed where applicable.
- The achievements and challenges of welfare services were discussed with reference to key issues such as increasing access to services; community based services; generalist services and partnerships and institutional issues.

CRITICAL THINKING QUESTIONS

1. Conduct a comparative analysis of the social treatment and developmental welfare service models and identify their salient features.
2. Select any one of the client populations discussed in this chapter. What are the key developmental strategies needed to meet the needs of this client population?
3. A gender-sensitive approach was integrated throughout the discussion in relation to the different client populations. What needs and issues were identified and what gender-sensitive approaches were proposed?
4. Sloth-Nielson identified key points that are pertinent to the promotion of the rights of children growing up in child-headed households on page 181. The stance taken in this instance is that the impact of the epidemic on families is so grave that child-headed households are a reality and the policy principle should be to support them in fulfilling this responsibility rather than removing and separating the siblings. The argument against this view is that society should protect children from assuming child-rearing responsibilities prematurely and that this is inconsistent with children's rights. What are your views on this and why?
5. What do you think are the achievements and challenges of the transformation of social welfare services to the development paradigm?

Bibliography

AIDS Review. (2001), Who cares? Centre for the Study of AIDS. University of Pretoria. Series Editor: Mary Crewe, Tim Trengove-Jones.

Bilton, T., Bonnet, K., Jones, P., Lawson, T., Skinner, D., Stanworth, M. and Webster, A. (2002), *Introductory Sociology.* 4th ed. Houndmills, UK: Palgrave Macmillian.

Brocklesby, M., and Fisher, E. (2003), Community development in sustainable livelihoods approaches – an introduction. *Community Development Journal*, 38, 185–198.

Business Day. (2004), Companies act on HIV/AIDS. February 18:11.

Centre for the Study of AIDS. *AIDS Review 2003.* Pretoria: University of Pretoria.

Centre for the Study of AIDS. *AIDS Review 2001.* Pretoria: University of Pretoria.

CASE (Community Agency for Social Enquiry) (1998), *Social Security for People with Disabilities.* Researched for the Department of Welfare by Marguerite Schneider & Susan Marshall.

Connel, R.W. (1995), *Masculinities.* Cambridge: Polity.

Crowley, M.L. (1995), Crisis as challenge: counseling counselors, persons living with HIV/AIDS and survivors. *Journal of Social Development in Africa,* 10, 35–52

DEPARTMENT OF SOCIAL DEVELOPMENT (2001), *Information on capacity in facilities, government funded community and NGO community projects.* Pretoria.
DEPARTMENT OF SOCIAL DEVELOPMENT (2002), *National Guidelines for social services to children infected and affected by HIV/AIDS.* Pretoria.
DEPARTMENT OF SOCIAL DEVELOPMENT (2002), *National guidelines on home based and community based care.* Pretoria.
DEPARTMENT OF SOCIAL DEVELOPMENT (2003), *Progress Report, Building a people's contract to strengthen families and communities for a better life for children.* Pretoria.
DEPARTMENT OF JUSTICE (1996), National Crime Prevention Strategy. March. Pretoria.
DEPARTMENT OF WELFARE (1996), *Interim Policy Recommendations of the Inter-Ministerial Committee (IMC) on Young People at Risk.* Pretoria.
DEPARTMENT OF WELFARE (1997), *The White Paper for Social Welfare.* General Notice 1108 of 1997. Pretoria: Government Printers.
DEPARTMENT OF WELFARE ANNUAL REPORT. 1999–2000. RP 86/2000. Pretoria: Government Printers.
DONAHUE, J. and WILLIAMSON, J. (1999), *Community mobilization to mitigate the impacts of HIV/AIDS.* UK: Displaced Children and Orphans Fund.
DRUG STATISTICS IN SOUTH AFRICA (2003), A Doctors for Life Publication. www.dfl.org.za/issues/drugs/drug_page.htm (11 July 2004)
EDU (ECONOMIC DEVELOPMENT UNIT) (2003), *Framework: Johannesburg City Safety Strategy – final draft.* Johannesburg: City of Johannesburg.
FRANCIS, D. (2004), HIV: A pervasive system of oppression. *Social Work/Maatskaplike Werk*, 40:1, 61–71.
GIDDENS, A. (2001), *Sociology* 4th ed. Cambridge: Polity Press.
GOLDBLATT, B. (2004), The right to social assistance and gender – a study of the implementation of the child support grant. Paper presented at the Gender and Social Security Seminar hosted by the Centre for Applied legal Studies on 6–7 December 2004. Johannesburg: University of the Witwatersrand.
GRAY, M.M.A. (1996), The importance of community development. *Social Work/Maatskaplike Werk Journal,* 32, 193–204.
GREEN, S. (1997), Assessment of the psycho-social needs of clients with physical disabilities. *Social Work/Maatskaplike Werk,* 33:4, 343–359.
GREEN, G.P. and HAINES, A. (2002), *Asset building & Community development.* Thousand Oaks CA: Sage Publications.
GRIGGS, R.A. (2002), *Preventing crime and violence in South African schools: A review of learning and good practice from eight interventions.* Commissioned by the Criminal Justice Initiative. Cape Town: Open Society for South Africa.
HADLEY, R. and LEIDY, B. (1996), Community social work in a market environment: A British-American exchange of technologies and experiences. *British Journal of Social Work,* 26, 823–844.
HELPAGE (1999), *The ageing and development report: A summary.* London: HelpAge International.
HELPAGE (2000), *The mark of a noble society: Human rights and older people.* A briefing paper. London: HelpAge International. http://www.engender-health.org/itf/south_africa.html. (23 July 2004)
HSRC/NELSON MANDELA FOUNDATION AND NELSON MANDELA CHILDREN'S FUND. (2002), *The Nelson Mandela/HSRC study on HIV/AIDS – Executive Summary* www.hsrc.ac.za/research (25 May 2004)
HUMAN SCIENCE RESEARCH COUNCIL (2004), *The National Household HIV Prevalence And Risk Survey Of South African Children.* www.hsrcpublishers.ac.za (9 July 2004)
INTERNATIONAL LABOUR OFFICE (UNDATED). *Guide for community-based vocational rehabilitation of disabled people . The case of the Philippines,* Integrating disabled people into the community. Geneva: ILO.

IRIN (2004). *South Africa: New report highlights the plight of the elderly.* www.irinnews.org/report (15 June 2004)

KGANAKGA. M, (2003), Home based care. Lecture given at Rand Afrikaans University on 17 September 2003.

KIRST-ASHMAN, K. (2003), *Introduction to Social Work and Social Welfare: Critical Thinking Perspectives.* California: Brooks/Cole.

KIRST-ASHMAN, K. and HULL, G.H. (2002). *Understanding Generalist Practice.* California: Brooks/Cole

LANDON, P.S. (1995), Generalist and advanced generalist practice. In R. L. Edwards (ed.), *Encyclodedia of social work* 19: 2, 1101–1108. Washington, DC: NASW Press.

LEGIDO-QUIGLEY, H. (2003), Exploring the role on poverty alleviation in households affected by HIV/AIDS. Conference paper for the 4th International research conference on Social Security. Antwerp, Belgium, 5–7 May.

LESHILO, W.M. (2004), The feelings of people with physical disabilities regarding discrimination in Tembisa. Unpublished MA dissertation in Social Work (Health Care). Pretoria: University of Pretoria.

LOFFELL, J. (2001), Generic vs Specialist Approaches in the Social Services. Unpublished paper presented at meeting of Welfare Summit Task Team on Generic and Specialist Services. 19th March.

LOMBARD, A. (1996), Developmental social welfare in South Africa: A theoretical framework. *Social Work/Maatskaplike Werk Journal*, 32, 162–172.

MALAKA, D. (2003), A life skills awareness project for grade 7 learners on substance abuse and HIV/AIDS: An intervention research project. *Social Work/Maatskaplike Werk,* 39 (4): 381–391.

MALHERBE, B.R. (2002), Indigenous knowledge and practice in HIV/AIDS education and prevention with particular reference to women. *Social Work/Maatskaplike Werk,* 38:4, 337–353.

MARITZ, A., and COUGHLAN, F. (2004), Developmental social work: Exploring the attitudes and experiences of South African social work students. *Community Development Journal,* 39, 28–37.

MERTON, M. (2003), Shock figures on HIV/AIDS in the workplace. *Mail & Guardian*. May 30–June 5: 28.

METTS, R.L. and OLESON, T. (1995), Assisting disabled entrepreneurs in Kenya: implication for developed countries. *Small Enterprise Development Journal,* 6, 23–33.

MOKGATA, S. (2004), The financing and costing of welfare services beyond social security: issues and challenges. A perspective of private service providers. National Conference for Social Service Professions. 25–27 October 2004, Pretoria.

NAIDOO, S. (2004), *An analysis of MODE's services for entrepreneurs with disabilities.* Johannesburg: MODE

NATIONAL DEVELOPMENT AGENCY (2004), http://www.nda.org.za/ndaVm.htm. (5 December 2004.)

NATIONAL COUNCIL FOR CHILD AND FAMILY WELFARE. (2002), Cape Town: Cape Town Child Welfare Society.

NOUMBISSI, A., and ZUBERI, T. (2003), *Household structure and aging in South Africa: A research note.* Research note prepared for the Virtual Conference on African Households: An exploration of Census Data, Organised by the African Census Analysis Project, Population Studies Centre, Philadelphia: University of Pennsylvania, November 21–23.

PARRY, C.D.H. (2000), *Alcohol problems in developing countries: challenges for the new millennium.* www.sahealthinfo.org/admodule (14 April 2004)

PARRY, C.D.H. and BENNETTS, A.L. (1998), *Alcohol policy and public health in South Africa.* www.sahealthinfo.org/admodule. (13 April 2004)

PATEL, L., NOYOO, N. and LOFFELL, J. (2004), *The Human Development Situation in Johannesburg*. Centre for Social Development in Africa. Johannesburg: Department of Social Work – Rand Afrikaans University.

PATEL, L. and WILSON, T. (2003a), A perspective on the transformation of social welfare 1994-2002. *Social Worker Practitioner/Researcher*, 3:219–232.

PATEL, L. (2003b), Challenges of restructuring social welfare in a post apartheid South Africa. *Social Worker Practitioner/Researcher*, 1:1–11.

PATEL, L. (2003c), Social Development in a society in transition. *Social Development Issues*, 25: 1&2, 151–161.

PELTZER, K., MALAKA, D. and PHASWANA, N. (2002), Prevalence of substance use among first year University of the North students in South Africa: baseline assessment for primary prevention intervention. *The Social Work Practitioner-Researcher.* 14:1, 67–79.

PROUTY, T. (2002), *Perilous Complacency*. A Contemporary Survey of Workplace HIV/AIDS Policies and Practices in South Africa. Southern African Catholic Bishops' Conference. Occasional Paper 9. July.

REPUBLIC OF SOUTH AFRICA. The Constitution of the Republic of South Africa. 1996. Act 108 of 1996. Pretoria: Government Printers.

REPUBLIC OF SOUTH AFRICA. The Domestic Violence Act, 1998. Act No. 116 of 1998. *Government Gazette*. Pretoria: Government Printers.

REPUBLIC OF SOUTH AFRICA. The Drugs and Drug-Trafficking Act, 1992. Act 140 of 1992. *Government Gazette.* Pretoria: Government Printers.

REPUBLIC OF SOUTH AFRICA. Juvenile Justice Bill.

REPUBLIC OF SOUTH AFRICA. Probations Services. Act 116 of 1991. *Government Gazette.* Pretoria: Government Printers.

REPUBLIC OF SOUTH AFRICA. (1999), Financing Policy. Developmental Social Welfare Services. *Government Gazette.* No. 19888. Republic of South Africa: Government Printers.

REPUBLIC OF SOUTH AFRICA. (1997), White Paper on an Integrated National Disability Strategy. Office of the Deputy President. Pretoria: Government Printer.

ROTHMAN, J. (1995), Approaches to community intervention. In J Rothman (ed.), *Strategies of community intervention,* 5th ed FE Peacock Pubs Inc.

SACENDU (2003). *Research Brief Phase 14.* www.sahealthinfo.org/admodule /sacendu. (23 April 2004).

SOUTH AFRICAN NATIONAL COUNCIL FOR CHILD & FAMILY WELFARE (2002), Second Progress Report on the Transformation of the Child Welfare South Africa, SA National Council for Child and Family Welfare. Johannesburg: Unpublished Report.

SALEEBEY, D. (1997), The strengths approach to practice. In D. Saleebey (ed.), *The strengths perspective in social work practice* 2nd ed. (49–73). White Plains, NY: Longman.

SANCA (2004), Ahanang Correctional Services Project. Launch of Second Phase. Johannesburg: SANCA.

SHRUEDER, L. and KALIS., A. (2002), Second Progress Report on the Transformation of Child Welfare South Africa,. South African National Council for Child and Family Welfare. Unpublished.

SLOTH-NIELSEN, J. (2004), *Realising the rights of children growing up in child-headed households: A guide to laws, polices and social advocacy.* Western Cape: Community Law Centre.

SOUTH AFRICAN POLICE SERVICES (SAPS) Crime Statistics (2003), *Crime in the RSA for the financial years 1994/1995 to 2002/2003.*www.saps.gov.za/8-crimeinfo/200309/rsato2.htm (11 July 2004)

SOUTH AFRICAN NATIONAL DRUG MASTER PLAN (1999), Pretoria: Government of the Republic of South Africa.

THE STAR. *Top officials hitting NDA's pockets.* (23 June 2004.)

THE PEOPLE'S VOICE.(1998), *National speak out on poverty hearings.* March–June 1998.

THEJANE, T. and MUTHUKRISHNA, N. (2000), Investigating the lives of children with disabilities in the Qwaqwa Region: Implications for service provision in a rural context. *Social Work/Maatskaplike Werk,* 36:2, 157–167.

UNAIDS (2004), *Global estimates of HIV and AIDS as of end 2003.* www.unaids.org/bangkok2004/GAR2004_pdf/Globalestimates_en.pdf (11 July 2004)

UNITED NATIONS (1988), *Guiding principles for developmental social welfare polices and programmes in the near future.* New York: United Nations Department of Public Information.

UNITED NATIONS (2002), *Second world assembly on ageing.* Madrid: 8th to 12th April 2002.

UNDP (United Nations Developmet Programme) (2004), *The challenge of sustainable development: unlocking people's creativity.* Oxford: Oxford University Press

VAN DER BERG, S. (1998), Fiscal implications of the transformation of social welfare. *Social Work/Maatskaplike Werk Journal,* 34, 35–43.

VAN DER BERG, S. and BREDENKAMP, C. (2002), Devising social security interventions for maximum poverty impact. *Social Dynamics Journal,* 28, 39–68.

WEYERS, M.L. (2001), *The theory and practice of community work: A South African perspective.* Potchefstroom: Keurkopie.

WHO (WORLD HEALTH ORGANIZATION.) (2001), *The World health report – Mental health: new understanding, new hope.*

ZEHR, H. (2002), Listening to victims: implications for restorative justice practice in the US and abroad. Seminar sponsored by the Center for Restorative Justice and Peacemaking, University of Minnesota.

PART

3

Social development practice

CHAPTER

7

Social development practice model

LEARNING OUTCOMES

After you have read this chapter you should be able to:

- Describe and discuss the two stage model of social development practice. This will entail the ability to define social development, its character and organizing themes and discuss the integrated practice frame of reference of developmental social work and social services with reference to its key concepts, purposes, mandate, knowledge, skills roles and values.
- Describe the multi-modal approach to developmental welfare intervention
- Discuss the social development planned change process.
- Identify questions for critical reflective thinking

Introduction

Since social development is an emerging approach in social welfare, social work and the social services, there is a need to provide a conceptual framework that will guide social development practice in the South African context. A two-stage social development practice model is formulated in this Chapter. Part 1 of the model defines social development and outlines its character and organising themes. The second part of the model builds on Part 1 and sets out an integrated practice frame of reference to guide developmental social work processes and the delivery of social services.

Potgieter (1998) devised a holistic process model to inform social work practice from a developmental perspective. The process model is informed by empowerment, human diversity, a concern with human needs and generic integrated practice, which are core social development concepts. The social development practice model outlined in this Chapter builds on these concepts and integrates the theory of developmental social welfare discussed in the preceding chapters of the book. The model is intended to guide developmental social welfare, social work and social service practitioners in the how of social development in a changing national, regional and global context. The model is also rooted in the history, meaning and contextual realities of the country and connects disparate perspectives, issues and concerns with a desire to build a new nation based on democracy, social justice, peace and social and economic development. This practice model is a heuristic device to show how social development theory and concepts might be infused into developmental social work processes and the delivery of social services.

A model is a conceptual framework that identifies the key characteristics, ideas, values, processes and methods that inform practice. Its purpose is to discover and describe a phenomenon. It is however only a partial representation of what actually occurs in reality.

The driving force of the model is creative human agency or action and the power of the actors to bring about change in their lives and social conditions. Through this process individuals, families, groups, communities and organisations are able to explore new possibilities and ways of understanding their social situations, taking action to manage their conditions and optimise opportunities. This formulation of the practice model has been informed by Finn and Jacobson's (2003) conception of just practice based on key concepts such as meaning, context, power, history and the possibility of overcoming the fatalistic attitude that social conditions cannot be changed.

The translation of social development theory into practice requires ongoing critical reflection and engagement with others about the nature and meaning of social development. Implementation applications of social development are also important to find out what works and what does not work and why. In Chapter 8 innovation and best practice examples in the South African situation are discussed. Such reflection can lead to the affirmation of the social development approach or, through challenge and negotiation, new meanings might be created and recreated. An indigenous social welfare and social work practice model can only evolve through rigorous documentation and analysis of different practice modes and their appropriateness to the local and regional situation.

'An indigenous social welfare and social work practice model can only evolve through rigorous documentation and analysis of different practice modes and their appropriateness to the local and regional situation.'

Part 1: Organising themes of a social development model

The theory of social development was outlined in Chapter 1. Social development is defined by Midgley (1995:250) as 'a process of planned change designed to promote the well-being of the population as a whole in conjunction with a dynamic process of economic development'. *Social development* represents one approach to social welfare; other widely recognised approaches are the *residual and institutional* conceptions of social welfare. The two phrases – the social development approach to social welfare and developmental social welfare – are used interchangeably in this book and *refer to policies and programmes that meet needs, promote rights, manage social problems, and facilitate the maximisation of opportunities to achieve social well-being and the promotion of human empowerment and social inclusion*. The goal of developmental welfare is to achieve the wider societal and global goal of human well-being and human security. The social development approach to social welfare takes a broad view of social welfare and acknowledges the multi-sectoral nature of social development made up of different professionals and paraprofessionals in a range of fields such as health, education, social services, social work and social security.

The *character of social development* was explained in Chapter 1 in relation to its key dimensions. These dimensions were: the vision, goals, principles, programme type, auspices, views of clients and beneficiaries and the inter-relation between the national, regional and global dimensions of social development in the early 21st century.

Character of social development

Vision: empowered, humane, just and democratic society; focused on pro-poor change; challenges the unequal and distorted economic, social and political development nationally, regionally and globally; proactive involvement of governments in developmental social welfare.
Goals: promote social and economic development; participation of socially excluded in development efforts; achieve tangible improvements in the quality of life of the people; promote human development and social well-being.
Principles: social and economic justice; empowerment; collective action to promote public benefit; distributive and liberatory values.
Programme Type: activities connected with human, social, economic development and community development; building assets of the poor; local economic development; promote productive employment of the socially excluded; strengthen social capital formation; institutional development and promotion of good governance and democracy.
Access: universal coverage but with a focus on targeted interventions at the poor and socially excluded groups. Universal coverage may involve public, private and community oriented strategies.
Auspices: operates as part of a pluralist system – public, private and civil society; strong role for government in development action and facilitation.
View of providers and beneficiaries: both are active participants in development; change agents.
Local and global action: local, national, regional and global focus on human and social development; active involvement of international state and non-state actors in development.

'The South African approach to social development is socially constructed. This means that the idea of social development emerged from the social realities of the society and the involvement of many stakeholders in its formulation.'

South Africa's particular history and the conditions prevailing at the time when the new democratic society was instituted shaped the conceptualisation of social development locally. Currently, the country is also faced with further challenges of addressing new risks to human security and development arising from the globalisation process (discussed in Chapter 1). The South African approach to social development is socially constructed. This means that the idea of social development emerged from the social realities of the society and the involvement of many stakeholders in its formulation. Social development also has a meaning that is contextually relevant to the past and future society that is evolving. Social development therefore has a symbolic and a concrete meaning in the local situation, which is linked with the promotion of reconciliation and healing, the reconstruction and development of the society and the need to make good past wrongs and human rights violations. Other symbolic and concrete meanings of social development also refer to certain beliefs and principles that are valued such as equity and redress, *ubuntu* – the creation of a caring society, human agency, collaboration and partnerships and human diversity. Support for the most disadvantaged and least powerful in the society and securing an acceptable standard of living for all people is also widely endorsed. What that standard should be remains the subject of debate and the definition of social development is essentially a normative one, which is concerned with how things ought to be in the society. A distinguishing feature of social development is that it should also contribute to economic development through social investments in social programmes that enhance people's welfare through their participation in the productive economy and the achievement of social inclusion in the society.

In Chapter 4, the theoretical underpinnings of social development in the South African context were discussed. Social welfare in South Africa has been redefined around a new nucleus or a central concept, namely, social development, which is made up of the five organising themes.

'Social welfare in South Africa has been redefined around a new nucleus or a central concept, namely, social development...'

Firstly, the rights-based based approach was explained in terms of Marshall and Rawls's philosophical ideas of social and distributive justice and Drover's approach to active social citizenship. Drawing on the *Constitution of the Republic of South Africa and the White Paper for Social Welfare*, a caring, participatory, multicultural society that is geared to social transformation is envisaged. A second theme explains the theory of developmental social welfare based on Midgley's formulation of the inter-relation between social and economic development, social investment in human capital development through increasing human capacities to participate in the productive economy and society. A further axiom of the theory is that social capital or social networks based on friendship, kinship and community networks and organisations play a critical role in promoting sustainable livelihoods and in providing social support. The strengthening of financial and other tangible assets is also considered to contribute to human and social development.

A third theme in the South African conception of social development is the achievement of democracy and participation, which is indispensable to human development. Formal democracy refers to building a democratic and open society based on the will of the people through regular elections and good governance whilst participatory democracy is also encouraged through direct decision-making about matters which impact on people's lives through community-based services, civic engagement, social planning and policy formulation and advocacy. Democracy also confers rights and responsibilities on citizens. The notion of 'deep citizenship' can be achieved through active participation in all aspects of human life that is oriented toward democratic social relations in the family, community and social and economic spheres. Fourthly, a pluralistic approach to social development is envisaged involving the state, non-state actors including the private sector, individuals, families and communities. Unlike the welfare pluralism advocated by conservatives, a leading role for the state as the driving force of social progress in partnership with civil society, the private sector and other actors is envisaged.

A fifth theme addresses the importance of bridging the divide between micro and macro approaches in the process of analysing and addressing social problems; in this regard an integrated social development practice is proposed. Bridging the micro and macro divide also incorporates social development practice that attempts to bridge the gap between the *local and the global* levels of action. In a changing world, it is important to understand how meeting human needs locally are impacted by global developments and vice versa and to link the two levels in practice. These five themes draw on the theories of globalisation, social justice, developmental social welfare, democracy and human development, welfare pluralism and generalist practice discussed in Chapters 1, 4 and 6.

Part 2: Developmental social work and developmental social services model

Part two of the model sets out an integrated practice frame of reference for developmental social work practice and social services. It builds on the conceptualisation in Part 1 and defines key concepts and the purpose of social work – its mandate, knowledge, skills, roles and values.

Social development is considered to be multi-disciplinary and cuts across sectors such as health, education, economic development, social security and welfare services. Social work is one of the professions involved in the delivery of developmental social welfare. Other social service professionals involved in developmental social welfare in South Africa are community development workers, child and youth care workers, probation workers and auxiliary social workers. Provision in legislation is also made for auxiliary workers such as probation assistants. Community carers are performing community care and it is likely that a new category of auxiliary workers, referred to as community care workers, may be introduced. In view of limited resources, the new policy direction is to increase human resource capacity in the social services through the employment of auxiliary workers and paraprofessionals who will be trained and registered with the South African Council for Social Service Professions.

'Social development is considered to be multi-disciplinary and cuts across sectors such as health, education, economic development, social security and welfare services.'

The social development practice model incorporates developmental social work, community development and associated social service professions. The focus of part two of the model is on developmental social work and developmental social services.

Defining developmental social work and social services

Developmental social work is defined as the practical and appropriate application of knowledge, skills and values to enhance the well-being of individuals, families, groups, organisations and communities in their social context. It also involves the implementation of research and the development and implementation of social policies that contribute to social justice and human development in a changing national and global context.

Developmental social work aims to promote social change through a dual focus on the person and the environment and the interaction between the two. One of the purposes of developmental social work is to enhance problem-solving in human relations. This focus is shared with other mental health and social service professions in relation to social work with individuals and families. However, developmental social work also targets the environment to achieve social change through a range of mezzo and macro interventions. Secondly, social work from a social development perspective aims to balance needs with resources and promotes the optimal use of opportunities presented by the wider social environment and through tapping the assets, strengths and inner resources within the client groups themselves and the environment. Its concern is less with what people cannot do but with what they can do. Thirdly, developmental social work aims to:

'Developmental social work aims to promote social change through a dual focus on the person and the environment and the interaction between the two.'

- Meet needs, promote and protect the rights of client groups, especially those who are vulnerable and populations at risk of marginalisation in the society. Whilst developmental social work focuses on all people in the society, its emphasis on social justice means that it should address the needs of the most disadvantaged.
- Facilitate participation of client groups in managing and solving social problems.
- Promote social and economic inclusion through enhanced personal functioning and through strengthening human capital and the livelihood capabilities of individuals, groups and communities.
- Work collaboratively with all actors – individuals, families, groups, organisations, communities, non-governmental organisations, the private sector and government – to achieve its core purposes. Collaboration and working in teams, including social work and social service teams and multi-disciplinary and inter-sectoral teams, is also important in achieving its core purposes. Collaboration may also involve national, regional and international partnerships, exchange, collaborative action and standard-setting.
- Deliver services in an integrated fashion informed by the generalist approach to social work practice (Kirst-Ashman & Hull 2002) – also referred to as integrated practice (Parsons 1994). The generalist approach incorporates multiple levels of intervention with client groups of different sizes, and interventions with a diversity of client populations. This requires a variety of skills and the enactment of different professional roles. The notion of working at multiple levels of intervention is broadened to refer to intervention that also incorporates local, national, regional and global levels of intervention. The concept of empowerment draws on the strengths perspective and non-discriminatory practices that are central to generalist social work practice.

Developmental social welfare services refers to the delivery of integrated family-centred and community-based social services, facilities, social investment programmes and social protection – especially social assistance. The purpose of developmental services is to promote social justice, build human capabilities and enhance livelihoods and social functioning in order for people to lead productive and fulfilling lives. This approach breaks with the social treatment model of welfare services and its distinguishing features are described below.

- Services delivered from a rights-based perspective. Rights-based services include interventions such as the protection of the rights of populations at risk of oppression and marginalisation; the promotion of rights through education of rights and duties; facilitating access to rights; challenging policies and social systems that compromise rights and advocacy for needs and rights.
- Services delivered that are family-centred and community-based and that are integrated, decentralised and accessible at a local level. Service provision is balanced in its focus on psychosocial, protective, promotive, preventative and developmental goals with the family and the community being the main focus of attention and action. In this context, the family is understood in its broadest sense and incorporates new family forms and structures emerging in contemporary societies. The meaning of community refers to either a community of place or a community of common interest or concern and where there is agreement to collaborate to achieve common purposes.
- Services delivered from a generalist approach to service delivery. It incorporates multiple-levels of intervention; work with clients of different sizes, a diversity of client populations, needs and levels of social development. Its concerns are related to social and economic injustice, the abuse of power, discrimination and oppression. It incorporates an analysis of multiple, complex and inter-related factors that contribute to distorted development at all levels of human and social development as individuals, families, households, groups and communities interact with their environments. Generalist services are empowering of client systems, encourage participation in service delivery, build on the strengths of client groups and design and implement services from a critical reflective frame of reference. A variety of intervention strategies are also employed such as: face-to-face, one-to-one counselling with individuals and families, group treatment and support services. The mobilisation of communities to deliver services such as, peer and lay counselling, self-help groups, home-based and community care and volunteerism are other examples. Strategies may also include livelihood initiatives, educational interventions and the mobilisation of communities to meet needs through partnerships and a diversity of social networks. Work with and in organisations through stimulating community-based organisations, neighbourhood and

'Generalist services are empowering of client systems, encourage participation in service delivery, build on the strengths of client groups and design and implement services from a critical reflective frame of reference.'

village networks, the promotion of inter-agency collaboration, regional and global networking and policy and legislative interventions are other examples.

- Services that draw on the community development approach – that is, its philosophy, process, methods, techniques and skills to promote human development and improve the social, economic, cultural and environmental conditions of communities. With its focus on poverty reduction, sustainable livelihoods, empowerment, participation and human agency, it is well placed to contribute to social development. A variety of intervention modes are associated with community development, such as locality development, which includes poverty-reduction and livelihood strategies, community information, and education and communication strategies. Social planning and policy and advocacy are also intervention modes associated with the delivery of developmental social welfare services.

Mandate

The mandate of developmental social welfare, social work and developmental social services is derived from the Constitution of the Republic of South Africa of 1996 and various United Nations and other international standard-setting instruments adopted by the South African government. National policy and legislation discussed in Chapters 4, 5 and 6 also mandate and authorise social workers and the social service professions to implement policy and legislation. It also gives the social service professions the permission to perform certain professional tasks and activities and it defines the scope and the fields in which the social service professions may operate.

The Social Service Professions Act No 110 of 1978 and the Social Work Amendment Act 102 of 1998 provided for the establishment of the South African Council for Social Service Professions (referred to as the 'Council'). The 'Council' is responsible for the establishment and regulation of professional boards of the social service professions. Currently, only Social Workers and Auxiliary Social Workers are registered to operate in terms of the Act. Professional Boards for Child and Youth Care Workers, Community Development Workers and Probation Workers have been established. The 'Council' is responsible for the registration of social service professionals. It is also responsible for, among other things, the setting of standards as to what is professional and ethical conduct, enforcing good conduct, and facilitating professional development and quality assurance. Professional and paraprofessional social service personnel will be registered and regulated in accordance with 'Council' regulations, which are being established. This approach to professionalisation of the social services makes provision for the recognition of new types of professions and incorporates both tertiary level training and vocational training. It is a novel approach suited to local needs but it could also be criticised for creating hierarchies between the social service professions which could serve as barriers to collaborative action.

Many governmental, private sector and non-governmental organisations sanction social service professionals by contracting them to perform certain tasks. Private practitioners may practise as social workers in South Africa provided they are registered social workers with the South African Council for Social Service Professions. They may also register to work in certain specialised fields, such as adoptions. Social service professionals are members of professional associations and are a voice for the social service professionals. The real test of approval to practice comes from the public, who demonstrate their sanction of the social service professions by employing them and using their services.

'The profession has had to adapt to changing social conditions and has been challenged to become more relevant and appropriate in the local context.'

Formal sanction for social work exists as a profession based on its knowledge, skills and values. The profession has had to adapt to changing social conditions and has been challenged to become more relevant and appropriate in the local context. The transformation of the welfare system has raised many critical questions about the role and status of the profession in the society. Social workers have expressed the fear that the new policy directions could lead to deprofessionalisation and a consequent loss of status of the profession. In reviewing these issues locally and internationally Lombard (2000:330) calls for 'the profession to remain relevant as the socio-economic climate changes' and to grow the profession through maintaining high standards of ethical conduct and accountability.

The policy changes have presented the profession with a crisis of confidence arising from having to learn new ways of doing things and of functioning in a new policy environment, and this has led to a sense of marginalisation. Some of the reasons for this perception of marginalisation is that social work in the past was associated with apartheid, with casework and social control and with an excessive preoccupation with professional status and with keeping others out of the field (McKendrick 2001:106). McKendrick argues that social work is uniquely qualified to make an effective contribution to developmental social welfare in that its knowledge, practice skills, professional values and its focus on strengths and empowerment match the philosophy of developmental social welfare (McKendrick 2001:108). The new policy directions are motivated by the need to address the vast backlogs in addressing human needs in the South African situation and to increase human resource capacity effectively and in a cost-effective manner.

Knowledge

The knowledge base of social development practice is drawn from an interdisciplinary body of knowledge in the social sciences, economic and management sciences, behavioural sciences, development studies and social work. It can also be described as an eclectic knowledge base in that it draws on theory and research from other fields. Developmental social workers apply this knowledge to practice situations to help them to understand human behaviour and its complex and reciprocal interconnections with the environment. It also aids social workers in understanding and explaining social phenomena and informing and guiding practice.

Midgley (1995) identified three types of theories that may inform social development practice. Firstly, social development draws on representational theories, which are conceptual representations or images of social phenomena. These theories define key concepts and show what the relations are between them. Practice models, such as the social development practice model outlined in this chapter, constitute an example of representational theory (Midgley 1995:68–70). A second type of theory that informs social development is analytical theory that attempts to provide explanations for certain social phenomena. It asks why people behave in the way they do. On a macro level it may ask the question why globalisation leads to greater social inequality in contemporary societies. A third type of theory that is widely applied in social work, social policy and social development is normative theory. This theory is evaluative in nature and consists of principles or criteria to evaluate whether social interventions achieve their goals.

Social workers working from a social development perspective draw on a range of theories that could aid assessment, intervention and evaluation of practice with client groups of different sizes. Depending on the nature of the problems being addressed, the social worker may draw on macro, mezzo or micro-level theories. For example, large-scale theories, also known as macro or grand theories (such as systems theory, conflict theory, phenomenology and social constructionism and psychodynamic theories), may be used to aid assessment and intervention.

'Social workers working from a social development perspective draw on a range of theories that could aid assessment, intervention and evaluation of practice with client groups of different sizes.'

Macro theories are also based on different philosophies of how knowledge is created or epistemologies – positivism, post-positivist (also known as interpretivist) and critical theoretical frameworks (Henning et al. 2004). These philosophies also influence the social worker and the social service organisation's approach to practice. Social work practice approached from the *positivist framework* conducts assessments on the basis of the law of cause and effect, which is believed to be studied only by means of rational scientific methods, quantitative data and the use of scale technologies. Such an approach considers the researcher/practitioner to be neutral and objective. The *interpretivist framework* is a critique of positivism and argues that social workers should capture the lives of client groups in order to understand and interpret their meaning from the client group's perspectives. It involves working towards an empathy with client groups as social actors who create their own understandings of their situations with intervention being defined in an interactive way by the social actors themselves. This approach is based on the idea that human beings cannot be studied in the manner that the natural and medical sciences are, and that a different approach is needed. Interpretivists also challenge the notion that the social worker can be objective and unbiased, and they acknowledge the importance of values in social work practice. Lastly, a critical framework approaches social work practice from the point of view of the unequal distribution of power relations in the society, which is of a social, economic, political and institutional nature. Critical theories informing practice could be of a social justice, empowerment, anti-discriminatory and feminist orientation. They also question the unequal power relations between the practitioner and client groups where the worker is the expert. Neutrality of the worker is also questioned and a partnership between client groups and workers is envisaged.

There are also middle-range theories that are applicable at mezzo levels and that may inform practice: these include theories of organisations and communities or empowerment theories. These different types of theories and models enable the social worker to ensure that client groups have the benefit of a growing and progressive knowledge base and to apply this to several levels of intervention ranging from the micro to the macro level. In view of the complexity of human behaviour and its interconnections with the environment as well as large-scale social transformations that are taking place locally and globally, an expansive knowledge base, which understands people in their total social situation, is critical to developmental social work.

'This means that the social worker needs to have knowledge of a wide range of social work and other theories.'

Theories do not address all aspects of human existence. For this reason it is important to use a combination of theories that are relevant to the needs of client groups and the social situations in which they find themselves. Some theories may not be suitable for some clients and situations and the social worker who has a broad knowledge base is able to draw on those theories that are most relevant to the situation. This means that the social worker needs to have knowledge of a wide range of social work and other theories. Instead of relying only on functionalist, social systems, ecological and individualistic psychodynamic theories, which focus on social treatment only, Robbins et al. (1998) call for a more expansive approach to the knowledge base of social work practice in contemporary societies.

Theories are a powerful means of organising the thinking of the practitioner. However, theories that inform social work are not free of the interests, biases, and moral and cultural beliefs of those who promote them. In applying theory, the social worker should be mindful of theories that explain human behaviour in a simplistic way or perceive a social phenomenon from the point of view of a single discipline only. It is important to be discerning in using theory especially when these theories reduce causality to a single explanation or factor – often referred to as reductionism. The ideological underpinnings of theory should also not be underestimated, as theory has a powerful impact on the lives of people. For instance, during apartheid, theories to justify racial superiority were used to examine the link between school performance and race. Colonialism also resulted in the denigration of indigenous approaches to meeting needs and the uncritical application of theories not suited to the local context.

Given the scope and limits of theory discussed above, evaluation and selection of what theories are best suited to what situations and that are compatible with developmental social work and social services is a major challenge. The following guidelines could inform theory evaluation and selection (Robbins et al. 1998; Payne 1997).

- An awareness of worker values, goals, practice commitments, strengths and limitations should guide theory selection. This also involves an assessment as to whether the theory is consistent with the values and ethics of the social service professions.
- A wide knowledge of a range of theories is needed and a holistic approach should be adopted that takes all facets of human and social life into account. This includes the bio-psychosocial, relational, spiritual and political, ideological, economic, the physical and environmental context.
- The theories should be well grounded in evidence, which should enhance understanding, interpretation, description, explanation and possibly prediction of behaviour and social outcomes.
- An assessment of the relevance of the theory to the needs of client groups is needed and account must be taken of client goals and perspectives and the social context.
- A cautious, co-ordinated, systematic and planned approach to the application of theory in a given context is suggested. The social worker should make a professional judgement of the relevance and appropriateness of the theory in collaboration with the client where possible.
- Theories may be selected on the basis of the best fit of the theory with the social problems, issues or conditions requiring assessment and intervention. The most compelling ideas of the theories are usually used. Where a theory is limited, it can be complemented with other theories. A synthesis of different concepts, ideas and models may be conducted for assessment and intervention, research and policy analysis.
- Social workers are also encouraged to choose their theoretical approach and to complement this with other theories that are appropriate to the purpose for which they will be used. For instance, development social workers will tend to ground their work in a developmental orientation, and complement this with other relevant theories.
- This process of theory selection and application involves creativity and, in practice, Payne (1997) is of the view that social workers tend to construct informal theories that guide their actions on the basis of their own experience and values.

'The most compelling ideas of the theories are usually used. Where a theory is limited, it can be complemented with other theories.'

Social development theory, like social work theory in general, is fairly underdeveloped. It remains a great challenge to build the theoretical foundations and practice modalities of developmental social work and developmental social services. A more expansive approach to social work theory means that new possibilities are created for practice and research in different paradigms. The large-scale social changes that are taking place at a global level and in South Africa and the Southern

African region require an ongoing review of existing theories. A critical reflective review of social work and social development knowledge could lead to a renewal of existing knowledge or the creation of new knowledge in the course of action that is relevant to the changing context.

Knowledge: Developmental social work. Developmental social work integrates multidimensional theories that emphasise the interconnections between human problems, life situations and social conditions. It is informed by generalist conceptions of practice (Kirst-Ashman 2002; Sheafor, Horejsi & Horejsi 1997; Schatz, Jenkins & Sheafor 1990). It also requires a holistic assessment of the client system's social situation and the type and levels of intervention are decided after the problem has been identified, assessed and understood in its full context in dialogue and interaction with service users. The social worker is then able to define a generalist intervention strategy, which addresses the problem at multiple levels – micro, mezzo and macro levels. The micro level of intervention refers to social work practice with individuals, families and small informal groups. The focus of intervention is mainly confined to the local sphere of action and interaction. Social work practice at a mezzo level refers to work with formal organisations, groups and networks and its sphere of action may be local, provincial or national. Macro-level interventions take place at a much broader level. These refer to social work practice with communities, policy and legislative interventions and may operate in the national, regional or global realm. Developmental social work also bridges the micro–macro divide in social work and makes the linkages between the local and the global and vice versa. This approach can work best in agency environments that encourage generalist development practice.

Developmental social work is compatible with general systems and ecosystems perspectives as these provide for a holistic approach and for interventions with client groups of different sizes. It also enhances an understanding of the interconnections between the person and the environment. However, its limitations lie in its lack of focus on conflict and how social structures contribute to poverty, inequality, underdevelopment and social exclusion of individuals, families and communities. It is for this reason that general systems theories need to be complemented with other relevant social welfare, social work and development theories.[1] These are theories of social justice; empowerment; developmental social welfare; welfare pluralism – the role of the state and other actors in promoting development. Participatory and people-centred development[2] theories

Footnotes

1. For a more detailed exposition of social science, social work and developmental welfare theories mentioned above refer to Robbins, Chatterjee and Canda (1998); Payne (1997); Midgley (1995); and Johnson (1992).
2. For a discussion of poverty and development theories, refer to Allen & Thomas (2000).

(Korten 1995), with their emphasis on justice, environmental sustainability and inclusiveness, are highly relevant, as is human needs-centred development (Seers 1979), with its emphasis on realising human potential through meeting the physical, employment, and educational needs of the people. From this perspective, developmental social work takes the view that individual, community and macro change takes place incrementally and is driven by the people themselves in partnership with development agents such as social workers and community development workers involved in deliberate and planned change.

'From this perspective, developmental social work takes the view that individual, community and macro change takes place incrementally and is driven by the people themselves in partnership with development agents ....'

Figure 7.1 contains a mandala of developmental social work, which is presented in a circular symbol of the universe and reflects the search for unity and relatedness of developmental social work with its wider social environment. The four quadrants in the outer circle contain a constellation of theories grouped around a central concept. In the first and second quadrants, person-focused and environment-focused theories are identified (Robbins et al. 1998). In the third quadrant, social work theories are listed that include both person- and environment-focused theories, some of which are most suited to particular levels of intervention. The fourth quadrant identifies the development theories that inform development thinking and practice, some of which were discussed in Chapters 1 and 2. The circle in the centre integrates the theories and concepts that were discussed in Chapter 4 and combines these with generalist social work practice theory. The theories in the inner circle represent those that have the best fit with developmental social work, although they do not preclude the use of any of the other theories in the four quadrants in the outer circle. The skills, roles, values and intervention strategies of the model are discussed below.

In the selection of theories, it is vital that social workers and social service practitioners continuously ask critical questions about the assumptions, beliefs, values, issues, interests and practices of the range of theories identified above and to select those that are most compatible with the new developmental social welfare and social work paradigm. Such a process of questioning should be a positive and constructive one and the answers should assist the practitioner in deciding whether the perspective is consistent with the character of social development practice and the social development frame of reference. Schriver (1995) refers to this process as paradigm analysis and suggests that this be conducted through a process of critical questioning. The questions should serve as a filter in the selection of theories to identify those perspectives and ideas that are consistent with the social development approach.

Critical questions for paradigm analysis

Does the theoretical perspective:

- Assist us in understanding and working with client groups to achieve empowerment, social justice, pro-poor change and a humane and democratic society?

- Aid assessment and intervention that takes account of unequal social, economic and political relations and power in the society?
- Recognise the benefits of participation and collaboration between beneficiaries and service providers in working for change?
- Lead to interventions at multiple levels that will help us to bridge the micro macro divide?
- Allow for widening people's choices by creating opportunities that expand people's capabilities?
- Help us to understand the interrelations between the social and the economic aspects of people's lives?
- Encourage flexibility, creativity and a reflective practice?
- Does the approach assist us in examining our own perspectives and views and in understanding how these shape our practice?
- Inform local understandings and action that is relevant to South African conditions in a changing regional context?

Figure 7.1. Mandala of developmental social work and social services

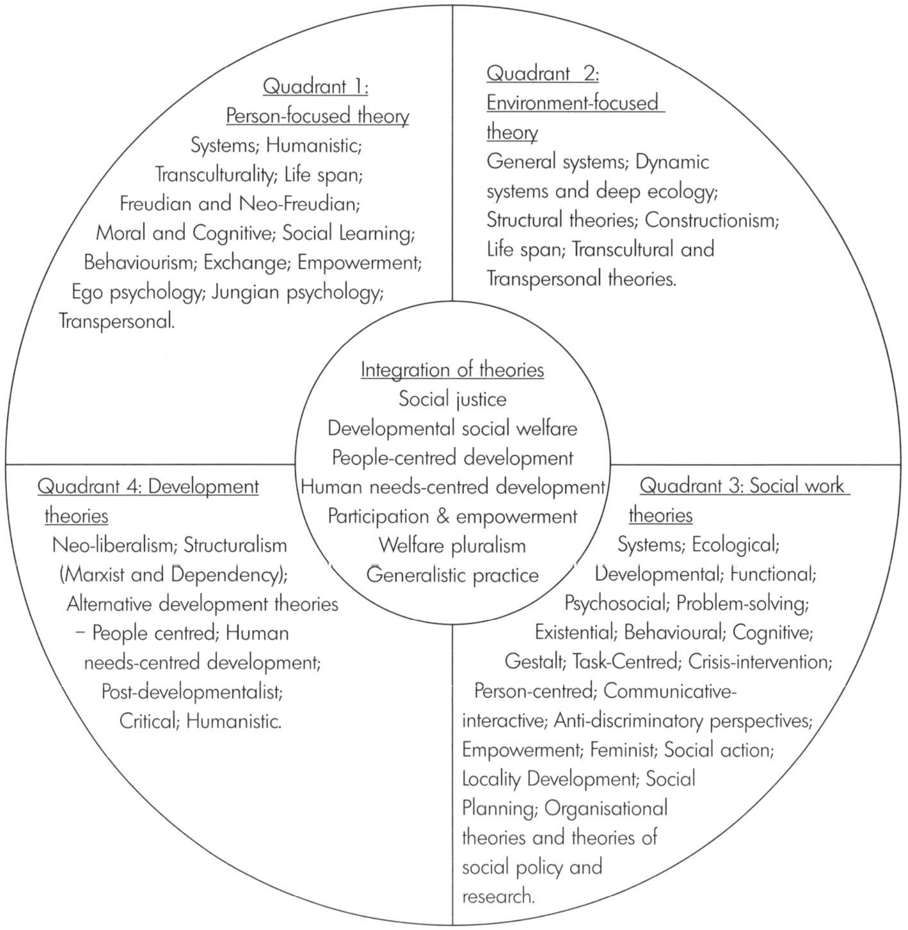

Source: Adapted from the theories discussed in Robbins et al. 398–400:1998; Midgley 1995; Johnson 1992.

Skills in developmental social work

Developmental social workers require a wide range of skills to work with client groups of different sizes and with a diversity of problem situations and populations at risk. Social work practised from a developmental perspective uses the knowledge, skills and values of social work and applies these at micro, mezzo and macro levels. More specifically, this requires drawing on the knowledge and skills of social work with individuals, families, groups, organisations, communities and policy and planning practice and infusing general social work processes with a developmental practice orientation and skills. This process is described briefly in relation to developmental social work at micro, mezzo and macro practice levels. The skills are transferable between the different levels.

Micro developmental social work skills (individual, family and small informal groups). Micro skills are those skills involved in relationship-building, effective communication, interviewing, counselling, and group work with small, informal groups. The groups may have different goals, including treatment, self-help, growth, socialisation, education and skills-building, advocacy and task groups (Kirst-Ashman & Hull 2003). Other micro skills include skills in accessing and utilising material and non-material resources (South African Qualifications Authority 2003).

Mezzo developmental social work skills (formal organisations, groups and networks). Mezzo skills build on micro skills of relationship-building, communication, interviewing and social work practice with groups. Additional mezzo skills such as organisational analysis and design, implementation and evaluation of organisational development and change interventions are needed. Other relevant skills in working in organisations are networking skills; working in teams including multi-disciplinary teams; mobilising, implementing and evaluating collaborative partnerships to achieve common goals; managing and administering developmental social service organisations and programmes; mobilisation of resources; decision-making; managing conflict; anti-discriminatory practice and reflective practice skills.

Macro developmental social work skills (community, societal and global action). Macro practice skills build on micro and mezzo skills. Depending on the modes of intervention adopted, a variety of community practice skills are used, including locality development, social policy/planning and advocacy (Rothman 1995). The locality development mode of intervention involves the mobilisation of a broad cross-section of people in solving their own problems through consensus strategies and community-building initiatives. The social policy and planning mode of intervention uses research and needs assessments to design, plan, implement and evaluate policies and programmes that solve substantive human development problems and concerns at a community, societal and international levels. Advocacy intervention strategies involve the mobilisation of people to take action against unjust social situations, to shift power relations and resources or to effect institutional change.

The skills required to implement these different modes of intervention are diverse, although some overlapping generic skills are applicable across the three modes of intervention. These are, firstly, research skills – particularly action research, which is usually conducted by communities and organisations to improve social conditions and solve social problems. It usually has a social change agenda. The second mode of intervention is designing, planning and evaluating intervention strategies, and managing programmes and projects. Thirdly, all three modes apply skills in the mobilising of people and resources. However, the tactics and strategies differ between consensual and conflict strategies or these strategies may be combined depending on the nature of the problem being addressed. Locality development involves working with small groups, the social policy/planning mode involves guiding large organisations, and cause advocacy mobilises large groups and mass organisations in social action.

In Chapter 8 innovation and best practice lessons learnt from the implementation of the social development practice model will be discussed. Some of the skills will be discussed and applied in the local context in Chapter 9.

Roles

Developmental social workers assume a wide range of roles across different levels of practice and with different client populations. Social work roles are linked to developmental social welfare goals and processes. Kirst-Ashman (2003:90) defines professional roles as consisting of the 'behaviours and activities involved in performing some designated function'. The generalist practice roles that are applicable to developmental social work are as follows:

- **Enabler and empowerment.** Parsons describes the enabler role as assisting or promoting client and client groups 'to make others able, to provide them with the means, opportunity, make possible or effective. It also implies education, facilitation and promotion of interaction and action' (Parsons 1994:188). This role is closely related to empowering individuals, groups and communities who face social exclusion in the society to take personal or collective action to address a situation. Kirst-Ashman (2003:21) defines empowerment as the 'process of increasing personal, interpersonal or political power so that individuals can take action to improve their life situations'. Empowerment also refers to the overall approach but for this purpose it refers to role enactment.

Example: MODE is an NGO that provides entrepreneurial training for people with disabilities, assists them with setting up their businesses, and provides ongoing support during the first year of operation. Close to 80 percent of the businesses succeed and individuals and their households are able to earn a livelihood and lead independent lives. The entrepreneurs say that they have grown in confidence and self-esteem, have learnt skills (including life skills) and have grown their businesses through their social networks.

'Turning dreams into reality' is the success story of MODE, an entrepreneurship training programme.

- **Mobiliser.** The social worker acts as the catalyst and brings community members together to identify their needs and issues and to take action to effect change (Kirst-Ashman 2003). This role is traditionally associated with community practice and effecting community change; however, the role may be used across client systems such as mobilising resources to meet needs or bringing together a group of technical experts to advise a community about environmental degradation. Mobilisation of parties to form a partnership to address a critical issue such as trafficking in children requires a local, regional and an international response.

'The social worker acts as the catalyst and brings community members together to identify their needs and issues and to take action to effect change.'

- **Facilitator.** The practitioner guides group experiences and facilitates interaction, decision-making and action (Kirst-Ashman 2003). It could be the facilitation of a support group for abused women and children or the facilitation of an organisational strategy to expand services to under-serviced communities. A social worker facilitated the participation and involvement of the women of *Impendle* in Kwazulu-Natal to participate in a poultry-farming project, which feeds 150 women and 200 children.

- **Educator.** The educator role involves information-sharing and exchange, skill transfer as part of lifelong learning and builds human capabilities to strengthen livelihoods, improve social functioning, build local institutions and enhance organisational effectiveness. Social workers assume many different educational roles such as mentoring and coaching; involving clients in skills training such as parenting skills, stress management, how to run a meeting, learning about accessing resources and how to apply for a job.
- **Counsellor.** The counsellor provides support and guidance to clients and assists them in helping processes and in problem-solving in human relations (Kirst-Ashman 2003:90). The counsellor role is applicable in social work with individuals, families and groups addressing issues of a psychosocial nature.

  Example: The father of Pumla'a child was recently shot and died outside her home. Pumla witnessed the shooting and is bereft and traumatised by the experience. She seeks help from the counsellors at the Centre for the Study of Violence and Reconciliation's Trauma Clinic where she receives short-term counselling and support.
- **Conferee.** The role of conferee identified by Parsons (1994) refers to 'participation in a conference' which could be any problem-solving situation where the client or client group and social worker confer or exchange ideas and make decisions about future action (Parsons 1994:168). Such a 'conference' could involve small and large groups. It may be useful in initial intervention processes to provide the mandate for the worker. However, it is equally applicable to intervention with teams, social networks, and organisational processes and in macro practice.

  Examples of situations where the conferee role is used are counselling; case and multidisciplinary team conferences; family group conferencing used with juveniles who are in conflict with the law; and policy consultation processes and think tanks. The gathering of elders in the village to discuss village concerns and governance has a long history and is known as the *Legotla*. Today, the term *Legotla* is widely used to refer to 'conferring' about matters of common concern and social service practitioners often assume this role.
- **Broker.** The social worker links clients' systems with financial, physical, educational, social service, technical and environmental resources to meet their needs. This could be in the form of a referral to a service or through facilitating client access to a resource such as an application for a social grant or identity documents (Kirst-Ashman 2003; Parsons 1994).

Example: In order to build the skills of development farmers who have limited resources, and access to finance and credit, the Land Bank assists by bridging the knowledge and resource gap of small farmers, especially women farmers. Mrs Eva Mashiane of the *Tafelkop Farmers Association* is a rural woman farmer who exports her goods. She was singled out and sent overseas to develop her skills and to broaden her export network, which was a very special learning experience (Corporate Social Investment 2003:39). Developmental social service practitioners may assist client groups by linking them with resources. In this example the link is made between Ms Mashiane of the local farmers association and the Land Bank. The broker role also overlaps with the role of educator.

- **Networker.** The role of networker involves the formal or informal linking between people and organisations to share resources, contacts and knowledge (Kirst-Ashman & Hull 2001). Networking could also involve partnerships between organisations to enlarge budgets to achieve a common goal; it could exploit organisational synergies to scale up the impact of programmes or expand service provision, or it could be a partnership to effect transformation. The role of networker requires an analysis of what needs to be done and to mobilise social development partnerships to achieve mutual benefits for the parties.
- **Mediator.** This role is assumed in order to resolve conflicts between parties and 'to promote reconciliation, settlement, compromise or understanding' (Parsons 1994:257). Social workers assume this role in many practice situations such as family counselling; victim-perpetrator mediation; community-building initiatives; depute-resolution over resources, and reconciliation through truth-telling. These are some contemporary ways in which social workers are involved in mediation.

Reconciliation through truth

The purpose of the submission to the TRC was to 'apologise to the people of South Africa, especially the poor and marginalised, for past social service practices, which were destructive to social wellbeing and the dignity of persons, families and communities, and for failures to take a firm stand against injustices' (Loffell 2000:53). The process of truth-telling was to enable the social service sector to contribute to national healing and reconciliation and to acknowledge the positive contribution of those who actively promoted social justice.

Source: Submitted to the TRC by: The Greater Johannesburg Welfare, Social Service and Development Forum; National Coalition for Social Services; SA Council for Child & Family Welfare; SA Interim Council for Social Work (May 1998).

- **Advocate.** 'One who speaks out on behalf of clients to promote fair and equitable treatment or gain needed resources' (Kirst-Ashman 2003:91). This is usually referred to as case advocacy. The practitioner may also advocate a cause, which could take the form of advocacy for a policy or a programme. The worker may also enable client empowerment through advocating for him or herself. The advocacy role is essentially about defending and upholding social rights. There is scope in the South African context for social workers to assume this role and many have done so through participation in policy and legislative processes and on a daily basis social workers are empowering individuals and communities to speak and act for themselves.

In search of safety, security and care – Social worker advocates for child refugees

Two Rwandan refugees recently escaped ethnic violence in their own country in search of safety, security and care in South Africa. Instead the two sisters were exposed to violence, sexual abuse and bureaucracy which may have resulted in them being sent back to Rwanda. A social worker at the Place of Safety where the girls were living, sought the help of the Centre for Child Law at the University of Pretoria. An urgent application was made to court to defer the deportation of the girls pending an application for asylum. The Convention on the Rights of the Child stresses the importance of giving special treatment to child refugees as children in need of care. The 'childcare worker Feziwe Bacela saved the girls from deportation when she realised their attempt to apply for refugee status was not being correctly handled by the SA authorities.'

Source: Carmel Rickard 'Shameful truth about SA's treatment of refugees', Sunday Time 6 June 2004. http://www.sundaytimes.co.za/2004/06/06/news/africa/

- **Social protector.** This role involves the protection of human rights of populations at risk by way of statutory processes. Examples include protecting children's rights, the rights of the elderly, people with disabilities and people who are HIV positive. Parsons (1994) refers to this role as the guardian role, which also involves the exercise of power and social control. This role is conferred on the social worker on the basis of the professional expertise of the practitioner or as a result of the institutional or positional authority of the worker usually derived from legislation.
- **Innovator.** This role involves the conception, implementation and evaluation of new ideas of practice and service delivery that are authentic and appropriate in a changing local and global context. Social workers experiment with new ideas in their organisations, which can be tested and later adopted as new directions for practice.

  Example: Home-based care programmes are currently being piloted nationally to develop best-practice models of community care. Storytelling is part of the African tradition and it is being used successfully in popular community education programmes. The Storyteller Group in South Africa is carrying out groundbreaking work, using comic stories as a tool to explore the gendered dimensions of violence in adolescent relationships. Innovative methodologies are used to reflect the realities of young people's lives while at the same time transforming harmful behaviour.

Values and ethics

Social development values are rooted in the values of the Constitution of the Republic of South Africa. The Constitution provides the desired ideal towards which the society needs to strive. The Constitutional values are a call to action to build the kind of society that meets the standards that the society has set for itself (Justice O'Regan cited in Ministry of Education 2001).

These Constitutional values and beliefs guide behaviour about what is right or wrong, good or bad. Ethics prescribe action based on values – it sets the rules that need to be followed to give effect to values. Social development practice embraces these values at an abstract level and also adopts principles to guide the implementation of developmental social welfare policies, programmes and services. These principles are contained in the *White Paper for Social Welfare* and include: Democracy, Equity, *Ubuntu* Non-discrimination, Human rights, People-centredness, Human Capital, Sustainability, Partnership, Inter-sectoral Collaboration, Decentralisation of Services, Transparency and Accountability, Accessibility and Appropriateness. How these principles are being implemented in the real world may present practitioners with value and ethical dilemmas, which occur when choices have to be made between two or more alternatives which conflict with one another. A dilemma is said to exist 'when there is no one answer that can conform to all ethical principles' (Kirst-Ashman 2003:30). For instance, most publicly funded old age homes are occupied by elderly people who are white and in need of care. How should their needs be balanced with the needs of black elderly persons for community services?

'Ethics prescribe action based on values – it sets the rules that need to be followed to give effect to values.'

The profession of social work can be described as a *value-based profession* (Kirst-Ashman 30:2003). Values inform how people are viewed and in turn guide practice in that they set *guidelines about ways of working with people*. The values of the social work profession locally and internationally have their origin in Judeo-Christian values (uniqueness of the individual, love, care and respect), humanism (service), capitalism (individualism and the work ethic) and clinical pragmatism, which acknowledges problems in human relations (Potgieter 1998:38).

Social development in South Africa has its roots in Constitutional values and beliefs that are generally accepted in the society and that emerged through a process of contest, dialogue and compromise. The Constitutional values are the 'glue' that holds the society together and attempt to break with the country's past; they posit alternative values that are pertinent to constructing a new society. Social work and social service values in South Africa reflect the inter-relationship between the individual and the society (Gray 1996).

Values are operationalised in the form of rules of good conduct, which are contained in professional codes of ethics. Social work in South Africa is guided by the Code of Ethics of the South African Council for Social Service Professions adopted in 1986. The Code of Ethics sets out a general approach and guidelines for ethical conduct, which is based on internationally accepted values and principles (Potgieter 1998:42–45). The South African Council of Social Service Professions (SACSSP) is revising the Code of Ethics for Social Services Professions and a code is envisaged that would be applicable to all social service professions registered with this body (SACSSP 2004). Drawing on moral theory for social work, Gray (1996) draws attention to the limits of ethical rules, and the fact that principles, although important, are often uncritically applied and do not take account of the complexity of ethical considerations. The existence of different worldviews in a society also leads to many different interpretations of values and ethics, especially in a society where new ideals have been recently embraced.

In order to define the primary values in education, the Ministry for Education engaged in a public dialogue known as *Saamtrek* (which means pulling together) and adopted a *Manifesto of Values in Education and Democracy* in 2001. The primary values of the Constitution which are considered to be most relevant to education are: Democracy, Social Justice and Equity, Equality, Non-racism and Non-sexism, *Ubuntu* (human dignity), An Open Society, Accountability (Responsibility), the Rule of Law, Respect and Reconciliation (Ministry of Education 2001).

A statement of values is needed that could guide social development practice. Based on the analysis in this book the following primary values are considered important in social development practice. These primary values are derived from the Constitution, international instruments, local and international codes of ethics (SA Council for Social Service Professions 2004, 1986; Kirst-Ashman 2003; Ministry of Education 2001; Potgieter 1989).

Primary values of social development practice

Social Justice. A commitment to social justice in the society by upholding and protecting rights, opportunities, obligations and social benefits equally for all citizens, especially the most disadvantaged. The practice of justice should result in social change. Social justice is defined in the *Social Work Dictionary* as 'an ideal condition in which all members of a society have the same basic rights, protection, opportunities, obligations, and social benefits' (Barker 1999:451). Social justice is also about ensuring that resources are equitably distributed.

Ubuntu (Humanity). Everyone has the right to human dignity and to have that respected and protected (Constitution of the Republic of South Africa 1996). Human dignity is a central value of the Constitution and is the foundation of justice and peace. The dignity and worth of the service user is impaired if the people are treated in a degrading or humiliating way. The Constitution, the Universal Declaration of Human Rights and the African Charter on Human and People's Rights use the term dignity in a broader sense as referring to the inherent worth and dignity of the person. The Code of Ethics (SACSSP 1986) affirms this value and it has been taken up in the Draft Code of Ethics Guidelines (SACCP 2004).

'The value of democracy is indispensable to social development in that there can be no social progress in the society if there is no representational and participatory democracy.'

Democracy and participation. This value is relevant to developmental social welfare in that it gives expression to the way in which social service professionals work with their clients. The value of democracy is indispensable to social development in that there can be no social progress in the society if there is no representational and participatory democracy. This view of society is based on open discussion, debate, understanding, active listening, tolerance, and the fostering of democratic social relations. The ways in which social service professionals engage with service users need to reflect human agency and active citizenship, recognising both rights and responsibilities. This value is not usually incorporated in social work codes of ethics but it may be implied.

Equality. All people should have access to services and benefits, but that access must be equal. Nobody may be unfairly discriminated against. This also means that the social service professional should understand his or her rights, but should also acknowledge the rights of service users and view them as equal to him or herself.

Non-discrimination. In view of past discrimination (especially of a racial nature), the value of non-discrimination is vital in ensuring the equal treatment of all people and in affording them the same opportunities irrespective of race, gender, sexual preference, age, disability or any other social divisions in the society. Social service professionals need to give effect to this value through a non-discriminatory social service practice and valuing diversity. Such practice is based on celebrating diversity in culture, language, gender, disability, sexual preference, national origin and race. Attitudes and behaviours that stereotype, marginalise, stigmatise or scapegoat people are contrary to non-discriminatory values. 'South Africa belongs to all who live in it, united in our diversity' (Preamble Constitution of the Republic of South Africa 1996).

Reconciliation. Social service professionals are concerned on a daily basis with the negative effects of the past on social well-being, which will be felt for generations to come. The value of reconciliation means that there is an acknowledgement of past hurt and a commitment to work for reconciliation between individuals, in communities and to address structural inequalities of power and social and economic inequalities. Reconciliation also requires active redress and reparation in the social welfare field.

Parable of the Bicycle

There was Tom and there was John. Tom lived opposite John. One day, Tom stole John's bicycle and every day John saw Tom cycling to school on his bicycle.

A year later, Tom walked up to John. He stretched out his hand. 'Let's reconcile and put the past behind us'. John looked at Tom's hand. 'And what about the bicycle?'. 'No', said Tom, 'I'm not talking about the bicycle. I'm talking about reconciliation'.

Source: Krog, A. (1997). Parable of the Bicycle. Mail and Guardian, 7th February 1997. Http://www.bard.edu/hrp/krog3.htm

Competence. Having the necessary knowledge and skills to work effectively with people and to strive for high standards of competence (SACSSP 2004; Kirst-Ashman 2003).

Integrity. This means that the social service professional conducts him or herself in a trustworthy manner and adheres to high moral ideals (SACSSP 2004; Kirst-Ashman 2003).

Professional responsibility. The Constitution reinforces the values of accountability, responsiveness and openness. This means that public social services should be governed by values and principles of professionalism, efficiency, equity, transparency, representivity and accountability (Constitution of the Republic of South Africa 1996 article 195). The way in which this value is institutionalised is through ethical codes, clarifying service-user expectations, ensuring good governance, accountability and the delivery of quality services.

Importance of human relationships. This value acknowledges 'the mutual emotional exchange; dynamic interaction; and affective, cognitive, and behavioural connections that exist between the social workers and the client to create the working and helping atmosphere' (Barker 407:1999).

Service. A commitment to service means 'providing help, resources, and benefits so that people can achieve their maximum potential' (Kirst-Ashman 31:2003).

Multi-modal approach to development welfare intervention

'Development is a vision of what a desirable society may be like.'

Development is a vision of what a desirable society may be like. It refers to a historical process of change in which societies are transformed over long periods and it consists of deliberate efforts to bring about change (Allen & Thompson 2000:40). The social development practice model involves deliberate interventions aimed at achieving human development nationally, regionally and globally. These interventions are about 'doing development' – that is, what development agents or actors do and who mandates them to 'do development'. Development agents are individuals, groups, organisations and development practitioners such as social workers, community development workers and other professionals and non-professionals engaged in development. Policy and legislation generally mandate them; this includes the agencies that employ them and the public who seek their assistance.

'The social development practice model involves deliberate interventions aimed at achieving human development nationally, regionally and globally.'

What are the development strategies that are employed in implementing developmental welfare and social work? Appropriate and innovative intervention strategies have evolved over many decades and especially during the 1980s (discussed in Chapter 3). During the 1990s, welfare and development organisations experimented with strategies to begin the shift from social treatment to social development. Various authors documented these initiatives, including new directions in community-based ways of caring and providing support for vulnerable groups, especially for orphaned and vulnerable children (Loening-Voysey & Wilson 2001; Smart 2000; Halkett 1999; Patel & Stewart 1998; Oliver & Soal 1997; Patel, Cachalia & Wilson 1995; Nell et al. 1993). Different modes of intervention emerged from these studies, and these are typically associated with developmental welfare and social work in South Africa. Based on the documented experience of developmental welfare programmes, five modes of intervention have been identified which describe different forms of developmental welfare interventions:

- Mode A: Poverty-reduction and sustainable livelihood strategies
- Mode B: Family-centred and community-based strategies
- Mode C: Community information, education and communication strategies
- Mode D: Social policy and planning strategies
- Mode E: Advocacy

These modes of intervention can be applied to developmental welfare practice with client groups of *different sizes* and a *diversity of client populations* using a broad social science, social work and developmental welfare knowledge base. Micro, mezzo and macro practice *skills* are applicable in any of the modes of intervention, including the range of social work *roles* discussed above. These modes are not exhaustive of all the possible interventions. Many of the modes can be interwoven and combined with other modes of intervention depending on the outcome of the assessment of the problem or situation. Rothman (1995) describes such an interweaving of interventions as a *multi-modal approach*. Developmental welfare intervention strategies are multi-modal in their nature and scope. Intervention strategies can also operate at multiple levels of intervention, which range from the micro to the macro, with the macro levels including societal, regional and global levels of action. Figure 7.2 depicts the multi-modal approach to intervention. In Figure 7.2.1 the separate modes are depicted and in Figure 7.2.2 the integrated multi-modal approach is depicted. The intersection of the five circles demonstrates the simultaneous use of all modes of intervention. Innovation and good practice examples emerging from field experience are discussed in Chapter 8, and demonstrate the different modes of intervention, including multi-modal interventions.

Figure 7.2: Multi-modal approach to intervention

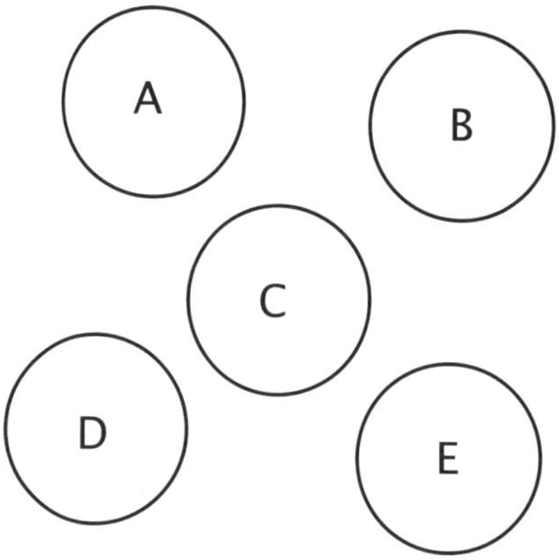

Figure 7.2.1: Separate Modes of intervention

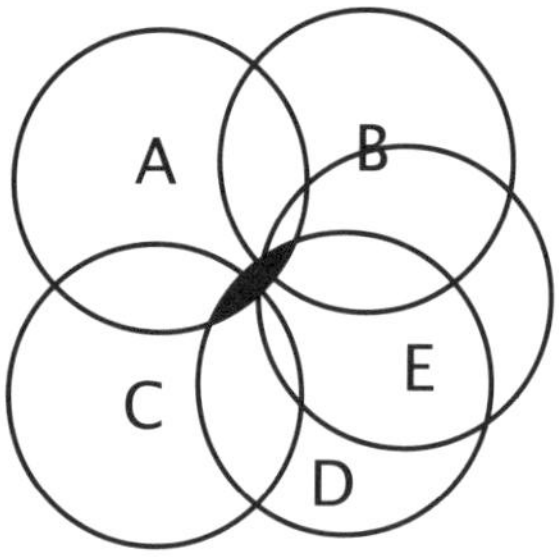

Figure 7.2.2: Multi-modal approach

Source: Adapted from Rothman (1995:46).

Social development planned change process

Social development frame of reference

The social development practice model is informed by a broad conceptual orientation that enlarges the vision and options of development agents to appropriately address diverse, complex and inter-related needs, problems and social situations in a society in transition. Part one of the model sets out the conceptual framework informing social development. This included identifying theories and models that are relevant to social development and the key organising themes informing practice. This multi-dimensional conceptual framework helps the practitioner to connect theory to practice and to be open to the use of a wide range of theories and interventions that focus on many levels of intervention from the micro to the macro and from the local to the global sphere of action. The organising themes that guide social development practice are social justice; social and economic development; people-centredness; human-centredness; participation and empowerment; social development partnerships and generalist practice.

Social development practice is also multi-modal in its approach and in the choice of intervention strategies. An interweaving of interventions strategies is proposed on the basis of multiple modes of intervention. The possibilities are unlimited, depending on the situation. This provides social service professionals with the scope to be flexible and creative, but also to be centred on what is possible. The multi-modal approach to intervention does not rely on one set of methods or skills to address complex and inter-related human problems, life situations and social conditions.

Part two of the social development practice model describes and explains the mandate, knowledge, skills, roles and values of developmental social work and social services. The organising themes for practice, the multi-modal approach to intervention and the mandate knowledge, skills and values provide the *practice frame of reference* of developmental social service practitioners. This frame of reference informs and guides the practitioner when engaging in a planned process of change.

Planned change process

A distinguishing feature of the social development planned process is that the *mode(s) of intervention* and the *level* of intervention are not decided until after carefully considering the different ways in which the client or client group's *problem might be defined and approached.* The planned change process follows a series of processes, starting with engagement and mandating of change processes; this is followed by exploration and assessment, goal-setting, planning, implementation and evaluation, termination and follow-up. The change process is widely acknowledged in social work and community development practice although there are variations between the authors of emphasis and representation of the process (Kirst-Ashman & Hull 2002:29; Parsons 1994:4). The social development planned change process is depicted in Figure 7.3 and combines the development frame of reference with the planned change process in the diagram to show the link between the two.

Figure 7.3 Social Development Planned Change Process

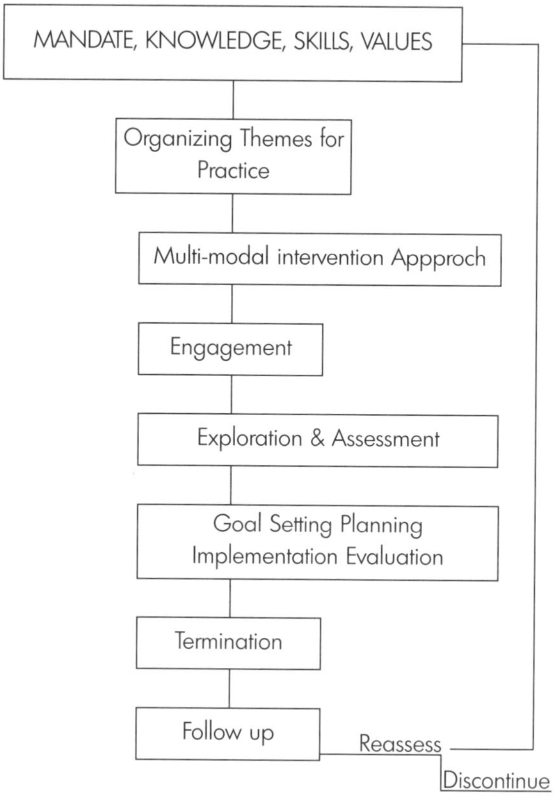

Source: Adapted from Kirst-Ashman & Hull 2002; Parsons (1994:4)

CHAPTER SUMMARY

- A two-stage model of social development practice is described and explained in this chapter drawing on the theories, concepts and models discussed throughout the book. Part one of the model sets out the conceptual framework of the model and part two provides an overview of the mandate, knowledge, skills, roles and values of social work and the social services from a social developmental perspective.
- A multi-modal approach to intervention is a critical component of the social development practice model. It allows for the interweaving of diverse modes of intervention: those based on critical reflective practice and those that are flexible, creative and contextually appropriate.
- This conceptual frame of reference informs and guides planned change processes and draws on widely acknowledged change and helping processes.
- A distinguishing feature of the social development planned process is that the mode(s) of intervention and the level of intervention are not decided until after carefully considering the different ways in which the client or client group's problem might be defined and approached. After analysis and problem assessment with the client or client group, a multi-modal intervention strategy is developed and implemented.
- The model acknowledges the inter-relatedness of human problems, life situations and social conditions.
- Local concerns that also connect with national and regional priorities and issues of global significance are addressed: poverty and inequality, sustainable livelihoods, HIV/AIDS, crime and violence, substance misuse, human rights and the needs and rights of populations at risk.

CHAPTER SUMMARY

- Social development is a value-based approach to practice that draws on a broad knowledge base, requires a diversity of skills and enactment of roles and intervention strategies suited to the situation. It allows for flexibility, creativity and the application of critical thinking in applying the model.
- An enabling organisational environment that sanctions the approach, competent staff and adequate financial resources to implement the model are needed. Social service professionals should be conscious of their limitations and should refer clients for more specialised assistance or tap the expertise of others to serve clients responsibly.

CRITICAL THINKING QUESTIONS

1. Discuss the five distinguishing themes of social development practice in the South African context.
2. What are the knowledge, skills and values of developmental social work?
3. Do you agree with the statement that social development practice is rooted in the history, meaning and contextual realities of South African society? Motivate your answer.
4. Social work is one among other social service professions including paraprofessionals. Do you support this policy stance? Motivate your position.
5. Think of a practice situation where you have experienced a value and an ethical dilemma. What values are in conflict with one another and why? What should the practitioner do to overcome this dilemma?
6. What does the *Parable of the Bicycle* tell you about reconciliation? Are we living in a reconciled society? Why is reconciliation difficult? How can social service practitioners promote reconciliation?

Bibliography

ALLEN, T. and THOMAS, A. (2000), *Poverty and development into the 21st century.* Oxford: Oxford University Press.

BARKER, R.L. (1999), The social work dictionary. 4th ed. Washington, DC: NASW Press.

CONSTITUTION OF THE REPUBLIC OF SOUTH AFRICA (1996), Cape Town: Constitutional Assembly.

CORPORATE SOCIAL INVESTMENT HANDBOOK 6th ed, Cape Town: Trialogue Publication.

FINN, J.L. and JACOBSON, M. (2003), Just Practice: Steps toward a new social work paradigm. *Journal of Social Work Education*, 39, 57–78.

GRAY, M.M.A. (1996), Moral theory for social work. *Social Work/Maatskaplike Werk Journal*, 32, 289–295.

HALKETT, R. (1999), *HIV/AIDS and the care of children*. Republic of South Africa: National Council for Child and Family Welfare.

HENNING, H., SMIT, B., and VAN RENSBURG (2004), *Finding your way in qualitative research*. Pretoria:Van Schaik.

JOHNSON, L.C. (1992), *Social work practice approach*. United States: Allyn/Bacon.

KIRST-ASHMAN, K.K. and HULL, G.H. (2001). *Generalist practice with organizations & communities.* 2nd ed. Wadsworth: Brooks /Cole.

KIRST-ASHMANN, K.K. and HULL, G.H. (2002), *Understanding generalist practice* 3rd ed. Wadsworth: Brooks/Cole.

KIRST-ASHMAN, K.K. (2003), *Introduction to social work and social welfare: critical thinking perspectives.* California: Brooks/Cole.

KORTEN, D. (1995), 'Steps toward people-centred development: Vision and strategies', in Heyzer, N., Rier, J.V. and Quizon, A.B. (eds.) *Government-NGO relations in Asia: prospects and challenges for people-centred development*, (165–189).

KROG, A. (1997), *Parable of the bicycle.* South Africa: Mail and Guardian, http://www.bard.edu/hrp/krog3.htm (7th February 1997).

LOFFELL, J. (2000), Truth and the social services. *Social Work/Maatskaplike Werk* 36:1, 53–68.

LOENING-VOYSEY, H. and WILSON, T. (2001), *Approaches to caring for children orphaned by AIDS and other vulnerable children: Essential elements for a quality service.* Report prepared for UNICEF by the Institute for urban primary health care.

LOMBARD, A. (2000), The Professional status of social work. *Social Work/ Maatskaplike Werk Journal,* 36, 311–331.

MINISTRY OF EDUCATION (2001), *Manifesto on values, education and democracy.* Pretoria: Ministry of Education.

MCKENDRICK, B.W. (2001), The promise of social work: directions for the future. *Social Work/Maatskaplike Werk Journal.* 37, 105–111.

MIDGLEY, J. (1995), *Social Development: The development perspective in social welfare.* London: Sage Publications.

NATIONAL COALITION OF SOCIAL SERVICES, CHILD WELFARE MOVEMENT & THE GREATER JOHANNESBURG WELFARE, SOCIAL SERVICE AND DEVELOPMENT FORUM (1999). Submissions from the Welfare Sector to the Truth and Reconciliation Commission, May 1999.

NELL, M., SHAPIRO, J., DE V SMIT A. and WEEKES, M. (1993), *From therapy to development: An assessment of the impact of the Independent Development Trusts funding on selected welfare agencies.* IDT Resource Centre.

OLIVER, D. and SOAL, S. (1997), *Report to the Independent Development Trust on the Outcome of a Limited opinion Survey in the Welfare Sector.* Johannesburg: Community Development Resource Association.

PARSONS, R.J., JORGENSEN, J.D., and HERNANDEZ, S.H. (1994), *The integration of social work practice.* California:Brooks/Cole.

PATEL, L., CACHALIA, C. and PELSER, T. (1995), *Report on non-government organisations and poverty alleviation in South Afirca.* Report prepared for the World Bank by Social Development Consultancy.

PATEL, L. and STEWART, M. (1998), *Working towards developmental welfare: lessons from the IDT's strategy to promote developmental social welfare.* Cape Town: Independent Development Trust.

PAYNE, M. (1997), *Modern social work theory,* 2nd ed. London: Macmillan Press Ltd.

POTGIETER, M.C. (1998), *The social work process: development to empower people.* South Africa: Prentice Hall.

RICKARD, C. (2004), *Shameful truth about SA's treatment of refugees.* South Africa: Sunday Times. http://www.sundaytimes.co.za/2004/06/06/news/africa (6 June 2004).

ROBBINS, S.P., CHATTERJEE, P. and CANDA, E.R. (1998), *Contemporary human behaviour theory. A critical perspective for social work.* Boston: Allyn and Bacon

ROTHMAN, J. (1995), Approaches to community intervention. In Rothman, J., Erlich, J.L., Tropman, J.E. and Cox, F.M. (eds), *Strategies of community intervention.* 5th ed. (26–63). United States: Peacock publishers.

SOUTH AFRICAN COUNCIL FOR SOCIAL SERVICES PROFESSIONS (SACSSP). (2004), Code of Ethics Guidelines Draft 2. Unpublished. Pretoria: SACSSP.

SOUTH AFRICAN COUNCIL FOR SOCIAL SERVICE PROFESSIONS (SACSSP). (1986), Code of Ethics. General Notice 292 of 1986, Government Gazette No 10205 of 25 April 1086.

SEERS, D. (1979), 'The meaning of development', in Lehmann, D. (ed.) *Development theory: four critical studies.* London: Frank Cass.

SHEAFOR, B.W., HOREJSI, C.R. and HOREJSI, G.A. (1997), *Techniques and guidelines for social work practice.* 4th ed. Boston: Allyn and Bacon.

SCHATZ, M.S., JENKINS, L.E. and SHEAFOR, B. W. (1990), Milford Redefined: A Model of Initial and Advanced Generalist Social Work. *Journal of Social Work Education* 26:217–231.

SCHRIVER, J.M. (1995), *Human Behaviour and the Social Environment. Shifting paradigms in essential knowledge for social work practice.* Boston: Allyn and Bacon

SMART, R. (2000), *Children living with HIV/AIDS in South Africa* – A rapid appraisal interim national HIV/AIDS care and support task-team.

SOUTH AFRICAN QUALIFICATIONS AUTHORITY (SAQA) (2003), *Standards for Social Work Education*. Government Notice 433 of 2003. Pretoria: Republic of South Africa. http://www.saqa.org.za/show.asp?main=/doc/legislation/nitices /2003/not0433.html

CHAPTER

8 Innovation and good practice

LEARNING OUTCOMES

After you have read this chapter you should be able to:

- Explain the meaning of innovation and good practice.
- Discuss the concept of the learning organisation as a framework to learn from experience through the use of critical reflective practice.
- Discuss the conceptualization and design of developmental programmes according to the logic model.
- Discuss exemplars of innovative developmental welfare strategies.
- Discuss the achievements and challenges of the national Flagship programme for Unemployed Women and Children under the ages of 15 years.

Introduction

Innovation is associated with the renewal of social work and social service practice from a social development perspective. *Innovation* is the conception, design, adoption, implementation and evaluation of new ideas and new priorities. Should these new ideas prove successful, the process will also involve facilitating the adoption of these ideas on a larger scale and the institutionalisation or mainstreaming of new ways of managing social problems.

Innovation can only be implemented in an *organisational context* that may consist of formal or informal organisations engaged in developmental social work and welfare interventions. It usually forms part of deliberately designed experimental or pilot projects of varying size and scope. However, many innovations are a response to real-life situations in communities and are not developed for experimental purposes. Social development innovation provides valuable opportunities for participatory organisational learning. Action research and programme evaluation research studies are also used to identify the learning from innovation and practice. Through a process of critical reflection on why some actions worked and not others, *good practice* can evolve which is tried and tested on an ongoing basis. Some of the innovative exemplars of developmental welfare programmes discussed in this chapter have evolved in these ways in urban and rural settings and at village levels in the South African context. Sometimes local efforts have been combined with the efforts of other partners such as governments, international organisations, non-governmental organisations, community-based organisations and faith-based groups.

'Social development innovation provides valuable opportunities for participatory organisational learning.'

The transformation of social welfare to social development has been experienced both positively and negatively. For some practitioners, the changes have generated insecurity and a belief that their work has little meaning and value. The overwhelming social problems, lack of resources and capacity constraints and skills have resulted in burnout and despondency with the new approach. However, the transformation process has also released new creative energy and the generation of new ideas and ways of managing social problems. Innovative practice ideas are discussed to encourage practitioners to embrace new roles and for organisations to provide an enabling environment for social entrepreneurship. The *innovator role* involves the conception, implementation and evaluation of new ideas of practice and service delivery that are authentic and appropriate in a changing local and global context. Innovation is also about the blending of new knowledge, skills and values, and evolves from real–life situations and experience that takes place in organisations where a learning culture and renewal is valued. It does not mean that everything associated with the former welfare system of the apartheid era is rejected. Innovation and learning from experience requires a break with those elements of the old system that are no longer meaningful, and the creation of new ideas and practices that blend the positive strands of the past with the new directions in developmental social welfare.

Learning organisation framework

Organisations can be described as social entities that are structured in a particular way to achieve organisational goals through a range of social and development activities that are co-ordinated and that interact in a two-way flow and influence between the organisation and its environment (Kirst-Ashman & Hull 2001). A *social service and development organisation* refers to formal and informal organisations, associations, groups and social networks of different kinds to facilitate the meeting of the needs of individuals, families, groups, organisations and communities. Such organisations also facilitate partnerships to find appropriate solutions to social problems and adverse social conditions facing them.

Innovation and the evolution of good practice take place in organisations that are reflective and that can be denoted as learning organisations. *Reflective practice* is defined by Schonë (1983:234) as the 'use of experience, knowledge and theoretical perspectives to guide and inform practice'. The reflective practitioner does not look for standardised, formulaic responses to situations, ready-made solutions and for the uncritical application of theory. Reflective practitioners are willing to break out of conventional parameters, and are comfortable working in situations that are complex, variable and uncertain. The use of simple technical solutions and the uncritical application of theory and practice to solve social problems are anathema to reflective practice.

'Reflective practitioners are willing to break out of conventional parameters, and are comfortable working in situations that are complex, variable and uncertain.'

Reflective practice involves the process of actively constructing solutions in an interactive fashion with all parties. Problem setting involves an assessment that addresses both the micro and the macro situation. Thompson (2002:238–239) refers to an assessment of the problem or social situation from the broader social, economic, political, cultural, local and global perspective as a 'high ground' analysis. This 'high ground' analysis should be linked to the actual situation, which he refers to as the 'low ground' analysis. This is one of the distinguishing features of reflective practice and it could be applied to assessment and intervention that is focused on practice with client systems of all sizes. It is a proactive way of working that involves the purposeful application of theory and good practice lessons in order to find appropriate and authentic solutions to real life problems and situations that people find themselves in.

'Reflective practice skills are also valuable in formulating and implementing innovation, developing good practice lessons based on experiential learning and in creating learning organisations.'

Reflective practice skills are also valuable in formulating and implementing innovation, developing good practice lessons based on experiential learning and in creating learning organisations. Senge (1990) popularised the notion of the learning organisation, a notion that can be applied to social service and development organisations to promote organisational change. Carnochan and Austin's (2001) research in the United States shows that organisations undergoing transformation are faced with many challenges such as resistance, fear and uncertainty and a lack of know-how in achieving these changes. This is also relevant in South Africa, which is undergoing large-scale change on all levels in the society simultaneously and where there are limited practice modalities to draw on. Senge's thinking about learning organisations provides a useful framework within which organisations can learn from experience – can learn by doing and reflection to inform future practice. Senge's principles of learning organisations are combined with Thompson's ideas (2002) on reflective practice. The principles outlined below may be useful in assisting organisations and practitioners that are leading change and innovation.

Principles in leading change

- **Dynamic systems thinking** (Robbins et al.1998) could aid an understanding of the complex inter-relations between systems and subsystems and in exploring the causes of social problems in a systemic and critical way. This involves bridging the divide between micro and macro systems in the analysis and in the construction of solutions. It also involves linking local experiences and realities to an understanding of globalisation and its potential risks to human security. An understanding of the social, human, economic and environmental impacts on local communities and how these could be integrated in intervention are also important to consider.
- **Mental models** are deeply ingrained and hidden in how we think and act. Senge calls for mapping these models, bringing them to the

surface and subjecting them to critical scrutiny and identifying the learning from the hidden maps. Through such a reflective process, the strengths in what exists can be identified and the old, which no longer serves the organisation, can be discarded. This process paves the way for developing new models or mental maps that blend the positive in the old and the new.

- **Building shared vision** is a useful way of developing a shared picture of the future that the organisation is seeking to create. This process involves building a shared vision, goals and principles and modus operandi of how the innovation and the change in the organisation will be implemented. A shared visioning process means that all relevant parties in the organisation – external and internal stakeholders – should be involved in such a process to promote ownership and commitment and to draw on all the available knowledge and expertise that could make a difference.
- **Personal mastery** is about continually clarifying and deepening personal and organisational vision, focusing energies, developing patience and maintaining objectivity. It is also about building skills, harnessing organisational talents and commitment to learn from experience and finding the connections between personal learning and organisational learning.
- **Team learning** describes a process whereby team members learn and work together, build trust and achieve a common purpose. They also engage in dialogue, critical reflective thinking and action as they build a culture of innovation and change.

These principles provide direction for a critical reflective approach to initiating and facilitating innovation in a changing environment.

Conceptualising and designing developmental welfare programmes

Choosing appropriate developmental service delivery strategies requires the identification and consideration of alternative interventions. The multi-modal approach helps practitioners to identify and select appropriate alternative interventions. Instead of relying on interventions that are known to practitioners, that are popular and/or appealing, practitioners should also search for new methods that have proved successful and that have potential (Lewis et al. 2001:58–59). This can be done through brainstorming and engaging in literature searches – journals, agency publications, programme evaluation studies and newspaper reports about innovation and best practice. Practitioners with a social entrepreneurial flair will be open to exploring new ideas.

'The multi-modal approach helps practitioners to identify and select appropriate alternative interventions.'

The multi-modal approach to intervention provides for the interweaving of different modes of intervention. The modes of intervention are Mode A: Poverty reduction and sustainable livelihoods; Mode B: Family-centred and community-based strategies; Mode C: Community information, education and communication strategies; Mode D: Social policy and planning strategies; Mode E: Advocacy (refer to Chapter 7). These modes of intervention provide an indication of what different social development interventions may look like in practice. Interweaving of strategies means that a combination of modes of intervention may be used in *conceptualising and designing developmental social welfare programmes*. Conceptualising developmental programmes involves the application of theory to inform programme design such as, What are the causes of the problem or social situation? What are the assumptions under-girding programme development? Based on such conceptualisation, a programme is developed which refers to the way in which various elements are arranged in a systematic fashion to achieve specific developmental goals and outcomes.

The *logic model* of programme development provides a useful framework for conceptualising and developing rigorous social development programmes. The skills used in developing poverty-reduction programmes are discussed in Chapter 9. The logic model is outlined as follows (Lewis et al. 2001:59; Alter & Egan 1997):

- **Problem/need** – define the problem or social situation and identify what needs to be changed. Conduct a situational analysis of the situation as it is. What are the causes of the problem or social situation? How are these connected to the theory or underlying hypothesis of the programme?
- **Goal** – formulate goals which set out what the desired state is to be achieved.
- **Objectives** – formulate sub-goals or mini-goals that are milestones that lead to the achievement of your larger goal.
- **Activities** – actual activities that the project will execute to realise the objectives.
- **Inputs** – identify the concrete and tangible resources that you need: money, staff, equipment, infrastructure.
- **Methods** – what service delivery intervention strategies will be used to achieve your goals and objectives?
- **Results** – what are the short-term impact(s) of using the above methods and inputs?
- **Outcomes** – what are the long-term impacts of using the above intervention methods and resources?

Table 8.1 sets out different modes of intervention that have been or are being used by welfare and development organisations in the South African context. In Chapter 3 the emergence of progressive social welfare services that gave rise to new modalities that informed future policies and programmes was discussed. Since the early 1990s, welfare and community-based and development organisations have experimented and continue to experiment with new intervention strategies to promote social development. Some of the contemporary practice examples were also described in Chapter 6. The intervention modes are not conclusive but may stimulate thinking about new ways of delivering services.

Table 8.1: Multi-modal social development interventions

Poverty reduction & sustainable livelihood strategies	Family-centred and community based development strategies	Community information, education & Communication strategies	Social policy and planning strategies	Advocacy strategies
- Social relief & social assistance - Small & micro-enterprises - Entrepreneurship - Business development - Credit & micro-finance - Savings schemes - Asset building - Income-generation - Food security - Employment programmes - Community-based public works - Social capital	- Counselling - Peer & lay counselling - Self-help groups - Social support - Community care - Home-based care - Volunteerism - Community & youth service - Help-lines - Community dispute resolution - Collaboration with and strengthening family & community networks - Capacity building	- Community education & prevention - Advice & information - Community education - Advice offices - Multi-purpose community centres - Community media - Mass media - Community theatre & storytelling - Capacity-building - Civic education - Community Education for empowerment	- Action research - Rapid appraisals - Consultation & participation in planning and decision-making - Designing & implementing developmental welfare programmes - Early-warning systems - Service development in underserviced areas - Community surveillance - Monitoring & evaluation	- Awareness raising - Capacity-building & education for empowerment - Organizing, mobilising and networking - Campaigning for social justice - Legal advocacy - Social justice research - Protection & promotion of rights - Human rights Education - Action Research

Exemplars of innovative developmental welfare strategies

Examples of innovation are discussed below with reference to some of the above modes of intervention. Good practice lessons are identified where information exists. Examples of the social policy and planning modes and advocacy are addressed in Chapter 9.

Poverty reduction and sustainable livelihood strategies

'Poverty has been described as an interlocking and multi-dimensional phenomenon caused by a lack of multiple resources such as employment, food, assets (housing, land), basic infrastructure (water, transport, energy), health care and literacy.'

Poverty in South Africa. Poverty is broadly explained as being caused by either individual pathology or structural forces which create and perpetuate poverty (Giddens 2001). Public policy in South Africa is informed by a *structural approach* which explains poverty in terms of the economic and political forces in the society. Poverty-reduction strategies are aimed at breaking the structural forces that cause poverty through the achievement of economic growth and human development, enhancing the capabilities of disadvantaged individuals, households and communities and through redistributive social development interventions (May 1998). These measures are designed to ensure a minimum standard of living for all people, to eradicate extreme poverty and to acknowledge the power of human agency in poverty reduction.

Poor people's *definitions* of poverty are also increasingly informing local and global understandings and perceptions of poverty. International and local studies on the perspectives of poor people are being conducted to take their views on poverty into account (Narayan 2000; Budlender 1998). Poverty has been described as an interlocking and multi-dimensional phenomenon caused by a lack of multiple resources such as employment, food, assets (housing, land), basic infrastructure (water, transport, energy), health care and literacy. The psychological aspects of poverty have also been highlighted by poor people, and these include humiliation, inhumane treatment and the emotional strain of living in poverty. The lack of a political voice that can be heard by society and decision-makers is another aspect that is important in defining and addressing poverty (Narayan 2000; Budlender 1998).

The *measurement* of poverty is shifting from a focus only on one dimension of poverty such as income to a broader view that incorporates the above conceptions and dimensions. Poverty research shows that people do not necessarily live in poverty permanently but may move in and out of poverty over time as a result of changes in the life cycle such as childbirth, early adulthood and ageing. Poverty may also be caused by changes in environmental conditions or societal processes that lead to the social and economic exclusion of people. Such factors include political change, the restructuring of the economy, seasonal changes and conflict and war. These poverty-creating processes, which lead to the vulnerability of people, may be of a short-term nature but can become chronic or lead to long-term exclusion. Personal misfortune, such as the loss of earning capacity due to physical or mental ill health, disability and the death of a breadwinner, are other poverty-creating processes.

Poverty studies in South Africa also measure poverty in relation to the extent of poverty in the general population and by race, gender, urban/rural distribution and age. The Human Development Index devised by the United Nations Development Programme (UNDP) is used to assess poverty using indicators such as life expectancy at birth, educational attainment and standard of living. Other measures that are also used are the *Gini Coefficient*, which is a measure of income inequality, and *Poverty lines*, which measure the income needed to achieve a minimum standard of living. Poverty lines set a basic income level that is needed by an individual or a household and may vary from time to time. Poverty lines have limitations in that they do not take into account the variations in the cost of living or employment in a society. For example, food prices and transport may cost more in some parts of the country than in others. Using the poverty line, the poor are defined as the bottom 40 percent of households and the very poor or 'ultra poor' as the bottom 20 percent of households. A *poverty gap* analysis is also used to assess the depth of poverty by determining how much money is needed to lift the poor to the poverty line through targeted transfers (May 1998).

Consider the following statistics on poverty and inequality in South Africa (extrapolated from the UNDP 2003:41–43).

- Using the national poverty line, income poverty has declined marginally between 1995 and 2002 from 51 to 48.5 percent. The total number of poor people in 2002 was estimated to be 21.9 million.
- An estimated 41.6 percent of the population is considered to be unemployed if a broad definition is used. More men are unemployed, about half of the African population is unemployed and unemployment is highest in the three poorest provinces in the country.
- Poverty has gender, race, family-type and spatial dimensions. A total of 54.4 percent of the poor are women. Of the total population, 56.3 percent of Africans, 36.1 percent of Coloureds, 14.7 percent of Indians and 6.9 percent of White people were living below the national poverty line in 2002. The poverty rate of Africans was 8 times that of Whites.
- Single-parent families and 'couples with children families' were over-represented among the poor. A larger proportion of poor women were found to live in poor, single-parent families.
- About half of the country's poor could be found in seven of the nine provinces. Poverty is most concentrated in the Eastern Cape, KwaZulu-Natal and Limpopo provinces, where 59 percent of the country's poor live.
- There has been an increase in the poverty gap between 1995 and 2002 but this was more marked for African men, 'single' families and in the Eastern Cape Province.
- Of the total number of households, 61.2 percent have a disposable household income of under R41 999 per annum, with 25.6 percent having less than R12 000 per annum. A small percentage of households (2.2 percent) had the highest disposable income of

R360 000 and above. Income distribution worsened within all race groups between 1995 and 2002 and income distribution among race groups has increased except in the case of Whites, in which it has remained more equal over the same period.

Poverty reduction and sustainable livelihood strategies. There has been much debate about what macro-economic and social policies are needed that will increase economic growth; create jobs not only for skilled but for the least skilled people; reduce the cost of living and assist the poor. Unemployment rates have reached critical proportions, which is a significant factor in declining living standards and rising poverty in the society. Many of the problems facing the economy go back to the economic structure and labour market of the apartheid era. Globalisation has also exposed the economy to economic risks that have resulted in employment insecurity and vulnerability of employees and their families.

The UNDP's Human Development Report on South Africa (2003) argues for the achievement of sustainable higher growth rates and the inclusive reorientation of the economy to address unemployment and poverty. The government is embarking on increased employment creation through labour-intensive public works programmes which are intended to create a million jobs through skills development strategies and through scaling up support for small and medium enterprises.

Table 8.1 sets out some of the poverty-reduction and sustainable livelihood strategies that government and welfare and development organisations are involved with. Most of these initiatives are micro-development interventions aimed at individuals, households, and communities. Some programmes link people with resources and focus on increasing people's capabilities, assets and activities required to earn a livelihood. *Sustainable livelihood strategies* are mostly concerned with identifying and accessing natural and other resources and activities required for a means of living (Chambers & Conway 1992). Sustainable livelihood interventions linked with community development thinking and practice could enhance the effectiveness of the approach (Brocklesby 2003). The approach is participatory and taps the strengths and assets of the parties. The outcomes sought by these programmes are geared to increasing income, reducing vulnerability, strengthening social capital, increasing food security and promoting general social, emotional and physical well-being.

The following concepts define the livelihood approach:

- **Social capital** – social networks and a relationship of trust such as family, neighbours, friends, kinship networks, associations.
- **Natural capital** – natural resource stocks, e.g. water, land, forests, grass, trees, vegetation, game.
- **Financial capital** – savings, income, credit.

- **Assets** – housing, land, livestock, jewellery.
- **Physical capital** – transport, shelter, energy, water, communications networks.
- **Human capital** – mental and physical health, skills, knowledge and labour.

Innovation and good practice

Entrepreneurship. Themba (not his real name) started with one shoe repair business and then expanded this to two. While running the shoe repair business he started manufacturing sandals. In 1999 he received a loan of R8 000 from The Medunsa Organisation for Disabled Entrepreneurs (MODE), an NGO involved in entrepreneurial development for people with disabilities, which he repaid within a year. Although the shoe repair business was shut down in 2000 due to a drop in trade when the taxi route was changed, he was able to diversify his business into sandal manufacturing. Recognising the move back to African styles, he started making shoes and sandals from local skins, and today he is unable to meet the demand with a production output of 40 to 60 pairs of sandals a day. Despite the output levels, his turnover is averaging R40 000 – R50 000 a month. Themba is having difficulties accessing finance to expand his business.

MODE has been operational since 1992. MODE's Entrepreneurial Development Programme is run over a ten-week period and is focused on learning through doing. On completion of the course, each graduate is given a grant of R1500. While the grant goes some way to addressing the start-up costs of the business, it does not provide a long-term solution to the need for financial services by the businesses. Following the course, all MODE trainees receive post-training counselling or after-care. These are home or site visits, which continue for the first year of the course. The extended post-training support ensures that trainees work at implementing their goals and have the means to solve problems. A recent assessment of MODE (Naidoo 2004) showed that their clients are consistently able to use the training they receive to a high level, and survive the challenges of a rapidly changing business environment.

Community development. The *PIN Project*, based in Richard's Bay, KwaZulu-Natal, is an income-generating community support structure. Its intention is to assist the growing number of grandmothers who are caring for their grandchildren without any support from their parents largely due to the increasing number of adults dying from AIDS-related diseases. A group of grandmothers are involved in making AIDS-awareness bead broaches and profits from the sale of their craft are put into an orphan assistance fund. The project falls under the auspices of the Zululand Crafters Association, who source the beads and manage the quality control. A market for the broaches has been established at local conferences and overseas outlets. A management committee manages the orphan assistance fund and reviews all the applications for assistance. The criterion for assistance is that a grandparent caring for children orphaned due to AIDS may receive support. Networking is done with other service providers such as NGOs providing home-based care and HIV/AIDS counselling, while the Department of Social Development provides social assistance. To date, a few needy grandmothers have been given a once-off payment to assist with school fees or uniforms. Members gain emotionally and spiritually from being part of a support group, which in turn encourages and sustains their care-giving efforts. However, it takes much time and effort for income-generation projects to become financially viable entities and members' involvement in the project needs to be sustained in the absence of immediate visible benefits.

Food security programme. The *Banareng Feed the Child Feed the Nation Environmental Project* began as a result of hungry children arriving at school complaining of headaches and dizziness. As a result, Banareng Primary School, in Atteridgeville, Pretoria, started a permaculture (organic) vegetable garden on the school grounds with the support of a corporate sponsor, BMW. After an initial investment of human and material resources the project is now fully self-sustaining: it feeds 670 children and has impacted positively on improved school attendance. Gardening has been included in the school curriculum and is part of an interactive educational programme. The project teaches pupils about vegetable production, water conservation, alien plants and recycling, which is shared with other schools. Children are encouraged to start their own organic food gardens at home. The project is an excellent example of integrated sustainable development involving teachers, pupils and the community, using natural resources to support livelihoods. The success of this project is largely due to the efforts of the dynamic, engaging, forward-thinking headmistress. It is possible that without her involvement in the project, it would not continue.

Good practice lessons in innovation and good practice

The three examples demonstrate what is possible through micro-development strategies that draw on the livelihood knowledge, skills and experience of the participants. The outcomes of these programmes were varied and led to tangible improvements in income and food security. Whilst Themba grew in his capacity as an entrepreneur, the grandparents used their skills in bead-making to earn an income and built a supportive social network, and the school-based nutrition programme reduced absentee rates and integrated food security initiatives with new teaching and learning methodologies. All the developmental programmes built on the strengths, assets and infrastructure available to the people. Participatory methods, leadership and networking were critical to the success of the programmes. The challenges varied from project to project. These were firstly related to a lack of access to financial capital. Secondly, sustainable income-generation programmes combined with building social capital may need sustained inputs for a longer period before they become viable. Thirdly, leadership is a critical success factor and leadership development is important to the sustainability of the projects. Finally, macro social and economic development policies should support micro development programmes as these provide tangible opportunities to improve the livelihoods of the poor and populations at risk.

These examples illustrate how important financial services and business support services are to the successful outcome of micro-development programmes focusing on poverty alleviation and sustainable livelihoods. Business development support services include: accounting; advertising; communication skills; computer services; counselling; import and export assistance; financial management; human resources; legal advice; management training; market information; marketing assistance; product design; public relations; technical training; and transport services. Social service practitioners have questioned whether this is their role, especially because social workers believe that they do not have the expertise in micro-economic development. Others have argued that economic literacy for social workers is a vital skill and that it should become part of the core curriculum. Many social workers that do not have these skills themselves draw on the expertise of specialist organisations working in the field of business development support. Social workers can also play a broker role by linking specialist service providers in micro-economic development with individuals and community groups.

'These examples illustrate how important financial services and business support services are to the successful outcome of micro-development programmes focusing on poverty alleviation and sustainable livelihoods.'

Family-centred, community-based care and development strategies

Community care and community development. The *White Paper for Social Welfare* did not define community care specifically. It advocated a strategic approach to *linking* the care and support needs of communities with community development interventions, however. This perspective follows from the assumption that all people need care and support at different times in their lives but that the intensity and the nature of the support may vary depending on the needs of individual, the family and the availability of support networks in the community. Community care and support may be aimed at the elderly, children, people with physical illnesses or mental illness, people abusing substances and people who are ill as a result of AIDS. Care and support in disadvantaged households can further strain resources and place additional pressures on women, who are the main caregivers. Generalist practice provides for a holistic assessment and intervention of the social situation at micro, mezzo and macro levels. Intervention alternatives are set out in Table 8.1. The options incorporate micro, mezzo and macro interventions with client groups of different sizes and working at different levels of intervention. At the one end of the spectrum, individual and family interventions such as counselling, peer and lay counselling and peer support and help lines are indicated. Mezzo and macro interventions such as self-help groups, volunteerism programmes, community mobilisation and service development strategies to meet community needs and promote livelihoods are also commonly implemented. The Scat model, discussed below, is an example of macro, community-level practice, which builds local development agencies in rural areas to respond to local social, economic and community development needs.

Innovation and good practice

Community care and support. Community care attempts to help people who need care and support to live with dignity and as much independence as possible in the community (Meredith 1995). A combination of care and support services is provided by governmental and welfare agencies, community-based organisations and volunteers to offer care and support for people in their own homes and communities. Options include home-based care, group homes, foster homes, community centres and hospices. Many organisations actively involve local support groups in caring and providing support. These include burial societies, prayer groups, community-based organisations, mutual aid support groups and volunteers.

The Thembalethu Home-based Care programme is an example of a community-care and support model. It provides care and support to children and families affected by AIDS. The service is accessible (nearest the home of the people affected), it encourages the participation of the people to respond to needs in the context of traditional community life, and it strengthens mutual aid opportunities and responsibilities.

Thembalethu Home-Based Care, Mpumalanga

A concerned resident, Sally McKibben, started the Thembalethu Home-based Care programme (referred to as Thembalethu) in 1998 to provide support and care to people infected and affected by AIDS. Two years later, Thembalethu was caring for 429 patients and 905 orphans.

The project relies entirely on volunteer care supporters to provide home-based care services. Volunteers are recruited from women's groups attached to churches – a strategy that has proved to be successful. In the recruitment of volunteers they ask the question: 'who in your church is committed to visiting the sick?'

The basic package of care provided by care supporters includes home nursing care, support, spiritual support, and the provision of food and referrals. Other services provided include maintaining the personal hygiene of the patient, such as washing clothes and collecting water, providing facts about HIV transmission and assisting with the drawing up of wills and getting papers in order. Care supporters are paid a stipend of R250 per month for their voluntary work as a token of appreciation. They also get a uniform to identify themselves in the communities, and transport and meals are provided at their weekly training meetings. Care supporter caseloads range from 5 – 29 patients and 7 – 49 orphans per care supporter.

A key function of the care supporters is to train a family member as a caregiver. This person is trained to assist the care supporter in any way possible. It works in some cases, but not in all. The family caregiver needs to be mature and should be able to give the necessary support. They receive no stipend but get on-the-job training.

The project also has an income-generating carpentry and craft programme, but this is hampered by the lack of buying power of the very poor.

Thembalethu networks with district health clinics and state hospitals. The level of success in accessing resources (finances, medical supplies) depends on the quality of the working relationship between the project facilitator and health officials. There are no other NGOs in the area to network with.

Thembalethu plans to develop an orphan-care programme. It identified 900 orphans scattered in 8 villages in 2000. The focus of the programme will be on food security and the promotion of health among the children, and access to food will be linked to school attendance.

Source: Loening-Vosey &Wilson 2001.

Peer support groups. *The South African Depression and Anxiety Group* (SADAG) has encouraged the establishment of peer support groups country-wide since its inception in 1995. According to SADAG, South Africa had only 320 psychiatrists for 44 million people and in the North West Province the problem is particularly acute, with a population of 3.6 million supported by only one full-time and one part-time psychiatrist. SADAG is working with marginalised communities in the province to establish grassroots support groups that enable people to learn self-help skills, medication compliance, accessing facilities, dealing with relapse and other important concerns. The organisation is also focusing on suicide prevention and support in rural and under-served communities targeting youth and has received support from the World Bank to further develop this model (SADGA 2004).

Building local development institutions – Scat model: *The Social Change Assistance Trust* (Scat) is an intermediary grant-making organisation that promotes social change through the development of sustainable rural communities. Its unique approach to funding is aimed at empowering the rural poor and strengthening civil society in these areas.

Scat works with a rural partner, usually a paralegal advice office in an isolated rural area with limited access to formal institutions. The offices provide advice on social security, housing and community security. These organisations are called *Local Development Agencies* (LDAs). Scat provides grant funding for the core services of community organisations and Scat fieldworkers facilitate capacity-building in the LDAs. In addition, Scat accesses funding for targeted programmes such as HIV/AIDS, youth development and local economic development. Based on the needs identified by the LDAs in the communities, Scat is able to apply for funding earmarked for these types of development projects. In order to encourage the mobilisation of communities to raise funds to promote community participation and to reduce the dependence of the LDAs on grant funding, a Financial Incentive Scheme was started in 1996. A reward is paid to LDAs to raise funds in the local community in the ratio of R5 for every R1 raised. This scheme has been extremely successful and has helped the LDAs to supplement the cost of services and to fund community and poverty-relief projects. Fundraising events such as dances, choral events, sports days, and meat sales on pension pay days are organised by the LDAs, which has connected the LDAs more strongly with the communities. The Scat model has strict guidelines for the efficient and effective management of funds. The field workers provide intensive development facilitation support that includes capacity-building in financial and project management and leadership training. Intensive support is provided to the LDAs in the first two years and this then tapers off as they begin to work independently.

A community business generates income and meets the needs of the people of Nababeep.

Good practice lessons in community care and community development. The assumption underlying community care is that there are families, or capable women, who are willing and able to provide the care. However, this is not always the case. For many women, poverty and poor public health services have turned this care burden into a crisis with far-reaching social, health and economic consequences (UNAIDS 2004). Community care is also not suitable in all situations. In instances where community and family care fails, institutional care may be needed. Finding the balance between institutional and community care is a challenge. If community care is not to turn into community neglect, systems and procedures need to be in place to monitor the quality of care provided, and to intervene where necessary. Community care and support strategies also require the management of stress and burnout of caregivers, who are mainly women. Support for caregivers, extended families and kinship networks is important in order to ensure the provision of quality care. Community care and support should be viewed as part of a co-ordinated and integrated continuum of care. In order for it to succeed, it needs an investment of resources, community ownership and appropriate partnerships with formal service providers.

'Support for caregivers, extended families and kinship networks is important in order to ensure the provision of quality care.'

The Scat model is an innovative rural development practice model. It has drawn on concepts of sustainable, people-centred development, empowerment and the building of viable, community-based institutions in poor and isolated rural areas. The model was designed, implemented and evaluated over a twenty-year period through the use of collaborative and reflective experiential learning methods. It is a viable and appropriate practice model that could be replicated in the African context. It demonstrates what can be done with very little. It also illustrates that there is no quick fix in development practice: development requires long-term and sometimes intensive work with local partners to build sustainable local institutions that can respond appropriately to local needs. The components of the model include resource transfers, development facilitation support and training and capacity-building.

Information, education and communication strategies (IEC)

Concepts and approaches to IEC strategies. New technologies such as computers, the Internet, cell phones and telecommunication have the potential to increase access to information and knowledge to promote development. However, the gap between those who have knowledge and those who do not is widening in a globalising world where knowledge is the new asset. People with higher incomes and levels of education, and who are male and English-speaking are more likely to participate in the networked world (UNDP 1999). Many poor countries, especially on the African continent, have the least access to the new knowledge-based world (UNDP 1999; World Bank 1989). It is vital for these countries to have increased global connectivity, community access to knowledge and capacity-building to participate in the information society through the creative adaptation and use of new technologies.

Knowledge and access to information and innovative ways of communicating with client populations can be a powerful tool in promoting social development. Many people lack information about where and how to access resources such as social grants, housing subsidies and micro-finance. A lack of knowledge about infectious diseases and the risks of substance abuse and how to combat these are

'Information failure and the knowledge gap are widely recognised to be major obstacles to improved well-being and the empowerment of client populations.'

some of the barriers to improved social functioning. Information failure and the knowledge gap are widely recognised to be major obstacles to improved well-being and the empowerment of client populations. What information and knowledge people need and how best to communicate such knowledge and information to them remains a key challenge.

Education and prevention programmes in promoting health and social well-being are widely used in the social services. Health promotion models have been adopted in the social services to help prevent social problems and to achieve individual behavioural change. However, theoretical models to guide education and prevention programmes are not well developed (Nutbeam & Harris 2004). The most developed approach is the *psychosocial model*, which focuses on individual behavioural change. This model draws on the health belief model and cognitive and social learning theories to inform education and prevention programmes. It postulates that people are likely to change their behaviour if they perceive the benefits of behavioural change to outweigh the risks of ill-health and compromised social functioning. Education and prevention programmes based on this model focus on the knowledge and beliefs of individuals and communities and have informed public health education programmes such as HIV/AIDS, immunisation and substance abuse. Although the model is considered to provide an important reference point for education and prevention programmes, it has some limitations in that it does not acknowledge the importance of social, economic and environmental factors in influencing health actions and social functioning. The limitations of the health belief model have resulted in the incorporation of organisational change, inter-sectoral, community organisation and community-building strategies and the consideration of other models such as communication-behaviour change, social marketing, advocacy and policy action. Nutbeam and Harris (2004)[1] are of the view that no one model can adequately guide the development of education and prevention programmes as multiple factors have a bearing on behavioural change. The authors recommend the use of different models applicable to the local context that draw on local knowledge and experience, research about community needs and the factors that influence behaviour. Multi-level interventions are proposed, although this may not be possible for all practitioners. They nevertheless provide pointers for different strategies of intervention.

Social workers and social service practitioners spend much of their time sharing information and providing education. The educator role was discussed in Chapter 7. Despite this, the theory and practice of information

Footnote:

1 For a more detailed discussion of the theories informing health behaviour change; theories of change in communities and communal action for health; theories of communication-behaviour change; organisation and public policy change, refer to Nutbeam and Harris (2004).

exchange and education in social work is underdeveloped. One model of education that has been widely used in the local context is the *popular education model*. This model has been adapted locally and internationally and evolved from the popular education movements in Latin America in the 1970s (Poertner 1994; Freire 1972). Popular education refers to the real-life experiences of marginalised and oppressed people. It requires an understanding of the experience of oppression and its meaning for those affected. Through dialogue, critical thinking and reflection on their social situation, these people achieve an understanding of the reasons for their marginalisation. This process is referred to as consciousness-raising and the development of political action to change an oppressive social situation. Popular education is change-oriented and participatory, and the methodology was used to build grassroots social movements in the struggle against apartheid. Popular education has been adapted to inform social work practice through concepts such as empowerment and gender-sensitive, non-discriminatory practice. It has been used to promote the empowerment of women by women's groups, disability rights movements, HIV/AIDS movements and community action campaigns to improve community conditions. Popular education methods are also informed by the real-life experiences of the people. They draw on culturally specific knowledge in their methods of communication through the use of popular storytelling, music, drama and images that reflect local life.

'Popular education refers to the real-life experiences of marginalised and oppressed people.'

Innovation

Education and prevention programmes such as life-skills education, parenting, communication and sexuality education programmes are generally provided by social service agencies. Development workers also engage in community-building skills that strengthen local community organisations and develop individual and community assets. In this section some examples of the different approaches to information, communication and education strategies are discussed to stimulate ideas about practice. Strategies to communicate information and provide education to client populations are varied and include community advice offices, multi-purpose community centres, community radio, community newsletters, murals, storytelling and community theatre.

Education and prevention programmes.

- **Soul City** is an educational entertainment intervention, which is broadcast on national television in South Africa, reaching millions of people. Its popular education programming is aimed at effecting individual and community social and behaviour change. The Soul City approach does not view health and well-being as the responsibility of individuals only. In its programming it tries to create a supportive environment within which sensitive issues can be explored and that may stimulate personal and public dialogue and debate, community action, organisational change and the development of social policies that

'Soul City incorporates advocacy in its programming through the active encouragement of individuals, communities and law-makers to adopt behaviour that promotes health and social well-being.'

promote healthy lifestyles. Soul City incorporates advocacy in its programming through the active encouragement of individuals, communities and law-makers to adopt behaviour that promotes health and social well-being. The target audiences are varied depending on the programmes. A wide range of social issues of concern to communities and the society are addressed – from HIV/AIDS and violence against women to substance abuse and volunteering. The strength of the approach to education and prevention is that it is informed by theories of health promotion and social change, research on the information needs of people and an analysis of their situation, which in turn informs interactive programme design. Monitoring and evaluation of the programmes and its impacts on the target audiences is also critical to Soul City's success.

- **loveLife** was launched in 1999 to promote healthy adolescent lifestyles and to reduce HIV risk among youth in the 15 to 20 year age-group. It is a brand-driven, sustained multi-dimensional national programme focused on making condom usage part of the youth culture. It uses national communication campaigns and incorporates broadcast, print and outdoor media. Its programmes also include telephone help lines, event-based activities such as 'love tours', loveLife games and service provision through community-based Y-centres, adolescent-friendly clinics, and peer education including programmes focused on parents. loveLife combines well-established public health approaches with innovative marketing techniques. Its success also lies in its approach to young people: it speaks to them in a language that they can relate to and by the tone of optimism that is conveyed rather than scare tactics. The programmes also harness the power and influence of South Africa's youth culture through television, music and sports to promote healthy living (Parker 2003).
- **Community advice and information centres**. Advice offices run by NGOs and multi-purpose community centres (MPCCs) are some local examples of development information and communication programmes. The Black Sash is a voluntary women's organisation that was formed in 1955 to protest against the introduction of apartheid legislation. During the apartheid years the Black Sash delivered services to thousands of African people who were affected by oppressive apartheid laws. Through its advice offices, it provided advice and information to people to apply for social grants. Paralegal services were also provided by volunteers. This direct contact with people affected by apartheid laws provided the activists of the organisation with information that resulted in peaceful protests. They also raised many questions in parliament through their representatives to register human rights violations. Since 1994, the Black Sash has continued to provide paralegal advice and information services, rights education and human rights advocacy.

Multi-purpose community centres

In order to move services closer to people in remote or disadvantaged communities, the government has introduced the concept of multi-purpose community centres (MPCCs). These are one-stop services that offer a range of government services under one roof, and simplify the processing of applications for passports, identity documents and social grants.

Four years since the initiative was launched, 54 (MPCCs) and seven satellite services have been established in every province. The MPCCs house the services of different government departments and are accessible to local communities. Besides information exchange, skill development programmes are offered and community members can also learn how to use information and communication technologies such as the Internet. The Mapela Telecentre in Limpopo province has a satellite-connected network that provides state-of-the-art computer training courses for members of the community. Some MPCCs offer banking services, primary health care, HIV/AIDS education, and support to entrepreneurs to set up small businesses on the premises.

The centres also serve as venues where community events such as education campaigns, exhibitions and other activities can take place. Helping people get information that they can use to improve their lives and to develop their communities is one of the aims of the centres. Through the MPCCs, community members access information from government, but the system also empowers them to talk back to government about their needs and aspirations.

Source: http://www.southafrica.info/ess_glance/social_delivery/mpcc.htm accessed 24th May 2004.

- **Community radio.** Community radio stations have mushroomed in the new South Africa. Community radio is defined as 'radio that is owned and operated by a community or members of a community. The main purpose of this type of radio station is to develop the community and to respond to the expressed needs and priorities of the communities' (AMARC Africa 1998). Each community radio station is unique. Some may reach a very small area with their broadcasting while others reach large urban communities and remote rural areas. Radio stations vary in their focus. Whilst some stations focus on special areas of interest, others focus on broader community concerns. However, most community radio stations are underfunded and the majority of workers in the sector are untrained volunteers and so sustainability is an issue.
- **Bush Radio** was started in the late 1980s when a small group of people interested in the development of alternative communication systems formed an organisation that recorded information onto cassettes in radio format, made duplicates, and distributed them in townships in and around Cape Town. The organisation was called CASET (Cassette Education Trust). Since its humble beginnings in a small office in Salt River, Cape Town, the initiators of the project always knew that the 'airwaves' would be integral to its long-term educational and empowerment objectives and community radio was the obvious solution.

Bush Radio Programme Highlights (89.5fm)

Sakisizwe – Building the Nation – 'Bou die Nasie'

Hosted by Lindiwe Magija, this programme has a finger on the pulse of the Cape Flats community. Featuring local community activists, development workers and other interesting people, Sakisizwe allows the community to interact directly with studio guests telephonically. Each day has a different focus, and gender, labour, human rights, business development and arts and culture are all covered over the course of a week.

Once a month, the station broadcasts from a local community site in collaboration with the local Red Cross Society. The Society provides the generators and a caravan, and the radio station provides the sound. During these outside broadcasts, health messages interspersed with music are conveyed to the listeners. 'We speak to people about HIV and AIDS. The community also becomes involved by bringing us refreshments and providing the power supply.'

Source: http://www.bushradio.co.za/ accessed on 24th May 2004.

- **Theatre of the Oppressed** (TO) is the overarching title given to the techniques and approaches to theatre pioneered by Augusto Boal, a South American popular educator. Theatre of the Oppressed seeks to harness the power of theatre as a force for change, particularly for those in oppressed situations. The arenas of application of TO range from the classroom to the council chamber, the union meeting to the therapeutic group, from the development charity to the homeless people's hostel. Forum Theatre is the best-known and most widely practised form of Boal's theatre that uses improvisation to enable people to reflect, to criticise, and harness their own power as agents of social change.

Storytelling for change

Violence in dating relationships has increasingly become an accepted social norm for men, women, boys and girls in South Africa. How can popular culture support work in schools and convince adolescent youths that it's cool not to be cruel?

The Storyteller Group in South Africa has carried out groundbreaking work, using comic stories as a tool to explore the gendered dimensions of violence within adolescent relationships. Innovative methodologies show how it is possible to diffuse the conflict between the need to reflect the realities of young people's lives and the need to transform harmful behaviour.

Within a storytelling group, students (aged 16 to 20 years) from Acornhoek High School in Mpumalanga Province were asked to write a love story about a boy and a girl in a rural village. Reflecting their own experiences, the students treated domestic violence, forced sex and having multiple partners within a relationship as the norm. Using Boal's Forum Theatre techniques, however, the students became active agents of change: acting out scenes from their own story, they started questioning and debating the actions they had given the characters. The students explored previously undiscussed topics such as rights over one's body, male violence, sexual double standards, teenage sexuality, and traditional gender roles. Thus a new story in comic form emerged – with an educational agenda, yet still retaining its popular status by remaining true to the social conditions created by the students (Shariff 1998).

Good practice lessons in information, education and communication (IEC). The range of ICE examples provides alternatives for the development of information, communication and education programmes. These interventions can be creatively incorporated in the educator and empowerment role of the social worker and the social service practitioner. Some pointers in the development of future programmes are outlined.

'The success of educational and prevention programmes requires the rigorous application of a planning, programme-development and evaluation cycle.'

- In relation to **education and prevention strategies**, the health promotion approach, which focuses on individuals, community and societal change, can be usefully applied in the development of some intervention programmes. It is a multi-level intervention strategy and can be used effectively with client groups of all sizes. The success of educational and prevention programmes requires the rigorous application of a planning, programme-development and evaluation cycle (Nutbeam & Harris 2004). It involves the application of a theory (or theories) to guide the development of IEC programmes. Health promotion theory and research assists in identifying the target groups to be served and in defining the educational needs and the problem to be addressed. It also assists in identifying the focus of the intervention and in the analysis of potential solutions. This process in turn informs the identification of what resources are needed to implement the programme and provides a framework within which programme benchmarks may be set. After implementation, the theoretical approach informing the programme also aids the assessment of the programme, the development of indicators and in assessing the outcomes achieved. The programme-development and evaluation cycle described provides a useful framework for designing health and social well-being programmes that are relevant in effecting individual and community behavioural and social change at organisational and policy levels (McGuire 1989).
- **IEC intervention programmes** also need to consider the source of the message: who does it come from and how it will be perceived? In order for the interventions to be accepted they should be credible. In addition, what is conveyed and how it is conveyed is as important as where the information and knowledge comes from. This requires sensitivity to community values and beliefs, religious and political views, language and social context. The channel of communication selected – whether it be print or broadcast media or popular community-based media – should also be appropriate. Defining the intended target audience is crucial for IEC interventions and the outcome to be achieved.
- **Organisational and community centre-based programmes** that are multi-purpose and accessible to local communities, that use volunteers and combine information-sharing with other relevant community and education services may be more cost-effective and appropriate, especially if they serve a large area. These types of services may also be grafted onto the community services of existing organisations.
- In all the examples, **collaborative strategies** were used. Organisations partner with other organisations to deliver services, share resources or

learn from practice experience. Partnerships were formed between government departments and between government and NGOs. Social service practitioners may also collaborate with specialised NGOs that have developed information and educational materials and government agencies to use in their intervention programmes.

- **Popular education theory and methods** may be usefully adapted in the development of ICE strategies and communicating appropriately with different client populations through storytelling, community radio, theatre, mass public education and edu-entertainment programmes. Popular education is a powerful way of communicating: it involves high levels of participation that connects with people's real-life experiences and draws on knowledge of their situation. It focuses on what learners are concerned about, it examines unequal power relations in the society and it moves from an analysis of the situation to encouraging collective action to change oppressive attitudes, beliefs and structures.

Case study of the 'Flagship Programme'

Pilot programmes have been designed and implemented across government departments to promote innovation and learning from practice. In order to contribute to the theory and practice of developmental social welfare, a national pilot social development programme targeting unemployed women and children under five years was developed and implemented.

The aim of the programme was to facilitate training and employment, and educational and training opportunities for women with young children through the empowerment of women and the promotion of self-reliance and social well-being. This was a government initiated and driven intervention incorporating multi-modal strategies such as poverty reduction and the promotion of sustainable livelihoods, family-centred and community-based strategies and educational interventions. The programme was implemented and evaluated over a five-year period (Jennings & Tsime 2004; National Population Unit 1999). A draft Best Practice Model and guidelines were formulated to guide project design and implementation and to increase the likelihood of success of the projects as they are implemented on a wider scale in the future (Department of Social Development 2001). The achievements and challenges of the national 'flagship programme' are discussed drawing on the evaluation research of selected sites and the draft Best Practice Model (Jennings & Tsime 2004; Department of Social Development 2001; National Population Unit 1999).

A woman at work at the Flagship Programme for Unemployed Women with young children.

Achievements and challenges

Reach of the programme. A total of 18 pilot programmes were established in nine provinces reaching 1 407 women and 2 302 children over a five-year period. There appeared to be a high level of visibility of the initiative in the communities where the projects were implemented. This depended on how inclusive the community consultation processes were when the projects were initiated, however. It was a requirement of the programme that participants had to move off the programme after a year to create space for new recruits. The assumption was that the women would have acquired skills, which would be used to achieve independent livelihoods. This did not seem to materialise and many women were demoralised, as there was no 'exit strategy' for women who left the programme. At one of the rural sites the local farmers increased wages, and this attracted participants away from the projects. This was thought to be a threat to the project, but those who remained chose to do so on the basis of a self-selection process.

Targeting. The programme appeared to have been effectively aimed at poor, unemployed women with children under the age of five years of age. Almost three-quarters of the women interviewed by the external evaluator of the programmes indicated that they were selected because they were unemployed. Despite this, problems were encountered with the selection of participants, and this caused tension in some of the communities. In a few communities there were also accusations of favouritism in the selection of participants. Selection processes need to be transparent and the criteria fairly applied.

In the evaluation of five sites, Jennings and Tsime (2004) found that slightly more than a quarter of the participants had been in some kind of employment before they joined the project. This was more marked at some sites than others, especially those located in communities close to urban areas and towns. It is critical that employment programmes of this kind do not draw people away from existing jobs as they could lead to a distortion of local labour markets. This may also be an indication of problems with the recruitment and selection of participants.

Nature of activities. The types of livelihood activities that were most popular were vegetable gardening, bakeries, poultry farming and egg production, early childhood development projects, food production such as *amasi* (sour milk) and sewing projects. Other less common projects were leatherworks, a laundry, a hairdresser, overnight accommodation and a restaurant. Some of these activities proved to be more sustainable income-generation activities than others. For instance, the poultry farming projects were more sustainable because the chickens laid eggs for 18 months and after that they could be sold and the money reinvested in the business. The bakeries were also viable in areas where there were no shops that supplied fresh bread daily. Market analysis is critical in selecting viable activities.

Impact. The programme appeared to meet the needs of the targeted communities and there was agreement at five of the selected sites in the evaluation study that the project was owned and used by the communities (Jennings & Nsime 2004; National Population Unit 1999). These positive responses varied between the communities, however. At one end of the spectrum about half of the respondents felt that the community benefited, whilst at the other end of the spectrum, between 66 percent and 92 percent were of the view that they benefited. The financial impact at the household level was considered to be positive for those who were active in the programme, but former participants felt that those benefits were of a short-term nature.

Acquiring skills such as life skills and business and technical skills were also considered some of the benefits of the projects. Business skills transfer programmes were the most common forms of training. Here again the number of people who participated varied between the sites. The impact of the programme on the participants' children was rated less favourably and the evaluators were of the view that the child development aspect of the programme may have been too ambitious. In one of the remote rural communities, the 'flagship programme' appears to have made a positive impact on the nutritional status of the participants' children. A demographic and socio-economic survey of the children at this latter site indicated improved nutrition among the children born to participant mothers (Ndegwa 1999). The children ate more vegetables from the community garden, and at other sites the benefits to children identified included nutrition and payment of school fees.

Did participation in the programme build and strengthen community support networks? It appears that the participants in the programme were more likely to involve themselves in community networks and organisations, but those members who left the programme seemed to be more isolated than they were when they were actively involved. They perceived themselves to be at an economic and psychological disadvantage. This emphasises again the importance of managing the exit of participants from the programme and the need for providing financial, micro-finance and business support for those participants who have demonstrated the ability to run successful businesses (Department of Social Development 2001).

Sustainability. Many different factors were identified that had a direct bearing on the financial and organisational sustainability of the projects. Firstly, the type of activity selected had to be viable, and an analysis of the local market is therefore vital. The knowledge of community members needs to be tapped in making these decisions and technical advisers also helped to formulate viable business plans. Secondly, administrative and management challenges were identified in many of the projects; these included inadequate business and financial management systems and project management capability. Although many people had training in these areas, the content and approach need to be reviewed. Follow-up support was also lacking. Thirdly, organisational problems were also encountered which hampered the efficiency and effectiveness of the projects. Finally, the projects were implemented in some of the remotest and poorest communities in the country, where the household income of the majority of the people was well below the national poverty line. A lack of local buying power, infrastructure and access to financial capital to create viable businesses were the major constraints that were identified.

Many of the projects were dependent on government support and the *question must be posed as to whether income-generation projects of this nature are sustainable.* In some of the projects sustainability was achieved: the projects were well run and managed, they increased household income and they operated in a supportive community environment where the benefits of the projects were tangible resulting in participant and community goodwill. However, in one extremely remote area, development finance and community and businesses facilitation support appeared to be critical if the projects were to become viable in the longer term. One project secured funding from the National Development Agency, which funds development programmes, and the other projects used the technical expertise and training support provided by different government departments. This support function cannot be underestimated in the achievement of a successful outcome.

Community development process. After the launch of the national 'flagship programme' in 1996, a national task team made up of national and provincial government and voluntary welfare and development organisations engaged in a process to conceptualise and design the programme and to build a shared vision. Planning for each of the projects at local levels broadly followed the logic model of programme development. The vision, mission, objectives, targets, selection criteria were identified, as well as operational procedures, structures, implementation strategies and roles and responsibilities of the parties. Projects were required to select action committees to oversee and implement the processes. Business plans were developed and approved in order to secure government funding.

Government staff members facilitated the community development process at local community levels. Community consultations were to be held with all parties, including traditional leaders who had to be consulted. This occurred unevenly in the different projects and there were some projects where there were no community consultations in the early stages of the projects. The external evaluation indicated that three-quarters of the participants said that they were consulted when the projects were established. The successful projects appeared to have had far more extensive consultative community processes, which increased ownership of the projects and impacted positively on the sustainability of the projects (Jennings & Tsime 2004). Participatory planning and consultations were crucial in setting up the programmes and in sustaining them on an ongoing basis.

'The flagship model is a group-owned, economic empowerment model, which was implemented by external development facilitators. This is a workable model, but the challenge remains to build local ownership, capacity and goodwill for the projects to succeed.'

Power relations between project participants created difficulties for the successful management of the projects. There were misunderstandings about selection processes, roles and responsibilities, remuneration and benefits, all of which led to conflict and dissatisfied members leaving the projects. This highlights the need for skills in conflict resolution, mediation and group dynamics – all of which are core community development skills. The flagship model is a group-owned, economic empowerment model, which was implemented by external development facilitators. This is a workable model, but the challenge remains to build local ownership, capacity and goodwill for the projects to succeed. This does not mean that all income-generation interventions should be group-driven processes: there appears to be considerable scope for supporting the livelihood activities of individuals, as demonstrated by the MODE model.

Empowerment of women. The programme was designed to empower women through providing business and life skills, opportunities for employment and support services for children whilst women engaged in productive activities. Women were intended to run and manage the programmes and participate actively in the projects. It was also assumed that, through this process, they would build supportive social networks. Did the programme empower women and improve their quality of life?

The evaluation studies showed that training and skills transfer took place and that 72 percent of the respondents had some form of training that was highly rated by the participants (Jennings & Tsime 2004). HIV/AIDS knowledge and contraception was also assessed in the evaluation studies and there appeared to be a sound knowledge of HIV transmission and unprotected sex across all the sites, although in some cases inaccurate knowledge and beliefs were detected. The integration of HIV/AIDS knowledge needs to be integrated into the life skills programmes, especially in relation to myths and misconceptions about HIV and AIDS.

Employment opportunities were created and household income increased. The income from the project complemented other sources of household income such as social grants, migrant remittances, salaries, farming, hawking and beer-selling. In one of the programmes in the Limpopo province, it was found that 68 percent of households earn less than R500 per month and that the income of R200 per month from the project boosted overall household income and improved the quality of life of women and children (Ndegwa 1999). Close to 100 women who had left the projects was found to be worse off (Jennings & Tsime 2004). As regards childcare, three-quarters of the respondents indicated that childcare was provided on site, and this was viewed very positively.

The 'flagship programme' appears to have met its objective of promoting the participation of women in the governance and management of the projects. The women are actively involved in making decisions about the strategic direction and day-today running of the projects. Whether this confidence and experience of decision-making in the projects was translated into wider empowerment in the home was not assessed. However, some consideration was given to what impact their participation had on community involvement. Most participants had a high level of participation in local structures such as burial societies (48 percent), religious organisations (39 percent), women's groups (17 percent) and political parties (15 percent) (Jennings & Ntsime 2004). The impact of their participation in the project on their existing family and community networks is not known. An interesting finding of one of the evaluation studies was that the active participants in one of the programmes tended to have higher academic qualifications and social support from their families. Future studies need to probe these aspects, as there may be a link between higher educational levels and project success. Finally, in projects where women have had positive experiences and continue to be involved they perceived their participation as a privilege and an honour.

Bochum/My Darling

Sewela is a member of the Babinachuene Women's Multi-purpose Project in Bochum/My Darling in the Limpopo province. The project is situated in a deep rural area where extreme levels of poverty can be found. Sewela did not complete high school because she became pregnant. Her husband Matome was a mineworker in Johannesburg, but when the mining industry was not doing well because of the drop in the world price of gold, Matome was retrenched together with thousands of other workers. He returned home and for some time they lived on his retrenchment package and they were able to feed themselves and their three children.

But Sewela was not alone: there were other women who were also desperately poor in her village. One day they went to discuss their lack of a livelihood with the Headman and he sent them to the Ward Councillor. They learnt about the government's intention to help the women start a project for women who were unemployed and who had young children. They were encouraged to call a meeting of the women in the village and to identify what skills they had that could earn a livelihood (sewing, farming or baking bread). They elected a committee from among the women in the villages.

The social worker, Miss Moremi, provided valuable support and advice on drawing up a business plan and in linking them with other government departments that could help them. They were allocated a 10-hectare farm by the local *kgoro* (local authority) for a vegetable garden. They planned to use some of the vegetables for their families and to sell the rest to the Bochum market. Their business plan was approved and they were awarded R350 000 by the government to start their project. They learnt project management, business, financial management and marketing skills. The women were also trained in agriculture. They cleared the land manually, which was extremely labour-intensive, and provided work for 122 women who were involved at the start of the project.

The work in the community garden was very active, but it was seasonal work and of a short-term nature. So the women decided to start a bakery and a nursery school. All this started in 1996, and when the project was evaluated in 2004 it was found to be the most sustainable of all the 'flagship programmes'. After five years the projects received no further government funding, but by this time they were on their feet. In 2004, the community garden had a credit of R35 000 in the bank and the bakery had R25 000.

The project is now working well. The women have contributed to the income of their households. The children are healthier. Sewela and her colleagues have formed a saving society to which they contribute R50.00 per month. They hope to use this money for home improvements on a rotational basis for each of the participants. The women of Malebogo village are more optimistic about the future and they keep in touch with Miss Moremi, who monitors their progress and is always ready to listen and provide advice.

CHAPTER SUMMARY

- The innovator role in generalist social work practice has received scant attention. The fostering of innovation and learning through reflective practice is vital if developmental social welfare and social work is to expand and take root in the local context. Innovation and learning from practice are important ways of diffusing new ideas and practice in the welfare sector.

CHAPTER SUMMARY

- Innovation takes place in organisations that support a culture of innovation and that foster and reward innovation among staff. Senge's principles of learning organisations provide a useful framework to guide organisations in implementing new ideas and practices.
- The diffusion of innovation into welfare and development programmes can best be achieved through the conceptualising of social development programmes. The logic model provides a framework for designing development programmes that use theory and practice research to inform programme development.
- The multi-modal model of intervention was used to guide the analysis of exemplars of innovative social development programmes in poverty reduction and sustainable livelihoods, in family-centred and community-based interventions and in information, communication and education strategies. Good practice lessons in programme implementation were discussed in relation to the different modes of intervention.
- The first national pilot programme, which targeted women and children, and which was developed and implemented to contribute to the theory and practice of developmental welfare, was discussed with reference to its achievements and challenges. The analysis of the strengths and challenges of the programme was drawn from evaluation research on the programme and the draft best practice model that evolved through learning from experience and critical reflection on practice.

CRITICAL THINKING QUESTIONS

1. Identify a relevant innovation in your agency. Document and analyse this idea with reference to the key concepts, principles and methods of promoting, implementing and diffusing innovation into organisations. Also consider the following questions and prompts:

- What challenges can be anticipated if this idea is to be replicated on a wider scale in your agency?
- What practitioner roles are relevant in this situation?
- What qualities are important in fostering innovation?
- Can you identify five good-practice lessons in this example?
- What theoretical frameworks informed your understanding and interpretation of the idea?
- Identify one aspect that requires further research that may lead to the development and diffusion of this idea.

Bibliography

Alter, C. and Egan, M. (1997), Logic Modelling: A tool for teaching program evaluation. *Journal of Education in Social Work*, 33: 1, 103–117.

Amarc Africa (1998), The African Community Radio Manager's Handbook: A Guide to Sustainable Radio. AMARC Africa.

Brocklesby, M.A. (2003), Community development in sustainable livelihoods approaches – an introduction. *Community Development Journal*, 38: 3, 185–198.

Budlender, D. (1998), *The People's Voices. National Speak Out on Poverty Hearings. March-June 1998*. Johannesburg: CASE.

Department of Social Development (2001), Developmental Programmes for Unemployed Women with Children Under the Age of Fifteen Years: A Best Practice Model. Seventh Draft.

Chambers, R. and Conway, G.R. (1992), Sustainable rural livelihoods: practical concepts for the 21st century. Institute for Development Studies Discussion paper 296.

CARNOCHAN, A. and AUSTIN, M.J. (2001), Implementing Welfare Reform and Guiding Organizational Change. *Administration in Social Work*, 26: 1, 61–77.

FREIRE, P. (1972), *Pedagogy of the Oppressed*. London: Penguin Books.

GIDDENS, A. (2001), *Sociology*. 4th ed. Cambridge: Polity.

JENNINGS, R. and NTSIME, M. (2004), Baseline Study on the Flagship Programme. Report researched and written for the Department of Social Development. Pretoria: Strategy and Tactics.

KIRST-ASHMAN, K.K. and HULL, G.H. (2001), *Generalist Practice with Organizations and Communities*. United States: Brooks/Cole Thomson Learning.

LEWIS, J.A., LEWIS, M.D., PACKARD,T. and SOUFLÉE F. (2001), 3rd ed. *Management of Human Service Programs*. USA: Brooks/Cole Thompson Learning.

LOENING-VOYSEY, H. and WILSON, T. (2001), Approaches to Caring for Children Orphaned by AIDS and other Vulnerable Children: Essential Elements for a Quality Service. Report prepared for UNICEF by the Institute for Urban Primary Health Care. Pretoria: UNICEF.

MAY, J. (1998), Poverty and Inequality in South Africa. Pretoria: Interministerial Committee for Poverty and Inequality. Pretoria: Government of the Republic of South Africa.

MCGUIRE, W. J. (1989), Theoretical Foundations of Campaigns. In Rice, R.E. and Atkin, C. (eds.) *Public Communication Campaigns*. California: Sage Newbury Park

MEREDITH, B. (1995), *The Community Care Handbook. The Reformed System Explained*. England: Ace Books.

NAIDOO, S. (2004), An Analysis of MODE's Services for Entrepreneurs with Disabilities. Johannesburg: MODE.

NARAYAN, D. (2000), *Voices of the poor. Can anyone hear us?* United Kingdom: Oxford University Press.

NATIONAL POPULATION UNIT AND VAN RENSBURG, D. (1999), Baseline Population and Development Data for the Flagship Programme for Bekkersdal. Pretoria: National Population Unit.

NATIONAL POPULATION UNIT (1999), Baseline Population and Development Data for the Flagship Programme in Elliotdale. Pretoria: National Population Unit.

NATIONAL POPULATION UNIT (1999), Baseline Population and Development Data for the Flagship Programme in Fraserburg. Pretoria: National Population Unit.

NDEGWA, D. G. (1999), Findings from a socio-economic survey of participants in the Welfare Flagship Programme: Northern Province. National Population Unit: Department of Welfare.

NUTBEAM, D. and HARRIS, E. (2004), *Theory in a Nutshell. A practical guide to health promotion theories*. 2nd ed. Australia: McGraw-Hill.

PARKER, W. (2003), Re-appraising youth prevention in South Africa. The Case of Lovelife. Presented at the South African AIDS conference, Durban, August 2003.

POERTNER, J. (1994), Popular education in Latin America: a technology for the North? *International Social Work*. 37, 265–275.

ROBBINS, S. P., CHATTERJEE, P. and CANDA, E.R. (1998), *Contemporary human behaviour theory: A critical perspective for social work*. Boston: Allyn and Bacon.

SOUTH AFRICAN DEPRESSION AND ANXIETY GROUP (2004), New Bulletin. http://www.anxiety.org.za (24 May 2004)

SCHÖN, D. A. (1983), *The Reflective Practitioner*. Aldershot: Ashgate.

SHARIFF, P. (1998), Dialogue, gender and performance: producing a rural South African comic beyond the learner paradox. Ph.D Thesis. Johannesburg: University of the Witwatersrand.

SENGE, P. (1990), *The fifth discipline: The art and practice of the learning organization*. New York: Doubleday Currency.

THOMPSON, N. (2002), People skills. 2nd ed. Hampshire: Palgrave Macmillan.

UNITED NATIONS DEVELOPMENT PROGRAMME (UNDP) (2003), South Africa Human Development Report 2003. Pretoria: United Nations Development Programme of South Africa.
UNAIDS (2004), *Care, Women and AIDS.* Geneva: UNAIDS (Joint United Nations Programme on HIV/AIDS).
UNDP (UNITED NATIONS DEVELOPMENT PROGRAMME) (1999), *Human Development Report.* New York: Oxford University Press.
WORLD BANK (1998), *Knowledge for Development.* New York: Oxford University Press.

CHAPTER 9

Enhancing social development practice

LEARNING OUTCOMES

After you have read this chapter you should be able to:

- Identify and define a selection of generalist practice skills that will enhance your competency in social development practice.
- Describe and discuss the following skills in terms of perspective, application and challenges:
  - Initiating and managing organisational change;
  - Managing poverty projects;
  - Building and sustaining social development partnerships;
  - Mediation and conflict resolution;
  - Action research;
  - Advocacy; and.
  - Anti-discriminatory practice.

Introduction

Standards for Social Work Education were developed by the Standards Generating Body for Social Work and these were registered in terms of the National Qualifications Framework with the South African Qualifications Authority (SAQA). The Standards identified micro, mezzo and macro skills that are essential to competent social work practice (SAQA Standards Generating Body for Social Work 2003). According to SAQA, social workers and social auxiliary workers should have knowledge, values and skills that enable them to:

- Challenge the structural sources of poverty, inequality, oppression, discrimination and exclusion.
- Intervene at the points where people interact with their environments in order to promote social wellbeing.
- Promote, restore and maintain the social functioning of individuals, families, groups and communities to enhance their social functioning and their problem-solving capacities.
- Apply knowledge of human rights and social justice in action.
- Provide social work services to protect populations at risk.
- Implement the social development approach in social work services.
- Work effectively in social work teams including multidisciplinary, inter-disciplinary and multi-sectoral teams.
- Engage in critically reflective practice.

The social development practice model identified the knowledge, values and skills that are an integral part of the practice framework that is set out in Chapter 7. The generalist practice perspective informs social development practice and involves working with client groups of different sizes and at different levels of intervention. The integrated application of micro, mezzo and macro practice skills and of different modes of intervention is a key feature of the social development practice model.

Skills that will enhance the ability of social workers and social service practitioners to use knowledge and intervention techniques effectively are essential to competent practice. The *concept skills* refer to discrete sets of behaviours or tasks that are performed to achieve the goals of social development. It also involves the application of knowledge in action and it builds on a foundation of knowledge and social development values that were discussed in Chapter 7 (Carnouyer 2004; Thompson 2002).

'The concept skills refer to discrete sets of behaviours or tasks that are performed to achieve the goals of social development.'

The skills that have been selected have not been fully incorporated in social work and social service curricula and are pertinent to integrated micro, mezzo and macro practice. The focus in the first part of the chapter is on mezzo and macro skills that are relevant to the implementation of the social development approach in the social services. Mezzo and macro skills build on micro skills such as personal effectiveness, interviewing and interaction and communication skills. In the second part of the chapter, the integrated application of micro, mezzo and macro skills is demonstrated where applicable.

Practitioners are expected to implement developmental social welfare and social work programmes but many do not feel confident in using these skills in practice situations. The skills that have been selected could enhance the effectiveness of social development practice and could build worker confidence in applying new knowledge and intervention techniques. *The approach adopted is to stimulate thinking and action and to demonstrate the application of the skills in real life individual, organisational and community contexts.* The intention is not to provide a 'recipe' of how to do social development. The aim of this chapter is the facilitation of on going learning through critical reflective thinking and practice and striving for the highest levels of competency. A balance had to be struck between breadth and depth of content and a high level approach was adopted linking the 'high ground analysis' (macro) to the 'low ground analysis' (micro) and vice versa. The reader is required to do further reading and to refer to previous sections where concepts, theory and research was discussed. Finally, the range of skills selected is pertinent to the overall theme of promoting and facilitating the transformation of social welfare to social development and to promote social justice and human well being.

Initiating and managing organisational change

Perspective of organisational change

The transformation of social welfare has provided the impetus for the redesign of social service organisations. Organisations are expected to continue to deliver existing services whilst at the same time initiating and implementing new directions and achieving higher levels of sustainability. They are expected to play new roles that require different skills such as understanding and facilitating development, infusing human rights and social justice concerns into direct service delivery, forming partnerships and delivering more appropriate services within a developmental framework.

Some of the key organisational challenges faced by social service and development organisations in implementing welfare reforms include:

- Adopting a more inclusive, diverse and participatory organisational culture.
- Redesigning organisations with the participation of staff of all levels of the hierarchy, consumers and other stakeholders.
- Designing equitable, integrated and generalist developmental services that address new needs and demands such as the impact of HIV/AIDS on clients and staff.
- Scaling up the reach and impact of services and increasing human resource capacity through the employment of professional, paraprofessionals and volunteers.
- Developing new partnerships and collaboration with a wide range of partners including local government, community based organisations and the corporate sector.
- Using practice-based research and planning methodologies to inform the design, the delivery and evaluation of services.
- Responding to the demand for quality services, accountability and transparency in the management and delivery of services in a resource constrained environment.

Organisational change is informed by different theoretical perspectives such as classical theories of organisations that are more suited to business and not human service environments. *Classical organisational theories* such as the concept of bureaucracy help to promote an understanding of how bureaucracies are structured and organised whilst scientific management focuses on how work processes are organised. Classical theories also emphasise the importance of unity of efforts to achieve common objectives. Later the human relations school helped to shape an understanding of organisational behaviour and management practice leading to further theoretical developments about the importance of addressing the human dimension in organisations such as valuing the human resources of an organisation (Lewis et al 2001). Although these theories are not always appropriate in human service contexts and in working with small informal and community based organisations, they enrich organisational development and change thinking and action.

The perspective informing intervention draws on Senge's (1990) work on the *learning organisation* discussed in Chapter 8 and it provides a framework for designing and managing organisational change. It starts with an analysis of the organisation by drawing on dynamic systems thinking and also involves uncovering existing mental maps of how services are currently delivered through identifying the strengths and challenges arising from it. Through this process a shared vision of the future evolves and the entire process takes place through participation of all staff and stakeholders and is based on the principles of team learning. Senge emphases the importance of personal mastery, on going learning and refinement of skills through such a process.

Developing a transformation process

Although the Child Welfare movement actively voiced its opposition to the government policies of the past, most of its services did not benefit the most deprived communities and the structures of the organisation did not reflect representation of the majority of the population. The forms of service delivery were also found to be inappropriate. To address the situation, the South African National Council for Child and Family Welfare developed a structured transformation process in 1999 with the overall deliverable of 'The Transformation of the Child Welfare Movement'.

Source: Extract taken from South African National Council for Child and Family Welfare. Second Progress Report on the Transformation of Child Welfare South Africa (2002:2).

Application of skills: strategic planning

Skills in organisational transformation, design and change are important in steering organisations into new directions. The most important components of an organisational transformation strategy are a clear vision of the future and a well-considered plan describing the steps that must be taken today, next month and in the years to come in order to make the vision a reality.

The following section describes the strategic planning process that can be used by organisations to guide them from their vision of the future, through an analysis of the current situation, to concrete strategies and plans to achieve their goals. Strategic planning at its most basic level is about setting organisational objectives and then mobilising available resources and the integrated activity of staff to achieve these objectives. The strategic planning process needs to be carefully organised. It can vary from very simple processes in small and informal groups and organisations such as community-based organisations to complex planning processes in large public bureaucracies and private national social service organisations (Coulshed & Mullender 2001).

'When staff are involved in the planning process they are motivated to carry out the specific activities that all believe will lead to successful programmes.'

In large and complex settings it is preferable that the planning process is driven by the head of the organisation to ensure maximum buy-in from managers and staff. In order to conduct a successful planning exercise, the planning team selected will depend on the size and structure of the organisation. Plans are more likely to be realistic when staff are involved in the 'how to get there' part of planning. When staff are involved in the planning process they are motivated to carry out the specific activities that all believe will lead to successful programmes. It is important to involve service users and other key role players who could also inform the process. They may participate in the planning teams or be consulted separately.

The planning process can take anywhere from one day to a year, depending on the size and complexity of the organisation and the level of disagreement within the organisation about its future direction. The extent to which change in organisational strategy is necessary to adapt to a changing environment, is another factor to consider in the planning of the change process. These factors may also help an organisation to decide whether or not to bring in an external facilitator who can assist with guiding the process and ensuring maximum participation from all levels of staff. Planning processes also require people skills such as facilitation, managing of group dynamics, negotiation and mediation, and interaction and communication skills.

Steps in the strategic planning process include:

1. Stating the vision, mission or purpose of the organisation.
2. Analysing the external and internal environment.
3. Conducting the SWOT analysis.
4. Establishing goals.
5. Selecting strategies to meet goals.
6. Establishing objectives.
7. Selecting activities for each objective and preparing work-plans.
8. Developing a funding strategy and a financial plan.
9. Monitoring and evaluation.

Stating the mission or purpose of the organisation. This sets out the overall values of the organisation and what purpose it intends to serve. The vision statement should clearly define the particular need the organisation is addressing and its role in addressing this need.

Example of a Vision statement:

A transformed child welfare movement that distributes services equitably; is representative of the society in its staff and service user profiles; is inclusive and developmental in its approach; and that is appropriately and efficiently structured to meet the challenges of social and economic development in South Africa.

Source: Adapted from the National Transformation Programme developed in 1999 by the South African National Council for Child and Family Welfare.

Analysing the external and internal environment. The external environment analysis involves a systematic analysis of the current social context and the political and economic climate in which the organisation's welfare services are currently being delivered. This may include an analysis of demographic trends, changes in welfare policy, trends in donor funding, current best practices in making services more accessible and national and regional developments among others. This analysis may require some data collection from a variety of sources. The internal environment analysis involves evaluating any advantages or limitations the organisation may have – including a situation analysis drawing on agency data and service user profiles; evaluation of current programmes and their efficiency and effectiveness; organisational structure; staffing profiles; supervision systems; training requirements and management information systems.

Conducting the SWOT analysis. On the basis of the information collected through the internal and external analysis, the next step is to conduct an analysis of the Strengths and Weaknesses of the organisation as well as the Opportunities and Threats revealed through the external analysis.

Figure 9.1: SWOT Analysis

SWOT Analysis

	Positive	**Negative**
Internal	Strengths	Weaknesses
External	Opportunities	Threats

Establishing goals. The SWOT analysis can help the organisation to set a realistic *programme and organisational goals.* Programme related goals define in general terms the impact your organisation hopes to have on target populations by the end of the time period specified in the planning process. Organisational goals define the internal changes and improvements that the organisation should make in order to achieve its goals. For programme related goals, the analysis of internal programming capabilities will provide information on past performance and on the potential for the expansion of activities. The analysis of financing capabilities will let you know if you can expand services or need to reduce them.

Goal setting

In 1999, the South African National Council for Child and Family Welfare recognised the need for a fundamental shift in the way they did their work. Their goal was the transformation of the Child Welfare Movement from a 'problem-centered/pathology centered' organisation into a developmental organisation aimed at building people.

Source: South African National Council for Child and Family Welfare (1999)

'Organisations often make the mistake of designing strategies around an existing organisational structure rather than allowing the strategy to determine the structure.'

Selecting strategies to reach goals. Your strategies map the route your organisation chooses to take in order to achieve its goals. Developing strategies involves considering all the possible strategies and selecting one or more for each goal. The strategies that are decided on will help the organisation to decide how the organisation should be structured and what the staffing requirements are. Organisations often make the mistake of designing strategies around an existing organisational structure rather than allowing the strategy to determine the structure. The planning team can brainstorm to come up with several possible strategies to achieve each individual goal. Research on innovation and best practice models locally and internationally can also inform the consideration of alternatives. The team can then evaluate these strategies on the basis of whether they:

- Will help achieve the stated goal of the organisation.
- Are feasible given the SWOT analysis.
- Will have a positive financial impact on the organisation examining both its potential to raise revenues and its projected cost.

Selecting a strategy

To achieve their transformation goal, the SA National Council for Child and Family Welfare identified four strategies. Project plans were developed for each of these strategies. The key strategies included:

- The developmental social welfare approach.
- Employment equity and social redress.
- Equitable distribution of services.
- Appropriately structured child welfare movement.

The 'Council' recognised that it needed a different way of working to achieve these strategic shifts. It was decided that each strategy be treated as an individual project with project teams drawn from staff from different divisions in the organisation and from outside the organisation.

Source: South African National Council for Child and Family Welfare (1999).

Establishing objectives. Every strategy includes a number of objectives. An objective is a specific statement of the work you intend carrying out. Your objectives should be SMART:

Specific – to avoid differing interpretations

Measurable – to allow monitoring and evaluation

Appropriate – to the problems, goals and strategies
Realistic – achievable, challenging and meaningful
Time bound – with a specific time period for achieving them

Selecting activities for each objective and developing work plans. In order to meet an objective you need to determine which specific activities must take place and in what order, who will carry out these activities and when. In preparing the financial plan this list of activities will be useful as you determine what resources (human, financial and material) will be needed to meet each objective. The following template can be used to develop work plans for individual strategies.

Table 9.1: Work plans to implement strategy

Strategy: Transformation of the child welfare movement from a 'problem-centred' organisation into a developmental organisation aimed at building people.	
Objective	1. Research and develop material on the developmental social welfare approach
Activity	1. Compile a user-friendly training package on the new approach. 2. Develop project management capacity to implement developmental programmes 3. Develop funding proposals to present to donors
Time-frame	July 2000
Human Resources	Project team consisting of experts from child welfare movement, community, universities
Outputs	1. Uniform user-friendly training material. 2. Training provided to 30 percent of staff in year 1. 3. Funding proposals submitted to donors for developmental projects

Developing a financial plan. When the planning team members choose among the possible strategies, they could make rough estimates of the cost and revenue implications for each possibility to determine its feasibility. Once goals, strategies and objectives are defined, the planners can prepare a detailed year-by-year estimate of the revenues and expenses required by the entire package of strategies. This detailed estimate, or long-term budget is the *financial plan.*

This financial plan, together with the strategies, goals and objectives, can be used as the basis for developing fundraising proposals to submit to corporate donors and the government sector.

Monitoring and evaluation. There are two types of evaluations that organisations use, these are formative and summative evaluations. *Formative evaluations* refer to the monitoring of the process of managing change, the achievement of milestones and an assessment of problems and barriers to programme implementation. It also involves monitoring of risks, unintended consequences, ensuring that programme costs remain in budget, addressing staffing issues and staff development and stakeholder relations among others. Formative assessment takes place during the implementation phase to ensure the achievement of programme goals and objectives, to learn from experience and to take proactive corrective steps. *Summative evaluation* involves an assessment of the impact of the change management interventions. Did the programme achieve its goals? What are the consequences of the change interventions?

The National Council for Child and Family Welfare's National Transformation Programme was monitored and evaluated by a National Project team and it was driven by Provincial Teams from 2000 to 2004. These teams were responsible for both formative and summative evaluations and progress reports were produced for consideration by the Boards of the agencies and government. Quantitative and qualitative research informed the assessment of impact (outcomes) of the transformation programme and to identify challenges to inform continued and ongoing transformation.

Challenges

As organisations shift from the remedial approach to a developmental one, they may experience 'transition pains' as they are confronted with what such a change means for their organisation, its traditions, culture, structure, working relations and the allocation or reallocation of authority and decision-making responsibilities. The suitability of existing staff for the new roles are other issues that may need to be addressed. There are many vested interests in organisations that may resist the changes that have to be made (Carnochan & Austin 2001). If organisations do not recognise and manage resistance, the change process could be undermined.

Organisational and institutional changes all hinge on the individual attitudes, behaviours and methods of work of the social development practitioner. Therefore, one of the most important means to realise organisational change is through human resource planning and development. Kaplan (1996) describes development practice as an *art*, which is dynamic rather than linear or predictable. The art of development practice requires the practitioner to be critically self-aware, to respect others, and to value truth, trust and diversity. Human resource development programmes need to be designed in a way that emulates the development process itself and which is underpinned by the precepts of social development. Human resource development programmes can include a combination of the following staff training and in-service training, mentoring and coaching, and identifying staff who have the potential to take new roles. This is also referred to as succession planning.

'Therefore, one of the most important means to realise organisational change is through human resource planning and development.'

Finally, monitoring and evaluation of change management efforts is vital to assess progress and to proactively address problems in the implementation of social development activities. Programme evaluation skills are other critical skills in change management.

A transformation challenge

The South African National Council for Child and Family Welfare's Transformation Plan identified a number of risks that needed to be addressed when implementing the different strategies. For example, within the Developmental Social Welfare Approach strategy, the possibility that staff and management may be threatened by the changes and undermine the process, had to be anticipated. Additional projects were identified to address this risk namely providing for career progression opportunities for staff, staff development and training for management committees including cross-cultural training.

Source: South African National Council for Child and Family Welfare (1999).

Further reading/resources

COULSHED, V. and MULLENDER, A. (2001), *Management in social work.* 2nd ed, British Association of Social Workers. Houndmills: Palgrave.
SENGE, P.M. (1990), *The Fifth Discipline. The Art & Practice of The Learning Organization.* New York: Doubleday.
LEWIS, J.A, LEWIS, M.D., PACKARD and F. SOUFLEÉ, F. (2001), *Management of Human Service Programs.* Australia: Brooks/Cole.
OLIVE (2001), *Planning for Implementation.* Durban: Olive Publications.
OLIVE. (1998), Project planning for development. Durban: Olive Publications.

CRITICAL THINKING QUESTIONS

1. Social service practitioners, managers and leaders are continually involved in initiating and managing organisational change. Conduct an interview with your supervisor or a senior manager at your field instruction agency to learn about their experiences of facilitating and/or participating in change management processes.

- What lessons did they learn from this experience?
- Discuss the generalist skills that informed their practice?
- What do you think of this example of change management?
- Does it resonate with your own ideas of change management processes?

Managing poverty reduction projects

Perspective on managing poverty reduction projects

The reduction of poverty has been placed at the centre of global development objectives along with other human development objectives to improve people's lives through expanding their choices, freedom and their dignity. Many countries have developed poverty reduction strategies, which are overarching macro strategies implemented by different social and economic sectors in collaboration with the private sector and civil society. South Africa does not have such an over-arching poverty reduction strategy although it may be argued that the Reconstruction and Development Programme adopted in 1994 initially provided such a framework. Poverty reduction is a key national governmental priority and is mainstreamed throughout most government programmes. A lack of such an overall strategy and a plan that guides, co-ordinates and monitors macro and micro level poverty reduction interventions remains a significant constraint.

Social service and development organisations are key partners in the implementation of community based poverty reduction programmes in South Africa. Besides the funding of programmes through the budgets of government departments such as the Department of Social Development, the National Treasury allocates additional funds for the reduction of poverty on an annual basis. The respective national government departments allocate the funds to provincial governments based on an annual call for grant proposals. In order for grant proposals to qualify for funding, the proposals should meet the stipulated funding criteria and the beneficiaries should be people who do not have access to other government services, unemployed people and populations at risk. The funding proposals are required to be based on sound business plans and should demonstrate viability. The proposals also need to indicate how the organisations will manage the projects and the finances. Grant proposals are also required to be based on research and the following types of programmes were prioritised by the Department of Social Development: community development, food security, skill development and programmes targeted at youth that would reduce crime and violence, older persons and people with disabilities.

'In order to improve the efficiency and effectiveness of poverty reduction programmes, it is critical that project design and management capability be improved.'

Despite some achievements, the poverty reduction programmes nationally have not been considered to be a success especially programmes with an economic empowerment focus. An evaluation of the Gauteng programmes in 2001 identified major inefficiency and ineffectiveness in the design and the management of the programmes. An evaluation of 204 projects conducted by the Kagiso Trust in 2001 found a few successful projects, but most of the projects were under-performing. Whilst some jobs were created, food aid was facilitated and skills developed, the economic development projects were less successful. Many participants did not earn an income because the projects did not generate any profits. Many poverty reduction projects closed because they ran out of funds or members had misappropriated funds. Some projects received funds but the services did not materialise. In order to improve the efficiency and effectiveness of poverty reduction programmes, it is critical that project design and management capability be improved. Such improvements may enhance the success rate of these programmes and improve the standard of living of many poor and vulnerable people. The skill of designing and managing poverty reduction projects has therefore been selected.

Application of skills: project management

Project management is defined as 'a group of tasks performed within a definable time period to meet a specific set of objectives within a budget' (Koster 1996). It provides a logical framework that identifies a process and skills needed to develop, implement and evaluate poverty reduction programmes and projects. Poverty reduction projects are usually part of overall poverty reduction strategies and programmes and are derived from social policies.

It is important to understand the link between policies, programmes and projects. *Policies* are courses of action taken by societies and their governments to achieve the goals of social development. Policies also provide the rules and frameworks that govern people's lives and ensure that governments, communities and organisations run in a co-ordinated and predictable manner (Kirst-Ashman 2003). Examples of policies and legislation that are relevant to poverty reduction include: social assistance policies and legislation, small business development, local economic development, land reform, small scale agricultural development and community-based public works.

Development programmes and their component development projects are instruments that institutions can utilise to ensure the implementation of broader policies. The concept *'programme'* is often used synonymously with 'project'. However, there is an important distinction between the two concepts: a *programme* refers to a group of similar, related or allied projects. Programmes are usually larger and more comprehensive than projects. A development programme consists of a series of development projects. For example, an anti-poverty programme can consist of a series of anti-poverty projects linked by time, proximity and purpose. A programme can be made up of a number of poverty reduction projects such as food distribution, facilitation of access to child support grants; savings schemes and entrepreneurial training and micro enterprises.

Projects are the 'building blocks' of social development programmes. Each project should be well designed and managed to be effective. But the project should be connected and should form part of the broader whole.

The poverty reduction and livelihood approach discussed in Chapters 7 and 8 is the suggested framework for the design and management of poverty reduction projects. Briefly the livelihood approach focuses less on what people lack but on what they have - their assets and strengths - and how these could be mobilised to help people make a living and improve their well being. Development interventions based on a livelihood analysis attempts to strengthen how people are already coping and to improve these capabilities by making it more sustainable. The focus is on assets, strengths and activities that people are involved with and their capabilities to make a living and improve their lives. The community development approach and social development principles inform the development and management of poverty reduction programmes and projects.

'...the livelihood approach focuses less on what people lack but on what they have – their assets and strengths ...'

In order to develop sustainable projects, the project management approach is useful to design projects and to monitor implementation and evaluation of projects. The project management cycle consists of four distinct stages and is illustrated below:

1. Project conception
2. Project preparation
3. Project implementation
4. Project monitoring and evaluation

Project conception. This stage involves the identification of a project idea and the formulation of a project proposal. Some ideas used are community meetings, consultations with key informants, community organisations and faith-based organisations and NGOs. Project conception could also be a response to a request by the community, government or other interested parties. Social service agencies may also identify projects through their annual strategic planning processes. Organisations may respond to a new need which has arisen such as an increase in the number of street children in an area. This may prompt an action research study to understand the reasons for this increase in homeless children and to identify possible responses.

In the example below, project conception was initiated by a University/Community partnership and commenced with a research study to map community assets, capabilities and livelihood activities.

'Livelihood' survey in Bapong

The Department of Community Development at the Rand Afrikaans University (RAU) is involved in community development in the Bapong community in the North West province. The BaPo ba Mogale Traditional Authority and the LONMIN Platinum Mine invited RAU to assist them with community development facilitation and support.

A survey was conducted in 2003 in partnership with RAU and the University of Louisville in Kentucky (USA) to inform a community development and poverty reduction intervention in Bapong. A household survey was conducted of 771 households in nine villages using a livelihood analysis to assess what the people's activities, assets and capabilities were which could guide project planning.

Some of the findings in regard to income, assets and education are presented.

- Almost half of households received income from migrant remittances and social grants; 32 percent of households had members who were formally employed; 12 percent worked in the informal sector and 33 percent had no employment. Jobs currently held are low paying jobs in domestic service, mining, farm labour and driving. Unemployment due to disability was 3 percent.
- Respondents identified a diverse range of skills that they are known for in the community. The most common skills identified were: building and bricklaying, brick-making, gardening and farming, sewing/knitting, baking/cooking, hairdressing and crafts.
- The average level of schooling attained was Grade 8; there is a high drop out rate in the school system. About 15 percent of children live with relatives; it may be that their parents are migrant workers.
- When asked about the dreams and aspirations of the respondents, most indicated that their greatest concern was employment - they wanted a job, or to start a small business. They also wanted to access

government grants and improve education for their children. Basic community infrastructure such as electricity, water, drainage and sports facilities was also identified as a concern.

This scenario tells a story of unemployment, how very poor households survive and what they think their skills are. A problem with drop out rates in the school system and employment were identified as their main concerns.

Source: De Wet, T., Erasmus, Y., van Rooyen, C. (2003).

Community gardens contribute to food security. A group of Bapong residents proudly display their first harvest of vegetables in their community garden.

Project preparation. Developing a project plan is the most important part of project preparation. A good project plan is the core of project management. It serves as the road map for completing the project on time, within budget and within desired performance expectations.

The project plan should follow the logic of telling:

- What is to be done;
- Why it is to be done;
- Who is to do it;
- How it is to be done;
- When it is to be done;
- In what order; and
- At what price.

The starting point for developing a project plan is to think about the desired end result. The clearer the end picture or vision is, the more effectively the plan can map the best route to achieve it. It is useful

'The clearer the end picture or vision is, the more effectively the plan can map the best route to achieve it.'

when developing the project plan to think about those external conditions that are not in the control of the project but are needed for a successful outcome. Factors such as community leadership support and access to donor funds are some extraneous factors that need to be identified. If possible constraints are identified early in the process, then actions to address these constraints can also be developed. The setting of performance indicators also happens at this stage. Indicators describe the basis for measuring how well the objectives and activities have been achieved and form the basis for project monitoring and evaluation. Indicators may be defined qualitatively or quantitatively and should be linked to the overall objectives and results of the project.

Once the project plan has been developed, work responsibilities need to be allocated through work breakdown structures. Realistic time schedules also need to be established. This activity of scheduling and managing resources is necessary to ensure smooth resource allocation and avoid resource overloads or under-loads. There are many project management tools and software that could be used depending on the level of sophistication of the organisation which are not discussed.

Developing a project plan based on the Bapong scenario[1]

The Centre for Community Development, the Traditional Authority and local community organisations and leaders called a meeting to report back on the research findings from the 'Livelihood' survey in Bapong. An action committee was elected at the meeting and through consultations between the community and its partners, agreements were reached to work on a poverty reduction programme which included the following projects: beekeeping; training in small business development targeted at unemployed people and a community garden. The Centre for Community Development was also asked to assist the community in developing a project to reduce the drop out rate of children from school. A project plan now needs to be developed for each project and a budget to submit to the Department of Social Development.

The action committee and the community worker developed a project plan for beekeeping. Presently there is a demand for local honey producers as South Africa imports honey. The project plan provided for the training of members of the community in beekeeping. It also included the need to learn the skills of beekeeping. The intention was to start their own small businesses by selling honey, beeswax, and beeswax candles. The action committee anticipated that marketing and a lack of business skills would be a great challenge. So the project plan included activities such as marketing and small business training. The idea seemed viable as partnerships could be forged between the local communities, local city council, local tribal authorities, the Department of Agriculture, the Agricultural Research Council (ARC) and local churches. The Department of Arts, Culture, Science and Technology indicated that they would fund the bee keeping projects. The ARC implements and manages the projects.

Footnote:

1 The project development phase is in the process of being implemented. The scenario sketched is a simulated exercise based on the research findings. A community garden and bee keeping projects are currently being implemented.

Project implementation. After developing a project plan and the funds are approved, project implementation commences. This involves monitoring project performance against baseline plans, outputs, milestones that have been set and exercising control if required. Exercising control means monitoring progress, reporting and evaluating the consequences of deviations from project goals and objectives, and taking corrective action. Problem-solving skills are vital to deal with implementation and unforeseen obstacles that may arise. If the planning was thorough, these should not be so significant as to take the project off course. The project manager or co-ordinator is responsible for managing the project team members. This involves building and supporting teams, providing leadership and direction, motivating staff, resolving conflicts and holding team members accountable for deliverables. Facilitation and mentoring skills are important including formal and informal communication with team members. Participatory project management is a more appropriate approach with work teams and flatter structures although it is important that project managers have responsibility and authority to ensure the achievement of goals. Managing smaller community based projects requires all of the above implementation interventions although on a much limited scale. However, small informal organisations can be more flexible and participatory and less formal and bureaucratic. Projects usually report to a structure to ensure accountability and irrespective of the size and complexity of the project, managing communication, stakeholder relations and reporting are critical to project success.

Project evaluation. Once the project is complete, the project manager and the team needs to conduct an evaluation of what transpired during the project life cycle. This final phase of the project management cycle is often overlooked or neglected despite it being crucial to learning from experience and contributing to public accountability.

If an external donor funded the project, they may want to bring in an independent evaluator to objectively assess whether the project met its deliverables and had the desired impact. In the final stages of managing projects, there are reports to be submitted to donors and financial statements. Project evaluations may also involve research to assess the impact of the intervention.

Challenges

The following questions can be used as a checklist for a successful project:

- Does it address real problems?
- Are the objectives clear?
- Is the project based on well-formulated plans?
- Are the roles and responsibilities of team members clearly defined and understood?

- Will a competent and motivated team implement it?
- Is it located in an organisation with sufficient capacity to implement the project?
- Does it enjoy support from other stakeholders?

Based on an evaluation of poverty reduction projects in Gauteng by Kagiso Trust in 2001, projects were considered to be more likely to succeed if:

- A core group of highly committed project members existed. Most of the projects started with a large membership, but many dropped out because of tensions, conflict, and dissatisfaction with earnings. Projects also took too long to generate an income and participants got frustrated.
- A viable business opportunity is identified and if the participants have access to reliable markets for their products and access to the materials and skills needed to produce and sell their goods and services.
- Project design connects with local economic development strategies and plans or development actions of key partners.
- On-going mentoring in project management, financial management and business support is provided. Capacity in these areas is very low and these skills take time to learn. The evaluation stressed that most of the marginally successful projects needed increased support.
- Sound financial management systems are in place to ensure that funds are not misappropriated.
- Participants worked for a regular income and increasingly earned more as the project's productivity and income increased. These types of projects were considered to have a better chance of success than those projects whose members do not have a direct stake in income generation and distribution. Labour issues are also more likely to come to the fore in these types of projects. Some members regarded themselves as employees in the projects and the ownership of the project is left to the members of the management committee.
- Participants have a basic education and skills to engage in entrepreneurial activities.
- Expectations of what participants are likely to earn are clarified at the beginning in order to increase participant retention in the projects.

Further readings/resources

DAVIES, A. (1997), *Managing for a change: guide to the management of development projects.* United Kingdom: ITDG Publishing

OLIVE. (2002), *Planning for Implementation. The Operational and Financial Planning Handbook.* Durban: Olive Publications.

OLIVE. (1998), Project Planning for development. Durban: Olive Publications.

CRITICAL THINKING QUESTIONS

1. What do you think are the pitfalls in executing poverty reduction projects?
2. What action can be taken to avoid these pitfalls?
3. Identify the micro, mezzo and macro skills that social service practitioners use in designing and managing development projects?

Social development partnerships

Perspective on partnerships

Social development partnerships are an emerging response to the social and economic development needs of societies in a more interdependent global world. Many social problems cannot only be addressed locally and nationally but require regional and international collaboration. A social development partnership is a voluntary and collaborative agreement between one or more organisations whereby all the participants agree to work together to achieve a common purpose or undertake a specific task. The key features of social development partnerships are sharing risks, responsibilities, resources, competencies and benefits. The partners recognise that they are mutually dependent on one another and agree to work together under a shared process of decision-making and joint problem solving. Social development partnerships could enhance the delivery of developmental welfare services through enlarging budgets and finding synergies between partner activities to meet needs and deliver services more efficiently and effectively. Partnerships to promote transformation through sharing best practice, pooling knowledge and experience to solve complex social problems and through mutual social influence are other benefits of partnerships. Through collaborative partnering, duplication and fragmentation in service delivery at local levels could also be addressed.

'The key features of social development partnerships are sharing risks, responsibilities, resources, competencies and benefits.'

Partnerships can take different forms and include the total spectrum of partner relations ranging from international and transnational partnerships; bilateral (government to government) and multi-lateral partnerships (involving many governments); regional partnerships such as the Southern African Development Community (SADC) to national intergovernmental partnerships involving different spheres of governance. In Chapter 4 social development partnerships was discussed with reference to the *welfare pluralist approach* and the *collaborative partnership model* between government and non-governmental organisations and the private sector. The concept partnership is also informed by *social network theory* (Trevillion 1999). Power is an inescapable feature of all human relations and is an important dimension that should be taken into account in understanding the power dynamics of partnerships. *Conflict theories* assist in understanding the economic, ideological, political and social aspects of power relations and how these impact on the relations between the parties in a partnership. It is important to understand the balance of power in the relations between partners, what interests exists and whether these interests could secure greater benefits for some of the partners. In the context of globalisation, new social movements are emerging and these movements also exercise power through social action such as environmental and anti-globalisation activism.

The focus in this discussion is however on social development partnerships at the agency and community level.

Application of skills: agency/community partnerships

'The most important assets of a community are its organisations and institutions.'

To achieve common goals agency/community partnerships bring together a wide range of formal and informal organisations from communities, social service and development organisations, religious organisations, universities, research bodies, government and the private sector. Finding these partners and mobilising them for com-munity building, renewal and development is a major challenge. Instead of identifying deficiencies in communities, the asset approach to community development alerts practitioners to working with community capacities, skills and assets. The most important assets of a community are its organisations and institutions namely community-based organisations, civic associations, faith-based organisations, clubs and societies and social, neighbourhood and friendship networks. Other partners that may be mobilised are schools, clinics, churches and businesses. Partnership development also depends on sound relationships and skill in relationship building.

Social service organisations form many different types of partnerships to achieve their objectives such as informal networks; community or special interest group forums and more formal inter-organisational relationships such as a consortium. The aim of the partnership will determine the type of partnership needed and certain types of projects are not possible without partners. The agency can also adapt a partnership to meet the particular needs and constraints of an organisation. To initiate a partnership, a catalyst is needed or a person to initiate the process and set it in motion. It is also important to emphasise areas of convergence and if there are differences of opinion, these need to be made explicit. Building and maintaining effective partnerships requires identifying common goals, maintaining frequent and open communication, learning from each other through mentoring and building honest relations between the partners. Problems in partnering often arise and it is important that the partners confront these when they happen. Strong personal, organisational and leadership commitment to the partnership; productive interaction in partner activities; a willingness to compromise and sensitive engagement with one another are critical to partnership building.

Skills that are important in partnerships are relationship building, networking, teamwork, running effective meetings, communication, record keeping and the implementation and management of partnership agreements. Some of the common problems faced in partnerships involve a lack of role clarification, dedicated staff to take responsibility for co-ordination especially if there are shared responsibilities for service delivery. Agreements on these aspects need to be established when the partnership is formed and reviewed on an on-going basis. It is also important to be sensitive to issues of power and domination in partnerships and differences in organisational culture may impact on the success of the partnership. Partnering organisations may also fear the loss of their identity and there is always the danger that small organisations may loose their autonomy or are controlled by larger bodies. Partnerships may require additional resources and can place a strain on already overloaded staff (United Nations Economic and Social Council 2003). It is therefore important to approach partnering in a strategic way and to assess the benefits and costs of the exercise.

'It is therefore important to approach partnering in a strategic way and to assess the benefits and costs of the exercise.'

Initiating partnerships

Scenario: The head of your organisation Ms Sibeko is keen to build an agency/community network to co-ordinate the delivery of services in Alexander Township outside the City of Johannesburg to deliver services to youth at risk. Ten public, private and community organisations met to discuss the idea. The first meeting was very chaotic, everybody spoke at the same time, many ideas were raised but at the end of the meeting there was no clear direction on how to proceed. It was also worrying, as some parties were more concerned about how the network would impact on their services and not what could be achieved through collaboration. The participants left the meeting feeling frustrated but with some commitment to meet again. The next meeting is scheduled to take place in a fortnight. Since this meeting was crucial to get the network moving, Ms Sibeko had a feedback session with staff members to review the previous meeting and to plan for the next meeting.

Feedback Session: The meeting considered a number of issues and questions such as, why is the partnership being formed? How can they build on the points of convergence or congruence between the partners? What is the purpose of the partnership and what are the benefits and risks for the parties. What is expected of the partners and what do each of the parties expect to get out of the network? What will they have to give up if they work together? How should the turf issues be addressed? What might be some activities that the network could start working on that is non-threatening. How should the network be structured? Should the head of the agency draw up an agenda or should the meeting set the agenda? Where should the meeting be held? These and many other issues and questions were considered before rushing into a partnership.

Postscript: After weighing up all the issues and challenges, the staff agreed that an action minute of the last meeting should be prepared and circulated to all the parties. Since the agency may have been perceived as wanting to dominate the partnership, volunteers were called for from the other organisations to consider the above issues and to work on an agenda. One of the other agencies offered to host a planning meeting and to provide the tea.

Challenges

The United Nations Economic and Social Council (2003:14) identified the following lessons that were learnt from recent experiences of social development partnerships:

- Partnerships could challenge partners to think and interact in new and different ways.
- Partnership gains may not always be easily quantifiable. Assessing partnerships only in terms of the measurable indicators may miss the long-term benefits of partnerships.
- There is no one model that applies to all types of partnerships. There should be scope for innovation and flexibility in the forms of partnerships, which should be determined by the needs that are being addressed.
- Partnerships involve change. This means that the partnership may be a response to social policy, legislation, economic and social changes in communities. Partners may also mobilise for change such as in the formation of coalitions formed to unite organisations to work in alliances to achieve a goal.
- Successful partnerships are not necessarily made up of formal and institutionalised relations between the parties. Local, national, regional or global partnerships such as Task Forces are often temporary and less formalised. Successful partnerships can therefore be temporary, dynamic and flexible leaving room for partners joining or leaving the arrangement as they see fit. Temporary partnerships may however decide to become more formalised as the relationship progresses.

Further reading

Bronstein, L.R. (2003), A Model for Interdisciplinary Collaboration. *Journal of Social Work,* 48: 3, 297–306.

Gilbert, N.(2000), Welfare Pluralism and Social policy. In Midgley, J., Martin, B.T. and Livermore, M. *The Handbook of Social Policy* (411–420). Thousand Oaks: Sage Publications Inc.

Lombard, A. and Jansen van Rensburg, A. (2001). Coalitions: A Practice Framework for Sustainable Development. *Social Work/Maatskaplike Werk,* 37:4, 325–342.

Patel, L. (2003), Social Development in a Society in Transition. *Journal of Social Development Issues,* 25:1/2, 150–161.

Trevillion, S. (1999), *Networking and Community Partnership* 2nd ed. Aldershot: Ashgate.

CRITICAL THINKING QUESTIONS

1. What lessons can be learnt from the scenario sketched in the box 'Initiating partnerships'?
2. What skills are important in forming and sustaining partnerships?
3. What is welfare pluralism? Discuss this approach with reference to agency/community partnerships. (Refer to Chapter 4)

Mediation and conflict resolution

Perspective on mediation and conflict resolution

Mediation is a process whereby a neutral third party helps disputing parties arrive at a mutually acceptable solution to their conflict. In the process, agreement and disagreements are carefully explored, information is shared, options are developed and the interests of each party are clarified. The decision-making power and responsibility remains with the parties and the goal is an equitable settlement based on consensus. Mediation is always voluntary and confidential. Mediation is not counselling, legal advice, punishment, psychotherapy or arbitration.

'The decision-making power and responsibility remains with the parties and the goal is an equitable settlement based on consensus.'

Conflict resolution has been usefully conceptualised by the Centre for Conflict Resolution (Sully 2000) in terms of a series of three developmental stages, with each stage representing a step in a continuum of effectiveness. The first stage is labelled *peace making* and it involves a reactive intervention strategy typically undertaken by a third party to the conflict. The immediate parties involved are not able to resolve the conflict on their own and it requires the intervention of an outsider to break the impasse or bring the parties to a point where they can deal with their differences and find a mutually acceptable solution.

The second stage, *peacekeeping*, is both a more anticipatory and a pre-emptive strategy. It typically still places the emphasis on the role of the third-party intervenor, but there is an attempt to address the causes of conflict at an earlier stage, in order to pre-empt the development or escalation of the conflict. The final stage, *peacebuilding*, moves beyond an interventionist, third-party model of conflict management. The task at this stage is to address the underlying causes of conflict and to build local capacity, understanding, skills, systems and structures to promote and facilitate peace.

There are many ways of approaching an understanding of the causes of community and civil conflict. Five components are identified that are relevant to understanding the causes of conflict (Sully 2000:7).

- **Resources**. Conflict is seen to arise out of competition over the ownership or allocation of, or access to natural and human resources.
- **Identity**. Differences in culture, ethnicity, religion and the power for self-determination act as key conflict-determining factors.
- **Power**. Political, economic and social differentials of power. Issues of domination, control and survival, involving both groups and individuals are common in conflict arising from power differences.
- **Social and economic change**. Changes in law and governance, changing value systems and the decline of traditional structures and values are significant factors contributing to conflict.
- **Gender and social status**. The influence of traditional gendered and social roles and values. Gender-based differences in perception and action often play an important part in the genesis and the management of conflict. In a similar way, generational differences may contribute significantly to conflict development.

Figure 9.2: The five components of peace and conflict

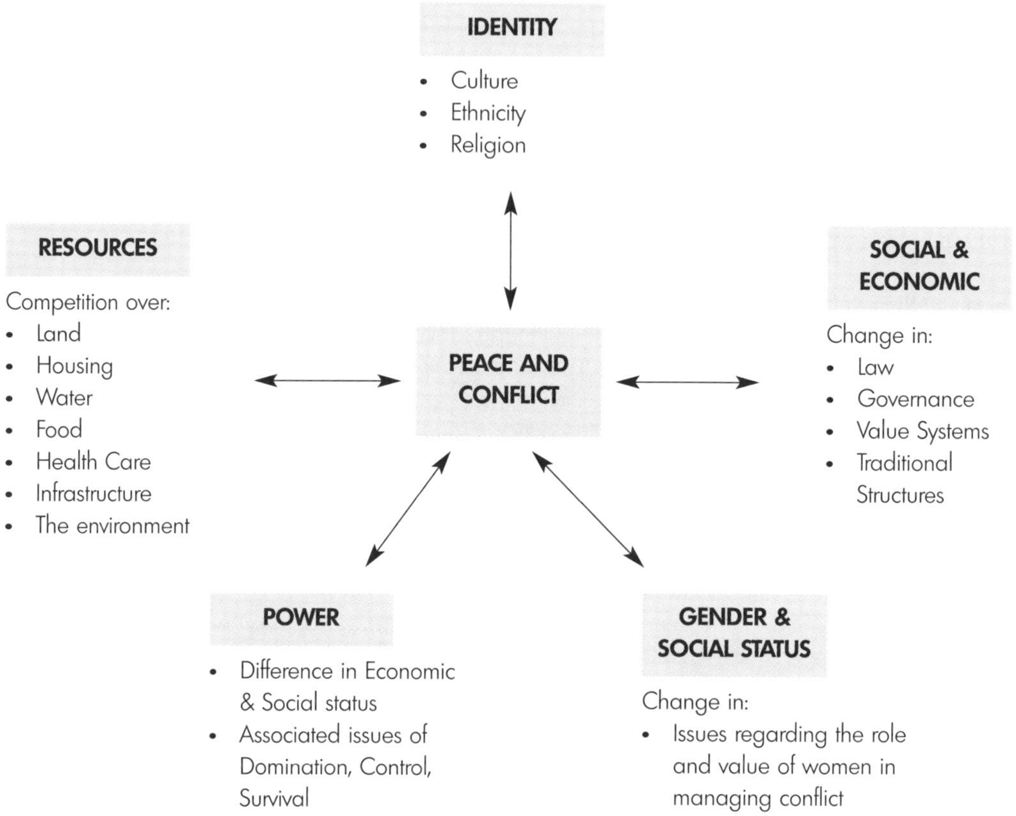

Source: Sully (2000: 8)

> *'Mediation and conflict resolution skills are vital to promote effective social development practice in a society engaged in reconstruction and development, reconciliation and healing.'*

Why is mediation important in social development? The emphasis of mediation on finding a 'win-win' solution resonates well with social work's core values of the dignity and the recognition of the worth of each person, the importance of human relationships and the pursuit of social justice. Evidence of this fit is seen in mediation outcomes. Parties to mediation report a higher level of satisfaction with the process and lower financial costs than parties who employ the traditional two-attorney system to resolve their differences (Severson 1998). Mediation and conflict resolution skills are vital to promote effective social development practice in a society engaged in reconstruction and development, reconciliation and healing. Conflict over resource allocation, service inefficiencies, discrimination and the way in which economic, political and social changes are managed could lead to tension in groups, organisations, work environments and communities. If not properly managed, it could escalate into conflict and violence that is destabilising. Social workers and social service practitioners use mediation skills to solve problems in human relations, groups and organisations. Community dispute resolution is also important to build a culture of community problem-solving. The following are some examples of situations where mediation is being used in the South African context:

- Mediation of school-yard conflicts. In some schools mediation has been introduced as part of the education curriculum and is conducted by specially trained peer group mediators in the same classes as the parties in conflict.
- Mediation in the juvenile justice system. For non-violent offenders, victim-offender mediation is a process where community volunteers, under the supervision of caseworkers, help both sides humanise and rehabilitate each other.
- Mediation as part of divorce counselling. This provides a way for families who are breaking up to learn to deal with the changes in roles, duties and new opportunities and to face those changes with emotional balance.
- Mediation as part of community action and conflict resolution involves the use of community mediation and dispute resolution skills to resolve conflicts between parties. The conflict between political parties and warring factions in Kwazulu-Natal and Gauteng communities in the 1990s was addressed through mediation and conflict resolution. Conflict of this nature can best be dealt with through the developmental stages referred to above and not through the judicial system.
- Mediation as part of labour conflict resolution that is aimed at finding a better way to end conflict and improve relations in the workplace.

Application of skills: mediation

Successful mediation involves the application of the following intervention options depending on the nature of the issue. (Alternative Dispute Resolution (ADR) Resources. http://adrr.com/adr1/essayf.htm):

Impartial third party facilitation. A third party neutral mediator is a person who makes the entire process work. The parties should trust the facilitator and be involved in the selection of the facilitator. All of these programmes work because the mediator is known to be either neutral or supportive of the parties and has no personal interest in the dispute. The facilitator assists the parties to find common ground around their own best interests. This type of mediation often takes place to prevent disputes from ending in the courts. If this is the case, the parties then agree to suspend legal action during the mediation. However, should no agreements be reached, the parties can revert to legal action.

Third party mediator to protect the integrity of the proceedings. This approach is used to ensure that the integrity of a process is preserved in order for people to have confidence in its outcome. Examples where this approach is used are election processes of organisations, the transparent application of criteria to select poverty reduction projects or the selection of beneficiaries to participate in development programmes. The facilitator also protects the confidentiality of a proceeding(s) and ensures that agreed procedures are followed. The mediator should not take sides against any party to the mediation and should preserve the integrity of the proceedings. This could be done through record keeping and in the drafting and adoption of a final agreement between the parties.

Mediation in good faith. In this type of mediation situation, the parties agree to work together with the intent to work towards a resolution. The rules are agreed to ensure that the parties do not use the processes for ulterior purposes. Both the behaviour and integrity of the impartial facilitator are important in creating, and preserving good faith.

All parties present. This approach is used when all the parties who are involved in a dispute need to be present and active in resolving the conflict. It requires the involvement of the people who have the authority to make decisions and act on those decisions to participate in the mediation process.

The above intervention options are commonly used in mediation and dispute resolution. The selection of the most appropriate option in a given situation requires careful assessment and consultation with the parties involved. A critical issue in mediation is that an appropriate or neutral site or venue needs to be agreed to between the parties. The site must be conducive to the process and a place where the process could be conducted in a neutral, confidential and inclusive manner. The place is as important as the persons who are a part of the process. The selection of the participants is also important to ensure that the parties to the conflict and those with authority and credibility are selected to participate.

'Training in mediation is critical if social service practitioners are to use mediation skills competently.'

The following generalist skills are applicable to mediation: interviewing techniques, active listening, communication, rephrasing and summarising skills, group work and facilitation of small groups, community dispute resolution and education in community problem solving. Training in mediation is critical if social service practitioners are to use mediation skills competently. Knowledge of conflict theory and how to balance power in groups where it is skewed is another important skill. The mediator needs to be aware of the importance of psychological factors and their impact on the process. An evaluation and reflection on the mediator role can improve the performance of the mediator. Since agreements are vital in the mediation process, the skills of crafting an agreement can facilitate dispute resolution. Finally race, ethnic, gender, age and cultural dimensions also have a bearing on a successful outcome (Severson 1998).

Challenges

Mediation is practised in different disciplines and settings such as law, family mediation, juvenile justice and labour relations in South Africa. Along side the official practice of mediation a grassroots approach has been popularised to defuse inter and intra-community conflicts in the transition period. Many communities have their own mechanisms of conflict resolution based on organic, traditional or African methods. In some communities residents associations and street committees perform these functions. An indigenous model of mediation is emerging that combines formal mediation with aspects of African tradition and a post-apartheid culture of conflict resolution through participation, negotiation and mediation. The focus is not only on collectives but also on the resolution of social and development concerns and issues.

There is scope for social service practitioners to broaden the conception of the mediator role and to infuse formal and less formal conflict resolution and mediation skills into practice. The role of the social service practitioner in mediation needs closer attention. There is scope for the integration of African methods of conflict resolution and community problem solving capacities in developing indigenous practice.

Further reading

Severson, M. (1998), Teaching mediation theory and skills in an interdisciplinary classroom. *Journal of Social Work Education* 34: 2, 185–194.

Sully, M. (2000), Using the Case Studies as a Means of Peace Building. In *African Case Studies Manual for Conflict Training* (7–9). Centre for Conflict Resolution. Cape Town: University of Cape Town.

CRITICAL THINKING QUESTION

1. Identify a scenario where mediation will be the most preferred method of intervention. Assess the nature and causes of the conflict situation and formulate an intervention plan to address the situation. Also identify what skills you are likely to use.

Action research

Perspective on action research

Action research (Greenwood & Lewin 1998), participatory action research (Strydom 2002; Kemmis & McTaggard 2000), community-based research (Chopyak 1999; Hall 1981) and practitioner-researcher-educator (Chan & Ng 2004) are some of the concepts and approaches that describe research with a social change agenda. It has its roots in struggles for social change in developing countries. Its theoretical foundations lie in critical theory and it evolved as a challenge to the dominant positivist research paradigm.

'Action research is biased in favour of those who face social exclusion from the mainstream of the society.'

The concept action research is used for the purpose of this discussion, as it is a broad umbrella concept, which allows for research that is participatory, community action oriented, facilitates learning and informs practice. It is used to describe an array of approaches to research that have as their basis the belief that collaborative participation by community members in the process of building knowledge is essential and central to any research-related endeavour (Van Rooyen 1998). The research process integrates three related activities: social investigation, educational work, and action with the ultimate goal of structural transformation and improvement of the lives of those involved (Hall 1981; Collins 1998). Action research is biased in favour of those who face social exclusion from the mainstream of the society. It also instils empowerment and social justice thinking in practice, research and education. For example, the social work practitioner-researcher-educator approach is being used in the implementation of an empowerment and problem based learning curriculum in the Department of Social Work and Social Administration at the University of Hong Kong (Chan & Ng 2004).

Action research is based on the following premises:

- Information empowers organisations and communities.
- Research can assist in solving social problems.
- Research can provide information to the community and can inform planning and assessment.
- Research is conducted with communities, for and by them and is a resource to organisations and communities.
- The goal is to democratise knowledge, learning and promote community action for social change. The relations between the researcher and subjects are less hierarchical recognising the knowledge that the parties bring to the process.
- The research process organises the community to come together to address needs, to map assets and to plan, implement and evaluate community interventions. The process also raises critical awareness about social conditions in communities that could inform advocacy.
- Its focus is on community mobilisation action, capacity building, and self-reliance and community participation.

Application of skills: action research

Action research is increasingly being used in a variety of practice and education settings to enhance practice and to respond to the current social context. Action research can be used when conducting or engaging in:

- Finding and mobilising community assets, skills and capacities;
- Needs assessments;
- Community development;
- Advocacy and lobbying;

- Social planning – programme design;
- Accessing resources;
- Formulating grant proposals;
- Programme evaluations;
- Providing client user feedback; and
- Social impact assessments.

University/community research partnerships

The African Self Help Association (ASHA) and the Department of Social Work at the former Rand Afrikaans University (now renamed the University of Johannesburg) signed a partnership agreement to collaborate in research and training. ASHA went through a process of organisational renewal in order to become more community-based in its approach. A needs analysis was conducted which informed the transformation of the organisation. ASHA and parents at the pre-school centres were actively involved in the research process and in the development of intervention strategies. The University also assisted with the training of community development workers and to date 1 000 community development workers have been trained in community leadership skills. They play an active role in the organisation and in facilitating community action.

Challenges

The major criticism levelled against action research is that it lacks scientific rigour and that it confuses social activism and community development with research. The association of action research with practice and activism has lead to the accusation that the research is driven by politically motivated outsiders and not disadvantaged communities who are taking the initiative to identify problems to be investigated (Kemmis & McTaggart 2000). Action research approaches research from a completely different research paradigm. It does not ignore formal research or epistemological issues that are important to valid social knowledge. Greenwood & Levin (1998:6) argues that 'social knowledge is derived from practical reasoning engaged in through action... action is the only sensible reasoning way to generate and test new knowledge'. Action research involves the use of a wide range of research methodologies and is also used effectively in conducting research in multi-disciplinary teams with community partners. For a full discussion of issues related to research design and illustrations of research studies refer to the list of further readings.

Further reading

Collins, K. (1998), *Participatory Research: A Primer*. South Africa: Prentice-Hall.

Greenwood, J. D. & Levin, M. (1998), *Introduction to Action Research. Social Research for Social Change.* Thousand Oaks: Sage Publications.

Strydom, H. (2002), Participatory Action Research. In De Vos, A.S., Strydom, H., Fouche, C.B., and Delport, C.S.L. *Research at Grass Roots*. Pretoria: Van Schaik.

Van Rooyen, C. (1998), Democratising Social Work Research. In, Gray, M. (ed), *Developmental Social Work in South Africa: Theory and Practice.* David Phillip Publishers: Cape Town.

CRITICAL THINKING QUESTIONS

1. Is action research unscientific? What do you think?
2. Engage in further reading and identify some of the difficulties in the practical implementation of action research.
3. What are the benefits and disadvantages of action research?

Advocacy

Perspective on advocacy

Advocacy is a social action tool, a community change strategy and a mode of social development intervention discussed in Chapter 7. It has the potential to empower individuals and communities to take action to address social, economic and environmental injustices. Advocacy is grounded in the social work profession's commitment to social justice (Finn & Jacobson 2003; Robbins, Chatterjee & Canda 1998). It is underpinned by the concept of empowerment which refers to the process by which individuals and groups gain power, access to resources, and control over their own lives. Empowerment theories help us to understand the structural barriers that prevent people from accessing resources necessary for health and well being. These barriers include the unequal distribution of wealth and power inherent in contemporary economies and societies and the effects of prolonged powerlessness and oppression on marginalised individuals and groups (Robbins Chatterjee & Canda 1998).

An advocate is someone who is willing to:

- Speak up.
- Help others to get benefits and services to which they are entitled.
- Challenge government systems and organisations when they do not work.
- Work for policies, laws and budgets that do work for people.
- Be a voice for others (especially those with troubled lives) with policy makers.

Source: Amidei 1992:7.

'Advocacy means to speak up, to plead the case of another, or to champion a cause.'

Advocacy means to speak up, to plead the case of another, or to champion a cause. It is a sustained effort organised by like-minded groups or individuals to work for systematic and peaceful change to policies or to other oppressive conditions or attitudes that affect people's lives. Generalist social workers should engage in advocacy at some level as part of their responsibilities to clients (Kirst-Ashman & Hull 2001). Two types of advocacy have been identified: cause advocacy and case advocacy (Kirst-Ashman & Hull 2001). *Cause advocacy* is a macro level practice skill that involves work on behalf of groups of people who lack the ability (resources, talent or skill) to advocate for themselves. Cause advocacy seeks to involve citizens in the process of change, especially through their participation in policy-making processes on matters that directly affect their lives. Advocacy builds support for change through dialogue and persuasion, not coercion, by using a wide range of methods and approaches to communicate a message. It aims to use people's own experiences and knowledge to persuade others to change. The Treatment Action Campaign is a good example of cause advocacy.

TAC's Advocacy Strategy

On 10 December 1998, International Human Rights Day, a group of about 15 people protested on the steps of St George's Cathedral in Cape Town to demand medical treatment for people living with the virus that causes AIDS. The group included people with HIV, a medical student, a 66-year-old grandmother, a former human rights commissioner and a selection of others determined to draw attention to the unnecessary suffering and death caused by the untreated epidemic. Passers-by were surprised. Not many of them knew that you could treat AIDS. They did not realise that AIDS medications were freely available in some countries. By the end of the day the group had collected over a 1 000 signatures calling on the government to develop a treatment plan for all people living with HIV, and the Treatment Action Campaign (TAC) was born.

But on 30 November 1998, when well known gay rights and AIDS activist Simon Nkoli joined the long list of South Africans to die of AIDS-related causes, his colleague and comrade Zackie Achmat knew something had to be done. Achmat spoke at Simon Nkoli's memorial service and announced that a protest and fast would be held on 10 December 1998 to launch a new campaign, under the auspices of the National Association of People With AIDS (NAPWA), to fight for access to treatment. In the years since it was launched, the TAC has attracted hundreds of volunteers and thousands of supporters around the country. It has opened branches in the Western Cape, Gauteng and KwaZulu-Natal. TAC volunteers come from all ages, professions and race groups. Their members also come from parliament and include lawyers, doctors, unemployed South Africans, scholars, students and pensioners. Many, but not all of their volunteers are HIV-positive.

There is no official membership list for the TAC, but volunteers are always needed to help out with a range of activities. Perhaps the TAC's greatest achievement has been to raise public awareness about AIDS treatments and to provide hope that poor people will be able to benefit from them. Through legal action, public protests, presentations to Parliament, regular media coverage, working with labour and religious groups and good old-fashioned campaigning, the TAC has put the issue squarely on the public agenda. Whereas a few years ago experts dismissed the idea of AIDS treatment in developing countries, this idea is now taken seriously – and is closer to being realized.

Source: Treatment Action Campaign: An Overview. http.//www.tac.org.za

Case advocacy is a micro level practice skill where the worker advocates on behalf of individuals or families. Often, a generalist social worker may notice that a number of individuals or families share similar problems and this awareness may set the stage for cause advocacy. Case advocacy may be as simple as the writing of a letter or the making of a telephone call to a person in authority or to a newspaper. Paralegal advice officers also assist welfare clients with grant applications and inform them of their rights. Sometimes, these organisations have joined forces with other human rights organisations such as the Legal Resources Centre to take legal action to enforce rights. *Legal action* can force change through the legal system by bringing cases to the courts and if won, could end certain practices or actions that violate people's rights.

Legal advocacy

The Constitutional Court judgement in the case of the Government of the RSA vs Grootboom in 2000 is a landmark judgement in the enforcement of socio-economic rights. In this case the respondents were evicted from low cost housing land that they occupied illegally. They took legal action and based their case on Section 26 of the Constitution, which obligates the state to take reasonable legislative and other actions to ensure that their rights were progressively realised. The Constitutional Court ruled that the socio-economic rights contained in the Bill of Rights placed a duty on the State and other role players to respect, protect, promote and fulfil these rights. Although the government's housing policy resulted in a significant increase in the number of houses being built, the Court held the view that the State failed to provide for temporary relief for those in desperate need.

Source: South African Human Rights Commission (2002).

A final approach is *social action*, which involves the use of more complicated, militant and confrontational strategies to achieve change. It is associated with the social action approach of Saul Alinsky (1971) which is designed to involve individuals and organisations in gaining power and control over their situations. Alinsky identified rules to guide social action that continue to raise many issues about the ethics of means and ends. This approach has resulted in differences of opinion as to its appropriateness in the social services and the moral and ethical dilemmas of professional involvement in social action campaigns (Mendes 2002; Kirst-Ashman & Hull 2001). The Code of Ethics of the South African Council for Social Service Professions adopted in 1986 provides no guidance to social service practitioners in addressing such dilemmas. South African social workers faced enormous and unusual ethical dilemmas in the practice of social work during the apartheid years and especially during the state of emergency in the1980s. Those who choose to participate in community action felt that they were morally and ethically bound to oppose unjust and oppressive laws and State action. The South African experience teaches us that if laws and regulations and the actions of governments and powerful organisations are unjust, social service professionals have little choice as to whether action should be taken. In his comments on the ethical dilemmas of community development workers in community action campaigns in Australia, Ife (1995:162-163) provides some practical guidance and says that three questions should be answered by social service workers as to whether they should break the law or not when engaging in community action. Firstly, is there a strong moral justification for breaking the law? Secondly, what are the personal consequences for those breaking the law? Thirdly, will the action advance the public cause that the social actionists are advocating? Ife argues that these questions must be carefully considered before embarking on social action and that principles of honesty, openness, integrity and non-violence should guide the practitioner in making such ethical decisions. 'These principles should only be violated if there are strong moral and practical reasons for doing so' (Ife 1995:256–261).

Application of skills: advocacy

Advocacy methods include awareness raising through the media, capacity building and educating stakeholders, organising, mobilising and networking, campaigning through demonstrations, boycotts, opinion polls, and petitions. The conventional model of advocacy is to achieve changes in official policies or legislation. However it is increasingly recognised that legislation changes little if people are either unaware of the changes or unable to use legal processes. Therefore advocacy attempts not only to change legislation and policies but also to impact on attitudes, behaviours and decision-making processes (Mayoux 2004). Some advocates form advocacy groups to address specific issues. They use local groups to show grassroots support and build coalitions with other groups to expand resources beyond the reach of any one group working alone.

'...advocacy attempts not only to change legislation and policies but also to impact on attitudes, behaviours and decision-making processes.'

The following five steps are pertinent to advocacy (Amidei 1992:31–40):

1. Identify the issue that will be advocated for and the goals to be achieved.
2. Get the facts to back up your case.
3. Develop an advocacy strategy.
4. Get to know the decision-makers and their staff.
5. Mobilise and broaden your base of support.

Identify your issue and goals. An issue is the problem that affects a significant number of people and that you wish to do something about. Some examples include child abuse, corruption, and inadequate social security coverage. The identification of your goals is of the utmost importance, that is, what is it that your organisation ultimately hopes to accomplish. For example, the TAC's goal was to ensure access to quality treatment by all people living with AIDS.

Get the facts. Good advocacy plans are based on solid facts, not anecdotes or guesses. A quick fact-finding effort could help establish whether the anecdotes are the exception or part of a pattern. Getting the facts may require some research and presents an opportunity to involve your volunteers in collecting and analysing information.

Develop a strategy. Once the issue has been clearly defined and the advocacy group has learnt as much as they can about the problem and who is responsible for it, its time to map out a strategy. Developing an advocacy strategy is similar to the process of developing a strategic and project plan – what do you want to do, by when, who will do it and how much will it cost? Deciding on what tactics to use and which tactics will be the most appropriate and effective, is an important part of strategy development.

An advocacy strategic plan should follow the steps needed to achieve the goals. It is almost always important to firstly create public support for your goals. This will be the basis on which your campaign stands or falls.

Get to know the decision makers and their staff. Knowing the players is not just a matter of being able to list their names. Effective advocates cultivate relationships with decision-makers and their staff over a long period of time. This facilitates access and communication.

Broaden the support base of the campaign. This is about finding ways to gather as many people and organisations together as possible in support of collective goals. It is not necessary to agree on everything in order to co-operate and to achieve a concrete goal. Make sure that all the partners in a campaign understand that this co-operation is about this specific goal and does not mean that they are tied forever on specific issues. One way to broaden the support base for social action is through *networking and partnering* as discussed above. This simply means going to the places and occasions where advocates can find out who the actors are that they want to approach in their campaign. It is about making the campaign known to all the possible actors: colleagues, NGOs, churches, policy makers, journalists, and influential community leaders. Networking enables the advocates to find out what the current debates are about, what the priorities of other organisations are and who their potential partners are. This will in turn inform the tactics and strategy of the advocates that should be assessed on an ongoing basis.

Forming coalitions is another way of broadening a support base. The key to a successful coalition is equality and respect. In successful coalitions, small and big groups, moderate and radical groups work together taking advantage of each other's strengths without ignoring differences.

Challenges

'Practitioners are sometimes reluctant to engage in advocacy for fear of controversy.'

Many welfare organisations have experienced a certain tension between service provision and advocacy. Practitioners are sometimes reluctant to engage in advocacy for fear of controversy (Kirst-Ashman & Hull 2001). If government provides funds for services it might seem unwise to criticise the government publicly. *Advocacy does not mean being anti-government.* Rather it means holding government accountable through constructive use of democratic processes and institutions. It means monitoring government policies, laws and actions on an ongoing basis – endorsing them when they are consistent with the organisation's objectives and priorities and criticising them when they are not. Regular liaison with key government departments and involving them in organisational activities or at least keeping them informed can help to build a climate of transparency, mutual confidence and trust. To advocate effectively, organisations should analyse and research how government is structured, how decision-making processes work, what its planning and budgetary cycles are and how legislative processes are conducted and scheduled. This is important if organisations are to participate effectively. For example keeping abreast of legislative programmes and public hearings on Parliamentary Bills is important to make the views of advocates known.

One of the criticisms levelled at advocates is that they 'neither share the social descriptive characteristics of their client community, nor consult with or account to the people they presumably represent, nor involve them in identifying the issues and in advocating for themselves (Checkoway 1995:12). As discussed above, social service professionals have a moral and an ethical responsibility to ensure that they respect the right of client populations to full and equal participation and that they are accountable for their actions. The South African Code of Ethics for Social Service Professionals could also provide guidance on ethical conduct in relation to advocacy and social action.

For as long as the society remains committed to the existence of a strong and vibrant civil society, democratic governance and peaceful processes of change, there will be a role for both case and cause advocacy which are important generalist practice and anti-discriminatory practice skills. In Africa and many other parts of the globe, citizens are still deprived of their rights and have unequal access to political power and economic resources. Many people in poor countries are hampered in their development and their ability to influence decision making because of deference to traditional authorities, customs, or prejudices. A lack of education and information are obstacles to full participation in society leading to individual or group interests being ignored. Whilst this situation prevails there are innumerable opportunities for advocacy.

Further reading

Alinksy, S. (1971), *Rules for Radicals.* New York: Vintage Books.

CARE USA (2001), Advocacy Tool and Guidelines: Promoting Policy Change. Downloadable as a series of pdf files from: www.careusa.org/getinvolved/advocacy/tool.asp#english. 24th May 2004.

Kelly, J. (2002), Research and advocacy for policy change: measuring progress. The Foundation for Development Corporation. http://www.fdc.org.au/publications/2002521_43.html. 24th May 2004.

Kirst-Ashman & Hull (2001), *Generalist Practice with Organisations and Communities.* United States: Brooks/Cole Thomson learning.

Mendes, P. (2002), Social workers and the ethical dilemmas of community action campaigns: lessons from the Australian State of Victoria. *Journal of Community Development,* 37,157–166.

World Bank (2003), Community Empowerment and Social Inclusion. http://www.worldbank.org/wbi/communityempowerment/Modules/Advocacy.html

CRITICAL THINKING QUESTIONS

1. Should social service practitioners participate in advocacy and social action? Why?
2. What are the value and ethical dilemmas for social service practitioners when they do so?

Anti-discriminatory practice

Perspective on anti-discriminatory practice[2]

South Africa was governed by a system of institutionalised racial segregation only a decade ago. Its history of colonialism and apartheid left the country with systemic social and economic inequalities. Racism was institutionalised, legalised and internalised. It was embedded in the operations, institutions and structures of the society. After 1994, the Mandela government began the difficult process of addressing racism embedded in the fabric of the society. Various measures such as policy and legislation and institutional changes were introduced. One of the most notable measures was the Truth and Reconciliation Commission (TRC) which is internationally acknowledged to be one way of promoting dialogue and reconciliation in post conflict societies.

Over 22 000 people participated in the TRC and told their stories of how they were victimised in the past, they spoke of their powerlessness in the face of state oppression and repression and its impact on their lives. These testimonies are an important historical record and a public acknowledgement of past human rights violations. The emphasis of the TRC was on building unity, racial harmony and reconciliation. However, critics say that national unity and the emphasis on uncovering individual crimes and instances of human rights abuses neglected the history of racism and segregation that affected not only individuals but also an entire population. This approach was believed to have had the effect of individualising human rights abuses while under-emphasising the systemic and institutional nature of discrimination and oppression. Mamdani (1996) argues that the TRC model resulted in a denial of responsibility by those who benefited from the system.

Ten years into the new democracy, South Africa has achieved a relatively stable transition but it remains a divided society. Racial prejudice, hate crimes, political intolerance based on political affiliation in areas such as Kwazulu-Natal and xenophobia between South Africans and foreigners, remain major challenges. Other challenges are related to inherited inequalities and social divisions in the society such as gender inequality caused by patriarchy, disability, ageism and HIV/AIDS status, all of which were discussed in Chapter 6. Despite

Footnote:

2 For a discussion and an introduction to the theory, concepts and themes of anti-discriminatory practice, refer to Thompson, N. (2001), *Anti-discriminatory Practice*. 3rd ed. London: Palgrave Macmillan.

the abolition of the Groups Areas Act, South Africans continue to live mainly in communities that are not racially integrated. At schools and universities, many students still prefer to interact with members of their own race and or ethnic group and bringing about change in the racial profile of service users and staff in social service organisations, has proved to be more difficult than initially anticipated. The legacy of apartheid will be felt for many more decades and may combine to form new forms of social division and racism. Scholars say that old forms of racism based on biological characteristics are being replaced with a *'new racism'* that is based on cultural differences that exclude certain groups (Giddens 2001:257).

'The legacy of apartheid will be felt for many more decades and may combine to form new forms of social division and racism.'

It is against this background that anti-discriminatory practice is critical in the South African context in view of the country's past history and continuing manifestations of social divisions in the new society. *Anti-discriminatory practice* (ADP) is informed by *conflict theory* and is 'an approach to social work which seeks to reduce, undermine or eliminate discrimination and oppression, specifically in terms of challenging sexism, racism, ageism and disablism and other forms of discrimination encountered in social work' (Thompson 1993:31). The approach recognises the impact of discrimination and oppression on people's lives and seeks to explore ways of avoiding the pitfalls of falling into practices which directly or indirectly result in the unfair treatment of individuals and groups. Those who are discriminated against are considered to be members of groups that experience a lack of power. The practitioner's focus is on personal and group empowerment through dialogue and an understanding of the totality of the experience of oppression and its manifestations on those affected by it (Langan & Day 1992:3). Thompson (2001) provides two main reasons why anti-discriminatory practice is particularly relevant for social service practitioners: firstly, social workers occupy positions of authority and secondly, as mediators between the state and its people, they may become part of oppressive state and non-state structures and knowingly or unknowingly reinforce discrimination. Thompson (2002) identifies three areas of intervention for practitioners starting with ways in which individual practitioners can imbue the anti-discriminatory approach into day to day practice. Effecting change in organisations, its policies and culture is an important area of intervention and lastly he proposes social and group strategies to influence both individual and organisational change.

Application of skills: Anti-discriminatory practice

The Promotion of Equality and Prevention of Unfair Discrimination Act 4 of 2000 provides a legislative framework that could guide social work practice in the South African context. The preamble to the Act states that 'systemic inequalities and unfair discrimination remains deeply imbedded in the social structures, practices and attitudes' of people in the society. The aim of the Act is to prevent unfair discrimination and to facilitate the transition to a caring, compassionate and democratic society based on principles of equity, fairness, social progress, justice, human dignity and freedom. Discrimination is defined in the Act (Chapter 1, Section 1) as:

> *any act, policy, law, rule, practice, condition or situation that directly or indirectly imposes burdens, obligations or disadvantage or that withholds benefits, opportunities or advantage from any person on the grounds of race, gender, sex, pregnancy, marital status, ethnic or social origin, colour, sexual orientation, age, disability, religion, consciences, belief, culture, language and birth.*

The Act stipulates what constitutes prohibitions on the grounds of race, gender, disability and hate speech. It also provides for the establishment of Equality Courts that would hear unfair discrimination cases and outlines the general responsibilities of public, private and civil society organisations in promoting equality. An Equality Review Committee is a requirement of the Act and its members are responsible for advising the Minister of Justice on the implementation of the Act. Social service practitioners could make representations to the Committee on matters of national concern and government departments are required to develop anti-discriminatory plans and to report against the objectives set. An Illustrative List of Unfair Practices in Certain Sectors of Society such as health, education, housing, insurance and pensions, professional bodies, partnerships and sport and recreation are contained in a Schedule accompanying the Act.

'Non-discrimination and the promotion of equality are primary values of social work identified in the social development practice model.'

This far-reaching legislation provides a sound platform for social service practitioners from which to approach the prevention of discrimination and the promotion of equality. The social development practice model discussed in Chapter 7 also provides a framework for intervention and to examine anti-discriminatory practice. Non-discrimination and the promotion of equality are primary values of social work identified in the social development practice model. Generalist practice with its focus on multiple levels of intervention at micro, mezzo and macro levels also guide the consideration of intervention and skills.

The point of departure of anti-discriminatory practice is on *practitioner* knowledge, sensitivity and awareness of discrimination and oppression in the African context – the historical and systemic nature of discrimination and an understanding of the key concepts and theories informing practice. Worker self-awareness and experiences of various forms of discrimination is vital in order to understand its impact on the self and populations at risk. Professional development also needs to focus on achieving greater congruence between professional and personal values. Thompson (2002) emphasises the importance of *recognising discrimination and oppression* as it is so much a part of the taken for granted world of people. The practitioner needs to have knowledge of the different *processes* that are associated with discrimination and how people experience it, what it means to them and how it impacts on their lives. For instance, people who live on the margins of the society do not participate fully in the society. There are certain factors and processes such as a lack of income, skills, racial prejudice, and beliefs of what certain groups of people can and cannot do that may lead to their *marginalisation* from the mainstream. People who are HIV positive may not be accepted in the community and ex-offenders may be stigmatised or perceived in negative terms when they apply for jobs. *Scapegoating* of foreigners occurs when a foreigner particularly from another African country is blamed for the escalation in crime and drug smuggling in communities. Scapegoating also occurs when there is competition for scarce resources and where groups of people feel threatened by others in relation to employment. In such situations they may vent their feelings by scapegoating others or projecting stereotypical thinking on them.

Key concepts in anti-discriminatory practice

- Discrimination refers to the unfair treatment of individuals and groups and behaviour that is prejudicial to their interests.
- Prejudice is based on preconceived views about individuals and groups that are not based on evidence and that may lead to the favouring of one group over another. It manifests itself in bias, unfair actions, intolerance and a devaluing of the esteem of the 'other'.
- Oppression means the inhuman or degrading treatment of individuals or groups; a denial of their dignity, rights and citizenship that stems from the political domination of one group over another.
- Racism is prejudice that is based on socially formed attitudes or behaviour of individuals and groups towards others whom they perceive to be inferior to them based on their biological characteristics. Racism is institutionalised when it permeates the structures and institutions and the social fabric of a society.
- Sexism is discrimination based on sex. It refers especially to discrimination against women and involves attitudes and behaviour that foster stereotypes of social roles that are based on sex (Merriam-Webster's Collegiate Dictionary 1994:1073).
- Ethnicity has a social meaning. It is based on the idea that ethic groups see themselves as culturally distinct from others due to their history, language, religion and life styles such as dress and food and the norms and beliefs of their communities. Ethnic and group identity is achieved through socialisation according to the cultural outlook and practices of the community. Ethnicity is often associated with minority groups - that is individuals and groups who belong to powerless groups. The concept is negatively associated with apartheid's ideology of racial and ethic segregation and the oppression of a majority. Ethnic conflict and hostility between groups has escalated into ethnic cleansing and genocide in countries such as Rwanda and Yugoslavia.
- Equal opportunities refer to the creation of equal opportunities for all people based on the value of equality. It refers to employment practices and equal access to resources, services and benefits.
- Stereotypes are rigid, biased and oversimplified conceptions of certain categories of people that are negative in tone and are linked to prejudice e.g. sex role stereotypes.

- Stigma is the categorisation of individuals and groups based on aspects of their circumstances or social and economic characteristics that are of a negative nature. It is associated with labelling and stereotyping.
- Xenophobia refers to animosity, hatred or fear of strangers especially people of foreign descent and is commonly associated with economic migrants, refugees and asylum seekers.

Sources: Giddens 2001; Thompson 2001; 1993.

An understanding of these concepts could enhance the practitioner's ability to identify discrimination and to explore appropriate interventions. *Micro level* interventions may include: dialogue, developing understanding, counselling, empowerment and self-help groups, consciousness raising groups, popular educational interventions, case advocacy to challenge incidents of discrimination and legal action. Thompson (2002) also refers to partnership building and to recognise social and cultural barriers to effective participation and partnering. Helping people to gain personal and collective power to counter the negative effects of discrimination are other forms of micro level intervention. Initiating reconciliation at micro and mezzo levels is another way of countering discrimination, which is being implemented in prejudice reduction workshops in schools.

Mezzo level interventions are focused on effecting organisational change in social service agencies and community based organisations. This may refer to policies and procedures of organisations in relation to resource allocation and service delivery guidelines in implementing non-discriminatory practice. Organisational level interventions are also relevant in the implementation of equal opportunity policies and in effecting changes in organisational culture. For example, agencies need to be sensitive about how language policies and religious practices or attitudes toward same sex partnerships may be barriers to access to services and experienced as discriminatory. The skill of managing organisational change is a key skill in enhancing social development practice. Community based organisations face different challenges to social service agencies as their services are generally located in local communities and may have been started by a specific social group in a community. For instance in the implementation of one of the flagship projects for unemployed women and children in an informal urban settlement, there were community perceptions that only people of a particular ethic group namely Xhosa speaking persons were allowed to participate in the projects. In order to address this perception, the social worker helped the action committee of the flagship project to clarify the goals and principles of the project to all parties by convening a community meeting. This example shows how an 'us and them' perception may be interpreted as unfair discrimination. This phenomenon is known as group closure and is particularly relevant in the allocation of resources and in gaining access to scarce resources. Thompson (2002) also suggests the use of group influence techniques to approach discrimination in groups and organisations through staff meetings, staff training, forming support groups of staff members to challenge discrimination in the agency and user participation in assessing services.

Working for policy, legislative changes and monitoring their implementation are *macro level intervention strategies*. Cause advocacy, legal action, popular education campaigns such as the Soul City and loveLife educational media programmes referred to above are other examples of macro practice. Action research is also critical to uncover the underlying reasons for discrimination; developing a deeper understanding of the issues and research to document best practice and monitor the implementation of policies, legislation and programmes. Community mediation and dispute resolution, cultural awareness and development groups and infusing anti-discriminatory thinking and practice into existing micro, mezzo and macro interventions are some ways in which equality and reconciliation might be addressed.

Case Example: Daniels v Campbell N.O. and Others

Mrs Daniels applied to the High Court of South Africa to acquire the ownership of her house where she lived for 28 years. She was married and following the divorce, the house was allocated to her in her own name. Later she remarried. However, because of the discriminatory housing policies of the City Council, she lost the title to her house because she got married and only married women who were breadwinners and rearing children qualified for access to housing. Mrs Daniels was married by Muslim rites.

Some time later her new husband Mr Daniels, bought the house because only the tenant could buy the house. When Mr Daniels died, the house became a part of his estate and since he had no will the estate was to be divided according to Common Law and not Muslim laws of inheritance. Mrs Daniels stood to loose her only asset as the estate was to be distributed between her stepchildren who threatened her continued occupancy of the house.

In 2003, the High Court of South Africa ruled in her favour. This ruling now provides protection for women married according to Mulsim rites to acquire ownership of their homes. The case 'illustrates the interplay between discrimination on the grounds of sex and gender and discrimination on the grounds of religious belief, and how such discrimination impacts on women's rights to housing' (De Villiers 2003).

Challenges

It is not known to what extent anti-discriminatory practice has been actively integrated into social work education and practice. There is a paucity of local literature and training material on the subject. South Africa provides a rich laboratory of ideas and experience to pursue research that could inform practice. This chapter has provided a cursory view of a complex subject that requires further in-depth exploration.

In the South African milieu where racial prejudice and race politics have and continues to occupy a dominant place in public discourse, there is the danger that anti-discriminatory practice may be equated with racial discrimination only. The approach is a broader one, which allows for the interaction of various sources and forms of oppression also referred to as 'multiple oppressions' and is acknowledged in current legislation. Practitioners may be reluctant to challenge unfair discrimination because of the sensitivity of the issues involved and because they are afraid that it may heighten tension and conflict in already socially and politically charged situations. This avoidance of issues of discrimination and oppression contributes to silence around these issues especially in relation to race and affirmative action. Professional education and continuing education and development programmes may assist practitioners in finding more effective and appropriate ways of raising awareness about discrimination and in relation to intervention strategies. Social service practitioners also need to have knowledge of the legislation and what constitutes discrimination in terms of race, gender, disability, age, harassment and the dissemination of information. Legal remedies can be sought where a person's right to equality has been infringed. The legislation also places the emphasis on prevention of unfair discrimination through public education and awareness programmes. There is significant scope for social service organisations to engage in prevention programmes of this nature. Anti-discriminatory practice is an integral part of social development practice with the aim of promoting equality.

Further reading

GIDDENS, A. (2001), *Sociology*. 4th ed. Cambridge: Polity Press. Chapter 9.
THOMPSON, N. (2002), *People skills*. 2nd ed. New York: Palgrave Macmillan. Chapter 17.
THOMPSON, N. (2001), *Anti-discriminatory practice*. 3rd ed. London: Palgrave Macmillan.
THOMPSON, N. (1993), *Anti-discriminatory practice*. London: Macmillan Press Ltd.
REPUBLIC OF SOUTH AFRICA. *The Promotion of Equality and Prevention of Unfair Discrimination* Act 4 of 2000.

CRITICAL THINKING QUESTIONS

1. Discuss some of the key concepts that inform anti-discriminatory practice and illustrate these with examples from your own experiences and from practice.
2. Discuss the skills and intervention strategies of anti-discriminatory practice.
3. The contemporary South African milieu both enables and hinders the implementation of the anti-discriminatory practice approach. Discuss this statement and motivate your response.
4. After reading this section, you may wish to explore your own values, attitudes, and behaviours in relation to individuals and groups other than your own. You could do this on your own or in a small group. Consider the following questions: identify some of your prejudices, consider what life influences shaped them. How do you feel about those prejudices? In what ways are they at variance with your professional values? Are you committed to challenging your own prejudices? If yes, what would you like to do?

CHAPTER SUMMARY

- This chapter identified generalist practice skills that could enhance social development practice in a changing local and global world.
- The skills meet the requirements of the Standard Generating Body for Social Work of the South African Qualifications Authority.
- The skills are an integral part of social development practice and build on the knowledge and values of developmental social work and social welfare.
- The skills are relevant in addressing the challenges of the transformation of welfare services to development, poverty and unemployment, peacebuilding, accountability of government, civil society and the private sector, and preventing and promoting unfair discrimination.

Bibliography

ADR (ALTERNATIVE DISPUTE RESOLUTION) RESOURCES. http://adrr.com/adr1/essayf.htm. 24 May 2004

ALINKSY, S. (1971), *Rules for radicals*. New York:Vintage Books.

AMIDEI, N. (1992), *So you want to make a difference: advocacy is the way.* 3rd ed. Washington: OMB Watch.

BRONSTEIN, L.R. (2003), A Model for Interdisciplinary Collaboration. *Journal of Social Work,* 48,297–306.

CARE USA. (2001), Advocacy Tool and Guidelines: Promoting Policy Change. www.careusa.org/getinvolved/advocacy/tool.asp#english. (24 May 2004)

CARNOUYER, B. R. (2004), *The Social Work skills Workbook*. 4th ed. USA: Brooks/Cole Thomson Learning.

CARNOCHAN, S. and AUSTIN, M.J. (2001), Implementing welfare reform and guiding organisational change. *Administration in Social Work*, 26, 61–77.

CHAN, C.L.W. and NG, S.M. (2004), The social work practitioner-researcher-educator. *International Social Work Journal*, 47, 312–320.

CHOPYAK, J. (1999), Community-based research: Research for action. *Harvard Family,* 4, 14–15.

CHECKOWAY, B. (1995), Six strategies of community change. *Community Development Journal,* 30, 2–19.

COLLINS, K. (1998), *Participatory Research: A Primer*. South Africa: Prentice-Hall.

The Conflict Resolution Centre: http://www.alaska.net/~cdrc/Hints.html (24 May 2004)

COULSHED, V., and MULLENDER, A. (2001), *Management in social work,* 2nd ed British Association of Social Workers. Houndmills: Palgrave.

DAVIES, A. (1997), *Managing for a change: guide to the management of development projects.* United Kingdom: ITDG Publishing

DE VILLIERS, C. (2003), Daniels v Campbell N.O. and Others. The long battle of a woman married according to Muslim personal rites to acquire ownership of her home. *Economic and Social Rights in South Africa*, 4: 3, 8–10.

DE WET, T., ERASMUS, Y. and VAN ROOYEN, C. (2003), *Bapong Household Survey.* RAU and the University of Louisville Kentucky.

FINN, J.L. and JACOBSON, M. (2003), Just practice: steps towards a new social work paradigm. *Journal of Social Work Education*, 39, 57–77.

GREENWOOD, J.D. and LEVIN, M. (1998), *Introduction to action research: Social research for social change*. Thousand Oaks: Sage Publications.

GIDDENS, A. (2001), *Sociology*. 4th ed. Cambridge: Polity Press.

GILBERT, N. (2000), Welfare Pluralism and Social policy. In Midgley, J., Martin, B.T. and Livermore, M. (eds.) *The Handbook of Social Policy* (411–420). Thousand Oaks: Sage Publications Inc.

HALL, B. (1981), Participatory research, popular knowledge and power. *Convergence*, 14: 6–17.
IFE, J. (1995), *Community Development*. Australia:Longman.
KAPLAN, A. (1996), *The Development Practitioner's Handbook*. London: Pluto Press.
KELLY, L. (2002) Research and advocacy for policy change: measuring progress. The Foundation for Development Corporation. http://www.fdc.org.au/publications/2002521_43.html. April 2004
KEMMIS, S. and MCTAGGART, R. (2000), Participatory Action Research. In Densin, Y. and Lincoln, Y. *The Handbook of Qualitative Research*, 2nd ed. California: Sage.
KIRST-ASHMAN, K.K. (2003), *Introduction to social work and social welfare: critical thinking perspectives*. California:Brooks/Cole Thomson Learning.
KIRST-ASHMAN, K.K. and HULL, G.H. (2001), *Generalist Practice with Organizations and Communities*. California:Brooks/Cole Thomson Learning.
KOSTER, M.J.F. (1996), *Introduction to practical project management*. Pretoria: University of South Africa.
LANGAN, A. and DAY, L. (1992), *Women Oppression and Social Work*. London: Routledge.
LEWIS, J.A., LEWIS, M.D., PACKARD, F. and SOUFLEÉ, F. (2001). *Management of Human Service Programs*. Australia:Brooks/Cole.
LOMBARD, A. (2001), Coalitions: A Practice Framework for Sustainable Development. *Social Work/Maatskaplike Werk*, 37, 325–342.
MAMDANI, M. (1996), Reconciliation without justice. *South African Review of Books* 46.
MAYOUX, L. (2004), *Advocacy impact. Enterprise impact news,* Issue 27, Jan/Feb 2004.
MENDES, P. (2002), Social workers and the ethical dilemmas of community action campaigns: lessons from the Australian State of Victoria. *Journal of Community Development,* 37, 157–166.
NEL, H. (2001), A project management approach to the implementation of development programmes within the local government sphere: an empirical analysis. *Development Southern Africa*, 18, 605–624.
OLIVE (1998), *Project planning for development*. Durban: Olive Publications
OLIVE (2001), *Planning for Implementation*. Durban: Olive Publications.
PATEL, L. (2003), Social Development in a Society in Transition. *Journal of Social Development Issues,* 25, 150-161.
ROBBINS, S.A., CHATTERJEE, P. and CANDO, E.R. (1998), *Contemporary Human Behaviour Theory. A Critical Perspective for Social Work*. Boston: Allyn & Bacon.
TREATMENT ACTION CAMPAIGN: An Overview. http.//www.tac.org.za (24 April 2004.)
SAQA (SOUTH AFRICAN QUALIFICATIONS AUTHORITY) (2003), *Qualifications for Social Work*. Government Notice 433 of 2003, volume 452, No. 24607.
SENGE, P.M. (1990), *The Fifth Discipline. The Art & Practice of The Learning Organization*. New York: Doubleday.
SEVERSON, M. (1998), Teaching mediation theory and skills in an interdisciplinary classroom. *Journal of Social Work Education*, 34, 185–194.
SOUTH AFRICAN NATIONAL COUNCIL FOR CHILD & FAMILY WELFARE (1999), *Transformation of the Child Welfare Movement: National transformation project*. Johannesburg
SOUTH AFRICAN NATIONAL COUNCIL FOR CHILD & FAMILY WELFARE (2002), Second progress report on the transformation of child welfare in South Africa. Johannesburg.
SOUTH AFRICAN HUMAN RIGHTS COMMISSION (2002), 4th Economics & Social rights report. Johannesburg.

STRYDOM, H. (2002), Participatory Action Research. In De Vos, A.S., Strydom, H., Fouche, C.B. and Delport, C.S.L. *Research at Grass Roots* (419–434). Pretoria: Van Schaik.

SULLY, M. (2000), Using the Case Studies as a Means of Peace Building. *In African Case Studies Manual for Conflict Resolution Training,* (7–9). Centre for Conflict Resolution. Cape Town: University of Cape Town.

TREVILLION, S. (1999), *Networking and Community Partnership*. 2nd ed. Aldershot:Ashgate.

THOMPSON, N. (1993), *Anti-discriminatory practice*. London: Macmillan Press Ltd.

THOMPSON, N. (2001), *Anti-discriminatory practice*. 3rd ed. London: Palgrave Macmillan.

THOMPSON, N. (2002), *People skills*. 2nd ed. New York: Palgrave Macmillan.

VENEKLASEN, L. and MILLER, V. (2002), A new weave of power, people and politics: the action guide for advocacy and citizen participation. World Neighbours. Excerpts and ordering info at: http://www.justassociates.org/ActionGuide.htm. 24 April 2004

VAN ROOYEN, C. (1998), Democratising Social Work Research. In, Gray, M. (ed). *Developmental Social Work in South Africa: Theory and Practice* (77–91). Cape Town: David Phillip Publishers

UNITED NATIONS ECONOMIC AND SOCIAL COUNCIL, COMMISSION FOR SOCIAL DEVELOPMENT (2003), *Forty-first session 10–21 February 2003: National and International Co-operation for Social Development*. Report of the Secretary General. New York: United Nations

THE WORLD BANK (2003), Community Empowerment and Social Inclusion.
http://www.worldbank.org/wbi/communityempowerment/Modules/Advocacy.html (24 May 2004)

CHAPTER
10

Conclusions: Future prospects for social development

Introduction

South Africa has embarked on an ambitious programme of restructuring the welfare system it inherited from the colonial and apartheid periods. The restructuring of the welfare system is part of a larger project to transform South African society to achieve peace and social justice, a caring, positive, participatory and a multicultural society aimed at overcoming the social divisions of the past. A bold new vision for social welfare was developed and is being implemented. Significant achievements have been noted in the policy and legislative domain, in the ending of racial discrimination in access to services and benefits, and in the creation of a nationally integrated single welfare system for all South Africans. Innovation and good practice lessons emerging from the implementation of developmental social welfare are other significant achievements that could inform the theory and practice of the new approach.

Despite these achievements, the expansion of social development has been hampered by multiple and inter-related factors ranging on the one hand from globalisation and macro economic, political and social factors to institutional issues and inadequate management and administrative capability on the other hand. A further challenge is the pressure from trade unions and non-governmental organisations to expand social assistance to address mass poverty and inequality. The restructuring of the administration of the social security system to improve efficiency and effectiveness through the creation of a national social security agency that will manage the delivery of social grants is an important development. However, the re-organisation of the social security system may impact negatively on the efficacy of developmental welfare services. Increasing demand and rising public expectations, low economic growth rates and constrained resources have placed increasing pressure on policy makers to respond to key priorities such as poverty and joblessness, rising levels of crime and violence in the society and the HIV/AIDS pandemic. Finally, the country is faced with a twin challenge of addressing the legacy of the past and new risks arising from globalisation and its attendant uneven and unequal development within and between countries and regions in the world. These issues and challenges were discussed in Parts 1 and 2 of the book.

It is against this background that the question needs to be posed as to what the future landscape of social development might be in a post conflict transition society and in a changing regional and global context? Is social development likely to thrive or will it stagnate or wither away? Are there particular factors and forces that either constrain or promote the expansion of social development? What are the challenges facing the society in the years ahead? One way of answering this question could be through constructing different scenarios about how the future is likely to unfold based on certain assumptions. Exercises of this nature are useful strategic planning tools to determine what needs to be done in order to achieve a desired outcome. Mayor & Binde (2001) caution against forecast models of this nature as they can easily lapse into 'futurology' and in reality a combination of scenarios are probably more likely. The future of social development in a rapidly changing world is uncertain, complex, unpredictable and it could evolve in many different directions. As indicated in Chapter 1, the future is not fixed and human agency also plays an important role in how social development is likely to evolve. While the future cannot be predicted, Ilya Prigogine, Nobel Prize winner, scientist and philosopher says that we can prepare it (Prigogine 1995). Many may argue that a focus on the present is the only option in an uncertain crisis ridden world whilst others call for preparation in order to respond to the challenges of coming decades (Mayor & Binde 2001). These authors advocate taking a long-term view rather than focusing on short-term realities only.

'The future of social development in a rapidly changing world is uncertain, complex, unpredictable and it could evolve in many different directions'.

The future landscape of social development in South Africa is examined below with reference to key themes namely:

- Social development: national and global perspective.
- Regionalism and social development.
- Social Policy.
- Institutional issues.
- Social security and welfare services.

Social development: national and global perspective

In Chapter 1, globalisation was defined as a process whereby economic, political, cultural and social relations take on a global form. Among its distinctive features is the spread of new technological tools of industrial production and communication that are the driving force of the new information age. While globalisation presents nations with new opportunities to promote social and economic development, it has far reaching negative consequences for the achievement of human security. Economic risks associated with the slow down in the world economy, lower levels of foreign investment, currency fluctuations, the volatility of capital and labour mobility are all factors that have a direct bearing on the South African economy and its capability to create employment and address poverty. These factors coupled with past economic, political and social policies continue to impact on the growth potential of the economy. Since 1994, an average growth rate of 1.7 percent has been recorded. This meant that public resources were constrained during this period. Earlier estimates indicated that roughly a 6 percent economic growth rate was needed to begin to achieve the social goals that have been set. Low economic growth rates have been accompanied by persistent unemployment and poverty on a mass scale, which is a threat to the stability of the society. The maintenance of small but steady levels of economic growth needs to be sustained, although there are indications of improved growth rates in 2005. The benefits of growth are however being redistributed to social development concerns. Social spending on health, education, social welfare and housing among others, is nearly half of total government spending. Social spending is considered to be high for a country of South Africa's level of development but given the magnitude of the social problems facing the society, critics have argued that it is inadequate to address the backlogs of the past and meet the present challenges.

A major challenge is to generate economic growth that will create jobs and reduce poverty. Policies and strategies are needed that will place employment at the centre of sustainable development (South Africa UNDP Report 2003). A bias to capital intensive methods of production and large-scale enterprises rather than the utilisation of labour intensive methods of production and small and medium enterprises are some of the barriers that may affect employment. Other barriers considered by the UNDP Report include the lack of the right mix of skills and a trade off between high wages and job creation - although this is disputed. There is no agreement between the social partners about the causes of unemployment and different policy options are advocated. Of particular concern are the employment and livelihood needs of persons who are less skilled, who have no work experience and those who are vulnerable and at risk of social exclusion. One of the premises of social development is the integration of people into productive employment through employment policies and strategies that will create jobs in the formal market economy and through public social investment programmes. But, even if employment could be generated in the formal economy to absorb the large numbers of the unemployed, there are many people who will not be absorbed into the formal economy especially those who are most vulnerable to social exclusion. Market driven strategies to create jobs are not the only solutions as market failure is also one of the causes of unemployment. For these reasons public social investments and enabling policies and incentives are also needed. Some examples of social investment strategies are support for education, skill and human resource development strategies, microenterprises, asset building and increasing access to credit, support for sustainable livelihood efforts, self-employment and public works. Social protection is also important especially for those who may not be able to integrate into formal and informal economic processes especially people living in remote areas.

In Chapter 7 social security was discussed and in Chapter 8 some of the innovative examples of poverty reduction and livelihood strategies in urban and rural communities were considered including some of the lessons learnt from these experiences. There is scope for further research on the economic activities of communities. Special measures are needed to support self-employment and non-formal community based economic development initiatives. The 'flagship programme' for unemployed women and children, the Social Change Assistance Trust (Scat) and the MODE models discussed in Chapter 8 demonstrate what is possible. However, the achievement of sustainable enterprises that are able to generate income especially in remote rural and underdeveloped areas requires an investment in the building of local capacities and institutions and infrastructure support. There is no 'quick fix' to realising the goal of sustainable community based economic development and unrealistic government funding norms and guidelines based on short term outcomes for micro-development interventions may actively work against skills building and empowerment efforts of individuals and communities. Expecting communities to achieve sustainability targets for projects in one year may be unrealistic especially in remote areas.

'There is no 'quick fix' to realising the goal of sustainable community based economic development.'

The ruling party, the African National Congress (ANC) won the 2004 general election with a two-thirds majority and with support from all classes and strata but principally from the poor and disadvantaged. Its election manifesto was a contract to create work and to fight poverty. In its third term in government, the ANC is now under enormous pressure to deliver on its election promises to its constituency. The trajectory proposed by the government is greater state interventionism through the massive expansion of its public works programme, skill development, micro credit, land reform and self-employment and the implementation of the decisions of the Growth and Development Summit of 1999 adopted by the National Economic and Labour Council (NEDLAC). The NEDLAC partnership between labour, business, government and communities exists to negotiate and implement agreements between the parties that will enhance the interests of all. However, can these measures meet the challenge of poverty and unemployment and associated inequality in the society? What combination of policies and strategies are needed to yield the desired results? Do the social partners have the will to confront some of the hard questions, policy trade-offs and compromises that are needed in order to generate growth, employment and poverty reduction? Failure to act could lead to disillusionment of the electorate, political and social instability, continuing crime and levels of violence placing further pressure on the welfare system. This scenario is not an option for the future. An appropriate balance needs to be found between the demands of growth and redistribution and between managing the challenge of economic globalisation and national needs. This may be an impossible task but 'the possible would never be achieved if, in the world, we did not constantly keep trying to achieve the impossible' (Max Weber 1919).

Regionalism and social development

Regionalism has become more prominent as a result of globalisation. The powerful regional trading blocs in North America, Europe and Asia are the main beneficiaries of globalisation. These processes have resulted in the exclusion and marginalisation of countries on the periphery and gave rise to the New Partnership for Africa's Development (NEPAD). South Africa is also playing a significant role in other international forums such as the India/Brazil/South Africa forum to challenge the dominance of the global economic system and the protectionist policies of these regional formations.

Of particular relevance is the Southern African Development Community (SADC) which is a formal regional organisation to enhance the political, economic, security, social and cultural integration and co-operation between member states. The social dimensions of regionalism in SADC were discussed in Chapter 2. Although the SADC countries have noted improvements in some indicators such as adult literacy, most of the countries fall within the low human development range. Political instability and conflict, the HIV/AIDS pandemic and mass poverty and underdevelopment are some of the key features of the regional social situation. The SADC has reorganised itself to address these challenges but it is hampered by institutional, resource and socio-economic and political constraints. Its approach to regional development is wholly government-led and heavily reliant on foreign donor funding. A weak private sector and civil society is a further limitation although in some conflict-ridden countries such as Zimbabwe, civil society has been actively undermined as it is perceived to be a political threat to the government. There is scope for mobilising wider social partnerships to promote social development regionally.

The transnational nature of many of the social problems in the world today demonstrates the complexity and limitations of finding local or national solutions to human conditions in a globalising world. Since the demise of apartheid, South Africa has also become less isolated from the rest of the world and is now fully interconnected formally and informally in the SADC region. Finding solutions to the challenges of regional migration and xenophobia, curbing the spread of HIV/AIDS, transregional crime and trafficking in drugs and small arms and the protection of children and gender equity and equality are some of the issues that require a regional response. Social policies and strategies to promote human development in the SADC region will in future require closer collaboration between the countries. Regional co-operation can however take many different forms such as formal and less formal networks, consortia and forums involving government and non-governmental organisations. The SADC Framework for Integration acknowledges the need for the harmonisation of social security and related social development policies in the region. This is particularly important, as regional integration will also lead to the creation of a Free Trade Area to compete globally and achieve more balanced economic growth and development between member countries. A Free Trade Area will be a significant development in the future and it presents a particular challenge for South Africa in view of the disparities between itself and other countries in the region. Social welfare and social development needs to occupy a more prominent place in the SADC Framework for Integration and South African policy makers and practitioners need to have a greater consciousness of social development and its regional dimensions. National social development efforts cannot afford not to take account of the interdependence between the countries in the region.

'National social development efforts cannot afford not to take account of the interdependence between the countries in the region.'

Social policies

Social development policy when it was initially formulated was focused on national needs and challenges and the implications of globalisation were not taken into account at that time. However, today globalisation and regionalism are at the centre of economic, political, social and cultural debates and should inform policy formulation.

The Reconstruction and Development Programme set the framework for social and economic development in 1994. The government's macro economic policy, GEAR, adopted in 1997 was criticised by the trade unions and sectors of civil society as a conservative neo-liberal economic policy that contradicted government's commitment to social goals. The focus was on building a globally competitive economy, attracting foreign investment to promote growth and privatisation of state assets and liberalisation of the economy. This was perceived to be a response to pressures from the private sector and international agencies such as the World Bank and the International Monetary Fund that espoused a conservative market oriented approach to economic and social policy. The government argued that the GEAR policy is a necessary measure to end the economic and political isolation of South Africa from the international community. Rebuilding the economy to be globally competitive, reducing the budget deficit and the country's debt burden, restoring confidence in the economy and the society and to achieve effective fiscal management and maintain a favourable macroeconomic balance, were other priorities that were identified. On the whole social spending increased gradually or remained constant in key social sectors. There was no significant retrenchment in social spending although reprioritisation of spending occurred with education, health and social development receiving the largest share of public resources. At the end of the first decade of democracy, the South African economy and society stabilised, growth rates have been small but steady and the national debt and inflation was considerably reduced. Resources have also been freed due to debt reduction, which have been redirected to other national social priorities. However, there is growing optimism that South Africa may be set for a period of sustained economic growth in 2005. These issues were discussed in Chapter 4.

'The South African approach to pluralism based on meeting needs through social development partnerships between the social market (public sector), the commercial and private sectors (civil society) in which the state plays a leading social investment and interventionist role to steer development, remains the most appropriate way forward.'

The ANC government, now in its third term, has renewed its commitment to a more interventionist state to meet its election promises. There has been considerable debate as to whether there has been a shift in government policy back to the Reconstruction and Development Programme, and if so, whether this shift could be attributed to public pressure to abandon the government's GEAR policy. The government has argued that the shift is in line with its earlier policy stance. However, there is no doubt that public pressure, the political and economic stability achieved in the first decade, the ANC's electoral victory and its need to be responsive to its mass constituency, are some factors that facilitated the shift to a new emphasis in policy. The President's State of the Nation Address of the 10th May 2004 set a firm economic and social agenda for the next five years and a clear shift in emphasis, which augurs well for social development in the short to medium term. The policy shift has prompted a debate between the government and the official opposition about whether the government is embarking on a 'statist' model of social development that is top down, that will squeeze out markets and civil society and ultimately compromise human rights. It is unlikely that this would occur in view of national resource and institutional constraints. The government cannot afford to go it alone. A mid-path is being sought between excessive economic control and economic liberalisation. The South African approach to pluralism based on meeting needs through social development partnerships between the social market (public sector), the commercial and private sectors (civil society) in which the state plays a leading social investment and interventionist role to steer development, remains the most appropriate way forward.

The rights-based approach to social development also shapes social policy including South Africa's commitments to international human rights and development. The Bill of Rights with its strong emphasis on socio-economic rights provides important protection for all citizens. While many of the Constitutional provisions recognise resource and institutional limitations, the spirit of the Constitution is that government and the society should take reasonable action to ensure that these rights are realised progressively within available resources and that the benefits should accrue to the most disadvantaged. The Bill of Rights does not prescribe how these rights should be realised and in this respect the government and its partners have the flexibility to design innovative policies and strategies to achieve the realisation of these rights. Finally, the Constitution is an important safeguard to promote and protect people's rights. A further safeguard is a vibrant and active civil society that will monitor and advocate for human rights. The rights based approach to social development policy is deeply rooted in the history of the country and will stand the society in good stead in decades to come. However, a human rights approach to social policy raises considerable public expectations about what the government is expected to deliver and what it can realistically deliver. Managing this tension requires making skilful policy choices and managing pressures from different interest groups. How far redistribution will progress and how far social rights will proceed will depend on the balance of power and pressure exerted by the parties and interest groups which may or may not lead to a compromise between them. It is in this respect that the future is uncertain and that public policy could move in different directions. While the current macro social policy and shift in emphasis provides an enabling environment for social development, institutional factors cannot be ignored.

Institutional issues

The dismantling of the apartheid institutions in all spheres of public, private and social life and replacing these with democratic and accountable institutions was an enormous undertaking and a significant achievement of the first decade of democracy. This involved formulating social development policy and legislation to dismantle the old welfare system and to construct new institutions that could implement policy efficiently and effectively. These developments and actions were discussed in Part 2 of the book. However, policies were often of an inspirational nature and could not easily be implemented. Some policies were ambitious and delivery targets were at times unrealistic. The *White Paper for Social Welfare* provided the policy framework for the transformation of the system to a developmental approach. A *Welfare Action Plan* was developed but not formally adopted and implemented. No systematic monitoring of the implementation of the policy is being conducted. Social development programmes were also not adequately costed and the financial and human resource and administrative and management implications were not always considered. Lack of knowledge and skills to implement the new policies have been a significant obstacle to its implementation and have also compromised the efficiency of the delivery of services. Policy implementation has also been limited by a lack of appropriate norms and standards, rules, procedures and mechanisms for enforcing them leading to a lack of co-ordination between government and its partners. The Financing Policy (1999) for instance provided no financial criteria for the financing of the diverse range of developmental welfare services and neither did it provide for the funding of new priorities. This was partly due to the fact that no additional fiscal resources were allocated to welfare services since 1994, although social security provision has expanded significantly. The lack of policy for the funding of developmental welfare services and the under-funding of this important governmental function resulted in the stagnation of developmental welfare services. A major constraint is the lack of an integrated national poverty reduction strategy, which is planned, implemented and monitored across all government departments and other sectors of society.

'A significant feature of social development in South Africa is the partnership model based on the idea of welfare pluralism or a mixed economy of social welfare.'

A significant feature of social development in South Africa is the partnership model based on the idea of welfare pluralism or a mixed economy of social welfare. The tradition of voluntary welfare and development organisations involved in service delivery in South Africa can be traced to the early part of the 20th century. This infrastructure is a national asset that should be nurtured and supported. The voluntary sector is a larger player than the public sector in service delivery especially in the more urbanised provinces. It has the knowledge, skills and experience to partner with government in the delivery of services but a limitation is that the service delivery model is not yet developmental. There are indications that this partnership is in crisis due to many factors: firstly, inadequate financing policy, a lack of skills and the under-funding of developmental welfare services are barriers to the growth of the sector. Secondly, community-based development partners have not been adequately incorporated as delivery partners due to financing constraints and a lack of enabling policies and procedures that could tap their comparative advantage and efficacy as service delivery partners with government. Appropriate, flexible and empowering policies and procedures are needed to build local community based institutions and local capacity particularly in under served communities and remote areas that are hard to reach. Innovation and good practice lessons discussed in Chapter 8 demonstrate the dynamism of local community development and community action as well as the challenges that they face. Failure to harness this resource to achieve proactive civic and development action is a lost opportunity. Thirdly, the relations between the partners are complex because government funds the voluntary sector partners to deliver services and they have contractual obligations to government to deliver services. This structural tension may lead to civil society organisations losing their autonomy and they may end up as quasi-governmental organisations that are reluctant to engage in advocacy. Finally, different interests and a lack of trust or 'social capital' between government and some of its key voluntary sector partners has been a barrier to partnership development. Resistance to change by some voluntary sector partners and an overly bureaucratic approach on the part of public officials to managing partner relations, coupled with competitive and dispersed interests between partners is a further barrier. Effective partnerships are based on inclusiveness, a voice, autonomy, mutuality, flexibility and interdependence, risk sharing and the balancing and co-ordination of different interests. Institutional arrangements are also needed to foster collaboration.

Voluntary organisations are also funded by the private business sector through Corporate Social Investment (CSI) programmes. In 2003, major listed South African companies allocated an average of one percent of pre-tax profit to CSI, which is below the international norm and there is scope for increased CSI allocations for social development. CSI is spent mainly in Gauteng, the Western Cape and KwaZulu-Natal provinces and there is a need to direct resources to programmes in rural areas (Trialogue 2003). The Broad Based Black Economic Empowerment (BEE) legislation aims to contribute to economic and social transformation by addressing racial inequalities in the ownership and control of the economy. Different business sectors are required in terms of the legislation to develop voluntary sectoral charters that should contain targets and time frames of how these objectives will be achieved. Performance will be measured by 2014 in terms of indicators such as, representivity of the composition of the Board of Directors of companies, black ownership, representivity of management and staff and procurement and CSI among others. The beneficiaries of these programmes should be black people including women, workers, youth, and people with disabilities and people living in rural areas. There has been grave criticism that the way in which the legislation is being implemented is favouring a privileged black elite that is politically well connected with the ruling party. The CSI target for the Financial Sector Charter is 0.5 percent of post tax profits. There is considerable scope to increase CSI allocations as part of promoting Broad Based Black Economic Empowerment because it is more redistributive and could benefit the target groups identified more directly. Furthermore, civil society organisations are increasingly involved in entrepreneurial activities to address funding shortfalls. Many are opting to become strategic business partners with black empowerment consortia involved in Black Economic Empowerment deals. Civil society organisations need to consider what these partnerships mean for them as development agents and for their independence and the vibrancy of civil society in an emerging democracy.

Social security and welfare services

The social security landscape and the features of the developmental approach to social security were discussed in Chapter 5. Briefly, these features include firstly the Constitutional right to social security and social assistance for those who are unable to support themselves. Secondly, social security includes social assistance and social insurance. Thirdly, a comprehensive approach to social security is envisaged where other governmental programmes such as nutrition and the subsidization of basic services form part of a package of benefits. Fourthly, these benefits are complemented by community development and livelihood activities and the strengthening of indigenous family-centred and community oriented development strategies and the promotion of parental responsibility for children. Fifthly, these measures point to a pluralist model (social insurance, social assistance, private savings and informal systems of support) which attempts to achieve universal coverage through different social security strategies. The South African approach to social security incorporates a range of strategies such as social assistance targeted at those in need, social insurance, informal systems of support combined with the rights based approach and productivist ideas. The developmental approach to social security has evolved historically and was built on the strengths of the old system combined with the new directions in the country to produce an approach that is unique to the local context. South Africa has a fairly developed system that is considered to be exceptional in a country of this level of development.

'The future direction of social security is not settled and is highly contested, as there are strong pressures from the grassroots to expand the safety net.'

The future direction of social security is not settled and is highly contested, as there are strong pressures from the grassroots to expand the safety net. The government's approach has been to expand the safety net for children, school nutrition and the provision of free basic services. Social security beneficiary numbers have increased from 3 million in 1995 to 9.1 million in December 2004, which is a phenomenal growth. It is the country's largest and most effective poverty reduction programme and is close to 4 percent of GDP – and reflects high expenditure trends in comparison with other middle-income countries. The restructuring of the social security delivery system to increase efficiency is a further priority for the future. A major shortcoming is the lack of social assistance for unemployed persons and a lack of access to social insurance for informal and non-standardized workers. There is scope to address the lack of coverage of informal sector employees by the private sector, as increased access to social insurance for disadvantaged groups is one of the requirements of the Financial Sector Charter. In the foreseeable future, the government has indicated that it will focus on growing the economy, and attempt to reconcile what is referred to as the 'first' and the 'second' economies. Other priorities will be to improve livelihoods and create work to 'ensure that over time, a smaller proportion of the society, in particular the most vulnerable, [do not] subsist solely on social grants' (President Mbeki, State of the Nation Address May 2004).

Internationally, there has been a shift in social security from a 'welfare state' approach to a more conservative residual approach. The developmental approach is a growing policy alternative advocated by Midgley (1995) and Sherraden (1991) as is Giddens' (2000) 'Third Way' approach to social welfare which attempts to find a middle ground between institutional and residual approaches. These approaches are considered briefly in order to capture the issues for social security locally and were discussed in Chapter 1.

The 'welfare state' approach to social security is concerned mainly with benefit transfers, universal provision to all people in the society and service provision based on entitlement or a rightful claim to social welfare derived from citizenship rights. The residual approach emphasizes individual responsibility, selective benefits targeted at those in need and seeks market-oriented solutions and emphasizes individual and family responsibility for social welfare. The developmental approach in contrast to the former approaches places less emphasis on entitlement rights as the rationale for social welfare but rather emphasizes social investments that enhance people's capacities to participate effectively in the productive economy. Developmentalists seek to enhance material well being through participation in the economy 'within the context of national policies that foster sustainable, people-centred economic development' (Midgley 2003:22).

'Developmentalists seek to enhance material well being through participation in the economy within the context of national policies that foster sustainable, people-centred economic development.'

The advocates for a Basic Income Grant have made a case for the expansion of social grants based on welfare state thinking. The government on the other hand has taken a more productivist view and has continued to implement a selective approach, which targets public benefits at the bottom 40 percent of the poor, as these measures are more redistributive in the local context than universal benefits. Universal coverage is envisaged through a combination of public and private measures. Affordability and the long-term sustainability of the social security system are considerations for the future. Demographic changes will lead to a doubling of the ageing population over the next two decades and the impact of the HIV/AIDS pandemic is expected to have grave social and economic consequences for future generations. A key question for policy makers is whether government can effectively implement the strategies proposed and make substantial inroads into mass unemployment, poverty and inequality in a short space of time while simultaneously maintaining social, economic and political stability.

The expansion of social security and the restructuring of the social security delivery system could have far reaching consequences for developmental welfare services. The growth in social security spending (estimated to be R168 billion over the next three years) means that there may be no additional resources for developmental welfare services, which is a significantly smaller programme. Furthermore, social security was previously a concurrent national and provincial competency and boosted provincial budgets considerably. Since 1994, social development at provincial level enjoyed a high political profile and visibility. The restructuring of the social security delivery system means that it will in future be a national government competency. This is necessary to improve the efficiency and effectiveness of the system.

There is however the danger that it could lead to the 'crowding out of welfare services', health and education, decreased funding and a waning political commitment that could lead to the downgrading of a vital social sector function at provincial level. If this occurs, social development will be reduced to social assistance and the payment of cash transfers while the empowerment and developmental thrust of social development will be lost. From this perspective, the future scenario for developmental welfare services is bleak.

The case for developmental social welfare needs to be made by the sector itself. Some of the arguments favouring social development are that social security and welfare services work together in a synergistic way to achieve the essence of social welfare that is, a state of human well being. Achieving minimum living standards for all people is a worthy social goal and is necessary but not sufficient to address the complex social, emotional, physical, intellectual and spiritual needs of people over the life cycle. Developmental social welfare services sets out to enhance social functioning and human capacities; promote social solidarity, participation and community involvement in social welfare; and promote social inclusion through empowerment of those who are socially, economically and politically excluded from the mainstream of society. Through the implementation of social legislation, the rights of populations at risk are protected and promoted. Oppression and discrimination arising not only from structural forces but caused also by social and cultural beliefs and practices may also hamper social inclusion. Anti-discriminatory approaches to development practice could make an important contribution to reconciliation in the society. Developmental welfare services could also contribute significantly to community building and local institutional development. Through its family centred and community-based approach, it strengthens the livelihood activities of households, facilitates the prevention of social problems and contributes directly to human dignity and the building of a caring society. Community-based rehabilitation is vital to social and economic integration in the society. The social and economic costs of social problems and loss of productivity caused by problems such as substance abuse should not be under-estimated. Substance abuse is also a significant contributing factor to the escalation of crime and violence. Strengthening and supporting families to promote child survival and development is vital to human development. Social security and welfare service strategies are intertwined and complementary. The necessary restructuring of the social security system and the expansion of benefits should not compromise the efficacy of developmental welfare services.

'Developmental social welfare services sets out to enhance social functioning and human capacities....'.

The case for developmental welfare services is a compelling one, but can the institutional constraints be effectively addressed? How can the resistance to change be overcome? How might universities, communities and development agents work more collaboratively for social change? Is there the will, the foresight and the commitment to a long-term vision to developmental welfare services?

Conclusion

In conclusion, South Africa's search for a new social contract and in achieving its social goals is a daunting one given the realities of its past and faced with the new challenges of globalisation and regionalisation. This book attempted to traverse this complex landscape and reflected on the achievements and challenges of a sector attempting to transform itself in a wider context of national, regional and global change. The transformation of social welfare to social development requires social service professionals who will be equipped with appropriate knowledge, skills, values and the imagination to work in a changing local and global world. The South African story remains an inspiring one and it demonstrates that the impossible is worth pursuing.

Bibliography

DEPARTMENT OF WELFARE (1998), Financing Policy. Developmental Social Services. General Notice 463 of 1999. No 19888. Pretoria: Republic of South Africa.

GIDDENS, A. (2000), *The third way and its critics*. Cambridge: Polity Press.

MBEKI, T. (2004), *State of the Nation address by President of South Africa, Parliament, Cape Town 21 May 2004*. htt://www.info.gov.za/soeeches/sotn2004.htm (28 August 2004)

MAYOR, F. & BINDE', J. (2001), *The World Ahead. Our future in the Making*. Paris: UNESCO Publishing.

MIDGLEY, J. (2003), Assets in the Context of Welfare Theory: A Developmentalist Interpretation. *Journal of Social Development Issues,* 25: 1/2, 13–28.

PRIGOGINE, I. (1995), 'Foreword" In Mayor, F., Forstenzer, T. *The New Page*. Dartmouth Publishing/Paris: UNESCO Publishing.

SHERRADEN, M. (1991), *Assets and the poor: A new American welfare policy*. New York: M.E. Sharpe.

TRILOGUE (2003), *The CSI Handbook. A comprehensive guide to corporate social investment in South Africa,*. 6th ed. Cape Town: Trialogue.

UNDP (UNITED NATIONS DEVELOPMENT PROGRAMME) (2003), *South Africa Human Development Report. The Challenge of Sustainable Development: Unlocking People's Creativity*. Pretoria: Oxford University Press.

WEBER, M. (1919), 'La Vocation du politique'. In Mayor, F. and Binde', J. (2001), *The World Ahead. Our future in the Making*. (19). Paris: UNESCO Publishing.

Index